SAP PRESS e-books

Print or e-book, Kindle or iPad, workplace or airplane: Choose where and how to read your SAP PRESS books! You can now get all our titles as e-books, too:

- ▶ By download and online access
- ▶ For all popular devices
- ▶ And, of course, DRM-free

Convinced? Then go to **www.sap-press.com** and get your e-book today.

Discover SAP®

 **PRESS**

SAP PRESS is a joint initiative of SAP and Galileo Press. The know-how offered by SAP specialists combined with the expertise of the publishing house Galileo Press offers the reader expert books in the field. SAP PRESS features first-hand information and expert advice, and provides useful skills for professional decision-making.

SAP PRESS offers a variety of books on technical and business-related topics for the SAP user. For further information, please visit our website: *www.sap-press.com*.

Olaf Schulz
Using SAP: A Guide for Beginners and End Users (2nd edition)
2014, 392 pp., paperback
ISBN 978-1-59229-981-2

Martin Murray
Discover Logistics with SAP: SAP ERP and SAP SCM (2nd edition)
2013, 412 pp., paperback
ISBN 978-1-59229-926-3

Manish Patel
Discover SAP ERP Financials (2nd edition)
2012, 604 pp., paperback
ISBN 978-1-59229-429-9

Srini Katta
Discover SAP CRM (2nd edition)
2013, 404 pp., paperback
ISBN 978-1-59229-836-5

Venki Krishnamoorthy, Alexandra Carvalho

Discover SAP®

Galileo Press

Bonn • Boston

Galileo Press is named after the Italian physicist, mathematician, and philosopher Galileo Galilei (1564—1642). He is known as one of the founders of modern science and an advocate of our contemporary, heliocentric worldview. His words *Eppur si muove* (And yet it moves) have become legendary. The Galileo Press logo depicts Jupiter orbited by the four Galilean moons, which were discovered by Galileo in 1610.

Editor Laura Korslund
Acquisitions Editor Emily Nicholls
Copyeditor Melinda Rankin
Cover Design Graham Geary
Photo Credit Shutterstock.com/158728976/© Pixfiction
Layout Design Vera Brauner
Production Graham Geary
Typesetting III-satz, Husby (Germany)
Printed and bound in the United States of America, on paper from sustainable sources

ISBN 978-1-59229-987-4
© 2015 by Galileo Press Inc., Boston (MA)
3rd edition 2015

Library of Congress Cataloging-in-Publication Data
Carvalho, Alexandra.
Discover SAP / Alexandra Carvalho and Venki Krishnamoorthy. -- Third edition.
pages cm
Includes index.
ISBN 978-1-59229-987-4 (print) -- ISBN 1-59229-987-3 (print) -- ISBN 978-1-59229-988-1 (ebook) -
ISBN 978-1-59229-989-8 (print and ebook) 1. Management information systems--Computer programs.
2. Business--Data processing--Computer programs. 3. SAP ERP. 4. Integrated software. I. Krishnamoorthy, Venki. II. Title.
HD30.213.C36 2014
658.4'038011--dc23
2014032359

Contents at a Glance

Dear Reader,

Are you a decision maker who's trying to decide if SAP is the right vendor for your software needs? Or a consultant who's just starting to use SAP software? Or maybe you've worked in IT, but your company has decided to change software vendors to SAP. Regardless of your role, this book will introduce you to the core SAP components, tools, and functionalities.

We know that the unknown can be a scary place, and that holds especially true for new or unfamiliar software solutions. We at SAP PRESS believe that with the right information in hand, you'll quickly understand the world of SAP. Yes, SAP has a vast portfolio of products. But yes, this book will help start your journey. You don't have to do it alone! Compiled by authors who are experts in their fields, this book offers friendly, easy-to-understand guidance and real-world examples that will help you to discover what SAP software really is and what it can do for an enterprise. Don't wade through confusing websites and blog posts that use all of the technical jargon you associate with software—everything you need is right here.

We're happy that you decided to start your SAP journey with *Discover SAP*. We hope you find the information you need, and welcome you to leave both praise and criticism at *www.sap-press.com*—your comments and suggestions are the most useful tools to help us make our books the best they can be.

Thank you for purchasing a book from SAP PRESS!

Laura Korslund
Editor, SAP PRESS

Galileo Press
Boston, MA

laura.korslund@galileo-press.com
www.sap-press.com

Contents

PART II   SAP Products

6 SAP ERP Human Capital Management 115

9 SAP Supplier Relationship Management 183

10 Ariba and Fieldglass 201

13 The SAP Strategy for Small to Midsize Enterprises ... 253

PART III Essential SAP Tools

14 SAP Reporting and Analytics 279

18 User-Friendly SAP: Duet, Alloy, Adobe Interactive Forms, and SAP Fiori 369

19 SAP NetWeaver as a Technology Platform 389

20 Preparing for an SAP Implementation 413

Preface

In this third, updated edition, we have tried to address what we felt was a gap in the available information about SAP by providing an easy to understand overview of SAP, its products, and its approach to enterprise computing. Our objective is to provide a simple and straightforward look at SAP and its products. We make every effort to explain SAP product features, not in technical jargon or by using marketing brochure product features, but by simply describing all of the benefits and by being specific about what these products can *do* for your business.

The following sections outline who can benefit from this book, how we structured the book, and what topics are covered.

Who Will Benefit from This Book?

If you're a business decision maker who is considering implementing SAP products in your business, this book will help you become familiar with the terminology, concepts, products, and technology you will encounter.

Decision makers

If you're a manager who is dealing with new SAP products in your group, and you want to help your people succeed and become more productive, this book gives you the information you need to appreciate how all of the various features and tools in SAP products might make your people more efficient.

Managers

If you're an IT person who has never worked with SAP technologies and products, you'll get a quick, solid grounding in both, and be able to make the connection between how those technologies and products solve business problems.

IT

If you're a consultant who is considering entering the world of supporting SAP products, this book can serve as a type of tutorial to help you better understand the SAP universe, including SAP's extended partner community and how it works to support customers.

Consultants

What You'll Discover

Our goal in writing this book was to introduce and explain enterprise computing concepts and terms in simple language, SAP as a company and how it approaches solving real-world business problems, the technology behind SAP products, and what you can expect during an SAP implementation.

We also provide an overview of each of SAP's major products with actual case studies so you can see how each product works in a real business.

We were careful to define the most current business and enterprise computing terms throughout the book so anyone from an IT specialist unfamiliar with business terms to a business person unfamiliar with technology terms can understand the information we provide. We also made every attempt to give you examples and case studies to make SAP and its products relevant to you, your business, and your industry.

Navigational Tools for This Book

Throughout the book, you will find several elements that will help you access useful information. We have used the following icons to help you navigate:

Tip: When you see this icon, you know that you'll find useful information as well as special tips and tricks that can make your work easier.

Note: Notes call out information about related ideas, other resources to explore, or things you should keep in mind.

Technical Information: This icon highlights technical details and issues related to SAP products that will help you in making decisions.

Newsflash: When you see this icon, you know you will be given some news, latest developments, or important information about SAP.

Example: Here you'll encounter real-life scenarios and exercises.

Additionally, marginal text provides a useful way to scan the book to locate topics of interest for you. Each appears to the side of a paragraph or section with related information.

This is a marginal note

What's in This Book?

This book is organized into three parts. We move from basic information about SAP and its approach to enterprise computing products and services, to more specific chapters on SAP products themselves. We then explore some of the tools you find in all SAP products that provide features such as self-service and risk management. Finally, we look at the technology behind those products and advise you about what to expect if you implement SAP solutions in your organization. Here's an overview of what the book covers.

Part I: SAP and Enterprise Computing: The Basics

This part of the book looks at SAP's history, evolution, and its current direction. We also discuss topics and trends that will impact future developments.

Read the book in sequence or go to specific chapters or sections as needed

Chapter 1

SAP: The Company is where we look at the history of SAP; that is, how it has grown and developed products to address various business processes over the years. We provide an overview of SAP today, including its different enterprise computing solutions.

Chapter 2

The SAP Approach to Enterprise Software is where we define enterprise computing and explain how SAP approaches finding and providing solutions to enterprises of all sizes and types.

Chapter 3

Business Suite 7 Overview explains how the modular approach to enhancing technical functionality can help companies reduce the costs and time associated with software implementations.

Part II: SAP Products

Each of the chapters in this part covers one or more SAP software products, explaining what the product is, how it fits in an enterprise setting, and specific product features and tools, as well as offering a case study with a real-world example of the product in place. Here are the products covered in these chapters:

Chapter 4

SAP ERP Financials addresses all of the financial functions of a business, which most readers will find very valuable. SAP ERP Financials is one of the most often implemented applications of SAP.

Chapter 5

SAP ERP Operations deals with product development and manufacturing, procurement and logistics, and sales and service products.

Chapter 6

SAP ERP Human Capital Management covers solutions related to human resources, again a very important part of the SAP landscape.

Chapter 7

SuccessFactors covers one of SAP's companies, who offers a cloud-based HR solution.

Chapter 8

SAP Customer Relationship Management helps you obtain, service, and retain your customers.

Chapter 9

SAP Supplier Relationship Management deals with the sourcing, procurement, and supplier enablement features.

Chapter 10

Ariba and Fieldglass discusses the cloud solutions for procurement.

Chapter 11

SAP Product Lifecycle Management covers the pieces of a product's life, from inception, to development, and through to obsolescence.

Chapter 12

SAP Supply Chain Management introduces features for keeping inventory moving in and out of your company in a way that can have a big impact on your bottom line.

Chapter 13

SAP's Strategy for Small to Midsize Enterprises deals with SAP's complete portfolio of solutions, including SAP Business One, SAP Business All-in-One, SAP Business ByDesign, and BusinessObjects Edge.

Part III: Essential SAP Tools

This part covers important tools that you might encounter in an SAP implementation. Let's get a quick recap of these chapters now:

Chapter 14

SAP Reporting and Analytics gives you a detailed look at the new BusinessObjects portfolio, including Enterprise Performance Management, Business Intelligence, Governance, Risk, and Compliance, and Information Management.

Chapter 15

SAP HANA introduces you to SAP's new in-memory database. This chapter is a bit more technical than the others, and will highlight the differences between traditional data processing and SAP's newest method.

Chapter 16

SAP Mobility provides helpful information on developing apps, mobile security options for the enterprise, and SAP's platform.

Chapter 17

User Productivity Tools for Information Workers is where you learn about role-based portals, which are work areas customized to each worker in your company to make them more productive. In addition, we explain how employee self-service (ESS) and manager self-service (MSS) functions allow your people to initiate many processes themselves, thereby saving them time and your money.

Chapter 18

User-Friendly SAP: Duet, Alloy, Adobe Interactive Forms, and SAP Fiori highlights tools intended for users of SAP software. Duet is a joint project between SAP and Microsoft, which provides the functionality of SAP through the Microsoft Office interface so familiar to knowledge workers. Alloy allows employees to continue using Lotus Notes while providing access to data within the SAP Business Suite. SAP Interactive Forms is software by Adobe that uses Adobe Acrobat technology to make easy-to-use interactive forms, which SAP embeds within business processes. And SAP Fiori is a collection of apps.

> Read all of the chapter descriptions to get an idea of what's included in each

Chapter 19
SAP NetWeaver as a Technology Platform introduces you to SAP Net-Weaver, the technology platform on which all other SAP products rest.

Chapter 20
Preparing for an SAP Implementation provides advice about how to prepare for putting SAP in place, from your assessment of your own company and its needs, to the programs, people, and services that can help you be successful.

Chapter 21
Preparing for an SAP Cloud Implementation provides advice about how to prepare for putting SAP in place in the cloud.

Chapter 22
An Introduction to SAP Rapid Deployment Solutions provides information on a third implementation option, in which you choose pre-configured software for a less expensive and quicker experience.

Chapter 23
SAP Solution Manager is a useful tool built into SAP NetWeaver that guides you through every step of your SAP implementation and even provides useful documentation about the specific solution you implement.

Appendix

We provide three useful appendices for your reference:

> **Appendix A**
> A glossary of SAP and enterprise computing terminology.

> **Appendix B**
> Provides information about various resources for help and information related to SAP and its products.

> **Appendix C**
> Gives you a useful collection of SAP solution maps that you can use as a quick reference for looking up the product and features you need.

Use the index as a navigational tool

In addition, the book includes an index that you can use to go directly to certain points of interest.

We hope that this straightforward overview of SAP and its technologies and products will give you the information you need to assess your own business needs, determine which SAP products and services to explore further with an SAP account representative, and help you take advantage of the many benefits that SAP has to offer for solving enterprise challenges.

Acknowledgments

The excitement of being asked to write a book is often followed by the realization of the enormity of the task: something that will need to fit an already over-committed work schedule.

If I got to the end of this journey with a product to be proud of, it is thanks to a very supportive husband, ever present during my many sleepless nights researching, writing, illustrating, and reviewing; my beautiful girls Lily and Bella, bringing joy to every step of the way; and my parents, who taught me to be focused, committed, and to face new challenges with passion and determination.

I must also thank my fellow SAP Mentors—a true source of inspiration, my colleagues at BI Group Australia for their support, SAP PRESS for bringing this perspective to my career, and above all, you, the reader. Knowledge is only valuable when it can empower people.

Alexandra Carvalho
Melbourne, Australia

This project draws inspiration from the efforts and support of many individuals. Without these friends and colleagues, this book would not have been possible.

Thank you to my friends at Galileo Press—for their guidance, patience and support. I would especially like to thank our editor, Laura Korslund, who made this book possible. Laura helped form this authoring team and has encouraged me to get the words onto the printed page.

I would like to say a big thank you to my co-author Alexandra Carvalho for her dedication and inclusion in this project. Her personal sacrifices ensured this project is a success and I greatly enjoy being part of this team.

Many thanks to the contributors Jawad Akhtar, Justin Ashlock, and Paul Ovigele for helping us complete this book. But for their timely help and contribution, this book would have taken longer to complete.

I owe the utmost gratitude to my family, who supported me during the writing of this book. Thank you for your love and patience throughout this project.

I owe a big thanks to Yasmine Abdallah, Arunkumar Timalapur, Muktar Ahmed Khan, Vivek Mahajan, and Apparao Kavuri, for their help in getting me the figures that are used in this book, as well reviewing some of the chapters for me.

This book has been reviewed and updated to the latest release, and we have included new chapters to explain about SAP Cloud, SAP HANA, and big data. I hope you find this book informative and it supports you in your SAP journey.

Venki Krishnamoorthy
Pittsburgh, PA

PART I
SAP and Enterprise Computing: The Basics

SAP: The Company

No product exists independently of its creator. This holds true especially for SAP, the origins, growth, and philosophy of which have had an impact on what it creates and how its customers benefit from its products. So let us start with an overview of SAP, the company, and its history to help you understand how to successfully interact with SAP today.

The Beginnings of SAP

SAP was founded in 1972 by five IBM colleagues who struck out on their own. Dietmar Hopp, Hans-Werner Hector, Hasso Plattner, Klaus Tschira, and Claus Wellenreuther founded SAP in Mannheim, Germany, where it began as a small regional company.

In the earliest days, the founders couldn't afford to buy computers, because they were so expensive. Instead, they arranged with another company—ICI, in neighboring Oestringen—to use their computers at night. This was long before the personal computer came on the scene. In those days, all of their work was produced on punch cards.

Tip

You can impress people with your SAP knowledge if you know that the company name SAP is the acronym for *Systems, Applications, and Products* in data processing. And remember, never pronounce SAP to rhyme with rap; instead, simply pronounce each of the three letters, S, A, P.

In an era of the development of simple business tools—such as calculating software, which evolved into spreadsheet programs, and relatively simple word processors—these five men recognized the need for more sophisticated applications that could support the way businesses function.

R/1 system   They spent the next year developing applications that would support real-time processing of business tasks. Their first product was a financial accounting software package. This software was at the core of what would later become known as the *R/1 system*. The *R* in this case stands for real-time data processing.

But R/1 was just the beginning; the next few decades were to bring about tremendous growth for SAP and the world of enterprise computing.

Examining the Growth of SAP

R/2 system, enterprise   During the 1970s, the term *enterprise* was just coming into general use, and today almost any business can be considered an enterprise if it has a focus on an ability to respond to changes in the market and innovate. SAP developed what it referred to as its *database and dialog control system*, which eventually became known as *R/2*. The system was essentially a business-application software suite that was run on a mainframe computer. R/2 was the cornerstone of enterprise resource planning (ERP) applications used by major companies throughout the coming decades.

SAP in the 1980s

In the 1980s, SAP grew quickly and moved into its first building in Walldorf, Germany, near Heidelberg. Early in the decade, SAP counted half of the top 100 German industrial firms among its customers, such as ICI, BASF, and John Deere, but growth beyond Germany's borders was imminent.

Development of R/2 systems during the 1980s took into account the potential of the multinational customer base, and SAP paid a lot of attention to enabling its products to handle a variety of languages and currencies, thus reflecting the huge amount of country-specific legal requirements. This multinational approach to software development continues today.

During this period, SAP technology also focused on making applications adaptable by programmers to fit into individual enterprises. For example, SAP development maintained a flexible approach, allowing the software to run on many different databases and platforms (operating systems) seamlessly.

Flexible approach to development

In the mid to late 1980s, SAP launched its first sales group outside of Germany (in Austria), passed the $52 million revenue mark, and began to make its presence known at major computer shows. In 1988, SAP GmbH became SAP AG and later that year began trading on the Frankfurt and Stuttgart stock exchanges.

The decade ended with SAP subsidiaries located in Denmark, Sweden, Italy, and the United States, thereby firmly establishing SAP's foothold in the international technology marketplace.

SAP built a successful business foundation during the 1980s, and in the 1990s, developed a truly international business approach and presence.

SAP in the 1990s

SAP grew internationally in the 1990s, with business outside of Germany exceeding 50% of its total income. Customers such as Shell Oil, Kodak, and Procter & Gamble joined SAP's European clients, and in 1998, the company was listed on the New York Stock Exchange.

R/3, introduced in the 1990s, was a giant leap in computing for business enterprises. It moved enterprise computing from the mainframe and the world of programmers writing code to the world of databases, applications, and interfaces that made SAP's offerings more accessible to end users.

R/3 system

SAP R/3 was based on something called *three-tier client/server architecture*. This is basically an approach to computer networking that divides the computer requesting data from the computer that stores the data and the end-user interface.

In this setting, a client computer (e.g., a computer at which a user sits working on a report) requests something from an application (this might be on a network or web server) that works with a database (the third layer, as shown in Figure 1.1). This division allows for a great deal of flexibility, as each layer is scalable in itself; if more database capacity is needed it can be added easily in the server layer, whereas the client layer is focused on other jobs, such as showing more sophisticated graphical reports.

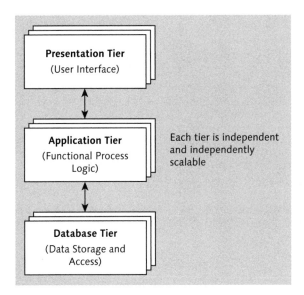

Figure 1.1 Three-Tier Client/Server Architecture

Client/server architecture became integral to creating web-based applications; for example, those in which services can be made available from the application layer.

Entering the New Millennium

Toward the end of the century, SAP announced plans to integrate its products with e-commerce and web technologies. Using the Internet model, SAP placed the end user at the center of enterprise computing. The growth of e-business had shifted the thinking of businesses toward establishing a more collaborative environment for users.

By 2004, SAP AG had revenues of €7.5 billion and was working with partners in 25 industries to develop its next generation of enterprise solutions. SAP became the third-largest independent software vendor in the world, after Microsoft and IBM.

Although it is useful to understand where SAP came from, to truly understand how it could work with your business you need to get a feel for what SAP is doing today.

SAP Today

Today, SAP is the number one business in enterprise computing and is still the third-largest software company in the world. In 2014, SAP AG became SAP SE, becoming a European traded company. The company produces business solutions for a wide variety of industries in every major market in the world. SAP's approach to developing software has become even more collaborative, in that it works with business partners to develop product features to reflect real-world computing needs.

In addition, SAP has made strong movement to become the leader in several different areas that are becoming more important to businesses in today's ever-changing economy. SAP is now the top cloud vendor, bringing more and more SAP solutions and applications to the cloud, rather than requiring the more bulky and expensive on premise solutions and hardware. SAP has also been a pioneer in developing mobility applications (mobile apps), helping businesses and employees to work on the go anywhere and at any time. We'll discuss these elements in more detail in Chapter 2.

If you have ever heard of SAP, chances are good that you've also heard about SAP HANA, SAP's game-changing offering for true real-time computing that was announced in 2010. With the help of SAP HANA, businesses can process huge amounts of data in mere seconds and accelerate analytics, business processes, sentiment data processing, and predictive capabilities. SAP HANA helps to make existing applications faster and also enables new types of applications that organizations could not run in the past.

SAP's Approach to Growing Its Business

One key to SAP's success has been the way it has collaborated with businesses and consultants to integrate best business practices into its software applications.

SAP Best Practices

SAP Best Practices make the technical implementation of business best practices in a workplace setting much easier. SAP Best Practices are documented prototypes on which you can base an enterprise solution, similar to the way an expense report template in a spreadsheet program saves you time by providing you with the structure of a standard business form.

Through these partnerships, SAP has been able to build an industry focus that allows its products to be used in a variety of industry settings, such as manufacturing, pharmaceuticals, and healthcare. SAP has also developed a huge support network of consultants, who are educated by SAP in how to work with their solutions through annual conferences, certification programs, and consultant education programs, such as SAP Academy.

 Tip

For a detailed list of support programs and information resources for SAP, see Appendix B.

Three communities that SAP supports are vital to these partnerships:

> **SAP Business Community**
> This is a forum for the exchange of ideas and solutions with member experts and business leaders.

> **SAP Community Network (SCN)**
> This network includes developers, consultants, and business analysts focused on sharing technical knowledge.

> **User Groups**
> These user groups are independent, nonprofit groups made up of SAP customers and partners who share knowledge and experiences through conferences and online interaction.

Customer Competence Centers (CCC)

In 1994, SAP created the CCC program to assist customers in setting up and optimizing their own support operations. The program focuses on sharing best practices, providing operational tools, and creating operations standards across all organizations involved with SAP IT service and application management.

Conclusion

In this chapter, we provided you with some context for understanding SAP as a company by discussing its history and providing a quick overview of SAP today.

In Chapter 2, we'll introduce some basic concepts and terms from the world of enterprise computing, discuss how SAP fits into that world with tools for integration and tools to support business processes, and look at where SAP is headed in the next several years.

The SAP Approach
to Enterprise Software

IT systems help enterprises implement their business strategies more effectively and optimize the coordination of their operational processes. The fundamental aim of enterprise software is to "pour" business processes into software; that is, to link technology with operational workflows within an enterprise.

This chapter provides an overview of the key concepts that relate to enterprise software. It introduces the central ideas and lays down the essential technical foundations. These include the SAP NetWeaver technology platform (on which all SAP applications can run), and technologies that help end users access SAP systems as part of their daily work. SAP's approach to the development of enterprise software is also presented.

Enterprise Resource Planning (ERP)

An *enterprise* is a unit or organization that operates as a commercial entity. Enterprises may range from charitable organizations with just two employees to large global corporations. Most enterprises use one or more software solutions. The scale of the requirements that must be fulfilled by these software solutions depends on the size of the enterprise and on the complexity and diversity of its business activities.

Enterprise resource planning
An IT system that supports business processes is referred to as an *ERP system*. ERP stands for *enterprise resource planning*. An ERP system comprises a range of software applications that are designed to support business processes, such as submitting a sales order or material procurement for production. SAP software, with SAP ERP at its core, is one of the ERP systems that is the most widely used by enterprises.

 Tip

Explanations of the various terms and acronyms used in enterprise resource planning are provided in the glossary in Appendix A.

SAP Business Suite
SAP software integrates functions and information in an enterprise. *SAP Business Suite* is a package of software applications that is designed to support the most prevalent workflows in enterprises. The SAP ERP portion of the SAP Business Suite focuses on financials, human resources, operations, and corporate services. Other portions of the SAP Business Suite handle customer resource management, purchasing, and other areas of enterprise functionality.

 How Large Does an Enterprise Have to Be to Use ERP?

The first implementations of ERP systems took place in large corporations with tens or hundreds of thousands of employees in dozens or even hundreds of locations. Enterprises of this size require software solutions that are capable of mapping diverse information and processes on a large scale. Today, however, many small and midsize enterprises use SAP. For more information, refer to Chapter 13.

The following sections describe the evolution of standard business software. Key terms and concepts are discussed in several places, which will give you a deeper insight into the world of the enterprise in terms of IT requirements.

The Origins of Standard Business Software

Applications were developed by SAP and other software providers to help enterprises more effectively manage and use information and business processes—for example, information about customers, products, or finances. These applications were called *business applications*. The foundations for their development were laid in the 1970s, and these applications served, above all, to support data processing in financial accounting and human resources.

Business applications

Centralized data storage and ease of access to information also enabled the creation of reports on this data. Thanks to the availability of very powerful processors, these reports can now be used to run analyses that provide a basis for strategic and operational decision making. Instead of merely generating a list of all customers, it is now possible, for example, to show which customer generated the greatest profit, or users responsible for customer accounts can access precise data that may reveal conflicting information about sales orders.

In the early years, SAP limited its software applications to accounting and HR. A little later, however, functions were extended to cover other areas within an enterprise. Today, ERP software can be used to help an enterprise manage finance, HR, logistics, sales and distribution, production, purchasing, and services. An ERP system is now capable of handling a wide range of processes, including anything from planning a business trip to tracking a sales order.

Areas covered by ERP

However, the need to cover various business areas was not the only challenge for ERP systems. It was also necessary to enable collaboration across departments, countries, or enterprises using the same data.

The Challenge of Integration

In the earliest years of enterprise software, huge data stores were created for each large department in an enterprise, so, for example, the finance department may have had a different set of customer data than the sales department. As a result, a sales employee was unable to access the accounting database to view billing data or the shipping department database to check whether an order had already been processed. Practically, though, all of the various people or departments that are involved in a business process in an enterprise need to be able to access the same data. It is not a particularly efficient way to run an enterprise if the purchasing department manages the order data and the marketing department has to ask the purchasing department to access this information on their behalf.

Avoiding data silos It was therefore essential to find a way to avoid this inefficient division of information. The answer was *integration*. SAP and other providers of ERP software searched for a solution to link the "data silos" that contained information and functions from different areas and to enable access to these across the entire enterprise.

In an integrated enterprise environment, a sales order is available to the sales department, finance, customer service, and shipping department to enable seamless processing and order fulfillment. As a result, the sales department can provide the customer with precise information about the order status and improve customer satisfaction. Centralized and fast updating of data means that the enterprise can be flexible in its response to change.

SAP NetWeaver The level of integration was consistently improved in each new product generation, from SAP R/1, R/2, and R/3 right through to SAP ERP. SAP NetWeaver (see Chapter 19) is the latest technology for data integration from SAP. All SAP products are based on this platform.

Overview of SAP NetWeaver

Technology platform SAP NetWeaver is the technology platform on which the SAP Business Suite runs. SAP NetWeaver essentially supports integration at the following four levels:

> **Integration of people**
> User productivity is mentioned many times in this book. Users need to be able to use the system without difficulty. It is therefore essential to provide them with an accessible user interface. A single user interface can be used for both SAP and non-SAP applications so that users can access all of the data they require.

> **Integration of information**
> All necessary information must be quickly and easily accessed within the enterprise and must be of a high quality. SAP NetWeaver Business Intelligence meets this information requirement.

> **Integration of processes**
> Efficient processes need to be universally defined across various systems or even across enterprises.

> **Integration of applications**
> Direct communication between various applications is ensured, and the popular programming language Java is supported in addition to ABAP, SAP's own programming language.

The SAP NetWeaver integrated technology platform is used to run all SAP applications and to exchange information with other applications. SAP NetWeaver supports the integration of business applications and data, and it offers tools for creating new applications. In other words, it represents a development environment for SAP applications.

SAP NetWeaver as a development environment

Moreover, SAP NetWeaver is a means of building a bridge between IT and business departments.

Uniting IT and Business Requirements

SAP NetWeaver acts as an interface between IT practices and business processes. A business process could be, for example, the creation of sales orders by a sales employee, and an example of an IT practice is the joining together of several applications originating in different systems with a single user interface. A key task for an IT department is to make it easier for users to use the system in order to work more efficiently.

The IT practice implemented in SAP NetWeaver is known as *User Productivity Enablement*. Increased user productivity is enabled, for example, by the SAP Enterprise Portal, which makes it easier for end users to access the SAP system thanks to various personalization options. This IT practice may include a range of specific options that can be implemented in SAP NetWeaver to support business processes. As a result, the customers and employees of an enterprise can optimize their access to the data they need.

User Productivity Enablement

Example

> You can create a website with SAP Enterprise Portal, and if you connect it to an order entry system, then your customers can use it to place orders. You can also use SAP NetWeaver on mobile devices, which sales employees use to enter orders while working outside of the office.

IT employees no longer need to program new solutions. Instead, they can build them from business process components, which means that employees from the IT department and other departments can finally speak the same language.

At this point, you should consider your own IT landscape and ask yourself if it could be integrated into an SAP environment. This integration is facilitated by the open application environment of SAP NetWeaver.

Open Application Environment

You can use SAP NetWeaver's open application environment together with a range of applications and technologies from various sources. This means that you can continue to use the technology that is already in place alongside SAP NetWeaver and save yourself the cost of purchasing a brand-new system.

Third-party systems

For example, if your environment includes systems from Oracle and SAP, SAP NetWeaver provides all functions required to allow these systems to communicate and exchange data. In addition to integration options, SAP NetWeaver also provides tools that you can use to create and modify your own businesses' applications, which are then known as composite applications.

Using Composite Applications

Applications that consist of various modules (known as *services*, which are explained in the next section) are referred to as *composite applications*. These applications are used to implement business processes. They allow you to reuse components from existing business applications to create new applications. A combination of functions from various applications then executes a business process (e.g., sales order entry).

In the past, changes like this required a complete reprogramming of the ERP system. Composite applications allow you to implement these changes more easily in your enterprise.

SAP Support for Business Processes

The unique feature of SAP's approach is the fact that it unites technology and business processes. This section provides more details of how this works in practice. By collaborating with a network of strategic partners, SAP became familiar with business processes that were used in many different industries, gained insight into the individual processes and best practices, and received feedback on its products from these partners.

The solutions that SAP developed (and continues to develop) are based on these best practices, which serve, so to speak, as the enterprises' individual recipes for success. However, the software still had to be modified to meet the requirements of each customer. To fulfill this requirement, SAP developed applications that could be tailored to meet the specific needs of individual customers while at the same time offering a framework for the needs specific to individual industries.

Application modification and best practices

 Tip: Best Practices

SAP Best Practices make the technical implementation of best practices in a workplace setting much easier. SAP Best Practices are documented prototypes on which you can base an enterprise solution, similar to the way an expense report template in a spreadsheet program saves you time by providing you with the structure of a standard business form.

Best practices comprise expert knowledge from various industries or relate to specific processes in an enterprise. SAP makes these best practices available in the form of technical and business-related documentation and preconfigured content in SAP systems. These can be regarded as "turnkey" resources that facilitate and accelerate the implementation process.

In the past, enterprises that had implemented an SAP system often required the assistance of external consultants to adapt the SAP ERP system to their specific requirements. It could take years for the implementation process to be completed. SAP optimized this process by integrating modification options and best practices into components or services that could be easily adapted.

To provide enterprise solutions, providers such as SAP first had to understand business processes and then learn how to implement these in a marketable software product; in other words, they had to develop software applications that could be sold as a package based on business principles.

Customizing Many SAP products previously required extensive modifications to make them match the individual requirements of an enterprise—a process known as *Customizing*. Today, many SAP ERP solutions are delivered as "out-of-the-box" solutions, which can be used in the organization with little or no modification. SAP also provides SAP Rapid Deployment solutions, which are industry-specific solutions that enable rapid implementation (read more about this in Chapter 22). However, the fact that SAP products come with preconfigured content makes them no less flexible or adaptable.

 Note

In Customizing, you adapt a standard software application to the specific requirements and organizational structures of your enterprise. Many SAP applications are only ready for use after you have made the necessary changes. Customizing settings are made when an SAP system is implemented or enhanced and also during release changes or upgrade projects.

Integrated best practices SAP products also come with *integrated* best practices that exist for the most frequently used business processes. This means that an application such as SAP CRM can be used with only very slight changes in customer service or in sales order processing.

Solutions for SMEs *SAP Business One*, *SAP Business All-in-One*, and *SAP Business ByDesign* include solutions that are designed especially for small and midsize enterprises. For more information, refer to Chapter 13.

Because SAP is itself an enterprise that is growing and learning all the time, new products and technologies will continue to evolve in the future. For this reason, we turn to a newer concept to which all software companies have had to adapt, and then discuss SAP's focus at the present time and for the coming years.

SAP and Big Data

The Internet allows us access to a huge amount of information. According to a 2013 article in *Science Daily*, 90% of the world's data was created in the years 2011 and 2012. Outside of merely browsing data available on websites, think about the data that is generated by people indicating their preferences on websites, using social media, and using tracking tools that document peoples' activities. The combination of all of the information that is generated (both technology and methods of processing the data) is now known as *big data*. Some of the aspects of big data are data acquisition, curation, storage, and optimization, as well as data analysis, visualization, classification, and prediction.

The generation of all this data also provokes some questions:

› How do we find big data?

› How do we analyze, use, and govern big data?

› How is big data helpful to our organization?

The first thing to realize about big data is that it is almost impossible to process it with traditional databases in a timely manner due to its sheer quantity. This has spurred a recent development in technology to create new architectures that hold huge quantities of data, process it quickly, and perform advanced analysis on it. Some of these technologies include Hadoop and SAP HANA. You can find more information about SAP HANA in Chapter 15.

New technology

Organizations can use different tools and applications that are provided by SAP to revolutionize the way they do business and take advantage of big data. By using the SAP HANA platform (on premise, in the cloud, or a combination of both), businesses can use new analytic tools to understand the business like never before and make more informed decisions, identify opportunities and expose risks, and use data science to make industry-based choices.

SAP HANA

Where Is SAP Headed?

SAP's focus remains firmly fixed on providing enterprises with technologies, software, and services to help them respond more flexibly to change, reduce operating costs, and enhance their internal processes to collaborate more efficiently with customers, vendors, and partners. One of SAP's key objectives is therefore to allow enterprises to acquire and analyze reliable data. Thanks to enhanced user interfaces and easy access options, SAP also makes it easier for end users to do their work in the SAP system and aims to make it even easier for users to consume information to help run businesses better.

SAP realizes these goals in various ways. Let us look into the issues currently in SAP's focus.

Cloud Computing

Cloud computing is the use of software applications that are delivered as a service over the enterprise network or over the Internet. These applications are accessed by users from anywhere by using a web browser, mobile device, or a thin client. The vendor providing the application is responsible for maintaining it as well the infrastructure that hosts it. The software as well the user's and enterprise's data resides in servers that are outside the enterprise firewall.

In the past, small and midsize businesses were often restricted by their budget; IT solutions can quickly become expensive. With the advent of SAP Cloud, however, the game is changing. Businesses of all sizes are afforded access to enterprise-quality services and solutions, because they don't have to worry about in-house costs and risks. Think of the dramatic increase of start-ups; they are, in all probability, using the cloud as a significant resource.

SAP offers many options for cloud computing. Organizations can transfer to be 100% on the cloud (private or public), but in many cases they are using a hybrid approach, with a portion of their applications on the cloud and a portion remaining on premise.

SAP is in the process of expanding their cloud offerings. A few examples of their current offerings (as of August 2014) include:

> SAP Sourcing

> SAP HANA Cloud Portal

> SAP Business ByDesign

> SAP Cloud for Customer/Financials/Travel

 SAP Cloud for Travel and Expense

SAP made its largest acquisition yet in September 2014. By acquiring Concur Technologies for $8.3 billion, SAP plans to further expand its cloud offerings for travel management. The SAP Cloud for Travel and Expense (T&E) simplifies planning and booking, and allows travelers to capture and submit business expenses on a mobile device. Travelers can get their money back easier and faster and the company can reduce complexity and cost, and increase compliance and transparency while relying on easy integration with SAP ERP. You can find this solution represented in a use case in Chapter 21.

If you are looking at implementing cloud-based solutions (HR or any other applications), then you need to be familiar with the following cloud terminology:

Cloud terminology

> **SaaS (Software as a Service)**
  This is a software delivery model in which the software or application and its related data are hosted on the cloud. Users can access the application from a thin client or over the Internet. SaaS is also referred to as on-demand software. SaaS applications are priced on a pay-per-use basis.

> **PaaS (Platform as a Service)**
  Cloud providers provide a development platform, which includes the operating system, an integrated development environment (IDE), a database, and a web server. Application developers can develop and run their applications using this platform without the added investment of buying and managing the underlying infrastructure and software. The added advantage of PaaS is that the computer and storage resources scale automatically to match the user demand, so the PaaS user does not have to manually allocate the resources.

> **IaaS (Infrastructure as a Service)**
  This is a service offering in which computer resources along with storage and network capabilities are offered as a service to customers. The infrastructure is owned and operated by the service provider.

> **Single tenancy**
  The users of the cloud application have their own instances of the database and the application. (Both the database and the application are hosted on the cloud.) Customers of single tenancy have the benefit of having a customized solution and enhanced security.

> **Multitenancy**
  Multiple customers have access to the same applications, and the related data are hosted on the same server. With proper security and authorizations, the users are restricted to viewing their data only. Because the same instance of the software is accessed by different customers, the software application is installed with basic configuration, and there is limited scope for customization or enhancements.

Mobile Computing

With most people now using smartphones, tablets, and other devices, it is no wonder that SAP provides mobile apps, platforms, and development tools to make businesses even more efficient. CEOs can securely view reports on the go, managers can approve in-office requests remotely, and consumers can avail themselves to business services 24/7.

By using mobile applications, users can perform activities such as launching a sales campaign, offering personalized rewards and recommendations to customers, and taking advantage of the quick processing time of SAP HANA and the Sybase development environment.

Mobile app
development

SAP is also offering a growing number of options to develop your own real-time mobile apps. These apps allow employees to access and exchange data with access to the actual SAP system. There are three options for development:

> **Native app development**
  Requiring the most time to create, these apps deliver the best-looking and quickest response time. These apps are device specific and must be downloaded to the device.

> **Web app development**
> These apps are not device specific and provide a mobile site for users to access.

> **Hybrid app development**
> This app looks similar to a native app; it is downloaded to the specific device, but the same app will run on any platform (iOS, Android, Windows, etc.).

Self-Services for Increased Efficiency

SAP NetWeaver and the applications in the SAP Business Suite provide enterprises with self-service areas. *Self-service* means that employees and managers can complete certain tasks without any help from other employees—just like in a self-service store. Self-services are comparable with Internet services that allow you to make purchases, find information, and communicate with other users without having to go to your local store, library, or post office.

These self-service functions are provided by the SAP Enterprise Portal, which allows users to access content via a browser interface. Tools are provided to guide users step-by-step through the process. These tools, referred to as *guided procedures*, will be familiar to you from using the Internet to perform tasks such as making reservations (e.g., to reserve plane tickets).

Guided procedures

Ex Example

If employees want to check their remaining vacation for the year, they usually have to request this information from the HR department and wait for an answer. With self-services, employees can check their remaining vacation in the system themselves and also request vacation time without having to contact the HR department. This procedure reduces the workload of HR staff, who can then devote more time to other tasks.

SAP offers self-services for both employees (Employee Self-Services; ESS) and managers (Manager Self-Services; MSS) in an enterprise. More information about self-services is provided in Chapter 17.

ESS and MSS

Another focal point for SAP, which was also mentioned earlier, is the enhancement of its product portfolio for small and midsize enterprises (discussed in Chapter 13).

Benefits of Using SAP Software

The purpose of enterprise software is to help enterprises meet their strategic objectives. Therefore, the way in which SAP ERP and other applications can enhance business processes is the primary concern, not the technology used. If you are considering implementing an ERP system, your focus will be on the capabilities of the software, which must fulfill your specific requirements.

ROI, TCO, compliance, and outsourcing

Therefore, the following concepts are all important when considering the use of enterprise software:

> **Return on investment (ROI)**
> The ratio of profit made on an investment in a software solution relative to the amount of capital invested.

> **Total cost of ownership (TCO)**
> The total costs involved in operating the software, which should be kept to a minimum.

> **Compliance**
> Adherence to various legal or internal regulations.

> **Outsourcing**
> The option of subcontracting parts of the business process to external providers.

Automation, business insights, and time to market

A key argument in favor of implementing an integrated enterprise software solution is the possibility of automating processes, a step that reduces costs while increasing efficiency. Thanks to centralized data storage, you can also run reports and analyses to help you make the right decisions for your business. For many enterprises, meeting customer requirements as quickly as possible is absolutely essential to remaining competitive in the face of market changes. In other words, the time it takes to position a product in the market after it has been developed (*time to market*) must be minimized to give the enterprise a competitive edge.

To sum up, the following core capabilities are essential to the success of an enterprise:

> **Differentiation**
  The ability of an enterprise to set itself apart from its competitors.

> **Productivity**
  The ability to work efficiently and cost-effectively.

> **Flexibility**
  The ability to react quickly to change.

These are all concepts that you will encounter again and again when using an SAP system or reading SAP publications.

Conclusion

This chapter introduced you to several fundamental concepts and terms relating to the SAP environment, including the following:

> Definitions of the terms "enterprise," "enterprise software," and "ERP"

> The history of the development of enterprise software and current concepts relating to ERP

> Cloud and mobile computing

> The meaning of data integration

> SAP's focus on business processes

SAP has developed an ERP system that offers a flexible approach to the use of services and is based on an open technology platform that facilitates the integration of users, data, and processes. To help you understand the technological basis of SAP applications, in this chapter we discussed the following topics:

> The role of SAP NetWeaver as a platform for SAP applications

> Tools such as portals and self-services, which help employees work more efficiently

Now that you are familiar with the basic concepts and technologies in SAP, let us move onto Chapter 3, which provides more information about SAP's applications that support common business functions.

3   Business Suite 7 Overview

Technology and its link to the global economy shows us just how quickly consumers' wants and needs change, and how that rapid change can have an impact on your company's ability to meet these needs in a timely fashion. To stay competitive, enter a new market niche, or maintain your current market share, you must be able to drive and direct how quickly your company adapts to new changes or meets current customer demands.

Keeping IT applications and business processes up-to-date and tuned to quickly respond to these needs is a challenge that many organizations face. Large enterprises today have to undergo three major phases before they are up and running with the latest and greatest software applications. First, a technical upgrade is needed to ensure that your hardware can handle the new applications. Next, many new software packages make you look at your current business processes and tweak them, add new processes, or retire old ones. Finally, you add the new software to get the desired new changes in functionality and then spend time training your employees on how to use the new package.

Meeting your customers' needs during changing market conditions

What does this mean to you? Extensive time and money will be spent on what turns out to be a full-fledged upgrade, which also includes a lot of features and functions that have nothing to do with the enhancements you wanted to make. When IT budgets are already under scrutiny and you are doing more with less, this becomes a tough business case to make. To help you reduce your total cost of ownership (TCO) and provide your organization with the ability to implement only those functions you need at the time you need them, SAP has developed the SAP Business Suite 7 package.

SAP's Business Suite 7 helps lead the trend away from costly and time-consuming upgrades. Released in 2009, SAP Business Suite 7 helps larger enterprises adapt a modular approach to enhancing their technical functionality while also reducing the costs and time associated with software implementations.

Modular upgrade approach
SAP Business Suite 7 is an integrated suite of products consisting of SAP ERP, SAP Customer Relationship Management (SAP CRM), SAP Supplier Relationship Management (SAP SRM), SAP Product Lifecycle Management (SAP PLM), and SAP Supply Chain Management (SAP SCM). (As of 2014, the integrated products are also on different enhancement packages, which we discuss later in this chapter.) This integrated lifecycle set of applications provides you with built-in business expertise and with tools and best practices that reduce efforts directed toward testing and customization. This allows you to deploy new innovations and products more quickly, which improves your response to changing market conditions and allows you to better meet your customers' needs. We will take a look at each of these applications next.

Overview of Business Suite Solutions

Modular implementation
As we've mentioned, one of the biggest draws to using the SAP Business Suite 7 solutions is their ability to be implemented in modular fashion. This allows you to focus on the critical areas of your business while keeping IT costs in line. Let us look at SAP ERP, the core product in the SAP Business Suite package. You will find more information about the individual SAP Business Suite components in Part II of this book.

SAP ERP

Align practices with corporate strategy
The SAP ERP application lets you hone your company's financial, human capital, operations, and corporate services practices to ensure

that they are aligned with the overall corporate strategy. SAP ERP consists of the following components:

> **SAP ERP Financials**
> Includes tools for core accounting and reporting capabilities, financial links to supply chain processes, functions to keep you in compliance with government and global financial regulations, and helps to monitor your incoming and outgoing cash flow while minimizing financial risks to your organization.

> **SAP ERP Human Capital Management**
> Empowers your employees to manage their personal information, such as marriage, birth of a child, and benefits coverage, and also events such as time recording and signing up for training (see Figure 3.1). Likewise, supervisors participate in the employee development and compensation processes and collaborate with other departments during the development of a corporate budget.

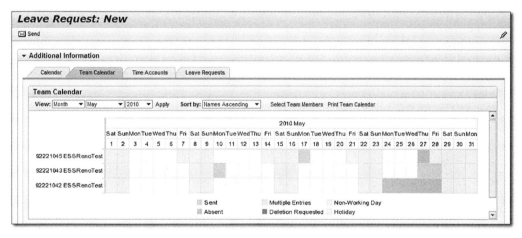

Figure 3.1 Manager Self-Service Portal for Leave Approval

> **SAP ERP Operations**
> Tools that help you manage and streamline the day-to-day activities within your organization. With SAP ERP Operations features, you can automate processes to reduce costs and waste, manage your production cycle, and provide self-service opportunities for your customers.

> ### SAP ERP Corporate Services
> Functions in the SAP ERP Corporate Services segment manage external activities that are associated with real estate, corporate travel, corporate assets, and environmental health and safety issues. If you have an international organization, the Global Trade Services portion of SAP ERP Corporate Services keeps you in compliance with trade, tariff, and documentation requirements.

The SAP ERP tools keep your organization running smoothly for your employees and management staff. We will go into more detail on each of these components in the following sections.

SAP Customer Relationship Management

The SAP Customer Relationship Management tools focus on one of your most important assets: your customers. To stay competitive, you need to find a way to maintain your current clientele and attract new customers by differentiating yourself from others in your industry. SAP's CRM tools can help you achieve your long-term goals in these areas:

Marketing, sales, service, and e-commerce

> ### Marketing
> Features in the marketing area help you with brand and loyalty management, market segmentation, managing your market campaigns, and finding new ways to reach out to customers through e-marketing campaigns.

> ### Sales
> These tools promote collaboration between your marketing and sales forces so that customer needs are met. Functions in the sales portion of SAP CRM help you determine what sales areas are profitable and how to deliver the most positive customer experience to build brand loyalty and return sales.

> ### Service
> With service tools, you take a proactive stance to servicing your customers by providing your staff with all of the information they need to know at just the right time. Other features allow you to manage your service agreements and contracts and set up alerts to notify customers when their contracts are about to expire. Inventory management tools allow you to keep track of the parts and materials on hand, which enables you to quickly address customer issues as soon as they arise. SAP CRM service tools also let you

establish secure web portals to provide an additional means of interaction between you and your customers.

> **Interaction center**
> Customers like to feel they have received personalized service from you. With the interaction center (IC) tools, you can deliver your sales, marketing, and service message to your customers over a variety of channels to meet their individual needs.
>
> IC supports telemarketing and customer support. IC is also used in areas such as telesales, customer service, and IC management.

> **SAP Web Channel Experience Management**
> You can take advantage of today's Internet technology to reach your customers. These tools provide a means for you to analyze trends that result from your e-commerce business and a way for your customers to order and track your products and report service issues online.

SAP CRM products help bring your business to the forefront for your customers and let your business prosper even during tough economic times.

SAP Supplier Relationship Management

Having streamlined your daily operations and developed prosperous customer relationships, SAP Supplier Relationship Management (SAP SRM) helps you focus your efforts on your relationship with your suppliers and vendors. Here you examine your procurement process to maximize efficiency from the initial contract bidding through the receipt of final payment. To help your staff have materials and supplies on hand when they need them, other features in SAP SRM help you evaluate your suppliers' performance and provide a portal for collaboration between your purchasing group and your vendors.

Procurement processes

The procurement solutions SAP offers are grouped for both on premise and the cloud as follows:

On premise and cloud options

> **Spend Analytics**
> You can analyze procurement data with this analytics tool.

> **Sourcing (Strategic and Operational)**
> Operational Sourcing is the day-to-day assignment of orders to applicable suppliers, based on product, product category, contract,

and/or availability. Strategic Sourcing focuses upon the optimization of large, critical purchasing activities.

> **Contract Management**
Contract Lifecycle Management in SAP Sourcing and SRM replicate the contracts to the applicable purchasing environments.

> **Operational Procurement**
This facilitates compliant buying with user-friendly catalogs, and automated requisition-to-payment processes.

> **Invoice Management**
This provides a central access point for all incoming invoices, including those with or without purchase order references.

> **Supplier Performance Management**
This enables supplier registration, qualification, and on-boarding. Once the supplier is registered, you can classify and manage the supplier's performance based on their value to your business.

> **Supplier Collaboration (Ariba Network and/or Supplier Self-Services [SUS])**
You can enable suppliers to maintain parts of their own record at your company, receive purchase orders and receipt notifications, submit purchase order responses such as shipment notifications and invoices, and maintain current catalog pricing and item data specific to your company.

> **Mobile Procurement**
The solution can be deployed on mobile-devices supporting a number of procurement-related activities such as shopping cart approval, supplier look-up, purchase request approval, and shopping cart creation.

SAP Product Lifecycle Management

Stay ahead of your competition by delivering innovative products with the help of SAP Product Lifecycle Management (SAP PLM) and the following features:

Innovative products

> **Portfolio planning**
Lets you monitor, manage, and control projects in your organization from inception through implementation. These tools also help you rank and prioritize your projects through collaboration

efforts between various department members to ensure that your projects align with strategic corporate initiatives.

> **Development and manufacturing**
Allows you to accelerate the development of new products by helping you with the design and manufacturing processes and the creation of technical specification documents.

> **Service**
Allows the service, warranty, and maintenance processes to be introduced during the product development stage, providing a view of the complete product lifecycle.

SAP Supply Chain Management

SAP Supply Chain Management (SAP SCM) has features to help your supply chain respond faster to market and economic changes while keeping the focus on the customer, including the following:

> **Planning**
Lets you optimize planning activities involving safety stock, the supply network, supply distribution, and supply chain design.

Planning, execution, and collaboration

> **Execution**
Monitors costs and efficiencies in your supply chain during order fulfillment, procurement, transportation, and warehousing.

> **Collaboration**
Connects you with suppliers, customers, and manufacturers so that information can be shared and your supply chain can function without disruption.

We have given you a brief overview of each of the SAP Business Suite 7 components and their features; now we will show you how they benefit your business.

SAP Business Suite 7 Benefits

SAP Business Suite 7 covers all aspects of your business and brings you tools to help you reduce costs, be more efficient, and bring new innovations to fruition faster. SAP also worked with its customers and partners to develop value scenarios, which are industry-specific processes that take you from end to end to achieve desired outcomes.

Industry-specific value scenarios

For example, if you are in the retail industry, customers' buying habits can determine how your business operates. With the "inspired shopping experience" value scenario, retail management learns how their business must change or adapt to maintain customer and brand loyalty.

SAP Business-Objects analytics

SAP Business Suite 7 has incorporated the analytics features from its SAP BusinessObjects portfolio (see Chapter 14) to provide you with better insight into how well your organization is performing and meeting its strategic goals (see Figure 3.2). The ability to monitor all aspects of your business provides you with the information and flexibility you need to make decisions or alter your strategy to meet your business objectives.

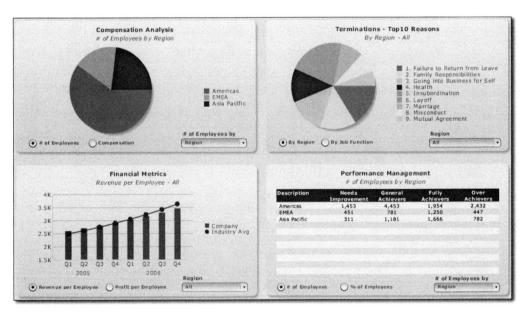

Figure 3.2 Analytics Reporting Using SAP BusinessObjects

Ability to get information from all sources

The SAP Business Suite 7 package components are built with SOA architecture and SAP NetWeaver technology (see Chapter 19). What this means is that the suite integrates with existing SAP applications and with your non-SAP applications. You can access data from all sources to help you in decision making, strategy execution, and product development.

In addition to helping you reduce costs and streamline processes through value scenarios, you can also reduce the need for extra training each time you add on another SAP Business Suite application. All SAP Business Suite applications are designed with the same user interface, which means they all have the same look and feel. Your employees will spend more time using the applications than trying to understand how they operate.

Harmonized user interface

Perhaps one of the biggest benefits of SAP Business Suite 7 is that it is less expensive to deploy than other options. Your company purchases only the application for the area it wants to improve, instead of purchasing an entire software application package. Your deployment is then a matter of switching on only those features within the component that contain the enhancements or functionality you need. When the enhancements are turned on, they are immediately incorporated into your current business processes. Enhancement packages then provide the opportunity for you to add additional industry-specific features to your system on an as-needed basis. Again, by turning on only the features you want, your company avoids the time and expense associated with a major system upgrade.

Reduce deployment time with enhancement packages

Regardless of which SAP Business Suite 7 applications you have purchased, SAP has synchronized the release of its upgrades for all applications. For example, if you purchased the SAP SCM application and then two years later purchased the SAP CRM application, you can upgrade your two components simultaneously when the next software release comes out from SAP. This ensures that your software always has the most current features and functionality and that only one upgrade is necessary for all parts of the SAP Business Suite.

Synchronized release schedule for all SAP Business Suite components

Being able to add software in an as-needed fashion helps your business react more quickly to market changes, pushes new products through the pipeline faster, and keeps your business prosperous even during rough economic periods. In the next chapters, we will examine the individual applications in more detail.

Conclusion

SAP Business Suite 7 applications connect all facets of your operation and provide you with greater insight and access to the information you need to analyze your business, make better informed decisions, and strategically position yourself for growth. With the ability to upgrade via enhancement packs and the inclusion of more than 24 industry-specific best practices, you will be able to reduce your TCO, more quickly realize the benefits to your company, and at the same time reduce inefficiencies and streamline your processes.

In the next chapter, we will begin our review of the SAP products, beginning with SAP ERP Financials.

PART II
SAP Products

4

SAP ERP Financials

SAP's first product offering back in the 1980s was the Financials package for enterprises. Because financial activity is vital to the life of any company in any industry, this was a logical starting point. Today, SAP ERP Financials is more robust than ever, with tools that allow companies to automate routine financial activities—such as managing their general ledger—and to improve their ability to budget and forecast by using analytics, to smooth their cash flow to make themselves more profitable, and to stay on track with local and global financial compliance requirements.

In this chapter, we look at the role of SAP ERP Financials in an enterprise and the specific features that SAP's financial software provides. We conclude the chapter with two case studies that show you how SAP ERP Financials provides benefits in real-world settings.

How SAP ERP Financials Fits in an Enterprise

For most business people, it is not hard to imagine the benefits of efficient, accurate accounting software tools. However, the scope of what SAP ERP Financials can do for an organization goes far beyond keeping numbers accurate. In this section, we look at the ways in which SAP ERP Financials helps you handle your cash flow better, deliver

Specific SAP
Financials features

69

reports and data that help you make key decisions, and support alignment with financial requirements to keep your company in compliance (Figure 4.1).

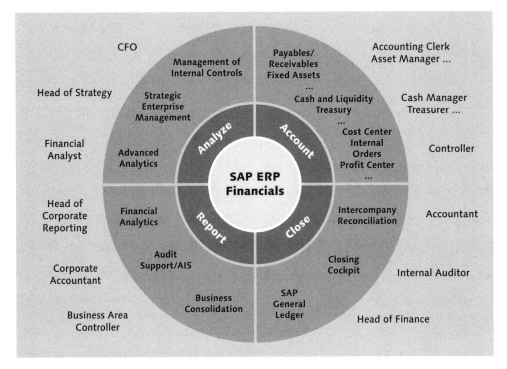

Figure 4.1 SAP ERP Financials

Optimized Cash Flow

Cash is the lifeblood of any organization, and keeping it flowing in a timely way is vital to your profitability and sometimes even to your survival. The ability to manage the cash in your enterprise is part of the SAP ERP Financials package.

Cash-flow cycle; financial supply chain

SAP ERP Financials includes tools you can use to manage the financial supply chain and cash-flow cycle from end to end. By automating several procedures, you can reduce the time it takes to collect cash from your sales, which can make a big difference to your bottom line. SAP ERP Financials consists of the following:

> **SAP Receivables Management (still known as Financial Supply Chain Management)**
> Provides tools to access online invoices and payments, analyze customers' credit worthiness, facilitate online billing disputes, and prioritize payment collection to reduce the number of overdue accounts.

> **SAP Business Planning and Consolidation**
> These functions help consolidate your individual department plans and budgets into one corporate plan while providing what-if scenarios to help you test your budget assumptions. At the same time, you have a well-documented audit trail to provide the compliance and reporting you need internally and externally.

Four key financial areas that SAP ERP Financials supports (see Appendix C for the SAP ERP Financials solution map details) are the following:

> **Receivables Management**
> This area enables you to handle electronic invoicing, payments, and dispute and collections management.

> **Treasury and Financial Risk Management**
> Provides tools for risk management, cash and liquidity management, and bank communication management.

> **Accounting and Financial Close**
> This area allows you to create and report timely financial statements as well as keep up-to-date with evolving financial standards. It includes submodules such as financial accounting, financial closing cockpit, intercompany reconciliation, and financial consolidation.

> **Management Accounting**
> This area enables you to handle activities such as cost and profit center accounting, profitability analysis, project accounting, and revenue and cost planning.

Of course, all of these management tools are very useful, but when it comes down to it the key to keeping your cash flow moving along in a productive way is having the information you need to make good decisions. That is where SAP ERP Financials' strong analytic tools come in.

Better Business Insight

Today more than ever, in addition to cash, information drives your business. With easy and instant access to financial data, employees can be more productive in their work. They have the correct information they need to complete transactions, report on their activity, serve customers, and plan future activities based on solid forecasts.

SAP ERP Financials rests on SAP NetWeaver

In describing SAP ERP Financials, SAP states that "SAP ERP provides a complete analytical framework to consolidate and dissect business information generated in your industry solutions or your core enterprise processes." This simply means that you can access business data in real time, use that data to make better business decisions, and produce impressive reports and analyses from that data. This is possible because of the data integration capabilities of SAP NetWeaver, the platform that SAP ERP Financials rests on, and the analytical tools built into SAP ERP Financials.

Portals, work centers

SAP ERP Financials allows all of the various sets of data and financial activities in your business to be integrated so that your employees can use *key performance indicators* (KPIs) in the context of their everyday work. By using the portal technology supported by SAP NetWeaver, individual workers can have reports and analytics pushed into their desktop work centers (i.e., their centralized online data, schedule, and tools page). Based on employee roles in the company, financial data that matches each person's needs can appear in work centers without anyone having to ask for it.

 Tip

> Because the design of SAP ERP Financials is intuitive, most employees have a fast learning curve and can get to work with minimal training.

SAP ERP Financials and Analytics

SAP BPC and SAP BW

What can you actually do with SAP ERP Financials and its analytic capabilities? You can get all kinds of reports, forecasts, and analyses that help you decide how and when to spend your money and make changes in your operations.

Through the use of SAP Business Planning and Consolidation (BPC) and SAP Business Warehouse (SAP BW), SAP ERP Financials allows you to perform the following analytical activities:

> Generate consolidated financial and statutory reports
> Plan, budget, and forecast
> Run cause-and-effect analyses
> Analyze profitability by criteria such as unit, profit center, or geographical location
> Calculate and manage risk
> Analyze product and service costing
> Review payment behavior
> Calculate overhead costs

In other words, if you have good information, you can use it in a variety of ways to help you manage your business. SAP ERP Financials not only provides the information, it also provides the tools you need to calculate, analyze, and display financial information to others.

The final piece of the SAP ERP Financials functionality is the ability to help you stay in compliance with a world of financial requirements in today's global economy.

Calculate, analyze, and display financial information

Improved Compliance

When you consider the financial scandals that have rocked the business world in recent years, the need to comply with regulations regarding your company's financials is pressing. If you are in senior management, you are well aware that corporate executives can be held personally responsible for not meeting current accounting standards.

Although the need for accountability is strong, compliance is not always easy. Different regulations exist when you are doing business in different countries or industries. The Sarbanes-Oxley Act (SOX) that is in effect in the United States, for example, does not provide a set of business practices so much as a guideline for what business records to store and for what period of time. It also includes regulations for the storage of electronic records, which has an impact on your IT department. If a transaction involves other countries, you must ensure that you are complying with all regulations for record retention.

Sarbanes-Oxley Act

73

One of the functions of SAP ERP Financials is to help you comply with regulations that demand quality financial reporting and strong internal controls, such as the SOX, the US Generally Accepted Accounting Principles (GAAP), the International Financial Reporting Standards (IFRS), and Basel II.

SAP ERP Financials, in conjunction with SAP BusinessObjects, provides several tools to help you stay in compliance, as shown in Figure 4.2.

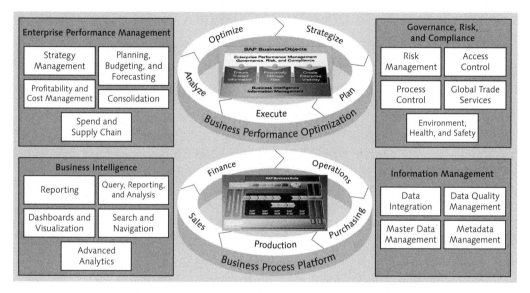

Figure 4.2 SAP ERP Financials Combines with SAP BusinessObjects

In addition, as you can see in Figure 4.3, you get tools for managing access control, global trade, environment, and process control in addition to risk-management features:

> **Protect information and prevent fraud**

  – Automatically eliminate access and authorization risks with out-of-the-box rules

  – Enforce segregation of duties across applications and departments

  – Prevent improper access instead of reacting to problems

> **Optimize operations**

  – Automate segregation of duties management

- Automate access management
- Promote IT and line-of-business collaboration
- Enforce accountability with review and approval processes
- Ease compliance and avoid authorization risk

> **Minimize time and cost for financial compliance**

- Provide proof and reliability with control tests and audit trail for SOD controls
- Report and review key risk indicators for system access

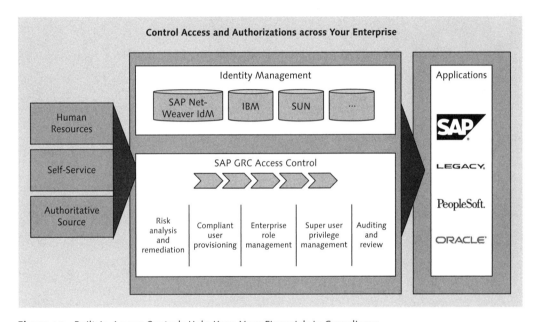

Figure 4.3 Built-In Access Controls Help Keep Your Financials in Compliance

With SAP ERP Financials and SAP BusinessObjects, you get tools to support the following compliance-related activities:

SAP BusinessObjects is covered in detail in Chapter 14

> Audit information systems
> Management of internal controls
> Whistleblower complaints
> Transparency to comply with financial regulations

Now that you have an overview of how SAP ERP Financials addresses cash flow, analytics, and compliance issues, let us look at the specific features in SAP ERP Financials that help you to achieve these benefits.

A Closer Look at SAP ERP Financials

Because you now have an idea of how SAP ERP Financials fits into a business, it is time to explore the specific functions and components included in SAP ERP Financials and see how they work in a real-world business setting.

Key Features and Functions

SAP ERP Financials provides a framework to help you manage the financial side of your business, but you may be wondering what exactly these features allow you to do. Here are some of the features and functions in SAP ERP Financials and how they support business activities:

> **Biller Direct**
> Give your customers online access to their monthly and yearly invoices, account status, bill itemization, and payment information. Customers can then save or print this information in a format that is useful to them. This data is also readily available to people in other departments within your company, such as call center agents, who may need it to resolve customer inquiries.

> **Cash and Liquidity Management**
> Manage and streamline your accounts receivable process so that your cash is available when you need it. Cash and Liquidity Management also enables you to pinpoint where and how your cash is being spent so that you improve your cash forecasting. Tools are provided to support electronic bank interfaces that help you reduce manual reconciliations and establish in-house banking to give you more control over your cash.

> **Closing Cockpit**
> Efficiently generate reliable and consistent financial closing information from all sources while providing one central point of data control and monitoring. Accurate financial reports are then available for regulatory and reporting purposes. The Closing Cockpit

automates many tasks associated with the closing process and reduces the reliance on manual processes and spreadsheets.

> **Financial and management reporting**
  Use this set of standard analyses that meet the reporting needs of a wide variety of roles in your organization, such as senior executives, line-of-business managers, and sales assistants. The usefulness of these reports is not limited to internal people; reports can be designed to meet the needs of shareholders, banks, and other financial institutions.

Meet financial reporting needs

> **Planning, budgeting, and forecasting**
  These tools handle anything from traditional budgeting to rolling forecasts. You can use Financials tools for collaborative planning, such as cost center planning. The Analytical Planning Workbench allows you to model planning scenarios and includes preconfigured planning applications that support your operational planning.

> **Strategy management and scorecards**
  Link and align operational and strategic plans and develop key performance indicators (KPIs) that support a number of popular *scorecard* methodologies. Scorecards are a type of financial report that typically color code and set up data so that it is easy to analyze. Supported scorecard methodologies include balanced scorecard, economic value added, and activity-based costing methods.

Scorecards

> **Cost and profitability management**
  Assign overhead costs, manage the costs of producing products and services, and analyze the profitability of various products and services.

> **Working capital and cash-flow management**
  Manage your capital with functions that support your processes and improve your liabilities and receivables management. You can manage cash flow, including cash-flow calculations and middle- and long-term planning.

 Tip

You can also manage receivables by analyzing payment histories and determining the Days Sales Outstanding (DSO), which allows you to optimize payment schedules.

To get an idea of the breadth of features that you get with SAP ERP Financials, Table 4.1 shows the various categories of functions that are included with the applications they contain.

Category	Application
Financial Supply Chain Management	› Credit Management › Electronic Bill Presentment and Payment › Dispute Management › Collections Management › Debt Recovery Management for Public Sector
Treasury	› Treasury and Risk Management › Cash and Liquidity Management › In-House Cash › Bank Communication Management
Financial Accounting	› General Ledger › Accounts Receivable › Accounts Payable › Contract Accounting › Fixed Assets Accounting › Bank Accounting › Cash Journal Accounting › Inventory Accounting › Tax Accounting › Lease Accounting › Special Purpose Ledger › Travel Management
Management Accounting	› Cost Center and Internal Order Accounting › Cost Element Accounting › Profit Center Accounting › Project Systems › Investment Management › Product Cost Controlling › Profitability Analysis › Activity-Based Costing

Table 4.1 SAP ERP Financials Solution Map

Category	Application
Corporate Governance	› Audit Information System › Management of Internal Controls › Risk Management › Whistleblower Complaints › Segregation of Duties

Table 4.1 SAP ERP Financials Solution Map (Cont.)

Industry-Specific Financial Management

In addition to all of the standard financial functions, SAP ERP Financials can also provide industry-specific financial management functions. SAP has developed sets of best practices in more than 25 industries, including automotive and pharmaceuticals, which help implement processes that match your business's core accounting and reporting requirements. For example, if you work in the automotive industry sector, dealer-management features and service-parts management are best practices tools that help you manage tasks specific to your industry.

Functionality for more than 25 industries

There are also cross-industry best practices available for functions such as customer-resource management and human-capital management.

Best practices

 Example

> Consider funds management in the public sector area. The traditional organization and processes of government agencies are under scrutiny today because of shrinking funds and more involved and savvy citizens. SAP ERP Financials can help a government entity to plan and control the flow of revenues and expenditures with a modern, double-entry bookkeeping method that increases cost transparency. The public sector solution also offers active availability controls to monitor financial appropriations (such as funds appropriated for specific initiatives). Special planning techniques uniquely useful in funds management make it possible to differentiate provisional budget plans, which may have to undergo a lengthy approval or vote process.

Keep in mind that SAP ERP Financials is an open solution that can dovetail with other complementary analytical solutions from SAP or third parties.

SAP Simple Finance

In June 2014, SAP announced the launch of *SAP Simple Finance*. This is a solution that is based on SAP HANA Enterprise Cloud and provides a simple end-to-end user experience, using SAP Fiori as a user interface. SAP Simple Finance simplifies complex financial processes by eliminating data aggregation tables, providing a single application for data processing and analytics, and leveraging a cloud-based platform for rapid deployment and easy access.

What does SAP ERP Financials look like in a specific company setting? We provide two case studies that demonstrate how the product works in two different industry settings.

SAP ERP Financials Case Study 1

Review Table 4.2, which gives you a snapshot of a case study, and then read the rest of this section to see SAP ERP Financials in action.

SAP ERP Financials in a real-world setting can help solve a variety of problems based on careful analysis of an individual business's needs and processes. In this case study, an international company that places strong emphasis on building brand identity was looking for a way to enhance its capital-management processes. The company had implemented some core components of SAP ERP, so it found that the SAP Treasury and Risk Management application in SAP ERP Financials provided a fit.

Company	International liquor distributor
Existing Solutions	Core components of SAP ERP
Challenge	To enhance its capital-management processes internationally

Table 4.2 SAP ERP Financials Case Study 1

SAP ERP Financials Case Study 1

SAP Solutions	SAP ERP Financials SAP Treasury and Risk Management application
Benefits	More consistent data for bank reconciliations, direct connection with bank payment systems to avoid lost data, automating of collection processes, linking of daily cash investments to daily cash positions, and more

Table 4.2 SAP ERP Financials Case Study 1 (Cont.)

The company went with SAP because it found strategic value in the integration of cash management, automated bank statements, accounts receivable, and accounts payable features. The company proceeded to implement pieces of the cash-management solution in four phases, which we describe next.

SAP Treasury and Risk Management

Phase 1: Cash, Debt, and Investment Management

In this first phase, the company focused on managing working capital. It set goals of reconciling bank accounts on a daily basis: concentrating cash, calculating an amount of cash to borrow or invest each day, improving control and accuracy, and reducing its workforce.

During this phase, every cash entry was set up to go through a single system. That system created automatic journal entries for the general ledger; this helped employees avoid repeated rekeying, which can introduce errors. Bank reconciliations became easier, because the general ledger and bank were always aligned.

SAP ERP Financials vendor payments

In addition, by using SAP ERP Financials authorized individuals could view the same current bank statement information, so no one had to route the information internally. Phase 1, the longest of the four phases, also implemented the following capabilities:

> **Vendor payments**
> These payments were set up to upload directly into bank payment systems, which helped to avoid lost data. Payment files are now saved in SAP data interchange file format (DIF) and can be sent using an electronic data interchange (EDI) translator so that they can be read by banking systems, which can then release payments.

> **Customer receipts**
> These receipts allow customer payments to be directly uploaded into SAP applications from bank systems. Customer receipts are automatically posted into customer records in the Accounts Receivable module and the General Ledger.

> **Global bank account information management**
> This now automates the collection and processing of global bank account information (refer to Figure 4.2 for an example) and reconciles accounts for the United States and most international accounts on a daily basis. Domestic cash balances are centralized into one account, which means that the company receives a higher overnight rate of interest. Reports about current and previous-day balances help management make decisions about how to fund disbursement accounts.

> **Reduction in number of bank accounts**
> This reduction was due to a function that allows for the postprocessing of bank statements to remove discrepancies. Without these discrepancies, it is easier to manage multiple complex types of transactions from a single account rather than maintaining separate accounts by transaction type.

SAP ERP Treasury
Management

> **SAP ERP Treasury Management for debt and investments**
> This feature supports the linking of investment contracts to daily cash positions along with performance reporting and investment-tracking capabilities. The system automatically calculates debt and investment interest or fees. Settlements are prepared for the treasury department's banking and financial institution business partners based on established settlement instructions. At the end of each month, the system automatically calculates and posts accruals and foreign currency revaluations for investments and for debt.

Phase 2: Global Cash Visibility

In the second phase of implementing SAP ERP Financials, the company focused on expanding the benefits of SAP ERP Financials by bringing six foreign subsidiaries into the reconciliation system. This centralization of account reconciliation helped make all financial information more visible to the company's accounting group. It involved uploading bank information for the subsidiaries to SAP ERP Financials to help the treasury department have access to worldwide cash positions. By centralizing this international banking activity, the company was able to close several more bank accounts. In addition, more and more payments were handled electronically, eliminating the need to maintain lockboxes.

Phase 3: Straight-Through Processing

Now it was time to tackle the *straight-through processing (STP)* payment process. Using this process, rather than uploading payments through banking software, payments are sent directly to the bank from SAP ERP Financials Accounts Payable payment data. This process works regardless of what form the payment might take, such as a foreign exchange draft or wire.

The resulting system is akin to an in-house bank that instructs an external bank to pay on its behalf. Because this cuts out some steps and automates journal entries, it keeps cash in-house longer and therefore lowers costs. STP also allows for better internal controls, because vendors' own banking information in the SAP ERP Financials Accounts Payable vendor master file is used to make payments.

The company also implemented an STP process for receivables. Because about 80% of domestic collections use Automated Clearing House (ACH) as its network for processing debits to customer accounts, the company can now send a payment file directly to the bank. This cuts out one internal processing step to save time.

Automated Clearing House (ACH)

In addition, during phase 3 the company improved vendor file accuracy using SAP Business Workflow to manage vendor master files, which eliminated duplicate activity and ensured better control of vendor file information.

Phase 4: Hedging of Foreign Exchange

To help deal with fluctuations in foreign exchange rates, all foreign exchange contracts are now recorded in SAP ERP Financials. Each exchange trade creates a trade ticket, which in turn causes a confirmation of trade to be returned to the system. During this phase, the company integrates its commodities by hedging contracts into their accounting system using SAP ERP Financials. This removes the need to use a third-party foreign exchange management system.

Foreign exchange rate fluctuations

SAP ERP Financials also enabled the company to use intercompany contracts, which allowed it to handle foreign subsidiaries that have to record foreign exchange hedge contracts locally. Those local contracts are now integrated with the company's core SAP data and with subsidiaries that report at the parent-company level.

Compliance controls

The company also was required to perform auditing reviews to comply with the Sarbanes-Oxley Act. Through careful implementation of SAP software, auditing tasks were simplified and controls were established to ensure compliance. Controls were therefore put in place at the front of workflow processes, so the company did not need controls at the backend.

The company implemented segregation of duties for payment processes required by SOX. One example of this was the way that the company controlled wire transfers to set up STP so that changed vendor information could not be accessed inappropriately.

SAP ERP Financials Case Study 2

Now look at another case study of SAP ERP Financials. First review Table 4.3, and then read the remainder of the section.

Company	Large European hospital
Challenge	To improve their ability to manage patient treatments, reduce administrative workload, and reduce costs
SAP Solutions	SAP ERP Financials with SAP Patient Management application
Benefits	Improved ability to organize care system, reduced treatment time and lower costs, negotiation with insurers, and enhanced view of all activities and services delivered

Table 4.3 SAP ERP Financials Case Study 2

This technologically advanced hospital was looking for ways to meet the growing needs of patients by modifying its care process. This is a large regional hospital with a staff of more than 3,000 and more than

1,000 hospital beds. They implemented SAP ERP, including the Financials features, to help keep rising healthcare costs under control.

The Challenges

Rising healthcare costs and an aging population are putting all medical organizations under pressure. Any new system had to support business and administrative processes as well as patient care processes.

Additional challenges involved dealing with a merger, changes from government to private funding, inflation, and the conversion to the Euro form of currency.

The SAP Solution

At the time, only one vendor offered a solution for the healthcare sector. The hospital implemented SAP Patient Management, an application from an SAP partner, and SAP ERP Financials to help them control their cash management, sales and distribution, and materials management. These solutions provided tools for electronic patient management as well as the ability to reduce administrative workload and save costs.

SAP Patient Management also helped the hospital make connections between treatments and costs, enabling the hospital to negotiate rates with insurance companies and reduce patient waiting lists. SAP Business Workflow capabilities helped the hospital work with patient records as a clinical pathway to enable the best treatment decisions.

SAP Patient Management

The improvements are being shared with other hospitals to help them also find a way to improved treatment and cost controls.

Conclusion

In this chapter, you learned about the following features of SAP ERP Financials that help to drive your enterprise:

> Financial and management accounting (including basic accounting processes)

> Corporate governance to keep your company in compliance with global regulations and requirements

> Financial supply chain management to ensure that you keep your cash flow as healthy as possible

In Chapter 5, we will explore another integral part of SAP ERP: SAP Operations.

5 SAP ERP Operations

Businesses today are focusing more and more on delivering products and services quickly and efficiently. SAP ERP Operations offers a way to make the entire operational product chain more efficient by providing functionalities and tools in six areas that help you control your operations:

> Product development and collaboration

Operational control

> Procurement

> Operations: sales and customer service

> Operations: manufacturing

> Enterprise asset management

> Operations: cross functions

In this chapter, you will learn how you can use SAP ERP Operations to automate your business processes, ranging from requisitioning and receiving materials to order entry, sales and production planning, and shop-floor management. You will also learn how you can integrate quality control and quality assurance in all the important business processes, such as procurement, production, or sales.

As with all of SAP ERP, you will also have access to analytics solutions from SAP (such as SAP BusinessObjects BI tools) and data management functions, which will allow you to stay on top of your operations and quickly modify them if necessary. In addition, you will find out how role-based self-service functions allow your employees to access the features of the system easily.

SAP ERP Operations Overview

Streamline and automate processes

SAP ERP Operations helps you streamline and automate operations-related processes, such as procurement and manufacturing, which goes a long way toward creating customer satisfaction and cost savings. Take a look at the three main areas of SAP ERP Operations and how they can work to benefit your business in the following sections.

Product Development and Collaboration

Product Development and Collaboration covers the entire lifecycle of your products, from conception and requirements gathering to retirement of the product. Having information about your products—such as specification documents, formula recipes, materials management, or compliance documents—readily available helps you to quickly adapt to changing market conditions and improve your strategic planning.

> **Ex Example**
>
> Suppose the requirements for the new machine you are developing include gold-plated fittings. You realize that the current price of gold now makes these fittings cost prohibitive. With SAP ERP Product Development and Collaboration, you can gather all documents related to this project and work with internal and external supply sources to find an alternative solution that meets your needs and maintains the quality of your product.

Document management

Because of document-management tools, all documents can be updated to the latest version and routed to the appropriate people for review and approval. The Documents Management System (DMS) in SAP ERP Operations completely integrates with important logistics, supply chain management, and operation functions of the company. For example, a purchaser can attach a relevant engineering drawing to the purchase order when placing an order of an engineering product with a vendor.

Procurement

Purchasing has become a highly complex area in which having accurate and reliable data can help you manage procurement in a way that can save you a significant amount of time and money. With complete support for procurement, you can manage end-to-end procurement processes, from self-service requisitioning to optimized flow of materials and a flexible invoicing and payment system.

End-to-end procurement processes

You can also manage all of your critical documents, including bill of materials, routing data, computer-aided design models, master recipes, project plans, and parts information.

Procurement in SAP ERP Operations caters to diverse business processes and scenarios. For example, in the subcontracting procurement process you hand over some of your company's products to a subcontracting vendor, who adds value to your product and returns the same. As long as the company's product remains with the vendor for value addition, the system continues to show the company's stock at the vendor's premises. The subcontracting vendor charges for the services rendered. Another business scenario in procurement is when one plant of a company requires materials from another plant of the same company. This business process is known as interplant stock transfer in SAP ERP Operations.

Subcontracting

Procurement in SAP ERP Operations helps your company efficiently manage the ordering, receiving, and financial settlement areas of purchasing and helps you to ensure compliance with regulations and collaboration with suppliers. For example, if your company manufactures MP3 players, then the Procurement features of SAP ERP Operations allow you to find the right supplier for those little plastic headphones that you package with your product, set up systems to receive and warehouse the headphones, pay your supplier, and control the distribution of the headphones to your various manufacturing plants.

Regulations and collaboration

Handling these procurement and logistics tasks helps you improve your customer service, because your products get out faster and information about orders is consistent and accurate.

Operations: Sales and Customer Service

Automate sales-ordering processes

Sales and customer service is where you put the focus on your customer orders. You can automate the sales-ordering process, including providing customers with quotations against their inquiries and generating orders and contracts. You can use the most profitable sales and interaction channels, reduce your administrative costs by automating sales-order management, and increase customer satisfaction by providing customers with access to on-time information about their orders.

This portion of SAP ERP Operations not only helps with products, but also supports services with service-order processing and service delivery. The ability to track sales and service activity for billing or cost analyses helps you to oversee your company's profitability. You can also manage aftermarket processing of warranty claims, service orders, and returns, as well as the calculation of incentives and commissions.

 Example

Imagine a retail appliance chain that has to keep track of after-sale issues, such as warranty expirations, service calls, and product returns. With SAP ERP Operations Sales and Service features, these tasks are all centralized and connected, leading to much greater efficiency in serving customers. Here, you also take care of a product's warranty, customer returns, and credit memos.

Operations: Manufacturing

Manufacturing is the area in which you can improve and automate your production planning and automate your manufacturing process. All of the documents and specifications for your products can be managed using these tools, and they can be connected with your shop-floor systems to ensure that you maintain quality standards.

Manufacturing in SAP ERP Operations covers four distinct production types, namely, discrete manufacturing, process manufacturing, repetitive manufacturing, and Kanban. Each production type caters to the specific production challenges and demands of a specific industry, such as automobiles, pharmaceuticals, chemicals, or pen manufacturing.

 Example

> If your company is in the business of delivering high-end espresso machines to consumers, for example, you might use manufacturing tools to plan, schedule, and sequence your production line to produce the highest quality machines on a faster schedule. You can also gather production information right from your shop floor to help you see how many espresso units are being produced each day and, therefore, keep a tighter control on the dispatching of parts such as filter baskets and steam valves throughout your manufacturing cycle.

In addition, consistent quality enhances customer satisfaction, and automating production processes can lower operating costs.

Refer to Table 5.1 to learn how discrete manufacturing (also known as shop-floor control or SFC) differs from process (also known as production planning for process industries or PP-PI) and repetitive manufacturing (REM).

When reading this table, ask yourself if the current production processes consist of the characteristics listed in the first left-hand column. If so, check the next three columns to the right to see which production type (SFC, PP-PI, or REM) support it. For example, a production characteristic "Material Quantity Calculation" is in frequent use in the process industries but has little or no use in discrete or repetitive manufacturing. The SAP ERP solution for PP-PI supports material quantity calculation. Companies using active ingredient management in their production process will find that implementing PP-PI benefits them, because they are immediately able to use material active ingredient functionality without resorting to any custom-developed solution.

Production types

Manufacturing comparison

Charactertistics of Production Type	Discrete Manufacturing (SFC)	Process Manufacturing (PP-PI)	Repetitive Manufacturing (REM)
Product stability/ complexity	Complex production process with intermediate storages	Complex production process and generally without or bulk intermediate storage (mostly continuous flow and liquid-based production)	High-volume or mass production, highly stable, and without any production complexities
Production flow	Order based and with intermediate storage	Order based and mostly used in producing materials that flow such as liquids (or cannot disassemble)	Lean (simple) manufacturing
Changeover from one product to another	Frequent	Frequent	Infrequent
Make-to-stock and make-to-order production method	Supported	Supported	Supported
Batch management	Yes	Yes (extensive use)	Yes
Active ingredient management	Not available	Available	Not available
Material quantity calculation	Not possible	Possible	Not possible
Completion confirmation (backflush)	For individual operations or orders	For individual operations or orders	Period-based confirmation with backflush
Order-related production	Yes (production order)	Yes (process order)	No (planned orders)
Production-based	Lot size–based production	Lot size–based production	Period- and quantity-based production
Cost object controlling	Order-based costing	Order-based costing	Period-based costing (using product cost collector)
Process management	Yes (process integration)	Yes (process management)	No (operational method sheet)

Table 5.1 Characteristics of Discrete, Process, and Repetitive Manufacturing Types

Enterprise Asset Management

Keeping your company running smoothly not only entails making sure that you have the materials on hand to manufacture your products and that your product line is churning smoothly, but also that elements such as your building and your fleet vehicles can handle your operation. Enterprise Asset Management lets you manage the life span of physical assets from purchase through their retirement, sale, or disposal.

Physical asset lifespan

The two distinct areas of Enterprise Asset Management in SAP ERP are Plant Maintenance and Customer Service. Plant Maintenance caters to a company's in-house assets maintenance, and Customer Service attends to a customer's assets maintenance and services.

Plant Maintenance and Customer Service

Operations: Cross Functions

The tools within Cross Functions let you establish standards that can be used across all operational aspects of your business, such as quality, safety, receipt and shipment of goods and materials, and project management.

Standardized processes

Collaborating with Value Chain Partners

One of the key features of SAP ERP Operations is how it enables you to collaborate with various entities and people in managing your operations. For example, scenarios will be developed for SAP ERP Operations that help you manage temporary staffing needs when you gear up your production line for high activity. You can also manage supplier order collaboration, which allows suppliers to use self-service features to negotiate and process purchase orders and verify payment status.

Supplier order collaboration

You can even work more easily with people or partners in the field through the use of mobile data collection technologies, such as RFID (Radio Frequency Identification). Figure 5.1 shows a solution map for such technologies. To see RFID in action, simply walk through your local grocery store and watch employees scan inventory into a handheld device.

Demand-Driven Planning	Demand Visibility and Intelligence		New Product Introduction and Promotions (NPI&P)	
Serialized Inventory Management	Inbound Processing and Goods Receipt	Outbound Processing and Goods Issue	Product Tracking and Authentication	E-Pedigree Support
Serialized Asset Tracking	KANBAN	Returnable Transport Item (RTI)	UID Enabled Processing	Tool and Asset Tracking
Manufacturing	Automated Packaging		Production Order Confirmation	
Warehousing	RFID-Enabled Unloading and Goods Receipt	RFID-Enabled Putaway	Stock Count (Standalone)	RFID-Enabled Packing, Loading, and Goods Issue
Event Management	Supply Chain Event Management	Railcar Management		Container Track/Trace
Serialization Date Management	EPCIS Repository	EPCIS Data Capture and Query	Business and Operational Analytics	Enterprise Serial Number Management
Device Integration (Partner)	Device Management		Device Controller	
Hardware (Third Party)	Tags	Readers	Printers	Sensors

SAP NetWeaver

Figure 5.1 Tracking Inventory and Sales Data with RFID and Other Technologies

 Tip

> SAP ERP Operations can work with SAP Manufacturing and SAP Product Lifecycle Management (SAP PLM).

In the following section, we will take a closer look at the features of SAP ERP Operations to give you a better idea of the specific tools you can use to achieve all of the benefits of SAP ERP Operations discussed so far.

A Closer Look at SAP ERP Operations

Exactly what tools and features provide the benefits we have covered in the previous sections? Let us start by reviewing the solution map for SAP ERP Operations, shown in Figure 5.2, to see what SAP ERP Operations consists of.

SAP ERP Operations Solution Map

Efficient management of processes

As seen in Figure 5.2, SAP ERP Operations consists of eight line items from the larger SAP ERP solution map: Human Capital Management, Financials, Product Development and Collaboration, Procurement, Operations: Sales and Customer Service, Operations: Manufacturing, Enterprise Asset Management, and Operations:

Cross Functions. Together, these areas help you manage your operations more efficiently.

Figure 5.2 SAP ERP Operations Solution Map

Key Features and Functions

Product Development and Collaboration, Procurement, Operations: Sales and Customer Service, Operations: Manufacturing, Enterprise Asset Management, and Operations: Cross Functions are the core functions you use to control the manufacturing and service of products in your organization. The benefits of each of these areas were already discussed, but an overview of the features of each is provided in the remainder of this section.

Table 5.2 outlines the key areas of SAP ERP Operations based on SAP's solution map, excluding SAP ERP Financials and Human Capital Management, which we covered in earlier chapters.

Category	Application
Product Development & Collaboration	› Product Development
	› Product Data Management
	› Product Intelligence
	› Product Compliance
	› Document Management
	› Tool and Workgroup Integration

Table 5.2 SAP ERP Operations

Category	Application
Procurement	› Purchase Requisition Management › Operational Sourcing › Purchase Order Management › Contract Management › Invoice Management
Operations: Sales and Customer Service	› Sales Order Management › Aftermarket Sales and Service
Operations: Manufacturing	› Production Planning › Manufacturing Execution › Manufacturing Collaboration
Enterprise Asset Management	› Investment Planning & Design › Procurement & Construction › Maintenance & Operations › Decommission & Disposal › Asset Analytics & Performance Optimization › Real Estate Management › Fleet Management
Operations: Cross Functions	› Quality Management › Environmental, Health, and Safety Compliance Management › Inbound and Outbound Logistics › Inventory and Warehouse Management › Global Trade Services › Project and Portfolio Management

Table 5.2 SAP ERP Operations (Cont.)

 Tip

If you need additional features for dealing with suppliers, consider SAP Supplier Relationship Management (SAP SRM), covered in Chapter 9. Also, the SAP Customer Relationship Management (SAP CRM) application (see Chapter 8) provides its own sales, marketing, and service feature set.

Product Development and Collaboration

The first area of SAP ERP Operations involves all aspects of product development and innovation within your organization.

Product Development

Product Development is the application that allows you to manage the new product development and introduction (NPDI) process. You can define what your product will be, set requirements, and locate supplier resources. Tools help you collaborate in the design and development processes, including tracking information that moves between various internal departments and external partners. A new range of coordination tools such as cFolders (Collaboration Folders) and cProjects (Collaboration Projects) in SAP ERP Operations help to connect relevant stakeholders, such as customers, suppliers, manufacturers, and indenters (or traders), who use the Internet to bring about greater business synergies by working together on a project with their shared knowledge and expertise.

NPDI process

Product Data Management

With Product Data Management tools, you manage the master data for all materials that are used in the production of your goods. For example, if there is an engineering change to a product, you will see all materials impacted by this change so that you can react accordingly if manufacturing and procurement orders need to be adjusted. Specifically, you take advantage of Engineering Change Management (ECM) functionality in SAP ERP Operations to bring out greater visibility and accountability to all the desired changes to master data.

Master data for materials

To validate master data changes using ECM, you can also integrate ECM with Digital Signature. Digital Signature is a paperless initiative in which the relevant business process owners accord their consent and approval to a process by entering their SAP ERP passwords. Digital Signature functionality also takes signatures hierarchy into account, in which, for example, a manager must first digitally sign a document before the general manager signs it. If SAP Business Workflow is in place, then the approval process gets further automation, with the right information going to right business process owners for further necessary action.

Digital Signature

Product Intelligence

Product Intelligence lets you retrieve all product data, both from internal sources, such as Finance and Supply Chain, and from your external sources, such as your supplier or distributor.

Product Compliance

Product Compliance features keep your products in compliance with global regulations throughout the world.

Document Management System

Central repository

With the Document Management System (DMS), you have a central repository for all documents related to your products, such as schematics, requirements, change notices, material orders, and parts lists. If a change is required, all documents can be easily retrieved and reviewed to help with the decision process. Consider how DMS in SAP ERP Operations can bring about business process improvements with some of the following features:

Business process improvements

> Store and retrieve all of a company's important documents in a central repository, which is immediately accessible and completely integrated with the business processes mapped in the SAP ERP system

> Check-in and check-out documents as needed

> Have multiple parts and versions of a single document for tracking purposes

> Index all documents for easy and comprehensive searches

> Track all documents by their statuses and have document statuses control business functions

> Search all documents by keywords in the long text of a document

> Organize all documents in a structured and hierarchical way

> Approve documents by individual digital signatures and also by a series of digital signatures

> Distribute documents to relevant stakeholders

> Access documents on the Internet (WebDocuments)

> Have the option of working with SAP Easy DMS via a Microsoft Windows Explorer interface

> Limit access of documents to only the relevant stakeholders through authorization options

Tool and Workgroup Integration

The Tool and Workgroup Integration segment allows integration of most major CAD/CAM tools with SAP ERP Operations. SAP DMS integrates with third-party engineering drawing tools, such as AutoCad.

Procurement

Procurement is all about ordering the materials or products you need to run your business. You can provide Employee Self-Services (ESS) through the catalog features, and you can connect product designers, suppliers, manufacturers, and customers to automate your procurement activities. The Procurement application shown in Figure 5.3 helps you manage the entire procure-to-pay process and includes the following:

Manage the procure-to-pay process

> Requisitioning

Features

> Purchase request processing

> Trading contracts

> Purchase order processing

> Invoice processing

> Delivery schedule management

> Sourcing

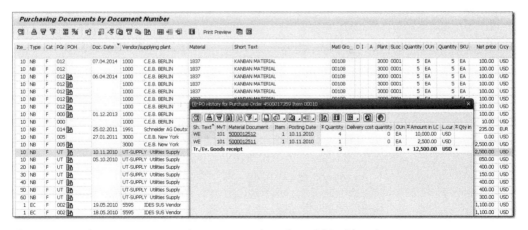

Figure 5.3 Tracking Various Stages of Procurement through Useful Dashboards

Employee role-based work center

In Figure 5.4, you can see how tools for finding and viewing information on a variety of procurement-related items are combined in one employee's role-based work center. This person can check information about purchase requisitions, purchase orders, and vendors and inspect items by delivery date, vendor, material code, and more. In addition, the system maintains complete visibility and traceability to every successive action taken in the entire chain of SAP ERP Operations. For example, a user who created a purchase requisition can see the current status if the procurement department has asked for requests for quotations from suppliers or placed purchase orders with specific suppliers and can even determine when the warehouse receives the goods against the same purchase requisition.

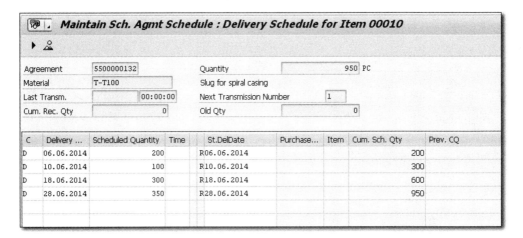

Figure 5.4 Delivery-Schedule Management with Sophisticated Tools

Purchase Requisition Management

Purchase Requisition Management contains the tools for creating a purchase requisition for products or services required by your company. Purchase requisitions can be created directly in the Purchase Requisition area, in which the requisitions information is manually entered, or the requisition can come in as a result of being triggered by another SAP component, such as Plant Maintenance or Production Planning.

Automatic creation with MRP

The system can also automatically create purchase requisitions when the user runs material requirements planning (MRP). MRP is a planning tool that evaluates the demand and supply of a material. If the demand is greater than the supply and there is an anticipated material shortage, then the system creates purchase requisitions for the shortage quantity. If the existing and forthcoming supply is enough to fulfill the demand of a material, then the system does not create any new purchase requisitions.

With the right system settings in place, you can tell the system what type of existing or forthcoming material supplies it should consider during MRP. For example, assume that you have stock of a material that still moves through quality inspection. Because the approval and acceptance rating of the material is so high or the material is normally not rejected due to quality reasons, you would like the system to consider quality stock when it performs material planning for a specific material.

Operational Sourcing

Operational Sourcing looks at the requisition and then determines the best source from which to obtain the products or services requested. There may be enough inventory on hand to cover the request, or an outside source can be automatically checked to determine if it has the desired quantity of product in stock. An important feature of Operational Sourcing is the source list. You can use the source list to maintain a comprehensive list of sources (suppliers or vendors) from whom you can procure a material. The source list is not confined to external procurement only; you can use it when another plant of your company produces a product or component that you use in manufacturing your own product. You can set quota management functionality in case you have multiple sources for a given material to ensure timely deliveries of materials and to diversify your supply sources of a material.

Purchase Order Management

Purchase Order Management lets you follow and monitor the purchase order as it is created and then sent to the supplier. Delivery schedules can then be created and tracked along with expeditors (reminders) to remind you to follow up with the supplier if necessary. The procurement process also enables automatic vendor evaluation, in which on-time delivery, quantity compliance to delivery schedule, and quality compliance to specification helps to calculate the vendor's performance score. The vendor-evaluation functionality allows you to effectively decide which vendors are reliable and should be offered more business and better or preferential payment terms.

Contract Management

Contract Management involves establishing contracts with your suppliers to set quotas on the amount of product they are to supply you with over a specific period of time. By doing this, you ensure that you do not run out of products at a critical time and that you have a backup supply ready should you need it. It also allows you to set up all of your vendor information in a central location.

Contract types There are two types of contracts:

> **Quantity contract**
A quantity contract binds the company to purchase an agreed-upon quantity of a material from a vendor at an agreed-upon price. The quantity contract also has a validity period. Each time the company is ready to procure material from the vendor and with reference to the quantity contract, it creates a Contract Release Order (CRO). When creating a CRO, the system checks to see if the contract is still within the validity periods and also whether the required procurement quantity of the material against the CRO was already used up during past purchasing activities.

For example, the company has a quantity contract with a pump manufacturer (vendor) to purchase 1,000 pumps at $5,000 each and within a one-year period (validity). The company has already purchased 700 pumps in the past. It now wants to buy 100 more pumps. To do so, it will create a CRO with reference to a quantity contract for 100 pumps. While doing this, the system checks to see if the contract is still valid. If so, it allows the business process owner to create the CRO. If the procurement quantity had been 400 pumps, the system would not have allowed CRO creation, because only 300 more pumps can be purchased against the quantity contract.

> **Value contract**
The value contract has all the features and controls of quantity contract, but it focuses on the overall total value of the contract when creating CROs.

Apart from contracts, SAP ERP Operations also offers scheduling agreements. A scheduling agreement binds the vendor to deliver a specific quantity of a material as per the agreed-upon and communicated delivery schedule. The user can create the scheduling agreement manually or can use assistance from the SAP ERP system, which can automatically create schedule lines during Material Requirements Planning (MRP).

Scheduling agreements

Invoice Management

When goods are received from your suppliers, you can use the Invoice Management tools to receive, verify, and process the invoices. The invoice is compared to the goods received for quantity and price and then, if correct, can be used for payment processing. This is known as three-way verification, in which an invoice is not only compared to a purchase order, but also to a goods receipt of materials. All data is then stored and updated in Materials Management and Financial Accounting. After invoice recording, the next logical step is payment processing of the vendor invoice, which is handled in the Accounts Payable subcomponent of Financial Accounting.

Operations: Sales and Customer Service

Each of the areas of Sales and Customer Service in SAP ERP Operations provides a rich set of tools, which we have discussed in the following sections.

Sales Order Management

Sales Order Management helps you handle everything from customer inquiries to quotations and placing orders. The e-commerce platform in SAP ERP Operations enables you to manage online orders. There are even tools to help you control sales incentives and commissions. Specifically, Sales Order Management includes the following:

E-commerce platform

> Account processing
> Internet sales
> Managing auctions
> Inquiry processing
> Quotation processing

> Trading contract management

> Sales order processing

> Mobile sales

> Inbound telesales

> Contract processing

> Billing

> Incentive and commission management

> Returnable packaging management

> Consignment

If you take sales orders, you will find these tools invaluable.

Aftermarket Sales and Service

Support your customers

Aftermarket Sales and Service deals with all of the details that come up after you have made the sale; this is the time when your customers are concerned with getting the product installed or arranging for ongoing service support. These tools help you support customers with planning issues, including production installation, service contracts, and warranties.

Operations: Manufacturing

This area of SAP ERP Operations includes Production Planning, Manufacturing Execution, and Manufacturing Collaboration. If you manufacture products, you can use this part of SAP ERP Operations to figure out your production processes, capture real-time production data, and work with other companies or vendors to complete the production process. The following features help you to automate your entire manufacturing operation:

Production Planning

> **Production Planning**

Helps you create strategies for your production sequence and schedules. With these tools, you can set up your factory floor optimally so that you can deliver customer orders as promised. You can use the following planning tools to optimize your production planning in SAP ERP Operations:

- **Material Requirements Planning (MRP)**

  MRP is a planning tool that calculates the net requirements of a material to evaluate if material shortage exists. If and when it finds any, it proceeds to create planned orders, which the user can convert into purchase requisitions for externally procured material or into production orders in case of in-house production.

- **Sales and Operations Planning (S&OP)**

  What company does not deal with the intensive and exhaustive exercise of creating annual sales and production plans? Let SAP ERP Operations help you prepare a sales plan that completely synchronizes with your company's production plan. You can use the S&OP planning tool to plan individual materials or even a group of materials, which is known as a product group.

- **Flexible Planning**

  This planning tool enables you to define your company's own key performance indicators (KPIs) so that your product gets to customers faster and in an efficient manner.

- **Long-Term Planning (LTP)**

  The LTP tool provides a comprehensive simulation environment to enable you to plan your future materials, capital, machine capacities, and resource requirements.

- **Forecasting**

  Leverage the power of forecasting by effectively using a product's historical sales or production or procurement data to predict how much to procure or produce. Various forecasting models, including constant, moving average, and seasonal moving average, are available.

> **Manufacturing Execution**

  Provides a tool for gathering actual production data, managing production processes, and allocating resources to get work done. You can keep track of inventory during the manufacturing process and dispatch inventory as needed. Manufacturing Execution completely integrates with several other logistics, supply chain, and financial components, such as Materials Management, Quality Management, and Product Cost Controlling.

Manufacturing Execution and Collaboration

> **Manufacturing Collaboration**
> Provides a means for integrating product data from outside
> sources into SAP. Integrating external software, such as Process
> Control System (PCS), with SAP ERP Operations enables you to
> bring about greater visibility to all stakeholders. There are two dis-
> tinct yet interlinked tools available that help to integrate data
> between an SAP ERP system and an external manufacturing collab-
> oration software. These tools are Process Management and Execu-
> tion Steps (XSteps).

SAP Enterprise Asset Management

Asset procurement, performance, and disposal

To manufacture goods or provide a service, you need physical assets,
such as land, an office or plant, machinery, computers, and perhaps a
fleet of trucks to deliver your products or cars for your sales force.
With the features of SAP Enterprise Asset Management, you can plan
for the purchase of these items and their maintenance and optimal
performance and manage their depreciation, disposal, sale, and
replacement when necessary. If your company is in the business of
providing maintenance and operations services to its customers'
assets, then the Customer Service component in SAP ERP Operations
is relevant to attend to those business processes. SAP Enterprise Asset
Management consists of the following applications:

Applications

> Investment Planning and Design

> Procurement and Construction

> Maintenance and Operations

> Decommission and Disposal

> Asset Analytics and Performance Optimization

> Real Estate Management

> Fleet Management

As previously explained, SAP Enterprise Asset Management distinctly
covers two different yet interconnected areas of SAP ERP Operations,
Plant Maintenance and Customer Service. Take a look at the business
processes in these two areas in the following sections.

Plant Maintenance (PM)

For its in-house maintenance assets, a company maintains the master data of equipment and also its functional location. Master data is the information that resides in the system for a much longer period of time and facilitates running day-to-day business processes. A functional location is a physical, process-oriented, or spatial location of company. Equipment is also often installed in functional locations. For example, the functional location "pumping station" may have several pieces of equipment, such as pumps, installed. The PM component can handle maintenance of both functional location and equipment. Standard maintenance tasks, such as preventive and corrective maintenance to ensure equipment is always in optimum working condition, are some of the standard features of the PM component.

Features and tools such as work permits and work clearance management (WCM) are available to ensure that before any sensitive work begins, the necessary permits and clearances are in place. For example, to lay a new water pipeline by cutting a road cross-section, a company needs permits and authorizations from relevant governmental, building, and regulatory authorities before actual pipe-laying work can begin. WCM takes care of all necessary authorizations.

Newer features, such as shift notes and shift reports, enable maintenance personnel to record important maintenance details and activities that happened during their shifts.

Customer Service (CS)

In the CS component, a company similarly maintains customer equipment and customer functional location data. The difference here is that the equipment category that the company uses for customer equipment allows for maintenance of sales-related data. This sales-related data contains information such as customer numbers and the specific sales organization or division within the company that deals with maintenance of customer equipment. The entire business process of customer equipment maintenance in CS is alternately known as resource-related billing, in which the customer quotation and customer billing are subcomponents of SD components of SAP ERP. Figure 5.5 shows how CS works in an integrated environment among various business functions.

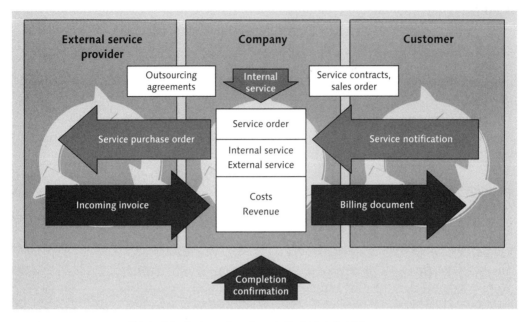

Figure 5.5 Business Functions in Customer Service

Operations: Cross Functions

The Cross Functions tools allow you to establish standards for your products and your company that can be applied across the board. This area includes the following:

> **Quality Management**
> Lets you set standard quality practices throughout your organization that also help you focus on prevention and process improvement. Quality Management integrates with your procurement, production, sales, and maintenance processes so that every operation gets the necessary quality inspection and checks needed for improved business processes. Companies can also use some of the latest offered functionalities, such as Stability Study, Failure Mode and Effects Analysis (FMEA), and Control Plan, to bring about more and improved quality checks to the entire supply chain's management and operations. Stability Study finds greater application in process industries, whereas FMEA and Control Plan apply to all manufacturing and procurement processes.

> **Environment, Health, and Safety Compliance Management**
> Practices for environmental, health, safety, and regulatory compliance and corporate responsibility. For stringent environmental- and health-compliance requirements, the EHS component in SAP ERP is here to attend to all compliance-related business processes.

> **Inbound and Outbound Logistics**
> Allows you to control the movement of products and materials into and out of your logistics and operations. You can manage your warehouse's in-yard activities and monitor the posting and distribution of outbound goods, including the calculation of duties and customs requirements. Inbound refers to materials that the company expects to receive from various external sources and is part of the Materials Management (MM) component in SAP ERP Operations. Outbound belongs to the Sales and Distribution (SD) component.

> **Inventory and Warehouse Management**
> Includes features to handle *cross docking* (a logistics procedure that avoids inventorying stock by breaking down received shipments on the dock and immediately shipping them out again), warehousing and storage, and physical inventory. You can keep close track of the value of inventory and control goods receipts, storage, picking and packing, and stock transfers.

> **Global Trade Services**
> Contains tools to help you stay in compliance with foreign regulations, import and export tariffs, customs regulations, licenses, permits, and trade agreements, such as NAFTA.

> **Project and Portfolio Management**
> Houses the functions for project selection, prioritization, resource allocation, budgeting, metrics, scheduling, and risk management. Because most organizations usually have multiple projects running at the same time, program managers can easily determine the status and progress of each project in their portfolio via the features in the Project and Portfolio Management area.

The following case study shows you how an agricultural firm gained substantial savings in time and money with SAP ERP Operations.

SAP ERP Operations Case Study 1

Table 5.3 provides a snapshot of the first case study related to SAP ERP Operations. You should review it before moving on to the rest of this section.

Company	Leading European agricultural firm
Existing Solutions	SAP R/3
Challenge	To unify business processes and extend them to international divisions
SAP Solutions	SAP ERP Operations, SAP NetWeaver
Benefits	Ability to track materials flow, use of analytics for strategic planning, reduction of manual input

Table 5.3 SAP ERP Operations Case Study 1

A leading European agricultural firm with almost 50 companies under its umbrella specializes in producing animal feed and feeding systems. The company is also involved in the industrial electronics industry.

The Challenges

Unifying business processes
With so many companies forming a single entity, it was important to find a way to unify the business processes across the entire enterprise. At the same time, the company was looking toward international growth and finding ways to deal with a changing market.

The company's international growth meant that it had to have standards in place for processes that could be extended to international divisions and offices.

The SAP Solution

The company implemented SAP R/3 in 2000, which went a long way toward standardizing processes. By upgrading to SAP ERP Operations, the company could take advantage of the new system's ability to support an entire business process throughout an organization.

SAP NetWeaver Application Server
SAP ERP Operations was put in place with about 80 users, but provided a connection for approximately 350 remote users by using SAP

NetWeaver Application Server (SAP NetWeaver AS). SAP ERP Operations was useful in several areas. First, the company built new production plants to extend its sales abroad and used the features of SAP ERP Operations to streamline its production line. In addition, features of SAP ERP Operations helped the company handle a variety of distribution methods in different countries. The company was able to flexibly adapt its systems to support these differences, including distributing from central warehouses or enabling salespeople to pick up and deliver products to customers.

A single, common IT system supports processes such as production and materials management for the whole international enterprise. Support for additional languages helped the company adjust to a more global business, and transparency of operations to satisfy international regulations further helped to support international expansion.

The Benefits

The company is using analytics in SAP ERP Operations to help find a strategic future for the company. The ability to manage the overall flow of materials using SAP ERP Operations has helped the company get a handle on internal transactions between divisions. Because this planning of the flow of materials is automated, manual input and administration of the system is much easier and less labor intensive.

SAP ERP Operations Case Study 2

Now take a look at Table 5.4, which shows you the highlights of the second case study in this chapter.

Managing the overall flow of materials

The largest plant of a major European car company produces all of the company's diesel engines. More than 590,000 engines are assembled there every year. The company employs approximately 2,600 people and has sales of €1.86 billion annually.

Company	Austrian car engine plant
Existing Solutions	SAP R/3 for Financials, Controlling, HCM, Production Planning, Materials Management, Sales and Distribution, Quality Management, and Plant Maintenance

Table 5.4 SAP ERP Operations Case Study 2

Challenge	To improve the recording of movement of goods and to record on-site rather than manually
SAP Solutions	SAP ERP Operations with mobile data entry (RFID) and warehouse-management features
Benefits	Faster execution of production processes and fewer errors in warehousing

Table 5.4 SAP ERP Operations Case Study 2 (Cont.)

The Challenges

The plant was aware of inefficiencies in the recording of goods movement. In addition, because data was not recorded on-site but instead was written and then entered into PCs, errors were being introduced in warehousing procedures.

Delays in recording goods information were causing slowdowns in production operations. The company needed a way to record information on the plant floor that would accelerate its operations and increase accuracy.

The SAP Solution

Radio-frequency and mobile devices

SAP ERP Operations allows integration of radio-frequency features via mobile devices equipped with scanners. This direct input of data helped to avoid errors that manual entry had introduced. These portable devices could be handheld or mounted on forklifts for ease of use.

The scanners were linked directly to SAP ERP Operations. Users quickly adopted the new system, and physical processes, such as shipping, engine assembly, and maintenance, occurred much faster and with a higher degree of accuracy. Because the system controls transport orders and organizes them in a logical way (to create the most efficient itineraries possible), all pick orders were triggered and sent out electronically.

The Benefits

SAP Console

Because data is sent directly from the SAP system and integrated into SAP ERP Operations, it is available immediately for analysis or processing. The solution was also cost-effective, because the mobile devices required no middleware to link to SAP ERP Operations via SAP Console.

Because the user interface is customizable for both look and language, users adopted the new system easily. The solution also made the company aware of new efficiencies that could be realized in change management, production control, and warehouse management. The company is already reworking its stock-receipt process to incorporate mobile devices and SAP ERP Operations.

Conclusion

In this chapter, we looked at SAP ERP Operations, which makes your entire product chain more efficient. There are three key pieces of SAP ERP Operations:

> Procurement and Logistics Execution

> Product Development and Manufacturing

> Sales and Service

Together, these areas of SAP ERP Operations provide features that allow you to handle your entire product lifecycle.

In Chapter 6, we will look at SAP's human management solution: SAP ERP Human Capital Management.

6

SAP ERP Human Capital Management

Every company in the world, whether small or large, involves people. In fact, *human capital,* as they are called, can be a company's greatest asset. People have the personal skills and experience that make your systems work. They bring vital social skills to your sales, customer, and vendor relationships. And they come up with new product ideas and enhancements for your company that enable you to make innovative leaps and stay competitive.

In recent years, great strides have been made to develop processes that help a company recruit, retain, and support talented people and also measure a workforce's productivity. Those who work in the human resources area at a company will find useful tools in SAP ERP Human Capital Management (SAP ERP HCM) for recruiting and retaining talent, running training programs, and administering compensation programs. In addition, managers can use these tools to record employee performance, attendance data, and more. Employees can use self-service tools for tasks such as checking available leave, educating themselves on benefits, and reporting their time worked on projects. This self-service aspect of SAP ERP HCM frees up human resource professionals to focus on other, more innovative tasks.

Recruit, retain, and support

In this chapter, we explore the value of efficient HCM systems for your organization, examine the specific features in SAP ERP HCM, and look at some case studies of SAP ERP HCM in action.

How SAP ERP HCM Fits in an Enterprise

SAP ERP HCM provides tools for human resource professionals and others in an enterprise that supports them in four areas: Workforce Process Management, Talent Management, Workforce Deployment, and End-User Service Delivery (Figure 6.1). We will explore each of these important areas in the following sections.

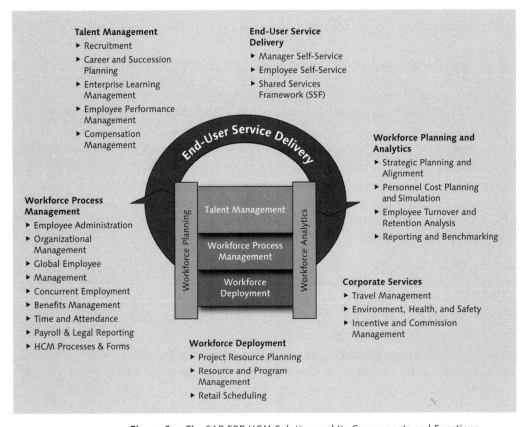

Figure 6.1 The SAP ERP HCM Solution and Its Components and Functions

Workforce Process Automation to Improve Efficiency

Workforce Process Management addresses several vital HR functions for any enterprise, including benefits management, time and attendance, and payroll.

Workforce Process Management is also the area of SAP ERP HCM that allows you to automate basic processes for managing employee information, such as vacation time availability or job training; managing your organizational structure and policies, including employee handbooks; and tasks such as coordinating employee relocation activities (i.e., the transition of employee records).

Automate basic processes

 Keeping Time under Control

An important feature of the Workforce Process Management element of SAP ERP HCM is time management. You can coordinate activities such as the calculation of wages or employee time accounts, in which employee vacation, sick time, and other time off is accrued. SAP ERP HCM also offers a special working environment for time administrators in which they can record bonuses, change working times, approve overtime, view time account balances, and so on from a single screen. Calendar views provide information about employee availability in a snapshot. In addition, by using web-based SAP Employee Self-Services (ESS), you can move time-management processes online so that employees can record their own time, request time off, and access their own data even while out of the office. Using web-based SAP Manager Self-Services (MSS), line managers can view all of their employees' time activities, approve employees' vacations, and so on from a single screen.

Improving Talent Management

Hiring the right people, growing their skills, and recognizing their usefulness to an enterprise is one of the most important jobs that human resource professionals do. The Talent Management processes included in SAP ERP HCM help you with tasks including recruiting, onboarding new employees, managing an employee's training requirements, helping employees improve their job skills, and career planning. This is all done while ensuring that employees get appropriate performance and compensation reviews so that you can develop the leaders you need to take charge of your enterprise in the future.

Recruiting, onboarding, and managing

Tip

You can also use SAP ERP HCM to link performance reviews and assessment ratings directly to compensation programs to help managers make more accurate decisions on pay changes.

With SAP ERP HCM, you can assign an employee's training courses as objectives in the the appraisal document. On successfully completing the training course, SAP ERP HCM will automatically update the appraisal document with the course results. When the annual appraisal process is completed, SAP ERP HCM will automatically update the employee's profile with the new skills the employee acquired when he or she successfully completed training.

More Efficient Workforce Deployment Management

Workflow and assignment handling

Workforce Deployment Management involves managing the human resources in your enterprise so that their workflow and assignments are handled efficiently. It also involves enabling employees to track their own activities, which can save project managers from having to rekey employee-reported hours and help prevent potential rekeying errors.

Note

SAP recently acquired Fieldglass, a cloud-based vendor management system (VMS). Companies can use Fieldglass VMS to better manage their nonemployee workforce, such as temporary staff, independent contractors, and any services provided through a statement of work (SOW). You can find more information about Fieldglass in Chapter 10.

End-User Service Delivery

The very nature of HR leads to high volumes of transactions and numerous HR, employee, and manager interactions. The End-User Service Delivery component is designed to ensure that your company can deliver its HR services to its customers in an efficient, standardized, and cost-effective manner. It can do this by providing employees and managers with their own web-delivered self-service tools to manage their own data and the tasks related to managing their team with little or no input from the HR team. Interactions between employees, managers, and the HR department that cannot be handled automatically by the self-service applications are handled by the SAP Shared Services

Framework for HR (SSF-HR), a powerful relationship management tool that enables companies to deliver consistent, standardized, and cost-effective employee and manager services from anywhere in the world.

 Note

SAP Shared Services Framework for HR (SSF-HR) is the newer version of the Employee Interaction Center (EIC). SSF-HR has all the functionalities that were previously available in EIC and provides better usability and web-based functionalities.

Beginning with SAP Enhancement Pack 6 (EHP6), SAP E-Recruiting is integrated with SSF-HR. Recruiting activities that were formerly handled by recruiters or by HR Business Partners (HRBP) can now be handled by personnel of the Shared Services Center (SSC). Both internal and external candidates are supported by this integration.

Gaining Insights through SAP ERP HCM Analytics

Although workforce analytics is no longer a separate part of SAP ERP HCM, it is important to note that you can use SAP analytic tools throughout SAP ERP HCM to improve reporting, analyze centralized data, and measure activities. Once you have access to vital HR data in useful forms, you can make better decisions about your HR initiatives.

Workforce analytics in SAP ERP HCM include the following:

> Workforce planning to monitor workforce trends and demographics

> Workforce cost planning and simulation

> Workforce benchmarking to measure workforce processes against external benchmarks

> Workforce process analytics and measurement for processes, including payroll, time management, and benefits

> Strategic alignment of business activities and overall business goals using a balanced scorecard framework

> Workforce analysis with reporting and analysis tools to monitor success factors and key performance indicators (KPIs)

> Talent management analytics and measurement to get a handle on your pool of talent, recruiting processes, learning, succession programs, and more

Make vital HR decisions

Now that we have provided you with a look at the types of activities that SAP ERP HCM can help you deal with, let us examine the specific tools you use to control these activities.

A Closer Look at SAP ERP HCM

As you have seen so far in this chapter, SAP ERP HCM offers capabilities to manage talent, including recruiting and learning how to use add-on packages.

Real-time access by managers and employees

SAP ERP HCM also provides improved workforce analytics and performance-management tools. All of these features of SAP ERP HCM can be combined with self-service capabilities (see Figure 6.2) that enable real-time access by managers and employees throughout an organization, giving them instant access to information and processes, freeing up HR staff time, and providing more direct access to work processes for users. In this section, we outline the specific pieces of SAP ERP HCM that help you achieve these results.

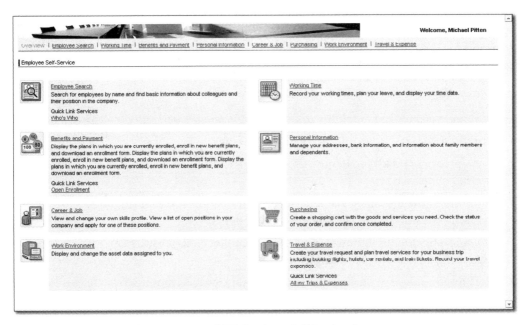

Figure 6.2 Typical SAP Employee Self-Services Page

Key Features and Functions

SAP ERP HCM provides capabilities and benefits in four key areas of your business. Table 6.1 outlines these areas based on SAP's solution map. The sections that follow explore these categories in more detail.

Category	Application
Talent Management	› Competency Management › Recruiting › Employee Performance Management › Talent Review & Calibration › Employee Development › Enterprise Learning › Succession Management › SAP Talent Visualization by Nakisa (STVN) › Compensation Management › Talent Management Analytics
Workforce Process Management	› Employee Administration › Organizational Management › Global Employee Management › Benefits Management › Healthcare Cost Management › Time and Attendance › Payroll and Legal Reporting › HCM Processes and Forms › Workforce Planning › Workforce Cost Planning & Simulation › Workforce Benchmarking › Workforce Process Analytics & Measurement › Strategic Alignment › SAP Org Visualization by Nakisa (SOVN)
Workforce Deployment Management	› Project Resource Planning › Resource and Program Management › Retail Scheduling

SAP ERP HCM solution map

Table 6.1 SAP ERP HCM Solution Map

Category	Application
End-User Service Delivery	› Manager Self-Services › Employee Self-Services › SAP Shared Services Framework for HR (SSF-HR)

Table 6.1 SAP ERP HCM Solution Map (Cont.)

Talent Management

The Talent Management processes in SAP ERP HCM include the following capabilities:

› Recruitment enabled by SAP E-Recruiting

› Career management to help managers review employee profiles and help employees manage their own career paths through self-service features

› Succession management to ensure that the right people are identified and actively developed so that new leadership is always prepared to step in

› Visualization of data enabled by SAP Talent Visualization by Nakisa (STVN) to help employees with their career planning

› Enterprise learning management enabled by SAP Learning Solution

› Employee performance management to handle tasks such as objective setting and employee reviews

› Compensation management to help you establish performance and competency-based pay and long-term incentive programs

Enable integrated talent management In the past, processes such as recruitment and training might have happened independently, with data stored in different systems. SAP ERP HCM makes it possible to have an integrated talent management system through a centralized data warehouse for every employee. With this integrated data system, all employee data is available to managers and HR professionals, ensuring a seamless system for hiring, training, and promoting people.

Imagine that you have a job opening in your department. Using SAP ERP HCM, you can search across a talent warehouse of potential candidates, and, after deciding on a candidate, you can easily transfer that person's data into your employee records upon hiring. After an employee is on board, you can offer predefined or personalized learning programs and use the data that a manager has entered about the employee to pinpoint areas of weakness or strength. You can also match the employee with the right training opportunity. HR can also use SAP ERP HCM tools to measure learning program effectiveness. Using self-service, your new employee can help to plan his own career and update skills data in his personnel records.

SAP Learning Solution can be used with SAP ERP HCM to integrate back-office ERP functionality with a learning-management system (LMS) and a learning-content-management system (LCMS). SAP Learning Solution supports e-learning with synchronous and asynchronous interactions and in-person training. Using SAP Learning Solution, you can author content and manage that content with a learning portal.

SAP Learning Solution

Training Administrators can manage learning schedules of employees (attendees) through a convenient self-service interface. SAP Learning Solution (LSO) provides a convenient self-service interface for employees and managers to access from ESS and MSS.

Analytical features allow you to build-in assessments of learning so that you can improve the quality of education that you deliver to your employees. You can also add a training simulation tool called *SAP Tutor* to the learning solution. SAP Tutor helps you create, edit, and deliver interactive electronic training. Because your employees can access this self-learning training, it frees up training or HR staff for other tasks.

SAP Tutor

SAP Visualization

SAP resells visualization solutions by Nakisa. Both solutions are able to be fully integrated with SAP ERP HCM. Similar to other SAP offerings, if you run into product issues with either of these two products you can open a ticket with SAP Active Global Support (AGS).

The visualization solutions contain two modules:

> SAP Org Visualization by Nakisa (SOVN)

> SAP Talent Visualization by Nakisa (STVN)

Both SOVN and STVN have user-friendly user interfaces and help to visualize the enterprise HCM data. We will discuss each of these modules in further detail in the following subsections.

SAP Org Visualization by Nakisa

SOVN provides a visualization of the enterprise reporting and organization structures to help HR staff, executives, and line managers effectively manage the enterprise. SOVN provides advanced search capabilities and connections with external social media sites to help employees easily communicate and collaborate.

SOVN consists of the following modules:

> **Org Chart**
> This is used for real-time visualization of organizational reporting structures and data. Managers can use this module to view key HR-related data, such as headcount, age, diversity, and compensation.

> **Org Modeler**
> This is used to model "what-if" scenarios and plan for organizational changes in reporting structures. As and when you create your "what-if" scenarios, you can use the built-in analytics to immediately calculate the effect the new structure will have on direct and indirect headcounts, salaries, and budgets. The module enables you to write the changes directly back to the SAP ERP HCM system.

> **Org Audit**
> This module was formerly referred to as the *Data Quality Console*. It offers 48 preconfigured template rules to audit your enterprise SAP ERP HCM data. You can create rules to identify data errors in Organizational Management, Personnel Administration, or Compensation. When the system identifies a data error, the module offers functionality to drill down to each error to view the category, severity, history, and details of inaccurate data in addition to tips on how to correct the error. Using this module, you can sched-

ule data extractions from SAP to ensure audits are performed on the most current data in your enterprise SAP system.

> **Team Manager**
  Managers can use this module to create and maintain position-employee relationships, plan future changes to positions by defining the effective date on which the new change becomes active, and manage any organizational changes.

SAP Talent Visualization by Nakisa

STVN helps enterprises engage in talent planning and establish a sustainable workforce by managing competency requirements, identifying critical positions in the enterprise, mitigating key role vacancies, and monitoring key performance indicators.

Sustainable workforce

STVN consists of the following modules:

> **Career Planning**
  Employees use this module for career planning. Using this module, employees can understand where they are currently, plan where they want to be, and understand how to get there. Employees can review their existing competencies, and then plan their careers by searching for jobs they are interested in and perform a profile match up to understand what competencies are required to become qualified for that job. Employees can also create and maintain their employee profiles. In employee profiles, employees can maintain details such as their mobility (willingess to relocate or travel) and their work experience.

> **Succession Planning**
  Managers and talent management specialists use this module for succession planning activities (see Figure 6.3). Using this module, you can identify what positions are critical for your enterprise and flag them as key positions. You can also identify successors for those key positions and identify their competencies, competency gaps, and their preparedness to occupy the key positions when they become vacant. Using this module, you can build the bench strength for the key positions. Managers will be able to perform talent comparison as well, which allows managers to compare two or more individuals against established criteria.

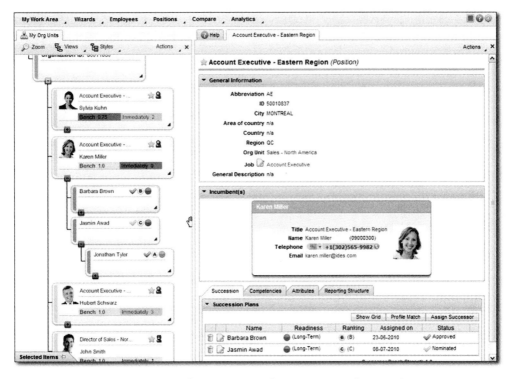

Figure 6.3 Perform Succession Planning Activities for a Key Position

➕ **Tip**

To implement SAP Visualization by Nakisa (SOVN and STVN), you should have organizational structures, including person and position data, available in SAP ERP HCM.

> **Goals and Performance**
> This is the newest module in STVN. Nakisa has provided new configuration steps in the SAP IMG to configure the Goals and Performance component. Using this module, managers and employees will be able to conduct the annual appraisal process.

Workforce Process Management

Workforce Process Management involves all activities that need to be processed to sustain a productive workforce. There are three categories of features in Workforce Process Management:

> The benefits management feature allows an organization to customize benefits offered to new employees and to define benefits plans on a broader level.

> Time and attendance features provide tracking, monitoring, record keeping, and evaluation of employee time data that you can tie into various projects.

> The payroll capabilities in Workforce Process Management support legal regulations in 47 countries to help ensure compliance and can easily handle issues of different currencies, languages, and collective agreements.

> The talent features in Workforce Process Management support end-to-end talent management. These features include talent acquisitions, learning, pay for performance, and succession management.

In addition, by taking advantage of the SAP Interactive Forms software by Adobe, processes such as hiring, termination, reassignment, and taking a personal leave of absence can now be handled without leaving a lengthy paper trail. Electronic forms can be transmitted instantly and are easier to track, complete, and modify. The forms-handling capabilities of SAP ERP HCM can be based on workflow templates that are included with the software. By using the concept of defined user roles, you can give the employees access to the forms they need.

Using electronic forms

Workforce Deployment Management

Workforce Deployment Management involves the vital area of resource management. Resource planning for projects and teams is accomplished with a workforce scheduling application.

In addition, you can align project tracking with employee time tracking and financial data. The workforce scheduling application also includes the capability to schedule retail staff. If you take into account customer traffic, shifts, and employee skills, you can allocate people in a way that matches your specific retail operation.

Workforce scheduling application

 Example

A chain of grocery stores that are open 24 hours a day with three shifts of workers will have different scheduling needs than a chain of walk-in clinics open from 9:00 a.m. to 4:00 p.m. four days a week.

End-User Service Delivery

End-User Service Delivery empowers both employees and managers to take responsibility for their own HR-related tasks via self-service applications and provides a powerful tool for enabling excellent customer service to employees through SAP Shared Services Framework for HR (SSF-HR). Additional details about each option are as follows:

ESS and MSS

> *Employee Self-Services* gives employees quick access to their own data through a simple-to-learn, employee-specific portal. Employees can maintain their own data, check their paystubs online, process leave requests, complete forms and checklists, and check their benefits entitlements. Changes to employee data completed via Employee Self-Services can be instantly reflected in the core HR system or sent for approval from either the HR team or the employee's manager.

> *Manager Self-Services* uses the benefits of the SAP Enterprise Portal to empower managers to take control of their own teams, giving them the ability to manage employee-related transactions, such as recruitment requests, team budgets, and project management tasks, and to produce their own reports.

> *SAP Shared Services Framework for HR* offers companies a centralized employee customer service program that provides an integrated tool to enable administrators to manage employee requests via phone, email, chat, or fax. It uses a sophisticated call tracking and monitoring tool to ensure that employees get excellent, correct, and consistent service no matter from where in the world the service is provided.

HR Renewal

HR Renewal is part of SAP's HR core renovation program. HR Renewal offers many functional and user-interface improvements.

User-friendly

It also delivers a new HR Professional role, which is different from the existing HR Admin role. With HR Renewal, users can process daily tasks in a user-friendly UI and with fewer clicks of the mouse.

Tip

> To implement HR Renewal, you need to be on ECC 6.0 and SAP Enhancement Pack 6 (EHP6). HR Renewal is also delivered-in an early shipment of SAP Enhancement Pack 7 (EHP7).
>
> You can upgrade to SAP EHP6 and choose not to implement HR Renewal.

To see how SAP ERP HCM functions in the workplace, read through the following case studies.

SAP ERP HCM Case Study 1

Table 6.2 gives you a quick overview of the first case study regarding SAP ERP HCM. Go through it before you read the rest of this section.

Company	British university
Existing Solutions	Older COBOL-based system
Challenge	To improve and lower the cost of payroll, to improve access to HR data, and to reduce errors in data entry
SAP Solution	SAP ERP HCM, SAP Employee Self-Services (ESS), SAP Manager Self-Services (MSS)
Benefits	Lower costs of payroll processing, freeing up HR staff, improved reporting and access to data, reduced errors

Table 6.2 SAP ERP HCM Case Study 1

A large British university located in London had a collection of legacy systems in place for HR and payroll procedures. They used a labor-intensive COBOL-based system that had been around for many years—so many years, in fact, that they were having trouble finding IT people who were trained to work with the system. The system left staff performing many calculations manually, and the awkwardness of the older system was costing the university time and money.

Moving from legacy
HR and payroll
procedures

SAP ERP HCM, with an SAP for Higher Education & Research industry solution portfolio, allowed the university to streamline its systems and automate its processes. The university also took advantage of the SAP Employee Self-Services (ESS) and Manager Self-Services (MSS) application. In this case study, we look at the challenges faced by the university, the SAP solution, and the benefits that resulted.

The Challenges

The university faced several challenges at the outset. First, it needed to improve its HR and payroll operations and reduce the cost of its payroll systems. In addition, the university sought to improve the way management controlled and reported employee activities. The existing systems allowed for duplicate data entry, which resulted in data errors that can occur when keying data. Finally, the university needed a way to improve access to important HR data to help management make good business decisions.

At the time during which the university was reviewing its existing system, there was also an increased need to improve reporting to meet government requirements. New funding regulations demanded more data and reports than the current systems could generate.

The SAP Solution

The university chose an SAP solution in part because of the company's track record working with universities, which have different needs from private-sector companies. Moreover, SAP's offerings could run on the existing Microsoft SQL Server database and could handle the UK's public-sector-specific payroll requirements.

Automate HR

The first goal was to automate manual HR and payroll activities. Then the university needed to set up ESS and MSS capabilities. Finally, the university needed to implement a solution that consolidated data entry and improved reporting capabilities.

To achieve these improvements, the university implemented SAP ERP HCM software, including payroll, recruitment, learning solutions, and succession management with SAP Talent Visualization by Nakisa features. University employees worked with a consulting partner with experience in higher education who trained the university's own team in how to work with this software.

The solution automated payroll calculations, which reduced the time it took to prepare payroll and also improved accuracy. In addition, the implementation consolidated several applications so that data would only be entered once. Data cross-checking and audit reports now help with correcting any errors that exist with the data.

Free up HR staff

The SAP ESS application the university put in place allows employees to update a great deal of their own personnel information, freeing up HR staff for more important activities, such as recruitment and maintaining employee relations.

The SAP MSS application enabled the managers to approve employees' learning requests and assign mandatory training requirements to employees.

Managers and HR used STVN functionalities to identify key positions and potential successors for them. STVN was also used to build bench strength for these positions and to identify skill requirements for employees to occupy the identified key/vacant positions.

Employees used the career-planning functionality in STVN to search for internal positions that they had interest in and to identify the skills required for those key positions and the training requirements that would enhance their skills.

Reporting features improved both the quality and accuracy of reports. The uniform interface the university adopted made the system simple for people to use. Interfaces that were built between the SAP software and a number of non-SAP applications allowed university employees to leverage the features of both. For example, the university's online recruitment website interacts with the SAP ERP HCM software, enabling users to export information onto the website and import it back into the SAP system.

Reporting

Looking toward the Future

The university hopes to build on its SAP solution by adding more ESS and MSS initiatives supported by the portal component of SAP

NetWeaver. This would enable people to complete processes such as performance appraisals and travel requests via the SAP application.

SAP ERP HCM Case Study 2

To help you understand how SAP ERP HCM works in real life, we have included a second case study. Table 6.3 gives you a quick snapshot of this study.

Company	German automobile manufacturer
Existing Solutions	Legacy systems
Challenge	To improve HR processes to better support flexible scheduling and sophisticated leave management
SAP Solution	SAP ERP HCM
Benefits	Improved system operation with a single interface and optimized personnel administration

Table 6.3 SAP ERP HCM Case Study 2

The Challenges

This German automaker has a reputation for innovative, flexible resource scheduling, including a very sophisticated leave-management operation. The company needed an HR system that could support optimized processing of all employee data, from new hires to payroll, for its 120,000 employees. The company also needed to manage pension programs for 75,000 retired employees.

The automaker decided to restructure its entire personnel-management, time-management, and payroll processes to achieve the speed, accuracy, and flexibility required.

The SAP Solution

The company assigned a group of 50 people to work with SAP Consulting to implement SAP ERP HCM. Using SAP's ASAP methodology, the group performed an analysis of existing processes and established a blueprint for meeting HR requirements using SAP's solution.

The in-house team created a quality-management system to check, recheck, and document test cases. They established 850 new work agreements and resource regulations to work with SAP ERP HCM. A production environment was created with hardware partner HP.

SAP solutions included organizational and time-management functions, tools for managing the company pension plan, and a web-based manager workplace.

The Benefits

Today, SAP ERP is used to process 750,000 transactions every day and can even handle peak operations of 1 million transactions. All HR-related legal requirements and work schedules are stored in a single system. Automatic workflows have improved work scheduling and helped employees to complete tasks faster.

Approximately 8,000 HR users can access payroll and time-management records easily. Because of built-in standard features in SAP ERP HCM, it is easy to modify processes as needs change, and such change requires little custom programming.

Conclusion

In this chapter, we looked at the Human Capital Management portion of SAP ERP, which helps your HR professionals manage your staffing and ongoing employee needs. This solution supports enterprises in the following areas:

> Talent Management, including features such as recruiting and career planning

> Workforce Deployment Management for planning and managing resource activity

> Workforce Process Management for dealing with issues such as benefits and time and attendance

> End-User Service Delivery to bring self-service capabilities to employees and managers

In Chapter 7, we will explore an alternative or add-on to SAP ERP HCM: a cloud-based HR solution called SuccessFactors.

7

SuccessFactors

SuccessFactors is a cloud-based HR solution that offers all of its applications in the cloud and focusses on advanced business execution and reducing TCO. SuccessFactors was founded in 2001 and was acquired by SAP in December of 2011. SuccessFactors continues to operate independently, but is now known as an SAP company. SuccessFactors has over 20 million subscribers and supports 35 languages, covering 177 countries.

In this chapter, we will explain the different components that make up SuccessFactors. We will then look at the tools that it offers to different businesses, and discuss how to access and deploy these tools.

SuccessFactors Components and the Cloud

SuccessFactors offers a unique HR suite called Business Execution (BizX). Customers can implement the entire BizX suite or pick and choose individual solutions for implementation. SuccessFactors provides 11 different solutions, which are grouped into categories:

> Core HR
  - Employee Central
  - Employee Central Payroll

> Analytics solutions
  - Workforce Planning
  - Workforce Analytics
> Talent solutions
  - Recruiting
  - Onboarding
  - Learning
  - Performance and Goals
  - Compensation
  - Succession & Development
> Social Collaboration
  - SAP Jam

 Note

SuccessFactors solutions are available only in the cloud; they are not offered as on premise or for on premise implementation.

Later in this chapter, we will discuss each of these solutions.

SuccessFactors focus areas

To execute the business strategy and attain business results, Success-Factors has three focus areas. The different modules are aligned with one of the focus areas, as detailed in Table 7.1.

Attract and Retain	Align and Perform	Learn and Develop
Succession Planning	Goals Management	Learning Management
Career Planning	Performance Management	Social Learning
Social Sourcing	Calibration	Content as a Service
Recruiting Management	Compensation Management	Extended Enterprise

Table 7.1 SuccessFactors Focus Areas and Alignment

A Closer Look at SuccessFactors

In this section, we will briefly discuss the different solutions in SuccessFactors and their functionalities.

Core HR

Employee Central is the core HR system of SuccessFactors BizX that is used by HR professionals, managers, and employees. The system combines HR transactions, processes, and data with social collaboration features and mobile functionality. Customers can use Employee Central to collect and manage personal information (see Figure 7.1) about employees (name, date of birth, address, dependents, etc.) and employment information (job- and compensation-related details). Managers and HR professionals can also use Employee Central to interact with employees.

Employee Central

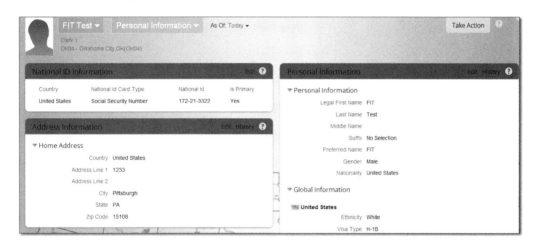

Figure 7.1 Capturing an Employee's Personal Information in Employee Central

Data maintained in Employee Central is effectively dated, meaning you can define when a recent change was made. When data is maintained in Employee Central, you can configure the module such that any changes made to the data triggers a workflow notification mentioning that a change is made, as well set up an approval process.

Note

Employee Central uses the Metadata Framework (MDF). MDF is a generic platform that enables users to define their objects, configure object relationships, and create rules and workflows via a rich, configurable user interface. Users and implementation teams use MDF to suit diverse customer requirements. SuccessFactors is moving more and more of their modules to MDF, thereby enabling users to configure the modules to suit their specific business needs.

By using permissioning, you can configure who can see the data, who can change the data, what type of changes can be made, and which employees can be managed by which user (i.e., determine the line of sight).

SuccessFactors has also developed the Employee Central Payroll function, so organizations can manage payroll on the cloud, and Employee Central Service Center, which was developed for HR service delivery.

Analytics Solutions

Planning   *Workforce Planning* enables customers to identify future state and workforce scenarios. Using Workforce Planning, customers can capture planning assumptions, forecast demand, create models, and perform gap analysis for skills across identified critical job roles. Workforce Planning also enables customers to identify critical gaps that pose a risk to the enterprise strategy execution. Workforce Planning provides a Best Practice Strategy Bank, which lists almost 100 different tactics and strategies that organizations can leverage to improve their attraction and retention processes.

Analytics   *Workforce Analytics* helps customers gain insights into workforce trends, risks, and opportunities and improves the distribution of talent-related metrics to frontline managers. Workforce Analytics can source data from SAP HCM, SuccessFactors Employee Central/BizX, or any other third-party application.

Next, we will break down the talent solutions into different subcategories.

Talent Solutions

Talent Solutions encompass functionalities and strategy for performance, learning, and recruiting. Customers can implement any of these solutions as needed as a standalone, or all of them for a seamless process. We will go through each of these solutions in the normal progression of recruiting and hiring, through maintaining and compensating.

Recruiting

SuccessFactors Recruiting Marketing offers social recruiting, social apply, search engine optimization, and talent community marketing. Customers of any recruiting solution (SAP E-Recruiting, other ERP recruiting solutions, or ATS) can implement Recruiting Marketing as an add-on to their current recruiting application.

Recruiting Marketing enables customers to create customized, branded pages for Facebook (see Figure 7.2) and other social networking sites. Using SuccessFactors Recruiting Marketing, customers can post job publications to these social media sites and to job boards and job aggregators. More importantly, job publications are displayed in search engine results.

Social network recruiting

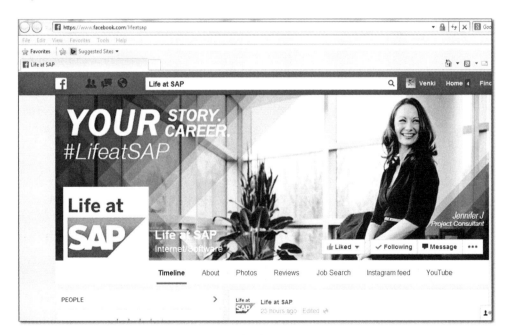

Figure 7.2 SuccessFactors Careers Page on Facebook

Customers can use SuccessFactors Recruiting Marketing to build a talent community and be in constant touch with their candidates.

Talent-acquisition lifecycle

SuccessFactors Recruiting supports the full talent-acquisition lifecycle. Customers can use SuccessFactors Recruiting to create requisitions, send requisitions for approvals, and create candidate portals from which candidates can search for and apply for jobs and keep track of their applications.

Recruiters can view the candidate applications, rank the applications based on job requirements, move the applications through the different hiring stages, generate offer letters from within SuccessFactors Recruiting, send the offer letters for approval, and release them to the successful candidates.

Hiring managers can view their requisitions, the number of applications received, and the status of the candidates, can enter interview notes, and can use Candidate Stacker to view the different candidates.

Onboarding

Once you've attracted and hired new talent, your organization still has some work to put in. Getting a new employee situated often falls to HR, but their role is only a small part of making a new hire feel comfortable and happy. *SuccessFactors Onboarding* is a new solution that was released in 2013. Customers can use SuccessFactors Onboarding to hire their successful candidates, help candidates to complete their initial paperwork, create welcome messages, and facilitate socialization. With Onboarding, the goal is to increase employee engagement and satisfaction and in turn, have a faster time to contribution.

Learning

Online courses

SuccessFactors Learning is a learning management system (LMS; see Figure 7.3 for a listing of courses in SuccessFactors LMS) that helps customers to take courses online and from anywhere. The courses can be accessed from any device as well (laptops, tablets, or smartphones).

In SuccessFactors, LMS can be integrated with your SuccessFactors Performance Management and Development forms as well. When LMS is integrated to SuccessFactors Performance Management, training courses from the LMS course catalog can be assigned as an objective for a particular employee. In this way, employees' training performance can be tracked and performance status set in the annual appraisal document.

Figure 7.3 Learning Catalog in SuccessFactors LMS

Ex Example

In regulated industries, such as life sciences and pharmaceutical, compliance is an area of importance, and customers are required to capture, store, and manage training data.

In regulated industries, LMS is deployed for career development, sales training, operational training, safety training, partner/supplier training, customer education, and cross-functional training compliance. SuccessFactors offers Validated LMS for regulated industries, which provide a secure, compressive system that supports audit processes, such as records storage, electronic signatures, GxP (Good Practice regulations and guidelines), FDA 21, and CFR Part 11.

SuccessFactors also provides a service called *iContent*, in which the organization's training courses are hosted by SuccessFactors. Those courses can be developed by the organization itself, or purchased from a third-party course provider. The only requirement is that these courses need to be SCORM/AICC compliant. When the training courses are hosted by SuccessFactors, the training courses are delivered anytime, anyplace, and anywhere with SuccessFactors LMS.

Customer trainings

Performance & Goals

SuccessFactors Performance & Goals helps organizations assign goals to employees, and monitor their progress. The solution provides in-depth employee performance information so organizations can retain, reward, and develop their talent. Its provides an intuitive user experience to develop clear and well-defined goals, ensure goals are aligned to organizational goals, and help managers with performance calibrations (see Figure 7.4).

Compensation

The *Compensation* solution allows organizations to keep tight reins over payroll and other compensation areas, such as pay-for-performance (determining bonus payouts to employees). Functionalities in this area include budgeting, hierarchy-based approvals, and total rewards statements.

Succession & Development

After cultivating your employees, it's always a shame to see them bring their talents to other organizations. Keep your employees challenged and moving up the ladder towards leadership with *SuccessFactors Succession & Development*. With this solution, enterprises can identify the key positions in the organization, identify successors for the key positions, identify positions that can be filled by external recruiting, conduct talent calibration, and have employees fill out their employee profiles.

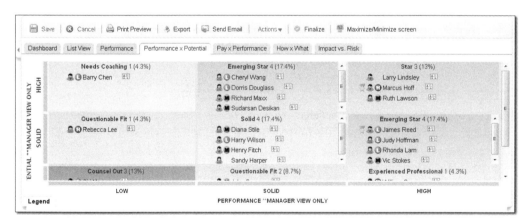

Figure 7.4   Performance vs. Potential Calibration in SuccessFactors

Social Collaboration

SAP Jam is SAP's social network solution that is offered in the cloud. SAP Jam facilitates collaboration between employees and teams in your organization while working on their day-to-day tasks and on larger projects.

The Jam instance includes the following tabs (see Figure 7.5):

> HOME
> This is the default landing page users see when they log in to Jam.

> PROFILE
> On this page, users can maintain their profile details. The profile wall displays the Jam activity of a user and his or her followers.

> GROUPS
> The GROUPS tab provides a virtual space for teams to collaborate on, share, and gather inputs on documents, share status updates, and share any information that is relevant to the project and tasks at hand.

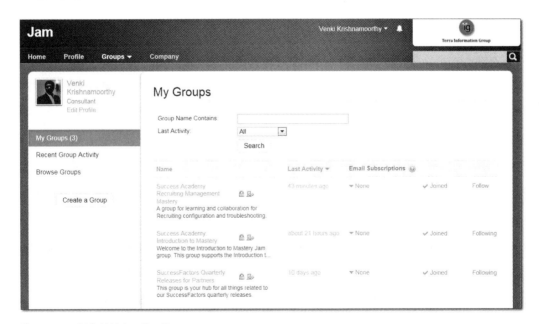

Figure 7.5 SAP JAM Landing Page

When a group is created, the group admin can invite project members to join the group. When an employee is invited to join a group, the employee will see the invitation in his or her INBOX displayed on the Jam HOME tab. All invites and group-related notifications will be automatically pushed to the employee's Jam wall.

As a member of the group, the employee can post messages and feed posts for other group members to read and respond to.

 Tip

While posting a message, a group member can use the @ symbol to specify the group member for whom this message is intended. The message will appear on the HOME tab of the specified group member.

When the group member uses the @@ symbol, then the message is delivered to all members of the group.

When a message is posted to the group wall, the message will be visible for all group members to read and comment on.

> COMPANY
This tab provides an overview of the network in the organization. You can use the DIRECTORY option to locate individuals or get an overview of employees who are registered in Jam. You can click on the DOCUMENTS option to review all the documents posted by the employees. The COMPANY tab also provides options such as COMPANY WIKI PAGE, DASHBOARD, GROUPS, LINKS, and so on.

Administration Tools

As a SuccessFactors customer, you will be required to form a SuccessFactors Admin group within your organization, which will be responsible for maintaining common SuccessFactors-related administrative tasks. Some common admin tasks include creating annual appraisal documents, assigning roles to individual users, changing user settings for users, and so on.

OneAdmin

You can process admin-related tasks from within the admin console (in SuccessFactors it is referred to as OneAdmin). As shown in Figure 7.6, the different administrative tasks are categorized by individual modules. Common employee-related admin tasks, such as updating user information and setting user permissions, are categorized separately.

Figure 7.6 OneAdmin Console

The OneAdmin console has online help and tutorials that can be accessed by users to learn more about the OneAdmin console and how to use its functions.

The RESOURCES & MATERIALS portlet available from the same page that provides access to the OneAdmin Console contains links to HELP & TUTORIALS, RELEASE SUMMARY, and CUSTOMER COMMUNITY, along with documentation about ROLE-BASED PERMISSIONS ADMINISTRATION.

In the following sections, we will discuss some of the specific administration tools.

Provisioning

Every customer will have their own provisioning environment, which allows an organization to configure SuccessFactors for specific

Configure
SuccessFactors

business needs. SuccessFactors only provides access to the provisioning environment to the implementation teams; customers will never get access to the provisioning environment.

In the provisioning environment, the implementation team will set the required configuration settings, as captured in the configuration workbook.

XML Programming

When consultants have to customize SuccessFactors applications (e.g., when creating a new field), they will make the changes in the XML file (see Figure 7.7). The changed XML file will be uploaded into SuccessFactors from the provisioning environment.

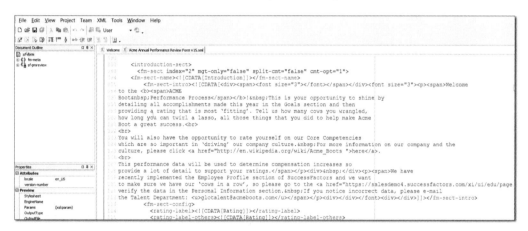

Figure 7.7　Sample XML Code

 Tip

You do not need to have extensive experience with XML programming to configure SuccessFactors. There are many excellent self-learning tools and guides available online.

To read XML files, you need to use an XML editor. There are many XML editors available at no cost from the Internet.

SAP HANA Cloud Platform

SAP offers SAP HANA Cloud Platform (HCP) as a platform-as-a-service solution for its customers. Using HCP, developers can develop applications that leverage the speed and scale of SAP HANA. HCP is provided on a subscription-based pricing model.

SAP HANA Cloud Platform provides the following:

> A JVM (Java Virtual Machine)-based integrated development environment

> An application container

> An application extension package of shared services and APIs

> Access to SAP partner ecosystem

As seen in Figure 7.8, HCP provides an IDE (Integrated Development Environment) that can be used by the partners to develop applications in the cloud that can be easily deployed by customers in their SuccessFactors and on premise solutions. For example, SuccessFactors currently does not fully offer U.S. Benefits. A partner of SuccessFactors has developed a U.S. Benefits application using HCP. Customers interested in implementing U.S. Benefits can purchase that app and deploy it in SuccessFactors. Any HCP-based applications purchased from the SAP store will be deployed in the cloud.

Applications in the cloud

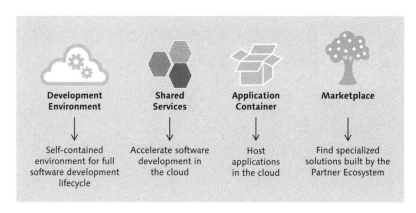

Figure 7.8 An Overview of the SAP HANA Cloud Platform (HCP)

Deploying SuccessFactors

Many existing SAP customers have more than one deployment option when they implement SuccessFactors solutions.

> **Note**

As of mid-2014, SuccessFactors does not provide the Benefits solution in the cloud. Customers who wish to implement Benefits in the cloud can implement one of SuccessFactors' validated solutions, such as Benefit-focus. This third-party solution will then be integrated with SuccessFactors Employee Central.

SuccessFactors does not provide a time management solution, either. Currently, SuccessFactors only offers Absence Management in the cloud. However, you can implement SuccessFactors Employee Central in the cloud and integrate Employee Central with your current time management application.

SuccessFactors offers EC Payroll for its customers. EC Payroll requires Employee Central as a prerequisite, and there is an additional subscription fee for EC Payroll. Currently, EC Payroll supports 27 countries, and SuccessFactors is continuing to add available countries.

Deployment options

As shown in Figure 7.9, the three options to deploy SuccessFactors are:

> **Hybrid HCM**
In this model, the customer implements all the SuccessFactors talent modules in the cloud. Core HR remains on premises. The applications in the cloud can be integrated with the on premise core HR via the delivered integrations.

> **Side by side**
In this model, the customer might implement certain applications of SuccessFactors (core HR or talent) in the cloud and maintain other applications on premises. We could also have scenarios in which the customer will have certain regions in a full cloud HCM model and other regions in a hybrid HCM model. This scenario is very common in global rollouts. Customers might eventually move all their HCM applications in all the regions to the cloud, but in the interim certain regions might have a few applications in the cloud and a few on premises. When you deploy a two-tier HCM model, it is important to understand what your system of record might be and to plan your integrations accordingly.

> **Full cloud HCM**
>
> Customers can implement the entire SuccessFactors suite and move all of their HCM applications to the cloud. In a full cloud HCM, core HR (SuccessFactors Employee Central), the talent modules (SuccessFactors Recruiting, Performance/Goals Management, Learning Management, and Succession Management), and HR Analytics (Workforce Planning/Workforce Analytics) are deployed in the cloud.

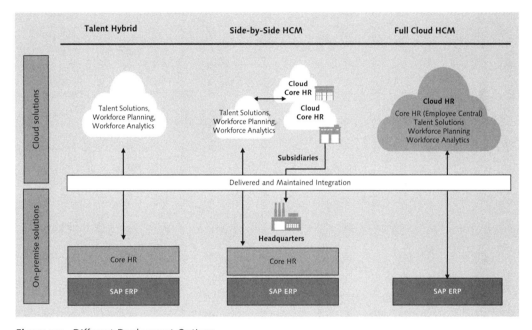

Figure 7.9 Different Deployment Options

SAP is encouraging its customers to move all their HCM applications to the cloud. As seen in Figure 7.10, all of the company's HR applications are based in the cloud. From the cloud-based HCM application, you can integrate with any of your on premise applications or even with other cloud-based applications. By moving to the cloud, customers incur a lower TCO (total cost of ownership), which enables them to concentrate their budget on their core business. SuccessFactors offers a consumer-grade usability experience compared to the on premise modules.

SAP recommendations

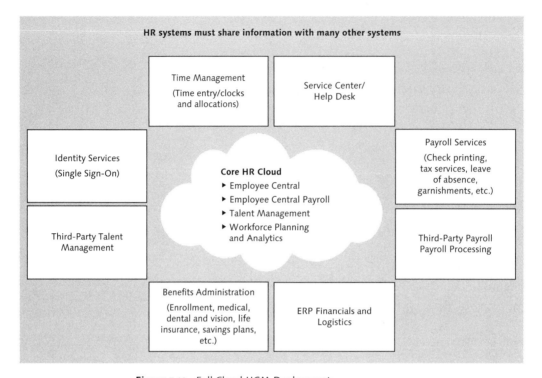

HR systems must share information with many other systems

Time Management
(Time entry/clocks
and allocations)

Service Center/
Help Desk

Identity Services
(Single Sign-On)

Payroll Services
(Check printing,
tax services, leave
of absence,
garnishments, etc.)

Core HR Cloud
▸ Employee Central
▸ Employee Central Payroll
▸ Talent Management
▸ Workforce Planning
  and Analytics

Third-Party Talent
Management

Third-Party Payroll
Payroll Processing

Benefits Administration
(Enrollment, medical,
dental and vision, life
insurance, savings plans,
etc.)

ERP Financials and
Logistics

Figure 7.10 Full Cloud HCM Deployment

SuccessFactors Integration with SAP ERP HCM

Very often, the SuccessFactors solutions are integrated with other applications. These applications might be on premise or cloud applications. Hence, integration with other applications is an important component in SuccessFactors implementations. An improperly designed and deployed integration might not provide the desired business outcomes for the customer.

Currently, SAP has delivered integrations for the pay-for-performance and attract-to-hire business processes.

Integration options   As shown in Figure 7.11, you can integrate SuccessFactors and SAP HCM in one of the three ways:

> **File-based integration**
> In file-based integration, the data is exchanged between Success-Factors and the SAP HCM by flat file uploads/downloads. You can schedule the upload/download as a nightly job.

> **Web services**
> For certain integration scenarios, delivered web services are available. These web services can be used for integrating SuccessFactors and SAP HCM.

> **Integration cloud**
> When you implement SuccessFactors, you also have the option to implement your integrations in the cloud. The integration tools SAP HANA Cloud Integration (HCI) and DELL BOOMI are both cloud based. SuccessFactors has a number of delivered integrations (commonly referred to as iFlows) between Employee Central and other modules that leverage DELL BOOMI. All the delivered integrations between SuccessFactors modules and on premise SAP ERP HCM are supported by SAP HANA Cloud Integration.

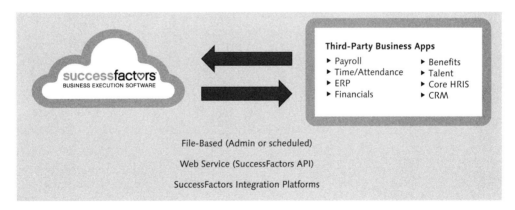

Figure 7.11 Different Integration Options

When you move your integration to the cloud, you will not need any dedicated hardware and there is no on premise footprint.

Tight integration between your HR system of record and other business applications is essential to enable efficient functioning of your enterprise-wide applications.

> **▶ Note**
>
> SAP HANA Cloud Integration (HCI) is a middleware integration platform from SAP that is available in the cloud. As shown in Figure 7.12, you can design real-time, bidirectional process and data integration by using HCI. The delivered iFlows can be implemented using HCI as well. HCI provides centralized monitoring and administration.
>
>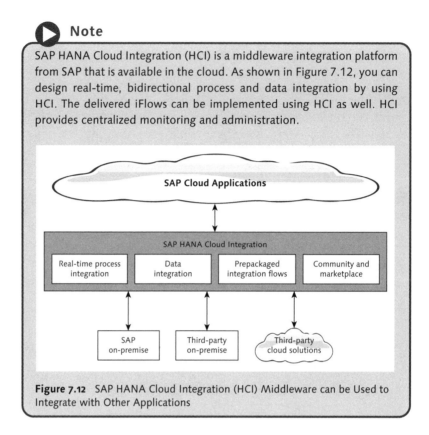
>
> **Figure 7.12** SAP HANA Cloud Integration (HCI) Middleware can be Used to Integrate with Other Applications

To see how SuccessFactors functions in the workplace, read through the following case studies.

SuccessFactors Case Study

Table 7.2 gives you a quick overview of the first case exemplifying SuccessFactors. Review it before you read the rest of this section.

Company	A manufacturing company
Existing Solutions	On premise HCM system

Table 7.2 SuccessFactors Case Study

Challenge	Currently, the annual appraisal process is done in pen and paper. The final scores are then uploaded into the on premise HCM system.
Challenge (Cont.)	The company currently uses an Applicant Tracking System (ATS) from a third-party vendor. HR feels that the ATS has outlived its utility and needs to be replaced with a more up-to-date technology.
	The company uses a learning-management system from a third-party vendor. This LMS is integrated with the on premise HCM system. The integration is painful, and very often the data is not updated correctly. Creating and maintaining online courses are also very cumbersome. The current LMS does not support social learning or virtual classrooms.
SuccessFactors Solution	› SuccessFactors Performance/Goals Management › SuccessFactors Recruiting › SuccessFactors Learning Management System
Benefits	› Employees more engaged in the annual appraisal process › Leverages new recruiting trends such as talent community, and social recruiting › Ability to create and maintain online courses; employees more participative through social learning and virtual classrooms › More accessible data enables improved reporting

Table 7.2 SuccessFactors Case Study (Cont.)

A manufacturing company based in the United States currently uses an on premise SAP HCM system. They have an annual appraisal process that is based on pen and paper. Their learning-management system is from a third-party vendor and is integrated with the on premise SAP HCM system. The ATS is from a third-party vendor and is fully integrated with SAP HCM.

HR has developed a new talent strategy and has presented it to the executive leadership. The executive leadership like the newly formulated talent strategy and encourage HR to implement the strategy. To support the new strategy, HR needs new talent applications that support mobility and social elements and an application that can be inte-

A new IT system to support the company's talent strategy

grated easily with their existing SAP HCM system, and it must also support easy reporting. After proper due diligence, the company's CIO decides to invest in the talent modules offered by SuccessFactors.

The added advantage offered by SuccessFactors is that the applications can be easily accessed from the existing SAP Employee Self-Services (ESS) and Manager Self-Services (MSS). Hence, training and change-management efforts will be minimal.

The Challenges

Because the current annual appraisal process is still on pen and paper, HR is not able to track the appraisal process effectively. HR cannot determine who has completed the appraisal proces and who is still in progress.

The current ATS is not popular with the talent-acquisition team or with job applicants. The talent-acquisition team constantly receives complaints from candidates about difficulty in completing the job applications, and difficulty in tracking their job applications. The ATS does not provide for questionnaire functionality, and so prescreening functionality is completely absent from the current ATS. The current ATS also does not support current recruiting trends, such as talent community or social recruiting.

The training team's biggest complaint about their current LMS is the inability to create courses. The training team currently uses third-party courses that are hosted by the vendor. Employees complain that the online courses are slow, resulting in frequent early termination of the courses. Notification of course completion is not consistent; often employees who have not completed the courses receive notification that the courses were successfully completed.

The SuccessFactors Solution

The manufacturing company decided to update their technology solutions to meet their business requirements and support current HR trends. After evaluating different software vendors and their solutions, the company decided to implement SuccessFactors. The company identified business owners of Performance/Goals Management, Recruiting, and Learning to support the implementation of SuccessFactors solutions. The business owners were requested to make themselves available at least three days every week to work with the team to determine the business requirements, testing, and change management.

The company assigned a team lead for each solution. The team lead will work full time on the project and work with the business users for project design, testing, and rollout.

Company preparation

For the appraisal process, the company decided to use two templates: one for managers and the other for all nonmanagers. Enterprise goals will be cascaded to the employees, and employees will be encouraged to develop personal goals and have their goals aligned to a team or enterprise goal. Managers will hold at least one formal meeting every quarter with each of their direct reports to determine the progress against each goal and to provide any support that will be required.

For a learning management system, the company decided to use iContent, SuccessFactors' hosting application for online courses. By using iContent, the company can develop courses and send them to SuccessFactors to be converted into SCORM format. The company will use WebEx to support virtual classroom training.

Based on the recommendation from SuccessFactors, the company decided to implement SuccessFactors Recruiting Marketing as well. By implementing Recruiting Marketing, the company was able to support recruiting best practices, such as talent community, social recruiting, and ability to publish job postings automatically to different job boards. During change management, the talent-acquisition team was trained to develop questionnaires and attach them to job requisitions. These questionnaires helped the recruiters to prescreen candidates and automatically rank the job applications based on their scores (responses) on the questionnaires.

Recruiting Marketing

With the implementation of these SuccessFactors solutions, the company was able to greatly improve their talent acquisition and retention processes. Some of the benefits include managers and employees who are more involved in the annual appraisal process, recruiters receiving a greater number of completed and qualified applications, and the training department's ability to create relevant training courses and make them available to employees. By leveraging the reports and ad-hoc queries available in SuccessFactors, HR is able to better track on the metrics and report on them.

Looking toward the Future

The company was very impressed with the results achieved by implementing SuccessFactors. The company is now planning to implement SuccessFactors Employee Central as well and move the employee data to it from their current legacy applications. This would allow the company to maintain all their HCM applications in the cloud, thereby enabling better integration between Employee Central and other SuccessFactors talent solutions. This tighter integration will enable the company to fully implement an integrated talent environment and gain better insight into their resources.

Mobile enabled The added advantage is that SuccessFactors is fully mobile enabled, and any workflow approvals generated from Employee Central can be viewed and approved on mobile devices. Mobile enablement removes bottlenecks that the company currently sees when the managers are travelling or on paid time off (PTO). With SuccessFactors Employee Central, the manager can nominate peers or direct reports as their delegates when he is on PTO, and all workflows are automatically routed to the delegates for further processing.

Conclusion

In this chapter, we looked at SuccessFactors and the different solutions it offers to HR professionals and to employees to manage their daily tasks. SuccessFactors supports enterprises (global, large, and small/medium businesses) in the following areas:

> Core HR applications to support your HR business fulfillment. This core HR can be integrated with your payroll, benefits, and providers.

> Talent management with solutions that support recruiting, learning, annual appraisal process, and succession-planning business requirements.

> An analytics tool to develop HR and talent-related dashboards for all your managers and executives.

> Self-service capabilities for managers and employees.
> Delivered mobility experience.

These applications provide features that enable you to support all of your HR-related requirements.

In Chapter 8, we will look at SAP Customer Relationship Management (SAP CRM). Whereas SuccessFactors helps you with supporting HR business processes, SAP CRM helps you take care of one of your most important assets: your customers.

8

SAP Customer Relationship Management

Without customers, most companies would be out of business. Gaining, servicing, and retaining customers are some of the most important activities any business can undertake. Managing customer relations begins when you market a product, continues through the entire sales cycle, and still does not end when the sale is complete. If you are good at maintaining customer relationships and focus on supporting your customers after they buy, your customer relationships can endure for years to come.

SAP Customer Relationship Management (SAP CRM) is part of the SAP Business Suite. SAP CRM allows for more efficient and effective interaction with customers, retailers, distributors, and others to help you support marketing, sales, and after-sales service.

In this chapter, we explain the role of SAP CRM in an enterprise and the specific features that SAP CRM offers you. We also provide case studies of real-world uses of SAP CRM.

How SAP CRM Fits in an Enterprise

SAP CRM is a very robust offering, and if you follow the solution map to its detailed level (see Appendix C) you will tally up perhaps a hundred or more features delivered by SAP and partner products. In this section, we look at the solution map for SAP CRM and general capabilities in each of its six major areas:

SAP CRM areas

> Marketing
> Sales
> Service
> Partner Channel Management
> Interaction Center
> Web Channel

These areas are outlined in the SAP CRM solution map.

SAP CRM Solution Map

The solution map for SAP CRM is a bit complex, so we will tackle that first. In Figure 8.1, you can see that there are three main areas of CRM functionality:

Main areas of CRM functionality

> Marketing
> Sales
> Service

To the right of these categories on the map are three vertical categories: Web Channel, Interaction Center, and Channel Management. Any of these three vertical categories might be used in any of the main categories, so they are considered cross-functional (and therefore listed vertically in the map). For example, you may sell via the web, but you might also use web commerce methods to market to customers or support them after a sale.

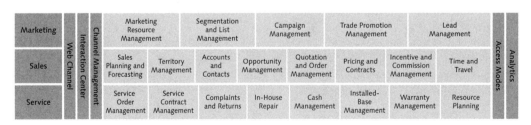

Figure 8.1 SAP CRM Solution Map

SAP CRM in an Enterprise

You may have heard the term *customer centric*. Essentially, this term describes a concept that many businesses use to drive their success. When you put the customer at the center of your business, you ensure that everything you do is an effort to gain and retain customer loyalty.

Customer centric

When you think about it, the customer is at the heart of most of the activities that a business engages in, from designing and building products to promoting products, taking and fulfilling orders, and providing support. Customer relationship management focuses on the areas in which you have the most direct contact with your customer—the marketing/sales/service portion of your business.

Using SAP CRM, you can centralize customer data to ensure that everybody from your salesperson to your order picker has the same information. You can streamline processes such as telemarketing, sales-account planning, and running customer interaction centers. You can set up customer self-service features to allow customers to register products online or track shipments. This self-service frees up your customer service people for other tasks.

Customer self-service

 Example

> An online clothing store that implements customer self-service features saves its employees from answering routine questions about products or order status so that they can spend time solving problems related to returns or cross-selling accessory products, such as handbags or jewelry.

SAP has built standard business processes into SAP CRM, including processes for handling customer complaints or product recalls, managing marketing campaigns, and tracking the results—even processing credit card payments and checking customer credit.

Standard business processes

The following section provides details about many of the features included in SAP CRM, divided into six key areas.

A Closer Look at SAP CRM

Each of the areas of SAP CRM, such as Sales or Marketing, has its own set of capabilities. In this section, we look at these capabilities in detail along with the types of business processes they help you manage.

SAP CRM Overview

Take a look at each of the major areas of SAP CRM listed in the solution map, each of which is discussed in more detail in the sections that follow. Table 8.1 outlines the key areas of CRM, based on SAP's solution map.

Category	Application
Marketing	› Marketing Resource Management › Segmentation & List Management › Campaign Management › Trade Promotion Management › Lead Management
Sales	› Sales Planning & Forecasting › Territory Management › Accounts & Contacts › Opportunity Management › Quotation & Order Management › Pricing & Contracts › Incentive & Commission Management › Time & Travel
Service	› Service Order Management › Service Contracts Management › Complaints and Returns › In-House Repair › Case Management › Installed Base Management › Warranty Management › Resource Planning
Web Channel	› E-Marketing › E-Commerce › E-Service

Table 8.1 SAP CRM Solution Map

Category	Application
Interaction Center	› Telemarketing › Telesales › Customer Service › IC Management
Partner Channel Management	› Partner Management › Channel Marketing › Channel Sales › Partner Order Management › Channel Commerce

Table 8.1 SAP CRM Solution Map (Cont.)

The features in this solution map cover the entire lifecycle of customer relations and include the following:

> Tools for marketing products and services to customers through a variety of campaign mechanisms

> Sales tools that help your salespeople plan, forecast, and follow through on sales efforts

> Services features that allow you to manage after-order service with service orders, service contracts, and repairs

> A range of tools for online selling and support

> Interaction tools to help you run your customer interaction operations with features for telemarketing and customer service

We look at each of these tools and features in more detail in the sections that follow.

Marketing

Whatever business you are in, marketing your product or services to customers is sometimes the first contact you have with them. The presentation of your message through a variety of customer touch points and the professionalism of your marketing activities can make a great impression or a poor one.

If you are involved in marketing, you are aware that it is a complex endeavor. You need sophisticated tools to plan, launch, and track

Features and tools

First contact

campaigns. The ability to have current data, integrated systems and processes, and robust analytics is important to your work.

The marketing solution in SAP CRM provides a way to integrate your marketing data and activities. SAP CRM Marketing offers a central platform for a variety of marketing activities, including the following modules:

> **Marketing Resource Management**
> Helps you in areas such as market research, planning (see Figure 8.2) and budgeting, cost and volume planning, brand awareness, and marketing project management.

Figure 8.2 Marketing Planning in SAP CRM

> **Segmentation and List Management**
> Involves managing and high-speed searching of customer and prospect information, generating predictive models, data mining, and list management and analysis.

> **Campaign Management**
> Helps you to plan and simulate campaigns, creating a marketing calendar, doing campaign-specific pricing and real-time response tracking, and performing analysis of target groups and campaigns.

> **Lead Management**
> Helps you manage multiple interaction channels, automate quali-
> fication, dispatch leads, use web-based lead generation, and auto-
> matically initiate follow-up activities.

> **Trade Promotion Management**
> Helps you to gain visibility and control of all trade-related pro-
> cesses. It also helps you increase your trade-promotion success
> with analytics and enhanced management of trade funds, promo-
> tions, claims, and retail execution.

Sales

The area of sales has its own challenges, including managing sales ter-
ritories, order tracking, and order processing. In a sales organization's
world, timely data and the ability to stay on top of prospective and
existing customer activity are essential. Having accurate data and analytical tools helps you break down current sales trends and forecast
future sales activity.

Sales challenges

Tools such as analytics and queries that collect key sales data in one
place save salespeople time, because they do not have to hunt down
data that is relevant to their customers from a variety of sources;
therefore, these salespeople can be more efficient and effective.

Sales features in SAP CRM include the following:

Features

> **Sales Planning and Forecasting**
> Provides capabilities for strategic planning, forecasting, collabora-
> tion, and account planning.

> **Territory Management**
> Allows you to manage market segmentation, assign and schedule
> territories, perform sales analyses by territory, and synchronize
> with your sales force via mobile devices.

> **Accounts and Contacts**
> Helps you plan sales visits, maintain an interaction history, use
> integrated email and fax features, manage relationships, and con-
> trol customer-specific pricing and analyses.

> **Opportunity Management**
> Helps you to manage team selling, organize competitive informa-
> tion, use account-specific sales processes, work with business

partners, set pricing, and analyze (see Figure 8.3) and follow up on sales opportunities.

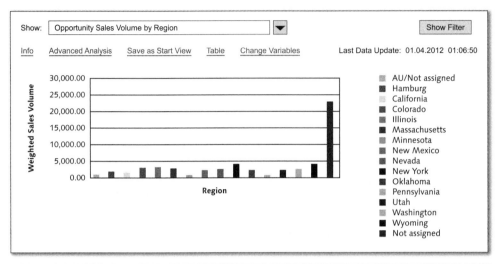

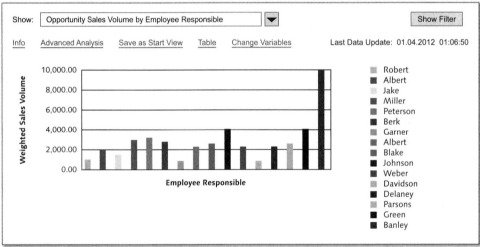

Figure 8.3 Analytics to Support Opportunity Management

> **Quotation and Order Management**
> Provides the ability to handle quotations, track order status, validate orders, run credit checks, and process credit card payments and rebates.

> **Pricing and Contracts**
> Allows you to work with value and quantity contracts, sales agreements, contract negotiation, release-order processing, and fulfillment synchronization.

> **Incentive and Commission Management**
> Includes direct and indirect sales compensation, incentive plan modeling, contracts and agreements handling, and commission-simulation tools.

> **Time and Travel**
> Helps you to track salesperson activities, including features for time reporting, managing expense reports, cost assignment, and tracking receipts and mileage.

These sales tools provide information and streamlined processes so that your sales force can spend more time selling and less time tracking data or filling out hardcopy expense forms.

In addition, SAP offers mobile apps for sales as of SAP CRM 7.0. SAP CRM mobile applications allow your field sales people and field service technicians to access SAP applications and customer data from a variety of devices. Mobile Sales for SAP CRM is primarily available via an occasionally connected mode for laptops and tablets.

Service

After you have connected with a customer and that customer has placed an order, you have to process that order and support your customer. That is where SAP CRM Service comes in. Depending on your business, everything from managing in-house repairs of warrantied products to handling complaints and returns may come into play here.

Order processing and support

SAP CRM Service includes the following areas:

Features

> **Service Order Management**
> Helps enterprises to support the complete service-processing lifecycle, including creation of service-order quotations, generating service orders, and delivering confirmations.

> **Service Contracts Management**
> Includes managing service agreements, service-contract processing, service-plan processing, usage-based contract management, and service-level management.

> **Complaints and Returns**
> This functionality enables dissatisfied customers to file complaints and return products. A guided activity helps the customer to file a complaint. A complaint can become the basis for a number of follow-up processes, such as return, credit memo, or debit memo.
>
> A guided activity helps the customer to return purchased goods. However, the customer can return only one item at a time, and the return should occur within the stipulated time frame.

> **In-House Repair**
> The customer users an interaction center or a web application to report a defective item that they want to send/bring in for repairs. A loan-device delivery to the customer, to bridge any long repair times, can also be created in this application.

> **Case Management**
> This functionality helps you to consolidate, manage, and process relevant information about a complex problem or issue in a central collection point. Case Management can also be used to process problems and issues that involve multiple processing steps or multiple processors.

> **Installed-Base Management**
> This functionality enables the representation of objects installed at the customer's location for which a service is provided. These objects can be devices, machines, or software. Installed-Base Management can also be used to manage objects within your organization.

> **Warranty Management**
> This functionality enables you to identify warranties within the processing of business transactions in service, check if claims on warranty services are legitimate, check if the newly created problem message is a case for warranty, monitor the cost of warranties, and identify the effect of warranties on pricing and billing.

> **Resource Planning**
> Service Resource Planning is used to execute project-based scheduling or service order–based scheduling using a number of resources. Using this functionality, you can determine and schedule the required resources.

If your operation involves after-sales support and you manage that support in-house, this set of features within SAP CRM will help you track data and fulfill service contracts efficiently.

SAP Web Channel Experience Management

Most companies have a web presence today. Customers have come to expect a range of e-commerce tools, including online ordering and order-status checking, online catalogs, and the ability to pay online.

Online features

The SAP Web Channel Experience Management solution, formerly called E-Commerce or Internet Sales, allows you to place your entire sales process online. You can provide easy-to-use sales tools and self-service features that give customers a personalized sales experience. You can also use features to streamline your backend fulfillment of online orders. Web Channel features are cost-effective for both business-to-business (B2B) and business-to-consumer (B2C) activities.

As you saw in Table 8.1, Web Channel breaks down into three main areas: E-Marketing, E-Commerce, and E-Service. The specific features you can take advantage of in each of those areas are discussed next.

Web Channel areas

E-Marketing

E-Marketing involves those aspects of your online store that promote your products or services. It consists of the following:

> **Catalog Management**
> Helps you create an electronic catalog of your products and describe their features and specifications.

> **Content Management**
> Allows you to create and manage content for your website that helps customers find what they need as they shop online.

> **Personalization**
> Allows you to create customer accounts and personalize their shopping experience.

> **Loyalty Management**
> Allows customers to enroll in loyalty programs and accrue and redeem loyalty points.

> **Email and Web Campaigns**
> Enables you to promote your products online.

> **Store Locator**
> Helps online customers find the nearest physical store location. This is a feature that companies with brick-and-mortar stores usually build into their websites.

If gaining online customers is important to your organization, E-Marketing features will be valuable to your e-store presence.

E-Commerce

Price and sell on the Internet

E-Commerce pertains to pricing and selling via the Internet. This group of capabilities includes the following:

> **Quotation and Order Management**
> Helps you set up a quotation system for products that are customized by product design or quantity discounts and to process related orders.

> **Shopping Basket Management**
> This shopping cart feature helps you manage your online customers' checkout process.

> **Pricing and Contracts**
> Helps you manage how you price your products and offer discounts and how you manage sales contracts for services or products.

> **Interactive Selling and Configuration**
> Allows you to set up live interaction between salespeople and online customers to help close the sale.

> **Web Auctions**
> Enables you to run an auction operation involving item postings, bidding procedures, and confirmations.

> **Selling via Partners**
> Provides tools for cross-selling through strategic sales partnerships.

If your company has online sales activities, SAP CRM E-Selling tools can provide a comprehensive solution to manage each aspect of your sales cycle.

E-Service

E-Service has all of the tools required to manage orders and support customers:

Manage and support customers

> **Knowledge Management**
> Helps you to manage data about online sales and produce reports about trends helpful for planning and forecasting.

> **Service Order Management**
> Allows support of online sale service order processing.

> **Live Support**
> Contains tools for setting up live support for your customers so that they can get answers to their problems in real time.

> **Installed Base**
> Helps you to measure the number of customers you have as opposed to your market share.

> **Complaints and Returns**
> Helps you handle customer issues efficiently to turn dissatisfied customers into satisfied ones.

> **Billing and Payment**
> Allows you to process invoices and payments for online sales.

> **Account Self Service**
> Gives customers the tools they need to get information without having to interact with a support person or salesperson.

E-Service tools round out the e-commerce capabilities of SAP CRM by taking your hard-won customer orders and handling them efficiently.

Interaction Center

Whether you call it your telemarketing group, customer service center, or telesales function, any area in which you interact with customers is managed via the *Interaction Center (IC)* portion of SAP CRM.

IC covers activities such as telemarketing and customer support. If you have a customer interaction center, whether you use such centers to actively sell products or simply support customers after the sale, this SAP CRM feature will prove invaluable. Next, we will discuss the

Telemarketing and customer service

various activities it supports in four areas: Telemarketing, Telesales, Customer Service, and IC Management.

Telemarketing helps you organize and manage outbound marketing campaigns, including the following:

> **Campaign Execution**
> Plan your marketing and sales efforts.

> **Lead Management**
> Manage data about sales leads.

> **Personalization**
> Plan ways to connect sales efforts with potential customers in unique ways.

Telesales includes tools to help you manage the actual telemarketing effort when you are selling directly to the customer:

> **Accounts and Contacts**
> Manage contact information.

> **Activity Management**
> Track sales activity.

> **Quotation and Order Management**
> Enable your telesales force to provide quotes and place orders.

After you have obtained a customer's order, *Customer Service* helps you work with your customers in these areas:

> **Help Desk**
> Provides assistance with product features.

> **Customer Service and Support**
> Helps support your customers after an order is placed.

> **Complaint Management**
> Deals with customer issues regarding product problems or defects.

IC Management is all about running your interaction center in these areas:

> **Knowledge Management**
> Controls data about your IC contacts.

> **Process Modeling**
> Helps you design efficient IC processes.

> **Communications Channels**
> Helps you set up efficient phone, online, and other communications methods.

If your company handles IC functions by itself or even works with an outsourcing partner for a portion of them, these features will help you implement more efficient procedures and streamline your customer interactions.

Partner Channel Management

What if you don't sell directly to customers? Many businesses work through partners to sell what they make. For example, companies such as jewelry manufacturers or book publishers primarily use retailers to sell their products. Other companies work with a franchise model or sell through third-party sales groups. How well these companies manage their partner relationships determines much of their business success.

Managing partner relationships

For example, Partner Channel Management allows you to manage your indirect sales channels—that is, your partners who sell for you. Tools for improved collaboration address sales, marketing, and service activities. In addition, analytics help you evaluate how your partners are performing.

Indirect sales channels

Partner Channel Management covers the entire lifecycle of a channel relationship, from strategizing your partnerships to providing information to your partners about your products, managing pricing, managing orders, and even setting up collaborative showrooms.

The various areas of SAP CRM Partner Channel Management that support channel management include the following:

> **Partner Management**
> - Partner Lifecycle Management
> - Partner Training and Certification
> - Partner Planning and Forecasting
> - Partner Compensation
> - Partner Networking

> **Channel Marketing**
  - Partner Communication
  - Catalog Management
  - Campaign Management
  - Lead Management
  - Channel Marketing Funds
  - Partner Locator

> **Channel Sales**
  - Accounts and Contacts Management
  - Activity Management
  - Opportunity Management
  - Pipeline Analysis
  - Deal Registration

> **Partner Order Management**
  - Quotation and Order Management
  - Interactive Selling and Configuration
  - Pricing and Contracts
  - POS and Channel Inventory Tracking
  - Collaborative Showroom
  - Distributed Order Management

> **Channel Service**
  - Knowledge Management
  - Live Support
  - Service Order Management
  - Warranty and Claims Management
  - Complaints and Returns Management

Keeping vital channel relationships running

Many businesses today sell through multiple channels. SAP CRM provides features for keeping these vital channel relationships running efficiently.

In the following section, we will briefly explore your options for an SAP CRM cloud solution.

SAP CRM Cloud Solution

If you want to transition to SAP CRM faster, consider checking into the SAP CRM cloud solution. This is a cloud-hosted solution that helps you switch to SAP CRM without having to implement the full solution in-house. These solutions are available in a subscription-based licensing model. You can expand your CRM features quickly and only as you need them. On-demand solutions from SAP use the same user interface as SAP CRM, so it is easy to shift the solution from a hosted one to a locally run, in-house solution down the road if you want to make this transition without having to start from scratch.

Expand your CRM features quickly

The SAP Cloud for Customer includes the following modules:

Cloud for customer

> Cloud for Sales
> Cloud for Service
> Cloud for Marketing

The SAP Cloud for Customer also includes industry-specific offerings. The following offerings are currently available:

Industry-specific

> **SAP Cloud for Customer for Retail (B2E)**
  This solution provides the following functionalities:

  – Enables the retail store employees to engage and enhance the in-store experience of their customers. The store employees will be able to provide personalized assistance such as unique offers, targeted product recommendations, and convenient check-out options.

  – Access customer history.

  – Look-up for products, prices, promotions and offers.

  – Time management, calendar appointments, tasks, store events, brand promotions, and social engagement are also fully supported.

> **SAP Cloud for Customer for Insurance**
  This solution empowers the insurance company's insurance agent to get more insight into the customer profile and help the agents with guided process flows for executing the entire sales cycle, from lead to quote and to policy. The solution provides the following functionalities:

- Create and maintain insurance products in SAP Cloud for Customer.

- Use standard interface with Camilion as the default insurance engine to calculate premiums, to source quick quotes, and to interface with SAP FS-PM (Policy Management) as the source for policy management.

- Simulate commissions for captive agents using the standard interface to SAP FS-ICM (Insurance Commission Management System).

- Using the Microsoft Outlook integration add-in, you can set up email workflow and other interaction web channels to maintain dialogue with customers.

> **SAP Cloud for Customer for Utilities**
  This solution provides a unified sales interface with business support for utilities and B2B support. The solution provides the following functionalities:

- Track leads and identify opportunities for key utilities accounts.

- Capture utility-specific technical master data, such as connection jobs, IBASE, and other relevant master data.

- Get detailed insight into a customer's buying preferences by using the 360-degree customer view and other analytics features.

- Manage utility contracts for a varied product portfolio by using the different configuration options and an integrated process interface to support various types of contracts and service products.

- Sell into specialized channels, such as educational markets, with the use of Channel Management.

In the following section, we look at the technical underpinnings that enable SAP CRM to provide some of its functionality.

SAP CRM Technical Details

SAP NetWeaver's open architecture

SAP CRM is supported by SAP NetWeaver, whose open architecture provides a web-based interface for accessing customer information. The SAP NetWeaver platform also enables interaction among various communication channels, such as telephone, email, chat, and short message system (SMS).

For example, if you want to set up a customer service operation, you will need a way to handle communication via telephone, email, and perhaps even a chat feature for real-time interaction with sales or service people and customers. These are all supported via SAP NetWeaver. See Chapter 19 for more on SAP NetWeaver's support for SAP products.

The analytics features of SAP NetWeaver are all about taking data and manipulating it to produce analyses, reports, and forecasts that provide consistent front- and back-office information. Integration services help users of SAP CRM connect with other SAP Business Suite solutions, such as SAP ERP, and with external systems. If, for example, you want to integrate your customer-order process with your backend financials, you can do that by using tools in SAP NetWeaver to integrate data from SAP CRM with SAP ERP Financials.

By now, you know that SAP CRM has a sound technical foundation and is packed with a long list of features, but you may be wondering how it works in the real world. The next section addresses this by presenting a case study that shows you how SAP CRM solved problems at one U.S. company.

SAP CRM Case Study 1

Review Table 8.2 to get a quick snapshot of a case study exemplifying SAP CRM.

Company	U.S.-based manufacturer of office equipment
Existing Solutions	SAP R/3, plus several third-party legacy systems
Challenge	To improve the access of customer service staffers to data about previous customer contact, to tie the online accessory store to the billing system, and to centralize customer data and connect systems

Table 8.2 SAP CRM Case Study 1

SAP Solutions	SAP CRM and SAP Business Warehouse
Benefits	Better control of customer record management and centralization of data

Table 8.2 SAP CRM Case Study 1 (Cont.)

Differentiation
through customer
service

SAP helped a U.S.-based manufacturer of office equipment—including printers, faxes, and multifunction products—to implement a CRM solution. The company employs 1,100 people and is a subsidiary of a larger company based in Japan. This U.S.-based manufacturer of office equipment sells its products through several channels, including mass merchandisers, dealers, distributors, retailers, and office superstores; however, all of its after-sales customer contact is handled in-house. Because this industry offers slim profit margins and has weak customer loyalty, differentiating itself via customer service was critical to the company's success.

The Challenges

The company faced several challenges in its customer relationships. Through its national service group, the company supports all customers and resellers, as well as parts distribution, returns, and customer contact centers. One of the key problems was that call-center staffers, who field almost 150,000 calls monthly, could not get records of previous calls. With a 20% repeat call rate, this caused huge problems, including a higher-than-industry-average rate of product returns.

The company's online accessory store was not tied into the main billing system. Orders were received via email and then entered into SAP R/3. Credit card checking was done after the receipt of the order. Decentralized customer data and disconnected systems were costing this company money and worse, customers.

The SAP Solution

SAP worked with the company to phase in a solution that included SAP CRM working with SAP Business Warehouse (SAP BW). SAP CRM handled the customer contact processes while SAP BW offered a method for centralizing customer data.

The solution was used across the organization; that is, in the customer service, technical support, parts distribution, and returns areas. Replacing disparate accounting, email, call center, and databases, the company integrated these into a single solution via SAP R/3, which the company had already implemented.

The centralized data supported inventory and order-status data, call logging, retrieval of customer data, a solutions database to provide call center staff with consistent answers, up-selling and cross-selling, and a universal customer number system for order fulfillment and follow-up support.

The company took advantage of *ASAP*, an SAP rapid implementation methodology, to deploy SAP CRM and SAP BW. The Directors of Parts, Operations, and MIS (Management Information Systems) headed the internal team, which implemented the following:

> *ASAP is an SAP rapid implementation methodology*

> Migrating data for 330,000 customers from SAP R/3 and other third-party and legacy systems to SAP CRM/SAP BW

> Deploying campaign-management features and a solution database for internal use

> Adding capabilities for managing inbound email

> Automating four call centers in a phased rollout

The Benefits

The solution reduced returns and improved the company's business process efficiencies in dramatic ways. Their rate of returns dropped while the industry rates were rising. The company could now execute a campaign in hours, rather than days, and with fewer resources. It could generate reports that helped get better leads. The average cost of a campaign was lowered by $4,400.

By using a single customer database, data was more accurate, providing for more consistent and accurate information throughout the customer support organization. SAP set up a system through which customers could register their products online themselves, saving employee time. This data fed into SAP CRM for immediate access by company staff.

Time spent on customer support calls dropped, and the volume of calls themselves dropped. Interaction was shifted from phone to email and was handled through the centralized SAP R/3 database, resulting in significant savings. Standardized processes for complaint management ensured that grievances were handled better and customer satisfaction was higher.

One important benefit of the new system was reduced employee stress. When an employee interacting with a customer is more confident that the information he is accessing is accurate, stress is reduced considerably.

Looking toward the Future

Other important SAP CRM features

The company hopes to build on its efforts by deploying other SAP CRM features. The company plans to use Internet sales features in SAP CRM to replace its own online store. In addition, the company wants to take advantage of telemarketing and mobile sales features. The company will add Internet access for their dealers to receive leads and schedule sales appointments more efficiently.

SAP CRM Case Study 2

Table 8.3 provides you with another quick overview of a case study; review it before we explain it in more detail.

This Asian company deals in pulp and paper products, runs 14 manufacturing sites, and has various subsidiaries and partners. The company sells to customers around the world and has a workforce of more than 20,000.

Company	Asian paper mill products
Existing Solutions	SAP R/3 for critical business processes
Challenges	To obtain up-to-date customer information for customer inquiries and to ensure minimum disruption to operations and customer services

Table 8.3 SAP CRM Case Study 2

SAP Solutions	Upgrade to SAP ERP, SAP CRM, SAP Enterprise Portal, and SAP BW
Benefits	Increased process efficiency, higher productivity, reduced costs, and reduced time spent on financial calculations and IT maintenance

Table 8.3 SAP CRM Case Study 2 (Cont.)

The Challenges

Salespeople and customer service people who had to work with customers of this large China-based company were not able to get the up-to-date customer information they needed to handle customer inquiries. Response times were not as fast as needed to keep customers satisfied.

The company had many self-designed forms and interfaces that had to be integrated or replaced all on a tight schedule. Moreover, the company had to ensure minimum disruption to operations and customer services.

The SAP Solution

One thousand users were upgraded to SAP ERP at 14 sites. SAP worked with an internal team to perform the upgrade in 15 weeks with little downtime. Besides implementing SAP ERP, the team integrated SAP CRM so that salespeople and customer service people now have timely access to information through customized interfaces. Enhanced system performance also allows for faster response times.

1,000 users upgraded to SAP ERP at 14 sites

In addition, SAP BW was implemented to improve the reporting available to managers for making key decisions about how to best serve customers and plan for the future.

The Benefits

Besides improvements in handling data, the company has realigned its processes for better customer service and increased productivity. The company's IT operation has less to do to maintain the system and make changes to it. The company's ability to more rapidly access and act on customer data has provided a competitive edge and laid the foundation for future growth.

Quickly access and act on customer data

Conclusion

In this chapter, we outlined the entire SAP CRM product and its many features for interacting with your customers, including the following:

> How SAP CRM fits into your enterprise

> The six key areas of SAP CRM, including both cross-industry (such as analytics) and SAP CRM–specific functionality in marketing, sales, service, interaction center, e-commerce, and channel management

> The technology on which SAP CRM rests

> How SAP CRM works in real-world settings

Serving your customers and collecting their orders is an important part of your business. But after you have those orders in-house, how do you ensure that you can fulfill them? In Chapter 9, we explore another useful tool that can help you to build your products and deliver them to your customers: SAP Supplier Relationship Management (SAP SRM).

9

SAP Supplier Relationship Management

SAP Supplier Relationship Management (SAP SRM) is SAP's principal on premise solution for procurement. SAP SRM helps organizations automate, simplify, and accelerate their business' procure-to-pay processes for goods and services. Procurement, particularly indirect procurement, is one of the "last frontiers" into which technology solutions and their corresponding efficiencies have not penetrated to a significant degree. Therefore, SAP's portfolio for SRM continues to evolve. SAP's SRM suite offers a comprehensive portfolio both for on premise and cloud-based approaches (the cloud-based approach is discussed in Chapter 10).

In this chapter, we will discuss the on premise solution for SAP SRM. First, we will discuss the different ways in which your business can implement SRM for different scenarios. We will then dive into the individual areas that compose SRM.

How SAP On Premise Procurement Solutions Fit into an Enterprise

Beginning with Materials Management in Procurement, SAP built a solution for procurement functions that is directly supported in SAP

ERP. In the following sections, we will discuss the ways in which you can implement SAP SRM to complement your business situation.

SRM "Flavors"

Ways to implement SAP SRM

You can deploy SAP SRM in a variety of ways, depending on your organization's business requirements:

> In the *Classic scenario*, SAP SRM can be tightly integrated with one or multiple backend ERP environments. This allows all leading documents to reside in the respective ERP system.

> In the *Extended Classic scenario*, SAP SRM can also serve as the main procurement area for an enterprise, housing the leading documents for the entire procure-to-pay process—except invoicing, which is typically supported in the applicable ERP environment.

> If integration with ERP environments is not required or possible, SAP SRM can also run as a *Standalone* solution.

Public sector

There is also a public-sector version of SAP SRM. SAP SRM Procurement for Public Sector (PPS) is a variation of SAP SRM that supports public sector–specific financial and procurement processes, policies, and regulations. Additional financial functionality includes integration with public sector funds management in SAP ERP, and supports earmarked funds, incremental funding, budget period, budget encumbrances at the time of shopping cart approval, and posting documents with a future date. SAP SRM PPS also includes support for two-envelope bidding, tender-fee processing, synopsis, and request for proposal, quotation, information, or tender (RFx) response evaluation using short lists for public sector–sourcing activities.

On the document-management-side, SAP SRM PPS is integrated with SAP Document Builder, a document-creation management solution supporting complex RFx, contract, and purchase order clauses, rules, and business content requirements typically found in public-sector procurement. For storing these documents and supporting documentation, SAP SRM PPS leverages SAP Records Management. Records Management stores the purchasing document, follow-on processes, and related documentation in a centralized manner, enabling central access for audit and storage requirements.

SAP SRM Scenarios

SAP SRM scenarios cover the main procurement areas found in the enterprise, from tactical/operational to strategic. Rather than implement every scenario in SAP SRM at once, you can choose which scenarios apply to your organization's business processes and build from this base. We discuss the supported SAP SRM scenarios in the following subsections.

Procurement areas

Self-Service Procurement

Paper or Microsoft Excel–based procurement processes are often cumbersome, time consuming, and error prone. In addition, workflow and signoffs in an unstructured environment may not conform to a company's general policies and best practices. SAP SRM's self-service procurement scenario enables your employees to create and manage their own procurement processes. The self-service procurement scenario in SAP SRM automates procurement activities for the user while increasing compliance and consolidating demand. SAP SRM provides a walk-up user interface with continuing enhancements, such as the SAP SRM UI, and support for complex workflow approvals on both device and desktop.

Catalogs are particularly relevant to the self-service procurement scenario in SAP SRM. External and internal catalogs allow you to search for and select items from a catalog or from multiple catalogs. External content and catalogs are also hosted by marketplaces. Internal catalogs lend themselves to additional controls and stock items from inventory management and material master data in the system along with correspondingly higher maintenance requirements. External and hosted marketplaces offer a less maintenance-intense approach and faster time to updates.

Strategic sourcing processes

Service Procurement

Services are a challenging yet promising area for procurement automation. They are challenging because the services scope remains difficult to define at the time of purchase, and promising because more and more services are being procured and managed in the system out of necessity. The demand for third-party services in the enterprise has grown exponentially since the adoption of core-competency models and outsourcing. SRM supports the services hierarchies in SAP ERP, as well as contract management around services, allowing you to manage more of your services procurement efficiently in the system.

Plan-Driven Procurement

Plan-driven procurement in SRM integrates and uses many processes from SAP ERP, including requirements from sourcing, order management, contract management, material requirements planning (MRP), collaboration, costing, and payment.

Once the demand is created from various sources and systems, the requisition is routed up to the SAP SRM Sourcing Cockpit for source-of-supply determination. The resulting purchase order goes through required approvals and is then issued out to the supplier. Plan-driven procurement allows you organize procurement activities and requirements that are driven by your operations and systems, and consolidate demand towards your designated procurement channels and strategies.

Strategic Sourcing

Traditionally, buyers have handled much of the sourcing activities outside of a system due to the complex nature of requirements gathering and grouping and negotiations. With SAP SRM, you can underpin efficiencies throughout the bidding process, while managing complex bidding events and types. Sourcing in SRM leverages a framework to support programmatic visibility, reporting, and savings tracking along with project management and inherent integration with follow-on activities, such as contract creation.

RFx   SAP SRM's RFx features include bid comparisons, weighting, bid types, and support for auctions. SAP SRM's auctions capabilities include support for multiple auction types (reverse, forward, and Dutch) and patented rules, live supplier communication functionality, and awards to drive best possible outcomes and pricing.

 RFx

> Request for proposal, quotation, information, or tender (RFx) is a customizable type of document that a purchaser sends out to potential bidders, soliciting a particular type of response.

Because SRM is an operations-oriented procurement environment, once a winning bid has been confirmed, a follow-on contract, purchase order, or further bidding event can be triggered directly in the system.

Central Contract Management

Contract management in SRM supports the creation of contracts from templates and clause libraries, configurable types, integration with sourcing process for contract creation, and workflow approval. For workload balancing and planning, SRM supports expiration alerting, repository search, and content-usage reporting. The reporting area is further augmented by performance- and audit-management reporting capabilities and integration with SAP BusinessObjects Business Intelligence reporting tools and data warehouses. The dashboard that is shown in Figure 9.1 is from just such a BI reporting tool.

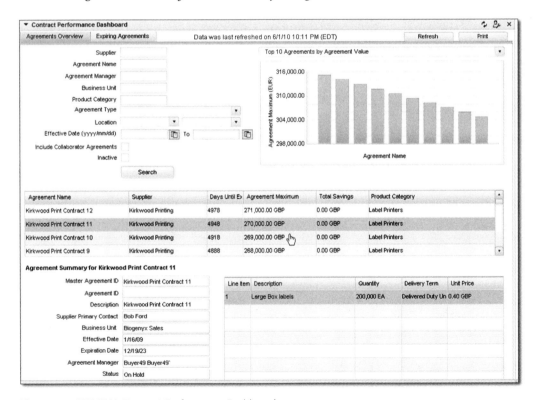

Figure 9.1 SAP SRM Contract Performance Dashboard

Hub functionality   SRM provides contract management hub functionality, allowing for central reporting, management, and distribution of contracts to integrated procurement systems for automated use of agreements. Centralizing the contract management in SAP SRM leverages its original design, which was built to consolidate procurement in multiple ERP systems onto a single SRM platform in order to distribute and manage contracts.

A Closer Look at SAP SRM

The main areas of procurement that SAP SRM helps organizations manage are outlined in Figure 9.2. There are a few additional on premise procurement solutions that augment SAP SRM, such as Supplier Lifecycle Management (SLC), Supplier Self-Services (SUS), and SAP Sourcing. We will discuss these in the next sections.

Figure 9.2 SAP SRM Areas of Coverage

Procurement   The procurement solutions that SAP offers are grouped for both on
solutions   premise and cloud as follows (and are discussed in detail in the following sections):

1. Spend Analytics: analysis tools and platforms

2. Sourcing: strategic sourcing and operational sourcing

3. Contract Management: complete contract lifecycle management

4. Operational Procurement: tactical procurement

5. Invoice Management: accounts payable

6. Supplier Performance Management: full supplier lifecycle management

7. Supplier Collaboration: Ariba network and/or supplier self-services (SUS)

8. Mobile Procurement: mobile platform and UI enhancements and adaptations

Figure 9.3 outlines the different on premise software requirements for each of these solutions, which we will discuss in more detail in the following sections.

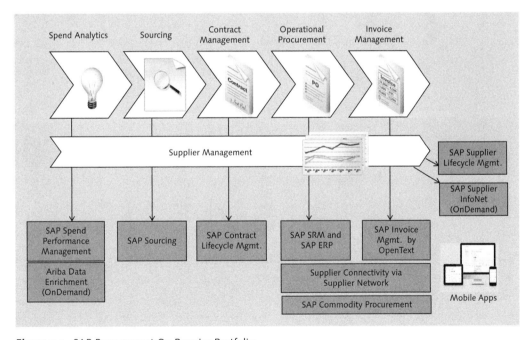

Figure 9.3 SAP Procurement On Premise Portfolio

Spend Analytics

Colleagues and company executives want to understand how the procurement operations are performing and how these operations can be improved. Rewards for savings and operations improvements can be substantial. One key insight gleaned from an enterprise's procurement data can often pay for the entire investment and implementation effort of a procurement solution.

SAP's main analytics solution areas for procurement fall into two categories. The first category is SAP's vast array of tools and reporting capabilities found in the standard reports in the individual systems and in the SAP HANA–driven SAP BusinessObjects Business Intelligence and reporting products. (You can find more information about SAP BusinessObjects in Chapter 14, and SAP HANA in Chapter 15.) SAP SRM comes with prebuilt extractors, enabling a company to extract data from the transaction systems into an SAP Business Warehouse for iterative reporting. With in-memory reporting capabilities from SAP HANA and prepackaged, procurement-specific reporting packages, such as Spend Performance Management (SPM), reports can be delivered and iteratively "sliced and diced" for every user type and company stakeholder. Figure 9.4 shows Spend Performance Management reports, which can be tailored midstream to yield actionable insights about purchasing operations and strategy.

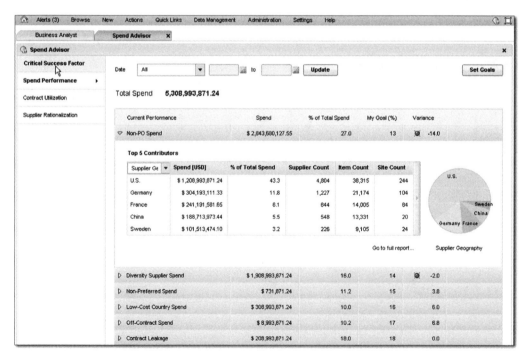

Figure 9.4 Spend Performance Management Reports

The second main category for analysis is the network of supplier and customer relationships themselves. "Big data," which we introduced in Chapter 2, is a major trend in technology solutions today, including procurement. When you combine data and transactions that occur inside the system with key data and transactions from outside of the procurement system, you have a whole host of new ways to analyze and act on data.

Analysis with big data

 Example

If your procurement system demand and order data is combined with up-to-the-minute oil-price trends and macroeconomic events that impact oil prices, then your company can react quicker to minimize losses and take advantage of pricing situations before your competitors can do the same. By incorporating supplier risk data, such as supplier credit scores and trends, with your supplier-purchasing strategies, you can mitigate potential supply issues and losses incurred from a supplier's insolvency.

SAP InfoNet is of particular importance to SAP SRM. SAP InfoNet leverages "crowd sourcing" among enterprises of supplier-performance data. This data is distilled into key performance indicators (KPIs) and benchmarks to minimize supply chain disruptions by proactively monitoring and predicting supply risks in real time.

SAP InfoNet

Sourcing

Once you have captured the need for an item or service via a requisition or a shopping cart, a supplier has to be identified, agreement reached on pricing and terms, and a purchasing document created to cement the transaction. Finding the right supplier and reaching agreement is the essence of sourcing.

Sourcing divides into two general categories: strategic and operational. Operational sourcing is the day-to-day assignment of orders to applicable suppliers, based on product, product category, contract, and/or availability. SAP SRM enables operational sourcing by assigning applicable suppliers based on a variety of drivers, such as contracts, vendor lists, sourced catalog items, and manual assignment of suppliers by the buyer. Building these assignment drivers around operational sourcing allows you to drive supplier consolidation while leveraging negotiated pricing and agreements with suppliers.

Operational sourcing

Strategic sourcing

Unlike the volume-based efficiencies of operational sourcing, strategic sourcing focuses on the optimization of large, critical purchasing activities that require supplier identification, invitation to bidding events, management of bid processes, and fair awarding of the bid to the winning supplier. As with Spend Analytics, one successful auction or request for proposal, quotation, information, or tender" (RFx) process can often pay for the implementation costs of an SAP SRM RFx and/or SAP Sourcing on premise solution.

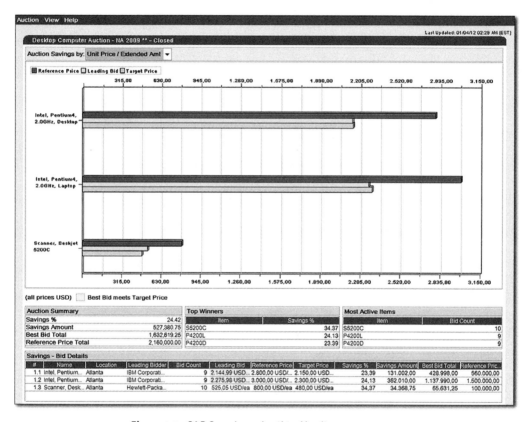

Figure 9.5 SAP Sourcing—Auction Monitor

Standalone or integrated

SAP Sourcing offers a sourcing environment for all of the upstream processes for complicated sourcing events, as well as contract lifecycle management and supplier management. As a standalone environment or integrated with SAP ERP/SRM instances, SAP Sourcing provides the flexibility and usability for complex sourcing events. SAP

SRM also offers a Sourcing Cockpit from which RFx processes can be initiated directly. Many SAP customers run both SAP Sourcing and SAP SRM, leveraging SAP Sourcing for complex contract negotiations and redlining and the Sourcing Cockpit for more operational sourcing events in response to requisitions/shopping cart requests. Both SAP SRM and SAP Sourcing also support various types of auctions for real-time, competitive bidding by suppliers. Figure 9.5 shows SAP Sourcing's auction monitor.

Contract Management

After using SAP Sourcing and the SAP SRM Sourcing Cockpit to nego-tiate the best contract possible with the supplier, you need to manage the contract through its lifecycle to ensure your company realizes all of the benefits. To do this, the contracts need to be "operationalized" and requests/demands routed to the appropriate contract in the sys-tem. If the contract is not used, then the negotiated pricing and agree-ments are for naught. Similarly, if a contract expires without the knowledge of the responsible buyers or the supplier disregards the terms, this undermines the agreement and efforts by purchasing to drive savings and efficiencies.

Negotiate the
right terms

Contract Lifecycle Management (CLM) in SAP Sourcing and in SAP SRM replicate the contracts to the applicable purchasing environ-ments and, in the case of SAP SRM CLM, centrally manage the con-tract for releases and renewals. This means that even if there are multiple ERP systems involved in the procurement process, the con-tract reaches these environments and captures the spend for the con-tract. You may have tiered pricing and other savings that are triggered at certain levels of spend. Rather than laboriously trying to calculate rebates and adjustments owed on a contract after the fact, this approach to contract management allows for dynamic application of contract rules at the time of order creation in a distributed landscape.

Operational Procurement

Operational Procurement is the catch-all scenario for the daily order-ing of goods and services by company employees and divisions. Tra-ditionally, businesses have targeted Operational Procurement as one of their implementation areas in order to realize immediate, large-scale efficiencies in their procurement operations. This is especially the case when moving from paper-based processes to an environment like SAP SRM. Paper-based processes are typically costly and error-prone, and given the massive scale at which indirect procurement occurs in a large enterprise, moving to a procurement system such as SAP SRM for these processes can translate into immense savings and efficiencies and corresponding enhanced profitability/margin.

System support for occasional users

However, it is also challenging to support casual users in a system, as many of these employees may only use SAP SRM once or twice per year, and have little or no training in creating SRM shopping carts. The Self-Service Procurement scenario in SAP SRM aims for a shopping experience like that which consumers enjoy when shopping online, but here the user assigns the expense to a cost assignment object, such as a cost center, and oftentimes goes through multiple levels of approval once the order is submitted. SAP SRM has over 130 integration points with the SAP ERP Central Component (ECC) backend system and its predecessor version, SAP R/3, including several checks and commitments in the finance and controlling modules. This allows companies to track spending and obligations in real time, driving more efficient management of budgets and cash flow.

Leveraging MM functions

Even when the procurement process is conducted in SAP SRM, most SRM implementations use at least some of the existing infrastructure in Materials Management for backend processes, such as accounts payable and inventory management. Operational procurement processes are also supported directly in the SAP ERP system under Materials Management—Purchasing (MM-PUR). Similar to shopping carts in SRM, users create requisitions. Once the requisition or PO is approved, a buyer sources the item and moves forward with issuing the PO to the supplier. There is also a shopping cart option directly in MM-PUR, which you can deploy if you do not require SAP SRM functionality.

Commodity procurement, sales, and risk management

A recent addition in this area is Commodity Procurement, which is part of a trio of solutions offered in Commodity Management. The other two solutions are Commodity Sales and Commodity Risk Management. Designed to manage the procurement of commodities with constantly fluctuating prices, Commodity Procurement uses its commodity pricing engine to automatically price and adjust pricing on commodities and its differential invoicing functionality to prevent overpayment of vendor invoices.

Invoice Management

Electronic invoicing is a fast-growing process in accounts payable. Switching from paper invoices to electronic invoicing reduces tedious rekeying work, typos, and misrouting of invoices and facilitates three-way matching in a system for accurate and auditable payments. SAP Open Text's Vendor Invoice Management (VIM) automates invoice extraction, manages the review and approval process, automates the invoice routing and sorting, and generates reports. Once Open Text transmits the invoice in ECC, it can be matched with a corresponding purchase order and goods receipt(s) and paid. On time, expedited payment avoids late-payment fees while positioning your company for further early-payment discounts. A solution that automates this negotiation process called SAP Ariba Discount Management will be discussed in more detail in Chapter 10.

Electronic and automatic invoicing

Supplier Information and Performance Management

Suppliers undergo a lifecycle with most companies in which they are identified and on-boarded into company-procurement activities to support direct or indirect procurement needs and processes. From here, a supplier either grows in strategic importance to the firm, gaining further goods and services revenue along the way, or is replaced by another supplier who expands their footprint at the company in a more efficient manner either due to a better quality/cost ratios for their products or via tighter integration with the company and its procurement needs. Most companies seek to centralize their supply base on a few core suppliers, finding the balance between volume savings and creating vulnerabilities to their business model in becoming overly dependent on a particular supplier.

Find core suppliers

SAP's Supplier Lifecycle Management (SLC) enables supplier registration, qualification, and onboarding. Once the supplier is in SLC, you can classify and manage the supplier's performance based on their value to your business. SLC also integrates with SAP SRM and Supplier Self-Services (SUS) to enable online purchase order and invoicing collaboration between your company and the supplier.

Supplier Collaboration

Transactional tracking to create footprint

Whether you need a supplier to respond to a detailed set of specifications during an RFx in a one-off scenario or you need to build a multi-decade partnership with suppliers in lockstep, you can leverage solutions to underpin these interactions and relationships. A transaction tracked through a standard business process in the system is much more robust than a phone call or a handshake and leads to cleaner processes downstream at the contract and operational procurement levels. Partnering, as well as the understanding and leveraging of key suppliers in a company's supply chain, can multiply a company's capacity and footprint far beyond its actual size.

Self service

You can enable suppliers to maintain parts of their own record at your company, receive purchase orders and receipt notifications, submit purchase order responses, such as shipment notifications and invoices, and maintain current catalog pricing and item data specific to your company via SAP's Supplier Self-Services (SUS) or the SAP Ariba Network. SAP SUS is the on premise approach to supplier collaboration and supports a "one-to-many" approach for managing suppliers. You maintain the SLC and SUS environments, and the supplier has to log in to these to interact with your company.

Mobile Platform and User Interface

Online retailers continue to set very high standards for purchasing in this area of a procurement solution. Casual users will not easily accept tools that require desktop-only access and two times the effort and training to complete processes that they can achieve at home in two or three mouse clicks or screen taps on any device. In order to increase the usability, adoption, and overall intuitiveness of SAP SRM, SAP has developed multiple user interface (UI) enhancements, including SAP SRM UI and SAP Fiori (see Figure 9.6), which allow for one-screen shopping and mobile applications to support different areas of the purchasing process on your smartphone.

SAP Fiori

SAP Fiori is a collection of apps with a simple and easy-to-use experience that is useful for broadly and frequently used SAP software functions. (You can find more information about SAP Fiori in Chapter 18.) The apps work seamlessly across desktops, tablets, and smartphones.

SAP also delivers Design Thinking workshops at customer sites to assist with the overall design of user interfaces for a company's particular processes and requirements.

The SAP Mobile Platform supports many of these UI-driven apps for SAP SRM and allows your developers to expand and tailor these offerings to your users. The platform automatically translates to apps on a wide variety of mobile devices, functioning as a middleware layer between heterogeneous backend data sources.

Figure 9.6 SAP Fiori

SAP SRM Case Study

Table 9.1 provides a snapshot of a case study that illustrates SAP SRM in action.

This producer of tobacco products has revenues of over €13.5 billion a year and employs more than 90,000 people in 180 countries. The company was experiencing out-of-control purchasing costs and needed a single system that would dovetail with its existing SAP system.

Company	Australian tobacco company
Existing Solutions	SAP ERP and multiple legacy systems
The Challenge	To enhance policies regarding purchasing and to improve purchasing department controls on spending
SAP Solution	SAP SRM
Benefits	Procurement spending reduced by €292 million a year; improved visibility and analytics

Table 9.1 SAP SRM Case Study

The Challenges

This company had no policy in place regarding its procurement processes across the enterprise. In addition, its purchasing department was not involved in many purchasing transactions, leaving no control over spending.

Because of maverick buying habits by various groups, purchasing costs were extremely high. The company sought a solution that would fit with its existing SAP system and also support the entire procurement process.

The SAP Solution

SAP SRM was rolled out in 19 countries in the first phase and then in another 31 countries in the second phase. The system was integrated seamlessly with existing SAP solutions. A country-based model provided both global consistencies and regional flexibility.

SAP SRM was configured in a single way for all users, providing a uniform procurement system across departments and countries.

The Benefits

With SAP SRM in place, the company reduced maverick buying habits and realized savings of €292 million annually. In addition, with consistent purchasing operations across the enterprise, the purchasing department was able to gain control of all procurement procedures.

The company was also able to gain visibility into its procurement data and generate analytics that helped make additional improvements to the company's processes.

SAP SRM Customer Fast Facts

Thousands of companies have realized immense savings and efficiencies by using SAP on premise procurement solutions. What kinds of bottom-line results might you expect to get?

Here are some quick examples of the types of savings companies have realized by using SAP SRM:

Savings examples

> › A major global diversified manufacturer consolidated more than 10 million spend records to gain over 90% visibility into its spending and subsequently has put controls in place over that spending within sourcing and procurement.

> › A paint company in China centralized procurement for its plants and branches on SAP SRM. This has resulted in 50% productivity gains for the procurement department and the reduction of non-compliant purchase orders to less than 0.01%. In addition, the company increased participation in its supplier collaboration activities and portal by over 90%.

> › One of the largest international telecommunications companies successfully leveraged SAP Sourcing to realize $12 billion in savings from merging processes. The company now has completely automated its sourcing processes.

> › An $18 billion consumer goods company reduced the sourcing cycle time by 67% and implemented best practices in its newly defined and automated sourcing processes.

> › One of the largest international pharmaceutical companies manages thousands of RFx and auction events, annually spending almost $10 billion. The company has reduced the timeline of each sourcing project by six weeks.

> › A $20 billion international insurer built a comprehensive contracts repository, gained visibility into contract expirations and projects, and reduced its Sarbanes-Oxley reporting effort by 75%.

> › One of the largest global office furniture makers automated its entire procurement process and reduced inventory by 60%, increased its automated invoice processing by 70%, and captured approximately 80% of its direct material spending.

> A major international conglomerate reduced its per-purchase transaction cost from about \$30 to only \$2 by automating the process while gaining insight into spending habits and formulating more effective sourcing strategies.

> One of the world's leading consumer products companies increased contract compliance from 75% to 95% by turning its contracts into dynamically updated catalog content and ensuring that employees purchased from those catalogs.

> The world's leading supplier of mobile systems cut purchase-cycle time by 80% and reduced the cost of order handling by 75%.

Every enterprise's results with SAP procurement solutions will vary, but one thing is certain: Implementing efficient, consistent supplier relationship procedures will have a positive impact on your profitability.

Conclusion

In this chapter, you were introduced to SAP's procurement solutions for on premise supplier relationship management, which cover a wide array of applications and procurement areas. We outlined the following:

> For requisitioning via catalogs and/or descriptive items and for operational sourcing, there is SAP SRM.

> For strategic sourcing, contract lifecycle management, and supplier management, there is SAP SRM and SAP Sourcing.

> For reporting, Spend Performance Management, Supplier InfoNet, and the standard reporting extractors found in many of the applications offer an assortment of options.

> For managing supplier onboarding, score carding, segmentation, and self-service maintenance/transaction activities, you have Supplier Lifecycle Management and Supplier Self-Services.

In Chapter 10, you will meet the cloud counterparts to all of the solutions discussed in this chapter.

10

Ariba and Fieldglass

The first generation of solutions streamlining the paper-based, cumbersome procurement processes of yore focused on email correspondence and web interfaces, but still required installation, configuration, and maintenance of software on premise. In the cross-company areas of exchanges and markets, locating these processes behind a corporate firewall à la on premise is a limiting option when deep collaboration is required between companies and systems. On premise solutions are thus at a disadvantage for truly integrated procurement before you even look at the maintenance and flexibility sides of the decision.

In Chapter 9, you learned about the on premise procurement solutions from SAP: SAP SRM. Future direction for SAP's procurement solutions points clearly towards the "cloud." No matter the size of your organization, the cloud solution for procurement will be a good option for you to evaluate as more and more transactions, partners, and analytics move to the cloud. For software as a service, *cloud* means multi-tenant, hosted solutions that can be accessed via a web browser on the Internet. In addition to maintenance advantages, the cloud offers the opportunity to further address two topics discussed in the previous chapter: data and usability. Users and suppliers generate enormous amounts of data, both explicit and implicit on an exchange and/or in a multi-tenant cloud environment. Explicit data is the data that is directly generated

Cloud for software as a service

from transactions, surveys, forms, and actions taken in the system. Implicit data is not provided intentionally, such as time spent on a particular page, paths taken in the solution or transaction, or extrapolations using explicit data generated in the system. Consolidating this data—by aggregating the data streams of transactions, for example—provides robust benchmark data on supplier performance and any number of business-relevant metrics.

On premise vs. cloud solutions

In this chapter, we will focus on the cloud half of SAP's procurement solutions, including both Ariba and Fieldglass. Ariba's solutions combined with Fieldglass cover a vast area of collaboration and processes between your company and its suppliers.

Overview of Ariba and Fieldglass

Internet-based procurement

Ariba began as a focused solutions provider for Internet-based procurement in 1996. Originally, Ariba offered many of its solutions as on premise software, similar to SAP SRM and other on premise SAP solutions. However, by the mid-2000s Ariba began charting a clear direction towards the cloud, buttressed immensely by the Ariba Network and a suite of cloud solutions.

In mid-2012, SAP announced the acquisition of Ariba. In March 2014, SAP also acquired Fieldglass, provider of the market-leading Cloud Vendor Management System (VMS), to further augment contingent and statement of work (SOW) labor-lifecycle capabilities. Fieldglass VMS has cross-functionality applications with both human resources (HR) and procurement, and is thus being integrated with Ariba for procurement and with SuccessFactors and SAP Human Capital Management (HCM) for HR uses.

Benefits of the cloud

Today, SAP offers a complete on premise and cloud solution portfolio for procurement. A cloud environment becomes "smarter" with use, much more so than a fragmented, on premise system. Use patterns and volumes can be identified in real- time, allowing for changes and optimizations to be made on the fly or in short interval upgrades. A cloud provider has direct incentives and the consolidated resources to stay involved at this level in the system across multiple customers/tenants, whereas an on premise implementation is usually one of many assets managed by a stretched IT department.

These solutions are grouped as shown in Table 10.1.

On premise vs. cloud solution stack

	On Premise Solutions	Cloud Solutions
Spend Analysis	SAP Spend Performance Management	Ariba Spend Visibility
Sourcing	SAP Sourcing and SAP SRM	Ariba Sourcing and Ariba Discovery
Contract Management	SAP Contract Lifecycle Management and SAP SRM	Ariba Contract Management
Operational Procurement	Materials Management in SAP ERP and SAP SRM; SAP Commodity Procurement	Ariba Procure-to-Pay, Ariba Services Procurement, Ariba Procurement Content, and Fieldglass Vendor Management System
Invoice Management	SAP Invoice Management OpenText	Ariba Invoice Management, Payment Management, and Discount Management
Supplier Information and Performance Management	SAP Supplier Lifecycle Management	Ariba Supplier Information Performance Management
Mobile Procurement	SAP Fiori	Mobile browser support for mobile device
Supplier Collaboration		Ariba Network

Table 10.1 SAP On Premise and Cloud Solution Stack—Procurement

As you can see from Table 10.1, Ariba combined with Fieldglass covers a vast area of collaboration and processes between your company and its suppliers. Beginning with Spend Analysis, this chapter's focus is the cloud half of SAP's procurement solutions.

A Closer Look at Cloud Solutions for Procurement

In this section, we will discuss the different solutions that compose the cloud offerings for procurement.

Spend Analysis

Ariba Spend Visibility allows you to extract, classify, and enrich spend data from SAP and other ERP providers, procurement cards, and legacy systems. Once you have the data, Spend Visibility provides dashboards, risk intelligence on suppliers, compliance/spend reporting (including diversity spend for federal and state reporting), peer benchmarking, as well as networking and knowledge sharing with other procurement professionals.

Visibility   Like all businesses, suppliers sometime experience cash flow problems that can have a ripple effect on your supply chain. Often there are no outward warning signs, such as delayed shipments or poor performance, prior to a supplier declaring insolvency. Via a partnership with Dunn and Bradstreet (D&B), Spend Visibility also contains a multidimensional data-enrichment approach that unifies data from D&B. This allows Spend Visibility to provide predictive warnings of supplier risk and estimates as to overall risk ratios in your supply base. Spend Visibility draws upon the vast data generated on the Ariba Network to provide benchmarks for suppliers and other key data points.

Sourcing

Strategic sourcing relies on supplier data being current, regardless of whether the information refers to the products a supplier offers or the supplier data itself. Having downstream options for operationalizing the outcome of a sourcing event are also key, as it does no good to award a bid and convert to a contract when the resulting contract is then never used by your company. Many organizations face challenges in keeping supplier information current as well as identifying new, promising suppliers for sourcing events to create competition and drive down costs.

Ariba Sourcing   With *Ariba Sourcing*, you conduct strategy development, negotiate,
features   source, and manage the resulting contracts and supplier data. Ariba

Sourcing currently supports over 295,000 companies conducting $340 billion in annual spending across 500 categories and has the following features:

> Request for proposal, quotation, information, or tender (RFx) Creation and Management

  - RFx types, including request for information (RFI), request for purchase (RFP), reverse auctions, and forward auctions

  - Integrated supplier discovery

  - Patented competitive bidding, sealed bidding, Dutch auction, and total-cost events

  - Matrix and tiered pricing

  - Team grading and collaborative scoring

> Category Management

> Sourcing Analysis and Reporting

> Integration with third-party systems using Web Services and file channels

> Savings and Pipeline Tracking

> Integration with Ariba Network for more efficient supplier discovery and interaction and with Ariba Exchange for networking and benchmarking with your peers

One of the bigger challenges in sourcing events is getting a mix of competitive bids from multiple suppliers. Ariba Discovery is an add-on service to SAP Sourcing that helps connect you to new suppliers during the sourcing process and distributed over 17 million sourcing events to suppliers last year alone. Suppliers register with Ariba Discovery and receive email notifications when you issue a new RFx with categories applicable to the suppliers' areas of coverage. Unlike with the on premise approaches, you rarely have to ask a supplier to register directly with your company; they are already registered on the Ariba Network and can be brought into RFx processes with little additional setup or prompting. Over one million suppliers across 20,000 categories and 190 countries participate in Ariba Discovery.

Contract Management

Ariba Contract Management supports procurement, sales, and internal contracts, leveraging the multi-tenant cloud environment to facilitate direct communication, negotiation, and agreement creation, as well as execution between your company and the supplier. Bringing contracts out of the paper world and into a complete, collaborative environment online can save you as much as 50% in contract-cycle time, 55% in additional spend compliance, and significantly reduced administrative, legal, and compliance costs. Much of your business is built on agreements and adherence to negotiated terms; Ariba Contract Management provides an end-to-end, integrated solution for this strategic area of procurement.

Request, authoring, and execution

Beginning with the request and authoring, Ariba Contract Management provides workflows and collaboration internally as well as via trading partners. Upon execution of the contract, the solution uses leading eSignature provider DocuSign to capture sign-off and provide an end-to-end document flow. No more printing, signing, and scanning a contract to send back to a supplier; with DocuSign, this all happens online. Once the contract is created, you need to fully apply it to your procurement activities to realize the value.

Integration

You also have the option to integrate Ariba Contract Management with external systems to operationalize contracts in addition to the native integrations with Ariba P2P and P2O. This means that the contracts get replicated in the appropriate purchasing environments (ERP and cloud environments) for usage, and the solution includes ongoing compliance and management via search, reporting, and renewal reminders/activities.

Operational Procurement

Once you have the executed contract defined with a supplier, your employees can start deriving value and savings with the help of several solutions. These operational activities are supported in several Ariba and Fieldglass solutions in the cloud, the first of which are Ariba P2P (Procure to Pay) and P2O (Procure to Order). P2P supports the end-to-end procurement process to payment in Ariba, whereas P2O integrates with an ERP backend system for goods/services receipts and invoicing/payments at the end of the process.

Ariba P2P and P2O offer a clear, straightforward interface with limited number of clicks and fields to fill out during the shopping process. The optimal, most efficient type of order is usually one that is sourced with a preexisting agreement from a defined item maintained in a catalog. Ariba Procurement Content (APC) provides a central area for catalogs and content integrated with P2O and P2P. APC supports fuzzy search, parametric refinement, and side-by-side comparison.

As per Figure 10.1, APC also allows suppliers to directly update their catalogs for your company via the Ariba Network, reducing your catalog maintenance burden, while driving contract usage and compliance. Over 750,000 catalogs have been delivered over the Ariba Network in APC.

Supplier self-service

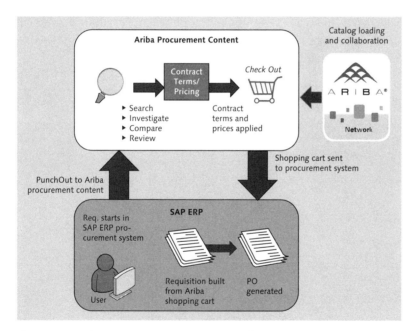

Figure 10.1 Ariba Procurement Content Process Flow

If a user cannot find an item in APC, further options exist. You can describe an item and have a buyer go and source it using the RFx capabilities in Ariba Sourcing.

Services procurement has additional functionality and support available in P2P, P2O, and Fieldglass. P2P and P2O can manage the procurement of all types of services, supported by pre-enabled catalog content of over 1,000 job descriptions in 14 categories. P2P and P2O also support fixed fees, time and expense, milestones, and/or a combination for SOW- and project-based procurement. Via Contract Management, P2P and P2O support complex pricing across materials, skills, geography, volume, tiers, and so on.

Fieldglass: Vendor Management System

In May 2014, SAP acquired Fieldglass, the recognized leader in services procurement and contingent workforce management. Fieldglass' cloud-based *Vendor Management System (VMS)* manages all categories of external labor, including contingent workers, SOW projects and services, independent contractors, and specialized talent pools. Fieldglass' VMS addresses the intersection between HR and procurement and helps organizations gain visibility into their contingent workforces (see Figure 10.2).

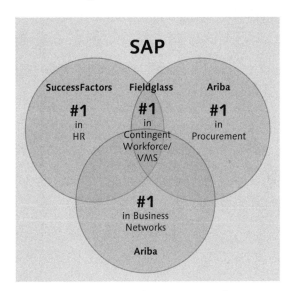

Figure 10.2 Intersection of Procurement and HR

Combined with the collaborative, network-based procurement capabilities of Ariba and the human resources expertise of SuccessFactors, SAP delivers a platform for businesses to manage their entire workforce—both temporary and permanent staff—from initial recruiting and onboarding to ongoing development, performance management, retention, and retirement.

Figure 10.3 depicts how Fieldglass elevates and integrates SAP's offerings for procurement, business networks, and HR.

Traditional VMS Capabilities

| Requisition | Candidate Selection | Work Order | Timesheets | Statement of Work | Invoicing | Reporting |

Figure 10.3 Traditional Flow and Capabilities of a VMS Solution

Fieldglass' VMS manages the entire lifecycle of procuring goods and services from the initial requisition to extensive reporting. The solution also goes beyond these with core functionalities in six key areas that are illustrated in Figure 10.4.

Core functionalities

Unified Platform	**Active Guidance**	**Consumer UX**
All Worker Types and Spend Categories ▸ Freelance marketplace; online staffing ▸ Region-agnostic sourcing ▸ SOW assisted workflow Applicant Tracking ▸ Built-in or existing hybrids ▸ Contingent | full-time interactions	Contextual Intelligence ▸ Embedded analytics enhancements ▸ Predictive analytics and modeling ▸ Rule-based auto-tuning Benchmarking and Data Services ▸ Peer benchmarking and gudiance	Mobility ▸ Mobile-first interface ▸ Time & expense ▸ iOS native enhancements Simple and Effective UX ▸ Zero training environment; adaptive learning ▸ "App in your inbox"
Enterprise Readiness	**Global-Local**	**Supply Ecosystem**
Interoperability and Reliability ▸ Cloud-to-cloud "drop-in" integrations ▸ Program office automation ▸ Supplier front-& back-office solutions ▸ API-first	Local Market Processes ▸ Asian expansions ▸ Additional languages	Ecosystem Enablement ▸ Supply base management ▸ Vertical/ consortium exchanges ▸ Job board portals ▸ Social networks

Figure 10.4 Fieldglass VMS Differentiators

Open integration platform Fieldglass provides an open integration platform that supports all major enterprise systems. With extensive experience in integration with both Ariba and SAP applications, Fieldglass can seamlessly fit into an existing SAP ecosystem and yield many process efficiencies through integrations with accounting or AP systems for invoicing or with Ariba for PO attachment and compliance to total-spend management policies.

Fieldglass customers realize benefits that cover the following pillars: cost, compliance, efficiency, and quality (see Figure 10.5).

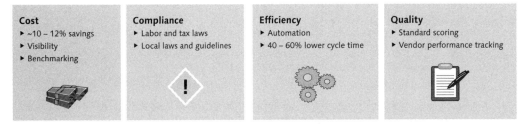

Cost
- ~10 – 12% savings
- Visibility
- Benchmarking

Compliance
- Labor and tax laws
- Local laws and guidelines

Efficiency
- Automation
- 40 – 60% lower cycle time

Quality
- Standard scoring
- Vendor performance tracking

Figure 10.5 Fieldglass Benefits to Customers

Invoicing Management

The final part of the procure-to-pay process resides with accounts payable. Traditionally, suppliers have submitted paper invoices in various formats, which creates a document-management challenge and inefficiency. This is overcome with the use of Ariba's invoice-management solution.

e-Invoice

Uniform invoice submission Ariba's e-Invoice solution leverages the Ariba Network, in which over one million suppliers, including many of your existing suppliers, already interact. Leveraging the Ariba Network and Ariba Exchange for community collaboration, Ariba e-Invoice enables uniform invoice submission by multiple suppliers. This includes invoice validation against 80+ business rules, invoicing against contracts and service-entry sheets, VAT/tax/legal compliance, account coding two-, three-, and four-way matching, invoice routing, approval, and reporting, and analytics. For bridging the final systems involved in invoice processing, Ariba e-Invoice offers invoice processing via supplier portal, Electronic Data Interchange (EDI), commerce Extensible Markup Language (cXML), CSV, and paper-conversion services.

Invoice-processing errors can impact the majority of invoices in paper-based environments. Transposing invoices into another system and misreading handwritten invoices or poorly scanned ones ends up creating errors and delays in payment. With Ariba e-Invoice, companies can achieve 98% invoice accuracy and automation. Customers have achieved up to 60% reductions in processing expense, 100% on-time payment performance, and a reduction in the time to receive an invoice from 21 days to two days.

Processing

Ariba Payment Management

Once you process the invoice, the next step is payment. Traditionally, paying suppliers has been challenging to automate, as suppliers cannot check on pending payments or where things are in the process and begin calling to get updates. Ariba Payment Management leverages the power of the Ariba Network to extend back-office systems to transmit ACH payments to suppliers. For suppliers, having Ariba Payment Management integrated with the Ariba Network provides updated information on the status of payments and allows them to update their account details directly.

Transmit ACH payments to suppliers

The capabilities of Ariba Payment Management cover the complete automation of your payment processes, including electronic payments, detailed remittance statements, a supplier self-service portal, and supplier bank-routing information verification. Using these tools, you can realize accelerated supplier-participation rates (in-house ACH programs often struggle with onboarding suppliers), increased accounts payable productivity and capability, and a reduction in fraud cases and late-payment fees. Combining e-Invoice with Ariba Payment Management delivers a one–two punch to inefficiency and waste in accounts payable. Using the rules and tools of e-Invoice, your accounts payable team can quickly return invoices with missing or erroneous information to the supplier for correction. With Ariba Payment Management, you further avoid late-payment fees and inefficiencies caused by paper checks.

Automation tools

Ariba Discount Professional

With these types of efficiency and agility improvements, you can turn your accounts payable department into a profit center. Initially, this is achieved via better management of Days Payable Outstanding

(DPO). In a high interest-rate environment, DPO management by itself provides you with cash flow and additional profitability. In a low interest-rate environment, in which returns on deposits are much less than 1%, obtaining and managing supplier discounts for early payments can provide the lion's share of profitability gains. Ariba Discount Professional automates early-payment discount management with a robust tool set from initial offer to agreement and a services arm, Ariba Working Capital Management Services, to support you in the formulation of an effective DPO-management program.

Ariba Discount Professional supports prorated, dynamic discounting, automatic and ad-hoc dynamic discounts, discount groups, full treasury control, alerts/notifications, and reporting. For suppliers, in addition to better cash flow management and control, Ariba Discount Professional also provides a cash-flow-optimizer tool and invoice/payment visibility. Ariba Discount Professional users have saved millions in early-payment discounts, increased DPO by 10 days on targeted spend, increased supplier participation, and increased annual discount savings by 10 times over pre-Ariba discount capture.

Supplier Information and Performance Management

Managing supplier information manually, let alone assessing performance, is a costly drain on your company's resources. Incorrect, out-of-date supplier records can lead to purchase orders and payments sent to incorrect locations, delays in deliveries, and difficulties in managing onboarding, segmentation, and reporting. If you send a PO to an incorrect location because you did not have the correct information, is the resulting delay attributable to a supplier's poor performance or to your processes?

Ariba Supplier Information and Ariba Performance Management

With Ariba Supplier Information and Ariba Supplier Performance Management, you can greatly reduce the cost of maintaining and updating supplier information, while focusing targeted efforts on managing the segmentation and performance of your supply base. Ariba Supplier Information features a supplier document repository for easy document collaboration, backend vendor master integration with third-party systems, single supplier record to use across all systems, and online buyer and supplier training.

Once the supplier records are actively and efficiently managed, you can focus on the strategic areas of performance management and segmentation. Ariba Supplier Performance Management (SPM) includes process management/collaboration capabilities, scorecards and KPIs, stakeholder surveys, and reports, alerting, and dashboards. Ariba SPM allows you to avoid critical supply issues through proactive monitoring and collaboration with key suppliers in an expanded scope and scale. Ariba SPM also provides your suppliers with visibility into performance issues and quality problems on a metrics-based level of reporting, providing your company stronger leverage in negotiations and resolution of issues.

Mobile Procurement and Supplier Collaboration

With its support of all major browsers, including Internet Explorer, Chrome, Safari, and Mozilla, Ariba users can access Ariba applications and subscriptions in the cloud from most devices with a browser and connectivity. In addition, smartphone apps in the shopping cart and approval areas of Ariba P2P are slated for release by the end of 2014.

 Cloud Procurement

In addition to mobile procurement, supplier collaboration is an increasingly important topic for procurement in the cloud. With Ariba Network (AN), we have saved the best for last in this chapter.

For a true, networked approach for managing supplier collaboration in which many suppliers interact with many customers, the Ariba Network provides the largest network of its kind. On the Ariba Network, a supplier can upload catalogs, receive and respond to purchase orders, respond to sourcing requests and RFxs, and submit invoices. You are able to realize enhanced portfolio and performance-management functionality on the Ariba Network without the maintenance and administrative burden of running the software in house.

Ariba Network

Figure 10.6 depicts the three main areas covered by Ariba solutions as a whole and by the Ariba Network in particular: buying, managing cash, and selling. To get an understanding of the size, momentum, and volume moving on the Ariba Network, think about this: As of mid-2014, over 1.4 million trading partners on the network were

Ariba main areas

conducting over $500 billion in annual commerce. This is twice as much as eBay and Amazon combined in the same period!

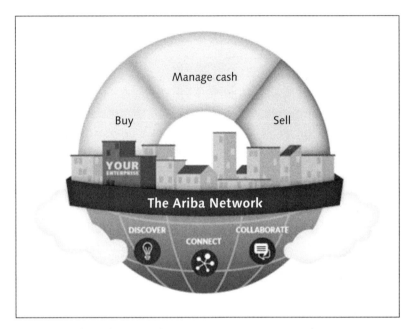

Figure 10.6 The Ariba Network

Trading

Trading on the Ariba Network allows for transparency and processing breakthroughs. Beginning with data validation, the Ariba Network prevents erroneous documents from being created, with over 80 customer-configurable rules for document processing and management. This validation in turn provides better compliance of invoices to orders and contracts and corresponding management of spend across all suppliers. With this speed and collaboration, suppliers and customers enjoy working-capital optimization, an ability to quickly transact with new partners, and strong trading-partner relationships.

Per existing customer and supplier experiences, conducting transactions on the Ariba Network allows buyers to compress invoice-processing cycles, reduce invoice-processing costs by up to 60%, prevent contract leakage to drive savings, and capture $3 million in early payment discounts for every $1 billion in spend. Suppliers use the Ariba Network to reduce Days Sales Outstanding (DSO) by up to six days, reduce PO-processing times to minutes, reduce invoice error rates by up to 83%, generate 65% more new business opportunities, and improve cash flow and forecasting.

SAP Ariba Case Study

Table 10.2 summarizes the case study of a large conglomerate's success in implementing Ariba solutions. The conglomerate operates in key segments of test and measurement, dental, industrial technologies, life sciences, and diagnostics, as well as environmental, with $19+ billion in revenues.

Company	Large design manufacturer of professional instrumentation, tools, and components, as well as large MRO distributor
Existing Solutions	Paper-based processes
The Challenge	To improve policies regarding purchasing to save money and to improve the purchasing department's control over spending
SAP Ariba Solutions	› Ariba Network › Ariba Procurement Solutions › Ariba Procurement Content (Catalogs)
Benefits	› Paperless purchasing adoption across 85% of operations (90 locations), reducing maverick spending and raising productivity › Significant supplier revenue growth directly related to innovative catalog approaches

Table 10.2 SAP Ariba Case Study

The Challenges

The company had manual, paper-based processes for procurement and was experiencing rising supply costs due to maverick buying and lack of compliance. In addition, both visibility into spending and products available for purchasing were extremely limited.

The SAP Ariba Solution

By implementing Ariba Network, Ariba Procurement Solutions (P2P), and Ariba Procurement Content, the company was able to move transactions with suppliers almost entirely online, enforce compliance, and streamline catalog data and searches to reduce time spent searching for products.

The Benefits

Adoption of paperless processes for supplier transactions saved the company millions over a three-year period, and the company's key suppliers also experienced substantial growth in revenues due to innovative catalog approaches underpinned by Ariba Procurement Content.

Conclusion

In a networked economy, more and more outward-focused procurement activities are moving to hubs in which suppliers and customers can interact in real time with fewer limitations placed on the transaction flow from disparate systems infrastructure, paper-based processes, and barriers to information exchange. In this chapter, you learned:

> The differences between on premise and cloud-based procurement solutions from SAP.

> How the Ariba Network and cloud-based solutions from Ariba and Fieldglass benefit your procurement organization and information technology, finance, and accounts payable departments.

> How suppliers' accounts receivable, sales, and marketing departments share in additional efficiencies and productivity.

In the next chapter, we will change topics and discuss product management with SAP Product Lifecycle Management.

SAP Product Lifecycle Management

The SAP solution Product Lifecycle Management (PLM) helps companies manage the entire lifecycle of creating a product, from the day the idea is conceived to the day the product is discontinued. During that time, SAP PLM provides support for managing projects, product-development tasks, documents, and strategic relationships. In addition, important regulations and health and safety provisions become easier to handle with SAP PLM's Corporate Services.

In this chapter, we will introduce you to the major features of SAP Product Lifecycle Management and provide examples of how it can fit into your enterprise.

How SAP PLM Fits in an Enterprise

Product lifecycle processes can be hard to get a handle on because they quite often cross various disciplines and groups in your organization. Management, designers, production, costing, and quality and sales teams, not to mention strategic external partners, need access to data about your product-development processes.

Product develop-
ment support

Through four applications, SAP PLM offers tools to handle just about everything involved with product development. In addition, support from other SAP products, such as SAP BusinessObjects, can introduce features to handle related tasks, such as analytics or product launches. In this section, we will explore these tools and describe how they can support product lifecycles in your enterprise.

Support for Discrete and Process Industries

If you talk to SAP representatives, you will hear how SAP PLM supports both discrete and process industries. However, let us clarify the difference between these two industries before we proceed further.

Discrete Industries

Tangible goods

Discrete industries (also referred to as *discrete manufacturing*) are often defined as those industries that produce items that you can see, touch, or count. For example, if you manufacture electronic products, such as radios, computers, medical equipment, cars, or furniture, you are in a discrete industry.

Process Industries

Chemical change

Process industries (also referred to as *process manufacturing*) are typically defined as those industries that involve a chemical change. Good examples of this type of manufacturing include the petroleum industry, chemicals, fertilizers, food production, and textiles.

Of course, many companies have processes that touch on both of these types of industry. But the processes used in building tables and processing petroleum, for example, can differ, and SAP PLM offers tools to support both, as you will see throughout the rest of this chapter as we delve into the features of SAP PLM.

SAP PLM Solution Map

The solution map for SAP PLM is shown in Figure 11.1. There are four areas of functionality:

> Product Management

> Product Development and Collaboration

> Product Data Management

> PLM Foundation

Each of these categories is discussed in more detail next.

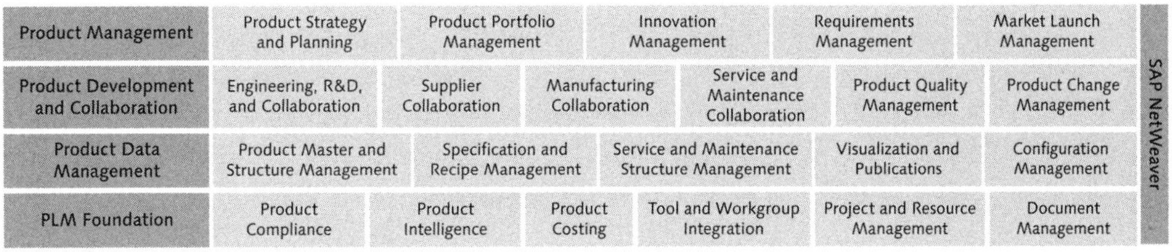

Product Management	Product Strategy and Planning	Product Portfolio Management	Innovation Management	Requirements Management	Market Launch Management	
Product Development and Collaboration	Engineering, R&D, and Collaboration	Supplier Collaboration	Manufacturing Collaboration	Service and Maintenance Collaboration	Product Quality Management	Product Change Management
Product Data Management	Product Master and Structure Management	Specification and Recipe Management	Service and Maintenance Structure Management	Visualization and Publications	Configuration Management	
PLM Foundation	Product Compliance	Product Intelligence	Product Costing	Tool and Workgroup Integration	Project and Resource Management	Document Management

(SAP NetWeaver)

Figure 11.1 SAP PLM Solution Map

SAP PLM's Value in Your Enterprise

Being able to deliver new products quickly and efficiently has obvious benefits for any organization. SAP PLM allows you to explore market opportunities, reduce the costs of product development, manage your processes efficiently, integrate with suppliers and partners, and ensure product quality.

SAP PLM also helps you ensure that the data about your products is consistent across your organization. Everyone from your product designers to your sales force will be aware of new developments and designs. In addition, document-tracking features help ensure that key data, such as engineering change orders, are handled with fewer errors. Now you can also integrate documents in all stages of not only product development, but also trial production and even in a product's quality inspections.

Document-tracking features

Integration with other SAP products, as well as MCAD and ECAD design tools, provides seamless process and information flow. With SAP PLM, you can develop prototypes and specifications to deliver to manufacturing partners and ensure that your products meet the necessary product guidelines and safety regulations.

A Closer Look at SAP PLM

Each of the areas of SAP PLM provides a set of features to handle various aspects of product development. In this section, we look at these features and examine how they help you get from the concept to the final product. Note that this is an overview; for each and every capability available, check out the detailed solution maps included in Appendix C.

Overview of SAP PLM

Take a look at each of the major areas of SAP PLM listed in the SAP PLM solution map, each of which is discussed in more detail in the sections that follow. Table 11.1 shows you the key areas of SAP PLM, based on SAP PLM's solution map.

Category	Features
Product Management	› Product Strategy and Planning › Product Portfolio Management › Innovation Management › Requirements Management › Market Launch Management
Product Development and Collaboration	› Engineering, R&D Collaboration › Supplier Collaboration › Manufacturing Collaboration › Service and Maintenance Collaboration › Product Quality Management › Product Change Management
Product Data Management	› Product Master and Structure Management › Specification and Recipe Management › Service and Maintenance Structure Management › Visualization and Publications › Configuration Management
PLM Foundation	› Product Compliance › Product Intelligence › Product Costing › Tool and Workgroup Integration › Project and Resource Management › Document Management

Table 11.1 SAP PLM Solution Map

Tip

The *Collaboration Folders* (cFolders) application in SAP PLM allows for document collaboration during product development. You can share information with internal staff as well as external vendors using cFolders, because it does not expose your backend system and therefore keeps confidential data secure. cFolders also works with the strategic sourcing features of SAP SRM.

The *Collaboration Projects* (cProjects) application in SAP PLM allows multiple stake holders managing a project to work together in a collaborative environment, thus bringing in greater efficiencies to the efforts involved. It also provides complete visibility of various aspects of a project, such as costs, timelines, and resources, to all the stakeholders.

Before we explore each of these categories in more detail, we will discuss how they are all related to functionality in other SAP products.

SAP PLM and Its Relation to Other SAP Products

SAP PLM is supported by SAP NetWeaver, the open architecture of which provides for a web-based interface for accessing product-development information. You can establish outside partners and vendors involved in your product development and allow them to access your latest documents and data via the web, thereby streamlining your project teamwork.

SAP PLM can now also manage large projects that span several sub-projects with overlapping dates, schedules, resources, and costs constraints. With features such as Gantt charts, it is easier to get a visual overview of the entire project and its dependencies.

The analytics processes supported by SAP Business Warehouse (SAP BW) and data warehousing allow you to have consistent product information, both across your business and with external partners or vendors. SAP NetWeaver integration functions help users of SAP PLM connect with other SAP Business Suite solutions, such as SAP Customer Relationship Management (SAP CRM), and with external systems.

See Chapter 19 for more on SAP NetWeaver

When you launch a new product, the integration of SAP PLM and SAP CRM is also useful. With these two SAP applications in place, you can support market launches of new products with automated delivery of the print materials that salespeople need and seamless order processing.

Integration with CRM and SCM

SAP Supply Chain Management (SAP SCM) can also be called on to help with top-down and bottom-up demand planning. This in turn helps you forecast product need in the marketplace.

In the following sections, we provide you with more detail about each of the major categories in the SAP PLM solution map.

Product Management

Define and execute project

Product Management is where your product-development project is defined and executed. Specifically, this module provides tools that help you brainstorm your new product design and make your business case for your management to evaluate.

 Example

> A software manufacturer can come up with the idea for new game software, begin to plan the product-development process, schedule the software engineers and other resources to work on the game, and strategize plans for this new product alongside other projects in the company.

Once underway, you can use SAP Project Management tools to help schedule, manage resources, and track your costs. You can also use project reporting tools to keep shareholders in the loop. If your company is managing several product-development projects, the strategic and product portfolio tools will help you keep a broader view of all of your projects and products.

Main features

The features in the Product Management area include:

> **Product Strategy and Planning**
> Helps you align new product concepts with your overall business strategies and goals. With the new product roadmap, you allow collaboration across departments and resources and also track risks and management of intellectual property associated with your new product.

Project Builder

> **Product Portfolio Management**
> Allows you to evaluate, based on current market conditions, which new products warrant resources for development, which products need to be maintained at their current level, and which

existing products need to be updated or retired. A relatively new functionality known as Stability Study helps planners decide which products need to continue the next rounds of product development or should be discontinued at a specific stage. Newer features, such as Control Plan and Failure Mode and Effects Analysis (FMEA), in SAP PLM bring a new round of controls and visibility to business processes.

> **Innovation Management**
> Helps you to study market potential for ideas, evaluate technical constraints in producing the product, and measure the potential return on investment of the new product. This entails creating trial bill of materials (BOM) and making use of preliminary costing functionality to see if it is viable to produce the product in-house or if it would be better to outsource some manufacturing processes.

> **Requirements Management**
> Captures all requirements—from business rules to functional and technical aspects—to ensure that your products meet the needs of your customers. Even market, competitor, and consumer surveys can become an integral part of requirements management.

> **Market Launch Management**
> Provides tools and strategies to help you successfully launch your new products in the market.

Product Management takes you through the product-concept and planning stage. The next area of SAP PLM helps you deal with the product development phase.

Product Development and Collaboration

This area of SAP PLM offers different benefits depending on the type of industry you work for.

If yours is a discrete industry, you can use Product Development and Collaboration to move requirement structures through to concept structures and finally into product structures. Integration with authoring environments, such as CAD systems, helps you move through design to prototype. You can collaborate with external business partners in a secure web environment. If your concern is strategic sourcing, you can look to integration with SAP SRM.

Collaborate with external partners

Prototype and configuration   A logical step in developing a new product is to create a product prototype. SAP PLM offers tools to ensure that you can procure the parts or supplies you need, produce the prototype, evaluate its design, and then move from prototype to final production. In this area, you also have the option to distinctly segregate the product in development into its costing, trial production, and stability study perspectives.

When you have your final product defined, you can get configurations to sales so that they can take the product to your consumers and provide equipment and technical asset structures to service and maintenance to support the product. SAP PLM also supports variant configuration that enables customers to choose from a large number of a product's offerings to suit their tastes, needs, and preferences. This also helps the company to quickly assemble and make available the customer-specific products.

Recipes   If your company is a process industry, you need to handle specifications and *recipes* (process definitions, such as how to process crude oil) at various levels. SAP PLM allows you to take enterprise-level recipes and implement them at the site and plant levels. You can manage process trials that ensure that these recipes are foolproof before you send them on to production. These business processes are covered in the Recipe Management area of SAP PLM.

Quality management and product-costing capabilities are important features for all types of industries and underlie the value of an integrated solution. Quality management integrates with important business processes such as procurement, production, and sales. Product costing integrates with production-planning components to determine the realistic and accurate cost of manufacturing a product.

Recipe Management is a comprehensive solution within the Production Planning component that caters to all aspects of new product development and introduction (NPDI), such as recipe management, trial production, product safety, and substance volume tracking. It also effectively integrates quality planning and inspection during all stages of NPDI.

Main features   Product Development and Collaboration features include the following:

> **Engineering, R&D Collaboration**
> This is a business process that enables cross-department development essentially by providing centralized data storage.

> **Supplier Collaboration**
> These tools help you manage and evaluate the ability of your suppliers to provide the required parts and components within the established quality standards and desired time frame.

> **Manufacturing Collaboration**
> This helps you to define your recipes and process definitions prior to sending them on to your manufacturing group. In this context, a *recipe* can be thought of as the steps and materials needed to build a product. A process definition defines a process such as quality control.

> **Service and Maintenance Collaboration**
> This is where you establish product maintenance records, maintenance manuals, and warranty claims and define the process for how your products are to be serviced.

> **Product Quality Management**
> This can be used with SAP ERP tools to define deliverables, quality measurements, and plan inspections for quality. The quality-notification tool helps you to detect, define, and report on quality problems. You can completely manage incoming quality certificates from vendors and outgoing quality certificates to customers. You also have complete visibility and control over products' batches before they expire, thus enabling you to take necessary actions, such as consuming products or selling them on a priority basis.

> **Product Change Management**
> This handles documents related to engineering change requests over the life of your products. These requests occur when things such as modifications to the original product are required to deal with market or product safety issues. A subelement of Product Change Management, Engineering Change Management (ECM), handles this effectively, and business process owners can even integrate Digital Signature to bring greater controls and validation to the entire process of product change management.

Example

> If your company makes ice cream, the product-development and collaboration phase is when you would test the recipes until the product met with your approval. After you complete the Product Development and Collaboration set of tasks, the next area of SAP PLM, Product Data Management, will help you document your product specifications and create the specifications that will allow you to produce that great flavor you created in every batch you produce.

Product Data Management

Handle documents throughout the life of your products

Product Data Management is the paper pusher of SAP PLM. This is the set of features that you use for handling documents throughout the life of your products, from planning and technical specifications to part management and bill of materials. Product Data Management includes the following tools:

> **Product Master and Structure Management**
> Involves the description of your product features in a product structure (a product structure describes how parts and components are assembled to create a product) and all of the data, drawings, and diagrams used in manufacturing processes.

> **Specification and Recipe Management**
> Involves managing the detailed product specifications and recipes (thorough descriptions of processes) for processes that connect the R&D function to product production.

> **Service and Maintenance Structure Management**
> Includes three processes: Phase-In Equipment, Corrective Maintenance, and Phase-Out Equipment. Essentially, you use this portion of SAP PLM to keep records over the life of various pieces of equipment used in your manufacturing process, including putting it into service, maintaining it, and retiring it from service. *Refurbishment* is also now part of the service and maintenance process. The refurbishment process entails uninstalling a piece of equipment from its location, repairing it, and then reinstalling it. Customer Service enables a company to offer maintenance services to its customers.

> **Visualization and Publications**
> The process for issuing documents such as repair manuals, training manuals, and technical publications. Features include document browser, document redlining, check in, check out, and extensive options to control who is authorized to view, change or download documents.

> **Configuration Management**
> Provides a history of all product changes made over the life of the product, including the management of parts catalogs and all documents detailing the individual components within your product. A single document in document management can have up to 999 parts and up to 99 versions. It is also possible to control the business functions of a document through status management. For example, a document with the status "approved" is locked for any further changes or updates. Similarly, a document with status "obsolete" is no longer available to business-process owners.

SAP PLM Foundation

In business today, where there are products, there are often regulations. Some of these regulations pertain to product safety, some to waste disposal in the manufacturing process, and still others to employees' health and safety when working with these products. The PLM Foundation portion of SAP PLM is where you find the tools for managing product and process audits to ensure that you are meeting set criteria.

Regulations

The various areas of SAP PLM Foundation are as follows:

> **Product Compliance**
> The tools in this area of SAP PLM include Product Compliance, Audit Management, Product Safety, Hazardous Substance Management, Dangerous Goods Management, and Waste Management. These tools ensure that your products meet and comply with regulatory and government requirements for product and consumer safety, transportation and disposal of hazardous waste and dangerous goods, and proper labeling of products containing such things as cleaning agents or drugs. With Audit Management functionality, you can effectively handle not only audits from external auditing firms, such Cotecna or SGS, but also internal audits.

> **Product Intelligence**
> Allows you to access and analyze all documents and information related to your products from all parts of your system, including SAP SCM and SAP CRM components. More advanced tools are online (Internet) collaboration and controlled access to important documents.

> **Product Costing**
> A functionality that allows you to break down or roll up the costs for products and services, including the costs incurred in each step of your production process. You can monitor orders and materials based on sales lots or individual sales documents. You can also incorporate additional costs such as manufacturing overheads in product costing through a costing sheet.

> **Tools and Workgroup Integration**
> Provides for the integration of applications such as CAD/CAM into your system for product development.

> **Project and Resource Management**
> Contains all of the tools necessary for the management of this new product-development process. You can manage the essential items, such as the project scope, time, costs, resources, and milestones. The SAP Project System (PS) component is the relevant component that takes care of all aspects of project management, including a project to develop a new product. Visibility of large-scale commercial projects with complexities such as resources and dependencies constraints is available through these tools.

> **Document Management**
> Provides a way to integrate documents with your processes and make them available to you in a variety of formats, including graphics, CAD, and text. Some of the business processes where documents can become available are purchase order, sales order, asset master, equipment, functional location, material master, and BOM.

Together, all of the tools provided in SAP PLM allow you to manage a product from its conception to its safe implementation in your workplace.

In the next two sections, you will find case studies to help you better understand how companies benefit from implementing SAP PLM in their enterprises.

SAP PLM Case Study 1

Table 11.2 gives you an overview of the first case study in this chapter.

Company	German medical equipment manufacturer
Existing Solutions	SAP R/3 and other SAP products
Challenge	To continuously innovate and deliver products to market quickly
SAP Solutions	SAP PLM, SAP Easy Document Management, Windows Explorer integration, and link between SAP PLM and the CAD system
Benefits	Design and production collaborate more easily, incorporation of outside resources in product development processes, and consolidated, accurate data

Table 11.2 SAP PLM Case Study 1

A German medical equipment manufacturer needed to deliver innovative products to compete successfully in the marketplace. The company implemented SAP PLM to accelerate its product development and to manage documentation more efficiently.

Deliver innovative products

The Challenges

The company, one of the leading medical equipment companies in the world, specializes in surgical equipment. In the medical equipment field, it is necessary to develop innovative, cutting-edge products regularly if you want to stay in business. A full 30% of this company's income-generating products are less than five years old, highlighting the need for constant innovation with new products.

This company had to find ways to deliver new products faster and determine how to integrate its CAD data into its product-development processes.

The SAP Solution

The company assigned four IT experts to a project team and implemented the solution in three phases. The first phase involved migrating development documentation for new products; the second phase connected SAP PLM with its CAD data and synchronized BOMs; the third phase addressed product change management to develop existing products. SAP Consulting helped with implementation and customization.

SAP R/3 to SAP PLM The parent company had been using SAP software solutions for many years and had used SAP R/3 since 1993. The company began to implement SAP PLM in 2002 to speed up its product development and handle documentation challenges. The company had an existing digital archiving system in its back-office operations but needed to address document challenges in R&D. The company took advantage of SAP PLM's digital product documentation and centralized database. By assigning a unique number to each product-related project, the company could track all relevant documentation in a standardized project folder created using SAP PLM. Templates and checklists were put in place to guide the document-management process.

SAP Easy Document Management was implemented to provide an easy-to-use interface for employees to access documents and data. This SAP user interface was integrated into Windows Explorer so that people could work in a familiar environment, thereby speeding up the adoption of the new system.

The company also linked SAP PLM to its CAD data. BOMs, 3-D models, and drawings were made accessible through SAP PLM, linking the development and production processes.

The Benefits

Because of tighter integration, the two processes of design and production, which used to be divided, now work together. Project teams can collaborate more easily and have access to the same product data.

In addition, the new system allows the company to bring outside entities, such as doctors and hospitals, into the process to give its R&D team the input necessary to create the next great product.

Having consolidated and accurate data helps the company know what its current product inventories are, what its current product costs are, and how changes in products affect sales.

Looking toward the Future

The company focused its SAP PLM implementation in one location, where most of its medical equipment R&D takes place. In the future, the company plans to expand it to other departments and divisions throughout the parent company. After that, the company hopes that consistent data will be available to divisions around the world.

SAP PLM Case Study 2

Table 11.3 gives you a snapshot of the second case study in this chapter. You should review it before proceeding with the rest of this section.

Company	Specialty chemicals
Existing Solutions	Multiple local systems
Challenge	To implement one ERP solution and comply with chemical industry regulations
SAP Solutions	SAP ERP and SAP PLM
Benefits	Chemical laboratory integrated into supply chain, reduced costs, and increased efficiency in product development

Table 11.3 SAP PLM Case Study 2

This German company generates annual revenues of over €5 billion and employs 22,500 people. The enterprise operates with more than 100 companies and has faced challenges in complying with health and safety management.

The Challenges

The company needed to streamline its multiple local systems with a centralized ERP solution. In addition, the company had to deal with multiple regulations for health, safety, and the environmental impact associated with its handling of chemicals.

The SAP Solution

SAP ERP provided the centralized ERP system the company needed and included important quality-management tools. The SAP PLM product integrated with SAP ERP easily and helped the company to meet legal requirements for health, safety, and environmental regulations efficiently.

The SAP solution also enabled the company to have faster access to master data in its operations around the world.

The Benefits

The company has achieved benefits in the areas of lower costs, faster access to data for more immediate decision making, and increased efficiency. By implementing a single solution, the company has greatly reduced the complexity of its IT landscape. As a result of this unified solution, customer satisfaction has grown, and data transparency has helped the company adhere more closely to industry regulations.

Conclusion

In this chapter, we explored the four major areas of SAP Product Lifecycle Management that can help you handle products from concept to implementation:

> Product Management

> Product Development and Collaboration

> Product Data Management

> PLM Foundation

We went into detail for each of these areas to give you a deeper understanding of how SAP PLM works and to show how it can be implemented in your own company. The case studies helped put SAP PLM in a real-world context so that you can fully understand the topic and the product.

In Chapter 12, we will look at how SAP Supply Chain Management (SAP SCM) can help you manage your supplier and procurement processes so that you can get the materials you need to make the wonderful products you planned with SAP PLM.

SAP Supply Chain Management

Supply chain management involves all of the business processes and coordination that is necessary to get a product or service from a supplier to a customer. This typically includes taking raw materials or various components and assembling them for delivery to the final user. In an enterprise, the supply chain process touches on several departments and often several companies, including those involved in planning and forecasting, sourcing (finding the right vendor), purchasing, inventorying, manufacturing, and distribution.

In this chapter, we will explore the many features of *SAP Supply Chain Management* (SAP SCM) that help your enterprise automate and streamline your supply chain to save time and money and deliver what your customers need, when they need it.

How SAP SCM Fits in an Enterprise

The various features of SAP SCM connect the areas of supply, planning, manufacturing, and distribution in an enterprise in a way that enables everyone involved, both inside and outside of the company, to have access to vital information (what SAP calls *visibility*). This sharing of knowledge and information helps companies adapt their supply chain processes to an ever-changing competitive environment

Connect supply, planning, manufacturing, and distribution

by helping them make decisions and execute them quickly. But to understand SAP SCM's approach to the supply chain process, you have to begin with the concept of an adaptive supply chain network.

The Adaptive Supply Chain

Shrinkage effect

In the past, supply chains were rigidly designed with processes, which were not easy to change because they were set up in a specific sequence. Due to the ever-changing nature of businesses today, the old supply chain model does not work very well. Companies that stay with the older model cannot make the quick changes that are necessary to stay competitive. In addition, the so-called *shrinkage effect* of today's tighter profit margins demands that the supply chain run as efficiently as possible to help make companies profitable. With newer and more agile supply chain models in place, companies can quickly react to the ever-changing regional or global challenges.

Collaboration

The goal of SAP SCM is to make it possible for a company to transform its traditional supply chain from linear, sequential processes into an adaptive supply chain network. The idea behind an *adaptive supply chain* is that the companies involved in the supply chain network optimally share information and resources in a way that helps them make adjustments quickly as market conditions change.

Linear vs. adaptive

SAP SCM also provides collaboration technology and easier access to data, which can help you reduce costs and improve your level of service.

 Example

> A large customer order for mobile computing devices comes in to your organization. In a linear model, you contact one supplier for information, such as pricing and delivery times for parts to fulfill the order, then you contact another supplier, and then you get back to the first supplier to see whether he can match the other price. You contact your salespeople and ask if another model or color would work for the customer. This linear approach is time consuming and inefficient. An adaptive model, however, allows you to contact your suppliers, manufacturers, distributors, and customers and share information in a collaborative fashion. Suppliers can work together to get you what you need. Consequently, you can respond to shorter, unpredictable lifecycles.

SAP has identified five key phases that constitute an effective adaptive supply chain network:

> **Planning**
  Involves planning and adapting to network-driven demand based on your enterprise business objectives. Planning also takes procurement lead times, a product's manufacturing time, and a product's delivery time into account to come up with realistic and reliable planning data.

> **Executing**
  Means putting your supply chain into action based on available or anticipated supplies and resources. If impeccable planning is in place, then executing the plan is certainly achievable.

> **Sensing**
  Relates to being aware of variations based on internal or external events and alerting people to these issues. This includes, for example, alerting the production team of a possible production delay when the vendor indicates an inability to supply the required raw material needed to manufacture the product.

> **Responding**
  Involves collaborating on and responding to demands and deviations across your supply chain network.

> **Learning**
  Relates to the previously mentioned four phases and means that you continually improve on your system from data generated in all of the phases. Companies can leverage the statistical reports and analyses tools available that provide comprehensive comparison between existing data in the system and more realistic data that can greatly improve planning and execution.

SAP SCM makes tools available to map to these phases, with features for planning and forecasting, analytics to help a company sense when changes are needed, how to respond to these changes, and how to improve processes, and tools for executing procurement, manufacturing, and distribution processes. Together, these features help an enterprise move toward an adaptive supply chain model.

Traditional vs. adaptive supply chain characteristics

Table 12.1, derived from SAP's white paper *Adaptive Supply Chain Networks*, will help you distinguish a traditional supply chain from an adaptive supply chain.

Characteristic	Traditional Supply Chain	Adaptive Supply Chain
Information propagation	Sequential and slow	Parallel and dynamic
Planning horizon	Days/weeks	Hours/days
Planning characteristics	Batch	Dynamic
Response reaction	Days/hours	Hours/minutes
Analytics	Historical	Real time
Supplier characteristics	Cost/delivery	Network capability
Control	Centralized	Distributed
Exception management	Centralized/manual	Distributed/automated
Integration	Standalone point solution	Intra- and inter-enterprise
Standards	Proprietary	Open

Table 12.1 Traditional versus Adaptive Supply Chains

The next step to help you see how SAP SCM works in an organization is to examine the concept of visibility.

Visibility of Information

Lifecycle of a customer order

Consider the lifecycle of a customer order that is placed via your website. In the perfect adaptive network, the customer order information would be instantly available to suppliers across the supply chain. Inventory is checked and rechecked. If the company can fulfill customer orders from existing stock, then that shortens the entire supply chain cycle. If a company needs to procure materials and then produce the product to meet customer order, then several supply chain stakeholders come into play. Every department and vendor involved in fulfilling that order could observe the order flowing through every stage into the supply chain system and back out to the customer. That ability to view the current status of the order is the essence of *visibility*.

The challenge here is that in most companies today, all of that data resides in many separate systems. Plus, outside suppliers are often not integrated into your enterprise's system. By using tools in SAP SCM to increase visibility, you can handle that order faster, automate many tasks, and deal with exceptions as they arise.

Adding visibility to your systems is the first step. Once you have visibility in your supply chain process, the next step that you have to take is determining how quickly you can respond to what you see. That is where velocity of response comes in.

Velocity of Response

Put simply, *velocity of response,* a phrase used in SAP SCM, is how quickly your organization can move in response to an event. For example, how quickly can you respond to an order to move the information, the materials, and finally the products through your supply chain and deliver this order to your customer? Companies such as Amazon have won great competitive advantage by embracing velocity of response as a key goal. The planning tools in SAP SCM can be vital for ensuring that your organization can quickly respond to and adjust plans to handle change.

How quickly can your organization respond?

That being said, most companies cannot respond quickly without the help of their business partners, such as suppliers and distributors. Connecting with them efficiently is another key to effective supply chain management.

Sharing with Partners

It is now the nature of supply chain management that companies have to break down walls between them to enable partnerships. Few companies design, market, manufacture, sell, and deliver a product in a vacuum or all by themselves. They have materials or components suppliers. They outsource one piece of their manufacturing process or use an outside distribution company.

Ex **Example**

Here is a good example of a specific process that SAP SCM can help you handle more efficiently. Available to promise (ATP) is a concept related to how you use inventory to fulfill a customer order. Inventory can consist of items on hand, inventory you have placed on hold to fill back orders, and inventory you have placed in reserve. Available-to-promise inventory is the inventory you can use to fill a customer order.

When you receive an order, SAP SCM uses the collaboration request/promise architecture to send a request to every vendor who could fulfill it. This could include in-house and external partners anywhere in the world. The required delivery date is verified, and if the item is not available, the customer is offered a substitute product or is alerted to the date when the company can fulfill the order. In other words, when a customer places an order and indicates when he wants the product, the system first uses backward scheduling to see if it can meet the customer's requested delivery date. If it is unable to meet that delivery date, it performs forward scheduling to come up with a realistic date by which it will be able to deliver the product to the customer.

Meanwhile, the transportation/planning engine routes requests delivery information to either an in-house or external transportation vendor to verify the shipment date. The order-promising engine picks which vendor to use to fulfill the order, notifies the production-scheduling engine, and sends a confirmation to the customer.

SAP SCM can help you build in alerts to this system if exceptions arise and even handle customer requests for changes. The specific engine that alerts the exceptions and deviations is known as Early Warning System (EWS).

This shared responsibility to get services or products to market requires that there be a degree of information visibility that is not snarled by firewalls or confidentiality policies. Having barriers among your partner systems means that your products do not get to your customers on time and that much of your time is wasted on miscommunication or the mishandling of your collaborative efforts.

Make-to-order and customizing

With challenges such as make-to-order processes and customization for the general customer population, being able to respond in a timely fashion demands a system that allows real-time information to flow freely through the entire supply chain. SAP SCM's collaborative tools enable this kind of interaction among departments, vendors, and customers.

When you consider the need for visibility, velocity of response, and integration with partners in the supply chain, you can appreciate the tools that SAP SCM offers to help you achieve these goals.

SAP SCM Solution Map

The SAP SCM solution map is shown in Figure 12.1. There are 10 areas of functionality, including the use of SAP's Duet, which allows users to work in familiar Microsoft applications, such as Excel and Outlook, to perform parts of the supply chain process.

Work in familiar Microsoft applications

Demand and Supply Planning	Demand Planning and Forecasting	Safety Stock Planning	Supply Network Planning	Distribution Planning	Service Parts Planning
Procurement	Strategic Sourcing		Purchase Order Processing		Invoicing
Manufacturing	Production Planning and Detailed Scheduling		Manufacturing Visibility, Execution, and Collaboration	MRP-Based Detailed Scheduling	
Warehousing	Inbound Processing and Receipt Confirmation	Outbound Processing	Cross Docking	Warehousing and Storage	Physical Inventory
Order Fulfillment	Sales Order Processing		Billing	Service Parts Order Fulfillment	
Transportation	Freight Management	Planning and Dispatching	Rating, Billing, and Settlement	Driver and Asset Management	Network Collaboration
Real-World Awareness	Auto-ID (RFID) and Item Serialization			Event Management	
Supply Chain Visibility	Strategic Supply Chain Design	Supply Chain Analytics	Supply Chain Risk Management	Sales and Operations Planning	
Supply Network Collaboration	Supplier Collaboration		Customer Collaboration	Outsourced Manufacturing	
Supply Chain Management with Duet	Demand Planning in MS Excel				

SAP NetWeaver

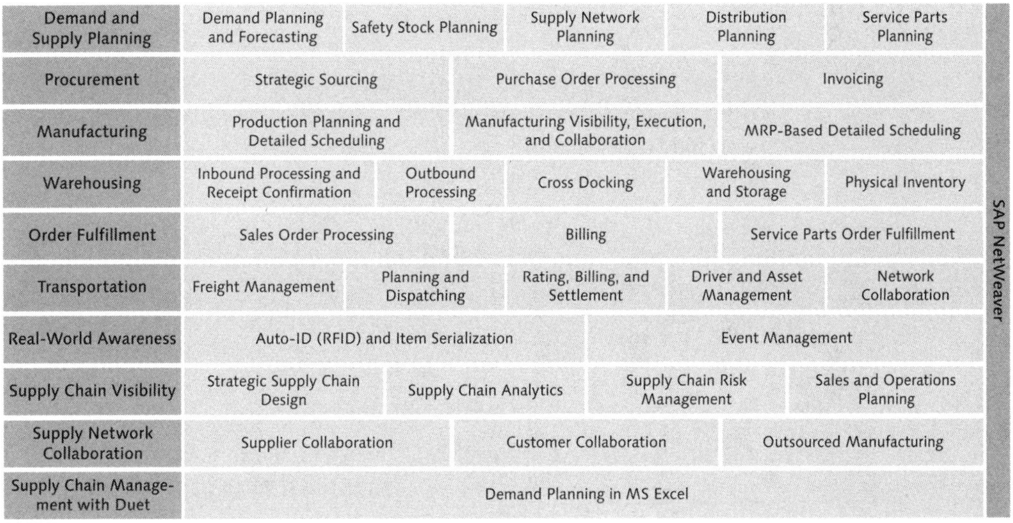

Figure 12.1 SAP Solution Map for SAP SCM

Note that two of the items on the solution map, Supply Chain Analytics and Supply Network Collaboration, are not part of the supply chain process itself, but rather provide tools for designing supply chains and collaborating with others in the chain.

In the next section, you will review the specific areas of SAP SCM and how they work to support your supply chain efficiency.

A Closer Look at SAP SCM

Each of the SAP SCM areas provides a set of features that you can use to manage various aspects of the supply chain network. In this section, we will examine these features and how they help you get from receiving a customer order to delivering a product or service. Note that this is an overview; for each and every capability available, see the detailed solution maps included in Appendix C.

Overview of SAP SCM

There are several major areas of SAP SCM listed in the SAP SCM solution map; we will discuss each of them in more detail in the sections that follow. Table 12.2 outlines the most current listing of key areas of SAP SCM.

Category	Application
Demand & Supply Planning	› Demand Planning & Forecasting › Safety Stock Planning › Supply Network Planning › Distribution Planning › Service Parts Planning
Procurement	› Strategic Sourcing › Purchase Order Processing › Invoicing
Manufacturing	› Production Planning & Detailed Scheduling › Manufacturing Visibility & Execution & Collaboration › MRP-Based Detailed Scheduling
Warehousing	› Inbound Processing & Receipt Confirmation › Outbound Processing › Cross Docking › Warehousing & Storage › Physical Inventory
Order Fulfillment	› Sales Order Processing › Billing › Service Parts Order Fulfillment

Table 12.2 Key Areas of SAP SCM

Category	Application
Transportation	› Freight Management › Planning & Dispatching › Rating & Billing & Settlement › Driver & Asset Management › Network Collaboration
Real World Awareness	› Auto-ID (RFID) & Item Serialization › Event Management
Supply Chain Visibility	› Strategic Supply Chain Design › Supply Chain Analytics › Supply Chain Risk Management › Sales & Operations Planning
Supply Network Collaboration	› Supplier Collaboration › Customer Collaboration › Customer Collaboration › Outsourced Manufacturing
Supply Chain Management with Duet	Demand Planning in MS Excel

Table 12.2 Key Areas of SAP SCM (Cont.)

SAP SCM offers a robust set of tools; in fact, if you go to SAP's website and view the solution map you will find that each one of the feature sets in the right column of Table 12.2 includes even more detailed features that we do not have space to list in this chapter. However, in the sections that follow, we provide overviews of the major areas of functionality in SAP SCM.

Supply Chain Planning

This area of SAP SCM allows you to synchronize supply to demand using both push and pull network-planning processes. Simply put, *pull* happens when you request information from your system, and *push* happens without any request coming from the user. In a supply chain environment, you can make a request (pull) to replenish inventory and execute production; alternatively, an action could be initiated using a push based on actual demand. Supply Chain Planning tools include the following:

Push/pull network-planning processes

> **Demand and Supply Planning**
> This set of tools in the Supply Chain Planning module enables decision makers within companies to perform strategic, tactical, and operational planning. Apart from SAP ERP, one of the more advanced planning tools available is SAP Advanced Planning and Optimization (SAP APO), which takes demand and supply planning to a much more detailed planning level.

> **Demand Planning and Forecasting**
> This set of tools helps you to assess the anticipated customer demand (including promotional activities) on a finished-product level. The Forecasting tool leverages historical data and also takes the forecasting model into account to come up with forecast values.

> **Safety Stock Planning**
> This helps you to secure delivery (see Figure 12.2) and improve customer service by balancing the uncertainties in the area of supply and demand. You can either manually enter the safety stock of a material, or leverage the system's capabilities to suggest the safety stock of a material. You can also leverage SAP SCM to suggest the reorder point of a material so that the company never runs short of required material.

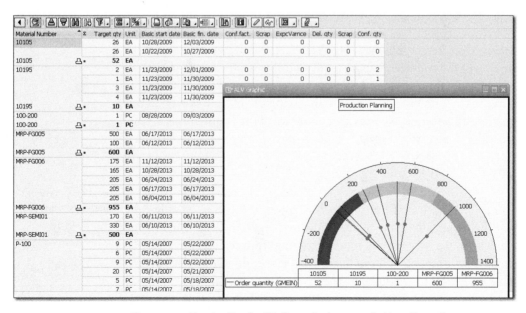

Figure 12.2 Keeping Track of Delivery Performance in Your Operation

> **Supply Network Planning**
> This set of tools helps you to manage and assign the best supply sources, distribute production over several plants (including subcontractors), select the best production resources in the plants, expand (drill down for more details) the bill of materials, and propose the procurement of components and raw materials.

> **Distribution Planning**
> This set of tools helps you to deploy the available inventory over the network, balance stock levels in situations in which you have excess inventory or shortages, and load transportation vehicles in the most efficient way.

> **Service Parts Planning**
> This delivers integrated planning capabilities to the service parts supply chain. Although Service Parts Planning provides capabilities for handling the large parts volumes that are often a part of an aftermarket supply chain, it also delivers a tight integration of the end-to-end planning process with other processes, such as supply network collaboration, procurement, warehousing, and order fulfillment.

> **Procurement**
> As you saw in Chapter 9, procurement is all about ordering the materials or products you need to run your business. As you add more visibility to your operation, your suppliers will want to have the materials ready to process your orders at just the time you need them. Likewise, because SAP SRM links to SAP ERP Financial Accounting modules, your suppliers' invoices will be paid in a timely manner.

> **Supply Chain Visibility**
> This category of tools provides analytic, process-management, and data-maintenance features to facilitate the Sales and Operations Planning (S&OP) process across your various departments. Processes such as Strategic Supply Chain Design, Supply Chain Analytics, and Supply Chain Risk Management feed into the S&OP process. This provides tools to help you analyze and adjust your plans to reflect the strategic goals of your organizations.

Planning is just the first piece of the supply chain operation. By building on good planning, you can execute on supply chain demands with another set of SAP SCM tools.

Supply Chain Execution

Adaptive fulfillment network

SAP SCM helps companies and individuals sense and respond to change through an adaptive fulfillment network. In such a network, distribution, transportation, and logistics are all driven by and integrated with real-time planning processes. Supply Chain Execution features include the following:

> **Warehousing**
> Helps your company manage the end-to-end warehousing process, including inbound and outbound processing, facility management and storage, physical inventory (see Figure 12.3), and cross docking. You can also take advantage of new data-collection technologies, such as RFID and voice recognition, and new workload-balancing tools that can make your processes more efficient.

> **Order Fulfillment**
> Enables you to track and monitor the entire fulfillment process, including inquiry, quotation, sales-order entry, pricing, scheduling, and proof-of-delivery processes. The system can promise orders based on best availability of goods and components in distribution centers, production sites, storage locations, and availability of transportation resources.

> **Transportation**
> Enables your users to consolidate orders and handle shipments across your company most efficiently to optimize your transportation dollars. Companies can share information and combine orders directly with carriers and forwarders over the Internet, which helps you to keep better control of your processes and maintain control of your plans.

With this variety of features of SAP SCM, you can get tighter control over your supply chain execution. In addition, SAP SCM provides several tools that enhance your collaboration with suppliers, distributors, and others, as discussed in the next section.

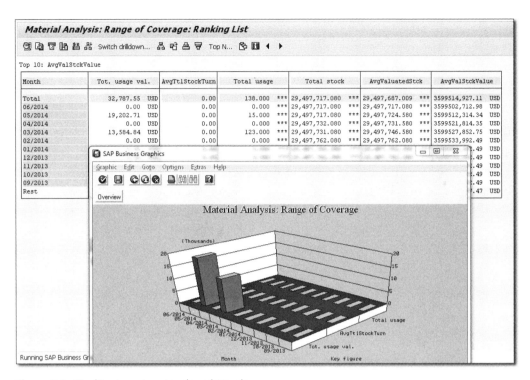

Figure 12.3 Tracking Inventory Levels and Trends

Supply Network Collaboration, Design, and Analytics

There is an old saying that it takes two to tango. In this spirit, the supply chain world is a highly collaborative one. To help you create a supply chain that encourages cooperation and efficiency, SAP SCM enables network-wide visibility, collaboration, and analytics across your extended supply chain.

Your company can align and synchronize operations with suppliers, partners, and customers to manage supply chain events and monitor performance. Collaborative capabilities include the following:

> **Supplier Collaboration**
> This helps your company connect to and collaborate with suppliers by providing third parties with easy and seamless access to your supply chain information. This capability also helps you to better synchronize supply with demand. Supplier Collaboration

Collaborative capabilities

245

also offers support for your raw material, component, and contract-manufacturing suppliers.

> **Outsourced Manufacturing**
> This is becoming commonplace in today's global business environment. This capability helps you connect to and collaborate with contract manufacturers by providing them with access to supply chain information and extending the visibility and collaborative processes to their manufacturing processes.

> **Customer Collaboration**
> This capability delivers an out-of-the-box, menu-driven approach to collaboration that customers can use immediately. You can even tailor the way you deploy these capabilities based on each customer's level of sophistication.

Setting up these collaborative tools will make your organization much more responsive and flexible. One of the sources of data you can use in your collaborative efforts is a technology tool called RFID, which is covered in the next section. SAP SCM also provides an option to integrate your company's weighbridges for all inbound and outbound goods movement and transfer relevant data directly into SAP ERP.

Using RFID in SAP SCM

RFID technology   *Radio Frequency Identification* (RFID) technology is being used today across the supply chain to increase efficiency. Companies use RFID tags, thin labels that contain a silicon chip that is something like the computer chip that drives your processor. When these labels are attached to items, such as products, packaging boxes, or pallets, they provide a way to track these items as they move through the supply chain.

Tags pass *read points* in the chain, and the item status is sent back to a centralized database. Think of the last time you tracked a package from an overnight shipper and observed its whereabouts as it left the central facility, appeared at a regional distribution center, was loaded on a plane, or sent off in a truck to be delivered to you.

RFID can save companies money and ensure that their information is updated to the minute. SAP SCM supports the use of RFID. SAP offers several preconfigured scenarios for RFID implementation and is building real-world-aware technologies into its business processes. For more information on how SAP is working with RFID, visit *http:// bit.ly/SAPRFID*.

Now look at how many of the SAP SCM features work in real-world settings through the following two case studies.

SAP SCM Case Study 1

Table 12.3 gives you an overview of a case study that will show the use of SAP SCM.

This European company produces not only packaging products, but also several types of value-added services for the materials. As a result, it has five business units that must work with many intracompany requests. The company needed a way to support these transactions more efficiently.

Company	European product packaging and value-added services
Existing Solutions	A variety of solutions that differed among divisions and groups because of many acquisitions over time
Challenge	To make the shift from providing only products to adding services and streamlining costs and response speed
SAP Solutions	SAP ERP and SAP SCM, along with a paper-machine-management software from an SAP partner
Benefits	Consistent data and processes across the enterprise and improved production planning and cost control

Table 12.3 SAP SCM Case Study 1

The Challenges

With a shift from simply providing products to providing services, the company had to deal with not only delivering a product but also meeting customer needs more efficiently. The company no longer simply delivered paper packaging. Now the company was trying to become a business partner that would deliver what a customer needed, in the time when it was needed, and in the amounts necessary to help its customers' own supply chain activities.

To add this kind of service, the company had to streamline costs and get its operations to move faster and more accurately. With many acquisitions over the years, however, the various units used different software products that were not very integrated. Furthermore, the company's supply chain operation in the paper packaging division was inefficient.

The SAP Solution

The company implemented SAP R/3 (whose functions are now available through SAP ERP) in all its business units. Then it implemented SAP SCM in its paper division, which supported the warehouse and quality-control processes, as well as production planning and order promising.

Holistic view of financial processes

SAP SCM was integrated with a software application from an SAP partner used to manage the use of its paper machines. The management system dealt with detailed planning and manufacturing tasks for the company's paper division. Using SAP SCM and SAP ERP across the various units gave its users a single, consistent interface. SAP's ERP solution gave the company a holistic view of its financial processes and improved visibility and analytics.

The Benefits

Using SAP ERP software allowed the company to gain consistent finance, customer-relationship management, sales, and distribution processes across units. In addition, SAP SCM and the third-party paper-machine-management software helped the company instantly share paper-machine data via SAP SCM to keep the shop floor in touch with other areas of the business.

A well-connected business

The ability to view and analyze its financial information helped the company keep costs under control. In addition, SAP SCM helped the company make improvements in production planning, which increased its productivity, providing further cost savings.

The company gained better visibility into its operations and inventory to collaborate more effectively with its customers and minimize waste. SAP ERP software and SAP SCM created a single place for all business information, which increased the likelihood of having more accurate and consistent data on which to base decisions. The solution has had the following effects on the company's business:

> Delivery accuracy went from 70% to 98%.

> Stock-rotation periods were reduced by six weeks.

> Working-capital requirements were reduced by 30%.

> The total cost of ownership (TCO) of its IT department went from 0.9% to 0.6%.

> Higher levels of service are being produced, and there is less stock to maintain.

SAP ERP helped the company change from being purely about products to including enhanced services, which has kept the company competitive and successful. SAP SCM provided the tools the company needed to align its manufacturing and supply chain processes with its customers' needs.

SAP SCM Case Study 2

Table 12.4 gives you a snapshot of the second case study in this chapter. You should review it before proceeding.

This U.S.-based company sells its line of health and beauty products and small appliances around the world. In this industry, customers demand frequent introduction of new products, which makes the supply chain a key element in business success.

Company	U.S.-based producer of health and beauty products and kitchen and appliance products
Existing Solutions	A variety of supply network planning systems and nonintegrated global operations
Challenge	To meet the demand for collaborative planning, to handle smaller orders with faster turnaround and direct shipments

Table 12.4 SAP SCM Case Study 2

SAP Solutions	SAP SCM
Benefits	Fewer canceled orders, freight cost savings, improved inventory returns, elimination of chargebacks from customers due to nondelivery of products

Table 12.4   SAP SCM Case Study 2 (Cont.)

The Challenges

Eighty percent of the company's orders currently arrive via electronic data interchange (EDI) or by fax, with the majority of orders coming through Europe.

Because customers today are placing smaller orders and expecting faster turnaround, this company, which sources products from contract manufacturers, needed a way to improve collaboration with its partners. The company had to reduce the time to get products on the shelves and incorporate direct shipments to do so.

Accurate forecasting   Furthermore, the company needed the ability to perform accurate forecasts in collaboration with manufacturing partners to help streamline inventory and cut down on returned products or orders that did not get fulfilled on time, resulting in canceled orders.

The SAP Solution

SAP SCM is now integrated with the SAP Business Suite so that, in addition to supply chain issues, the company can track pricing, credit, and delivery. The company first rolled out SAP SCM in Canada and then in five continental European subsidiaries. In the near future, they will implement it in the United Kingdom and the United States.

SAP SCM has provided a way for the company to integrate all of its operations and partners around the world to improve supply chain performance and adjust it to match market demand. The company gained visibility into forecasts, inventory, and production and made significant improvement in collaboration with manufacturers to ensure that supply will meet demand.

Each company sales unit worldwide now uses SCM to create a monthly forecast, and these forecasts are folded into a worldwide supply chain–planning document. The system has also been set up to issue alerts if a vendor has not received a shipment on time.

The Benefits

This international company is now experiencing some key benefits from its SAP SCM solution. The company has reduced the amount of obsolete inventory on hand and improved its ability to stock items that are in demand. The company is also noticing an improvement in customer satisfaction levels in addition to cost savings from reduced cancellations, penalty charges, and shipment inefficiencies.

Conclusion

In this chapter, we explored the many benefits of SAP Supply Chain Management, which addresses an enterprise's need for more efficient relationships with partners and suppliers. These benefits include the following:

> The ability to take advantage of an adaptive supply chain

> Increase in visibility and velocity of response

> Improved collaboration with partners

> Improved supply chain planning and execution

> Enhanced collaboration

Collaborative capabilities offered by SAP SCM help you respond to customers faster, find the best prices and suppliers for your needs, and improve cooperation across entire supply networks.

In Chapter 13, we will look at SAP's focus on small- and midsize-company products, including SAP Business One, SAP Business All-in-One fast start programs, and SAP Business ByDesign.

13

The SAP Strategy for Small to Midsize Enterprises

In the past, SAP products were thought of as primarily for Fortune 500 companies, despite the fact that about 65% of all SAP customers were actually small to midsize (SME) companies. But with the products SAP has developed for the SME market, SAP is known as a choice for any size business.

The truth is, all companies face the same issues—optimizing operations, increasing efficiency, cutting costs, and building lasting relationships with customers—so they all need quality solutions. SAP offers a complete portfolio of solutions, including SAP Business One, a single, integrated application to manage your entire small business; SAP Business All-in-One, a comprehensive, integrated industry solution to power your business end to end; and SAP Business ByDesign, the best of SAP, delivered on demand in a software-as-a service (SaaS) model. In addition, SAP now offers SAP BusinessObjects Business Intelligence (SAP BusinessObjects BI) software, Edge edition, as a core part of the solution portfolio that is specifically engineered, priced, and packaged to address customers' business-intelligence and performance-management requirements.

In this chapter, we will explore SAP's strategy to address the small to midsize market and discuss the functionality of and value delivered by each of the solutions offered in the SAP SME portfolio.

The Challenges Facing Small to Midsize Companies

Smaller companies have many opportunities that larger companies do not, simply because they are small and more nimble and have plenty of room to grow. However, these small companies also face challenges such as stiff competition and fewer resources. An efficient IT infrastructure can help these companies make the most of their assets and overcome some challenges.

Advantages and challenges for SMEs

For example, with a more global economy a greater number of smaller companies are competing against each other. However, with a bigger customer universe they are also finding greater opportunities. These greater opportunities of the global economy do bring new challenges, though, in terms of complying with regulations, taxes, and currencies, and smaller companies need help managing such issues. To grow, these companies have to run their operations as efficiently as possible so that they can attract resources, gain additional capital, and stay competitive. For these and other reasons, small and midsize companies require solid IT tools and systems; this is where SAP solutions can help, as we will demonstrate in the rest of this chapter.

Bringing Enterprise Computing to Smaller Companies

Advances in enterprise computing now make addressing the needs of this market easier than ever. SAP has over 40 years of gathering knowledge of back-office and front-office best practices, which is integral to their success with smaller businesses. In addition, SAP brings several technical features to the table:

> Preconfigured templates (*Best Practices*)

> Tools to accelerate the implementation of industry-specific solutions

> The SAP NetWeaver platform to support integration

> Easy-to-use interfaces

> A network of partners with proven industry expertise

SAP is a big believer in the idea that to make the best business decisions for your company you need to have as much information as you can get from all possible sources. To address this, SAP continually makes improvements to their solutions, and so, as we mentioned earlier, they now include SAP BusinessObjects BI, Edge edition in the offerings for small to midsize companies.

SAP Business-Objects BI, Edge edition

SAP BusinessObjects BI, Edge edition lets you perform interactive, *ad-hoc* exploration of data that resides in Microsoft, Oracle, PeopleSoft, and Siebel systems. You can generate highly formatted reports that can be accessed through familiar interfaces such as a web browser, Microsoft Office, a PDF document, or Microsoft SharePoint, monitor key performance indicators at a glance with visual dashboards that allow you to drill down into details that explain the root causes of trends and variances, and model scenarios to resolve problems or capitalize on opportunities by adjusting graphical controls.

Generate highly formatted reports

However, there have been many other changes and adjustments to the SAP midsize strategy, most notably back in 2007, when SAP committed its resources—and even launched a new business model that included a retooling of its own internal processes—to delivering solutions to a larger customer base further down in the midmarket. SAP Rapid Deployment solutions is a product offering that enables customers in the midmarket to deploy SAP solutions much more quickly. SAP provides rapid-deployment solutions for many of their core components and industries. We will discuss these solutions in greater depth in Chapter 20. For now, we will look at the SAP SME portfolio.

SAP Rapid Deployment solutions

The SAP SME Portfolio

Beyond the financial opportunities of the small to midsize market, SAP recognizes that the market is unique in its requirements. Small to midsize companies vary a lot in their structure, systems, and needs. Far from being simpler than larger companies, their needs are often just as complex; however, they are much less risk-tolerant because of their often tight profit margins and niche markets.

Consequently, SAP offers the small to midsize market a portfolio of solutions mentioned earlier: SAP Business One, SAP Business All-in-One, SAP Business ByDesign, and SAP BusinessObjects BI, Edge edition.

SAP Business One

The *SAP Business One* application is designed specifically for small businesses. It integrates the entire business across financials, sales, customer relationships, e-commerce, inventory, and operations. An important feature of SAP Business One is that it gives you access to SAP's extensive partner ecosystem, allowing you to extend the core functionality with over 550 add-on solutions that can help you meet your unique business and industry-specific needs. SAP Business One is the best fit for small businesses that have outgrown accounting-only solutions and are looking to streamline business operations with an integrated, on premise solution.

SAP Business All-in-One

The *SAP Business All-in-One* solution is the best fit for midsize companies with sophisticated business processes and industry-specific needs. This solution provides a comprehensive and flexible business-management option that has support for industry-specific best practices built in. It helps you manage everything from financials, human resources, inventory, manufacturing, logistics, and product development to customer service, sales, and marketing in one configurable solution. It is available from SAP and over 1,100 SAP partners in 50+ countries, and it can be readily configured to meet the business requirements of midsize companies in any industry.

SAP Business ByDesign

SAP Business ByDesign is the best fit for companies that want the benefits of a large-scale business-management solution without the large IT infrastructure. It is delivered on demand and fully managed by SAP. Because it is an on-demand solution, there are no upgrades to manage, no maintenance, and no up-front capital costs. SAP experts in world-class hosted data centers manage, monitor, and maintain it, so you do not have to invest time and money in any additional IT resources to build or support it.

In addition, the portfolio now includes the BI solutions of SAP Crystal Reports, SAP BusinessObjects Dashboards, and SAP BusinessObjects BI, Edge.

SAP Business-Objects BI, Edge

SAP BusinessObjects BI, Edge edition is also ideal for midsize companies. It consists of three elements: BI for improved business insight; SAP Business Planning and Consolidation for more efficient budgeting, planning, and forecasting; and SAP Strategy Management, which includes a scorecard feature to help you check your actual results against strategic goals. SAP BusinessObjects BI, Edge edition is offered in a standard version or in versions with added data integration and data-management tools, which we will cover later in the chapter.

 Note

Also included in the SAP BusinessObjects BI solutions are SAP Crystal Reports and SAP BusinessObjects Dashboards, but these will be covered in detail in Chapter 14.

In the next sections, we will provide a primer on each of these products and review their key product features to help you determine which product will meet your specific needs.

How SAP Business One Works for Smaller Businesses

SAP Business One is designed to be used in businesses with between 10 and 100 employees and minimal system requirements. The single-system design of SAP Business One keeps total cost of ownership (TCO) low and makes administration and system maintenance straightforward and simple.

Integrates with Microsoft Outlook, Word, and Excel

The really great thing about SAP Business One is that it is quick to install, simple to maintain, and, most important, easy to use. Because it works on any Microsoft Windows–based PC, it integrates with Microsoft Outlook, Microsoft Word, and Microsoft Excel. The Microsoft Outlook integration allows you to synchronize calendar appointments, contacts, and tasks between SAP Business One and Microsoft Outlook. You can connect to SAP Business One from Microsoft Word and then save an MS Word document as an activity in SAP Business One. You can also do this with MS Excel, enabling you to exchange and share data to keep all parties up-to-date about account developments and business opportunities.

SAP Business One has customers in a wide variety of industries, but does especially well in the macroverticals of wholesale, distribution, retail, light manufacturing, and professional services. SAP Business One has 40+ country versions and tens of thousands of customers. It is sold and implemented exclusively by its network of 1,000 certified channel partners.

Macroverticals

Releases

> The current (as of August 2014) release of SAP Business One is SAP Business One 9.0 and SAP Business One 9.0 for SAP HANA. The SAP HANA version helps customers to leverage business intelligence solutions that are based on SAP HANA. SAP Business One offers a mobile app that enables employees to get on-the-go access to the SAP Business One solutions.

The current version of SAP Business One includes several areas of functionality useful to a variety of industries.

The SAP Business One Solution Map

Manage core functions
SAP Business One organizes the features of the software into seven categories, four that address core business areas and three that deal with implementing and customizing the product. Together, these features help small businesses manage all of their core business functions, such as manufacturing, distribution, sales, and customer relationships.

 E-Commerce

> SAP Business One also includes e-commerce functionality that helps you set up an online store. E-commerce operations are fully integrated with inventory and financials and have tools for online catalog, shopping cart, order processing and notification, customer configuration, and online customer service.

The following sections break down the features of SAP Business One into core business areas, including Accounting and Financials, Customer Resource Management, Operations and Distribution, and Administration and Reporting. Let us start with Accounting and Financials.

Managing Accounting and Financials

Manage all parts of your financial operations
Financials is where SAP started when it delivered its first enterprise resource planning software product many years ago. There is a good reason for that: financials are at the heart of every kind of business, and managing them efficiently gives businesses of every size what

they need to start up, operate, and succeed. Some of the functionality that SAP Business One provides in this area includes the following:

> **Financial Accounting**
Perform all kinds of financial transactions, including general ledger, journal entries, budgeting, and accounts payable and receivable.

> **Accounting Postings**
Automate real-time accounting postings in response to relevant business events.

> **Banking**
Track all of your banking payments and reconciliations, including check, cash, and credit cards.

> **Financial Reporting**
Automate financial reporting for items such as profit and loss, cash flow, balance sheets, and aging reports.

> **Taxes**
Automate calculations and reporting, including sales, use, and value-added tax.

After you have your financials in place, you can focus on your customers.

Connecting with Customers

Customers are the lifeblood of any operation, and regardless of the size of your company if you do not set up your processes to acquire and retain customers you will regret it. SAP Business One provides functionality that helps you keep customers satisfied and ensures that those who serve them are well equipped to do so:

Keep your customers satisfied

> **Sales Opportunity Management**
The typical sales process moves through several stages. You can use SAP Business One to track sales opportunities from your first contact to the sales close. You can create quotes, enter orders, and provide better customer service from the office or online. Your sales manager can use SAP Business One to forecast revenue potential. User-friendly dashboards allow you to monitor and analyze sales opportunities and generate all kinds of sales reports.

Use dashboards to analyze sales

> **Microsoft Outlook Integration**
> You can manage and maintain customer contacts by synchronizing customer data from SAP Business One into Microsoft Outlook contacts or calendars, resulting in increased sales effectiveness and stronger customer relationships.

> **Marketing Campaigns**
> Use tools to initiate and execute marketing campaigns by using templates for mass emails.

> **Customer Service and Support**
> The customer service folks in your organization can use these tools to administer customer warranties and service contracts, manage service calls, and track all kinds of customer interactions.

> **Business Partner Management**
> Manage your master data for resellers and channel partners and allow resellers, partners, and customers to access relevant data over the web.

Once you have a customer order, you can fill it and deliver the goods using the operations and distribution features of SAP Business One.

Purchasing and Operations

Managing customer orders

SAP Business One offers a systematic approach to managing the procurement process, from creating purchase orders to paying vendors. You will find all the tools you need to manage the complete order-to-pay cycle, including receipts, invoices, and returns. You can also plan material requirements for production, control bills of materials (BOMs), and replenish inventory automatically. In this area you will find these features:

> **Purchasing**
> Use these features to set up and manage vendor contracts and all kinds of vendor-related transactions, such as sending out purchase orders, making updates to stock quantities, and handling returns and credits. You can also generate automatic production and inventory replenishment orders.

> **Production Planning**
> With this feature, your users can work with a simple-to-use process to manage your production material requirements; control

BOMs, including product descriptions, warehouse location, composition, and quantities; and work with MRP features.

Inventory and Distribution

SAP Business One also lets you manage your inventory and operations, including quotes, sales orders, shipping, and billing. You can perform inventory counts, monitor stock, and track transfers in real time and across multiple warehouses. Inventory and distribution areas include the following:

Effective inventory management tools

> **Sales and Delivery**
> When a customer expresses interest in your product or service, you can generate price quotes, and when they are ready to buy you can enter their orders, set up deliveries, and manage all billing and accounts receivables activities.

> **Inventory Management**
> You can use these tools to manage inventory levels with inventory counts, stock tracking, and transfers between warehouses by serial number, lots, or bin location. You can provide real-time inventory updates, inventory valuation, availability checks, and pick-and-pack processes. There are even features to streamline your pick-and-pack process.

Streamline pick-and-pack processes

There are, of course, some processes that exist not to get products to customers, but to support your administrative processes or help you develop your overall business strategy, which brings us to the final area of SAP Business One: Administration and Reporting.

Streamlining Reporting and Administration

There are certain tools that cut across your organization that everyone from the CEO down can benefit from, such as efficient procedures, easy-to-use software interfaces, and useful reports with up-to-date information, and these tools are what you will find in Administration and Reporting, including the following:

> **Human resources**
> These features help you organize a centralized place for maintaining and managing employee records and data, such as home contact information, time and attendance records, and training history.

Tip

The Drag & Relate feature in SAP Business One is handy for using all of your business data; it puts information into easy-to-understand formats. In addition, you can easily drill down to deeper levels of detail in your company's data.

Initiate credit checks and manage exceptions to workflow processes

> **Automatic alerts**
> Workflow-based alerts allow you to monitor, notify, and take action based on certain business alerts. You can define custom alerts and workflow processes by setting up approvals and procedures that make sense for your business, and you can set up SAP Business One to detect, log, and report on exceptions. You can even determine the steps that should automatically take place when a specified event happens. For example, you could set up an alert so that whenever a customer order exceeds a certain amount a credit check is initiated.

> **Dashboards and reports**
> You can create your own reports and dashboards for various areas of your business, such as sales, bookkeeping, inventory, financial statements, and customer interactions. You can also generate Microsoft Excel–based reports that allow you to drill down to deeper levels of details.

Note

Dashboards are user interfaces that provide a control center for working with data, such as a salesperson might use to check all relevant facts about a customer in one place.

Enabling E-Commerce and Web Stores

You can use SAP Business One tools to create an online presence that will help you level the playing field against larger competitors by allowing you to reach more customers. You can design, build, and configure online stores to get your e-commerce activities organized. E-commerce tools in SAP Business One include the following:

> **Design tools**
Use customizable templates and various tools to help you design, create, and configure your online store.

> **Online catalogs**
Create and manage online catalogs and build-in negotiated, customer-specific pricing.

> **E-commerce selling tools**
Incorporate special promotions and coupons, or build-in suggested selling techniques (such as indications of when customers who bought one product also bought another product).

> **Synchronize e-commerce**
Automate the synchronization of all online orders with the SAP Business One database.

 Note

> SAP Business One is the packaged solution ideal for much smaller businesses. If your organization is in the midsize category, however, there are two other solutions you can consider: *SAP Business All-in-One* and *SAP Business ByDesign*.

SAP Business All-In-One

The SAP Business All-in-One solution is a comprehensive and flexible business-management software with support for best practices built in along with updated messaging on the SAP website. It is for your company if you are looking for a comprehensive, integrated industry solution to power your business end to end.

Integrated solution to meet business needs end to end

Benefits of Using SAP Business All-in-One

Unlike other business solutions in the market, SAP Business All-in-One helps you manage everything from financials, human resources, procurement, inventory, manufacturing, logistics, product development, and corporate services to customer service, sales, and marketing in one configurable solution. Let us look at each of these benefits.

Improve Financial Management

SAP Business All-in-One allows you to accelerate financial closes, increase the accuracy of financial reporting, and maintain superior cash management. You can improve your ability to maintain a set of balanced books reflecting any business dimension. Support for international and local accounting standards also helps you reduce your risk of noncompliance.

Maintain Operational Excellence

Efficiency and effectiveness

With SAP Business All-in-One, you can improve your efficiency and effectiveness by streamlining business processes, enhancing service levels, and cutting costs and errors. The solution helps you shorten cycle times, increase order accuracy, reduce the volume of customer calls, decrease billing disputes, and lower inventory costs with better order-to-cash processes. You can resolve issues faster and boost customer satisfaction with low-cost interaction channels, such as web-based self-service.

Enhance Agility

SAP Business All-in-One allows you to respond more quickly to change, enhance customer experiences, and differentiate your company from your competitors. You can respond quickly to changing market conditions and customer demands by adapting your business processes. You can quickly launch new initiatives to speed time to market, and you can align your channels with your customers' interaction needs and preferences to provide consistency and convenience across all customer touch points. This customer insight in turn can help you drive innovation to set your products and services apart.

Unify and Simplify

All the functionality is integrated to simplify your business and IT landscape across functions, regions, and teams. By supporting streamlined business processes, SAP Business All-in-One enables you to complete a process from beginning to end. You might, for example, create an opportunity using customer relationship management (CRM) functionality, convert it directly into a quote, and then later convert it into a sales order—complete with product, pricing, billing, and delivery—using SAP ERP functionality. BI functionality gives you real-time visibility into your sales performance throughout the entire process. In addition, centralized data and business intelligence help ensure that you have a "single version of the truth," providing a 360-degree view of your operations, employees, and customers.

Drive Adoption and Improve Productivity

Additional advantages include faster adoption when working with SAP's partner network, increased productivity, and fewer errors. The integrated software and common desktop environment help your employees learn how to use the software quickly, and the integration eliminates manual data reentry between different functional areas, which can save time and reduce the risk of mistakes.

SAP Business All-in-One is Powered by SAP NetWeaver

Because SAP Business All-in-One is powered by SAP NetWeaver, you can quickly and cost-effectively add on to your existing solution as your business grows and your needs change with the help of SAP partners. SAP NetWeaver is also the ideal technology platform to integrate SAP and non-SAP software, reducing the total cost of ownership across the entire IT landscape.

SAP Business All-in-One features a user experience designed for maximum productivity and ease of use, including the following:

The user experience

> **User-friendly design**
> Intuitive web-like features and online tutorials help accelerate adoption and reduce the need for formal training.

> **Automated workflows**
> By automating manual processes, you will save time and money when, for example, generating an automatic alert on all contracts that are up for renewal or on customers with overdue payments. You can also escalate service requests for your most important customers and automatically route tasks between groups and departments.

> **Intuitive navigation**
> Role-based navigation, screen personalization, quick links to key data, snapshots of recent records, key reminders and alerts, and an advanced search help users perform daily tasks more efficiently.

> **Groupware integration**
> Integration with desktop tools such as IBM Lotus Notes and Microsoft Office allows users to manage their activities and

communications more effectively: any time, any place. Users can synchronize tasks, appointments, and emails and export customer and opportunity lists.

In addition, SAP Business All-in-One solutions offer the following integrated functionalities:

Integrated functionalities

> **Enterprise resource planning**
> The ERP functionality in SAP Business All-in-One is based on the SAP ERP application and includes comprehensive functionality to manage all aspects of your operations. It also delivers role-based access to business application data and analytical tools.

> **Business intelligence**
> Gain insight and improve decision making with tools for financial and operational reporting and analysis. SAP Business All-in-One offers best-practice reports, analytics, and tools to help satisfy the rigorous reporting requirements for financial accounting, logistics, customer relationship management, and more—all preconfigured by business role and business scenario.

> **Customer relationship management**
> The CRM functionality in SAP Business All-in-One is based on the SAP CRM application, so with the CRM functionality in SAP Business All-in-One you can boost marketing results with targeted messaging, close more deals with sales tools that improve effectiveness, and increase revenue and customer loyalty with superior service. Effectively manage all aspects of your customer relationships, from generating leads to closing a deal, including follow-up support and add-on sales.

SAP Best Practices by industry and function

> **SAP Best Practices**
> The SAP Best Practices package provides proven methods and tools for organizations to implement best business practices in key functional areas in a range of industries. SAP Best Practices are based on 35 years of experience in more than 24 industries worldwide. The result is rapid yet reliable solution deployment, which translates into less time, lower costs, and reduced project risk.

In addition to the overall SAP Business One solution, there is also the SAP Business All-in-One *fast-start program*. This program, which SAP partners can help you implement, brings the more robust features of

SAP ERP, SAP CRM, and SAP BusinessObjects BI functionality to the table for midsize companies with a smaller investment and faster ramp-up. It provides tools, methodologies, and pretested software.

What Is the SAP Business All-In-One Fast-Start Program?

The SAP Business All-in-One fast-start program is designed for manufacturing, wholesale distribution, and service companies that are seeking industry-specific functionality at a low cost of ownership and low risk. The fast-start program gives you a preconfigured, pretested software stack that includes SAP Business All-in-One, the low-cost SAP MaxDB database, and Novell SUSE Linux Enterprise Server operating system. In addition, SAP and select hardware partners, such as HP, IBM, Intel, and Fujitsu, have combined their latest innovations to deliver this software stack preinstalled on optimized hardware. As a result, you get a joint hardware and software solution.

Smaller investment and a faster ramp-up

With this program, you can improve the entire software acquisition process, shortening implementation times, speeding up your time to value, and reducing overall solution TCO. With this solution, you choose the functional building blocks that will determine your estimated solution scope and cost and then work with an SAP consultant to determine the next steps. A personalized demo will be created with your data, showing end-to-end scenarios to give you the full picture of what SAP Business All-in-One can deliver for you.

The SAP Business All-in One fast-start program offers your company:

Benefits of fast start

> **Simplicity**
> The pretested, preconfigured software is configured to select hardware, which simplifies the buying process.

> **Time savings**
> With preinstalled SAP software, it takes less time to get up and running, delivering rapid time to value.

> **Affordability**
> You get a lower TCO based on complete, pretested software.

> **Best practices**
> You receive the SAP Best Practices package for your industry, which includes templates and methodologies for rapid implemen-

tation and documentation and preconfigured support for business-process scenarios.

The fast-start program can be configured and customized to any industry or business

The fast-start program is easy to use and provides a fast path to improving user productivity. Users work with a simplified computing environment that has a user-friendly interface and role-based navigation. This ease of use provides employees with easy access to information.

Because the fast-start program is based on the SAP Business Suite, it can be configured and customized to adapt to the special needs of an industry or business. You can look to the SAP partner community to help you implement the fast-start program and also use vertical market partner solutions and third-party applications, which can be integrated with the solution. SAP has also enlisted hundreds of partners that will help you with their own add-ons for specialized applications.

In some countries, you can configure the fast-start program on the web.

Later in this chapter, we provide case studies of both the SAP Business One and SAP Business All-in-One fast-start program solutions so that you can see and compare them in action. For now, let us move on to the final SME offering: SAP Business ByDesign.

SAP Business ByDesign

The SAP Business ByDesign solution is the most complete on-demand business solution for midsize companies. It addresses the needs of your entire organization, is adaptable, and allows you to react quickly whenever your business needs change. In addition, it is personalized to improve productivity with a role-based user experience, built-in learning and support environment, analytics, and collaboration.

On-demand solution

SAP Business ByDesign is an on-demand solution that adds to the existing SME portfolio rather than replacing any existing products. Because it is an on-demand solution, there are no upgrades to manage, no maintenance, and no up-front capital costs. It is managed, monitored, and maintained by SAP experts in world-class hosted data centers, which means you do not have to invest time and money in any additional IT resources to build or support it.

An Adaptable Suite of Functionality

SAP Business ByDesign offers a complete integrated suite of functionality; it supports Financials, Customer Relationship Management, Human Resources Management, Supply Chain Management, Project Management, Supplier Relationship Management, Compliance Management, and Executive Management Support and includes useful features, such as analytics. All functionality is delivered through services, so external integration interfaces to web shops or supplier portals is easy.

However, rather than configuring a system with a team of consultants or by using sets of best practices, the idea behind SAP Business ByDesign is that the system is simply adapted to the needs of a particular organization (something SAP calls "configurable and extensible"). This adaptation takes various forms and can be easily modified along the way. Companies can choose the functionality and try it out to make sure it satisfies their needs. If not, they can adapt it until it does.

SAP Business ByDesign also offers an adoption catalog. You can configure your custom system by making choices from this catalog and responding to some specific questions about your business. This process should make both initial configuration and future changes and additions easier and more cost-effective.

> SAP Business ByDesign adoption catalog

In addition, customer service capabilities are built into the application and automated through a global service backbone. If your company expands globally, SAP Business ByDesign supports your growth with built-in compliance for countries around the world.

Underlying Technology

SAP Business ByDesign is a product built entirely with model-based development techniques. The result of this approach is a product that offers sets of application process components (e.g., order entry or invoicing) that you can combine to meet a particular business requirement. You can get these benefits on demand through a subscription fee.

> Model-based development techniques

Another difference is that SAP Business ByDesign uses a form of cloud computing; SAP hosts the applications you are using, and you access the functionality online through a SaaS model. This is a plus for you,

> Cloud computing

because by not having these applications onsite, your IT staff can focus more on your critical IT needs instead of having to implement, maintain, and upgrade these applications. Also, by having these applications hosted elsewhere, especially in today's economy, you may reduce or eliminate the need to purchase additional hardware, such as servers and disk storage. Instead, because SAP Business ByDesign is an on-demand solution, customers pay only for the pieces and user licenses they need on a subscription basis, which can be more cost-effective. Because of the hosted nature of the product, SAP expects to get an enhanced and faster feedback model from users, which it can use to make future improvements.

Although you can configure the software to meet most of your needs, you cannot modify the code as you can with SAP ERP or the SAP Business All-in-One fast-start program system. However, because it is based on services there are open interfaces that allow you to make interface changes to the system as necessary. SAP Business ByDesign is based on the SAP NetWeaver platform, and, as such, offers functionality that is useful to a wide variety of industries.

SAP Business ByDesign Integrated Functionality

With SAP Business ByDesign, you get a fully integrated solution that covers all of your core business needs, including the following:

> **Management empowerment**
> Gives managers an overall view of business performance and access to the organizational information they need. Management dashboards provide real-time, customized analytics and allow you to accurately track the most important aspects of your business.

> **Financial insight**
> Provides a single, up-to-date view of your financial condition through the integration of core business processes and financials. You can keep track of payables and receivables, payment and liquidity, inventory and fixed assets, taxes and expenses, compliance and reporting, and more.

> **Customer relationship management**
> Provides comprehensive, flexible support for customer-relationship-management processes that span marketing, sales, and service

activities to help you find the right opportunities and maximize customer satisfaction and revenue.

> **HR resources**
Helps ensure efficient HR operations and maximize the potential of your employees. Use employee and manager self-service features to streamline execution of daily tasks, and adapt HR services to changing business needs by adding, enhancing, and automating processes, including workloads, personnel, and payroll.

> **Supply chain management**
Helps you build an efficient supply chain so that you can respond quickly to changing markets. Optimize material flow by managing demand and supply and design, set up, and execute flexible warehouse and manufacturing processes to fit your products and business models.

Fully integrated solution to meet all business requirements

> **Project management**
Plan and track projects using graphical tools, such as Gantt charts and network diagrams. Share information among team members with workflow-driven task management and provide up-to-the-minute project data for easy tracking of costs, purchases, and employee and contractor hours.

> **Supplier relationship management**
Strengthen your relationships with suppliers and improve your procurement processes to reduce costs and turn suppliers into a competitive advantage. Identify and manage the best suppliers for materials and services. Gain insight into order management, supplier invoicing, and purchase requests.

> **Compliance management**
Keep up-to-date and compliant with changing laws and regulations using preconfigured tools for your company's accounting practices, applicable tax structures, and relevant labor legislation. Frequent and automatic updates help ensure that your financial books and government reporting meet regulatory standards.

> **Simplify IT**
Use built-in IT services, automated maintenance and support, and a quality-assured service model. Work with SAP experts to monitor and maintain your on-demand system. Take advantage of built-in learning and help provide easy access to resources.

Easy access to support

Tip

SAP Business ByDesign uses a concept called a mashup. A mashup is a website or a software application that uses content from several sources and integrates it into a single user experience.

This wraps up our discussion of the three SME business management offerings from SAP. Now let us look at SAP BusinessObjects BI, Edge edition.

SAP BusinessObjects BI, Edge Edition

Midsize BI solution SAP now offers SAP BusinessObjects BI, Edge edition to meet the BI and performance-management needs of the SME market. It is designed to help midsize companies improve business processes, discover new opportunities, and gain a competitive advantage. It offers solutions that address any business-intelligence requirement—from flexible ad hoc reporting and analysis to dashboards and visualization to powerful data integration and quality and prepackaged data mart solutions. Applications include the following:

Four versions available
> **SAP BusinessObjects BI, Edge Edition**
This application brings together the simplicity and speed of search with the trust and analytical power of BI to provide immediate answers to your business questions. Your users can leverage familiar keyword searches to find information hidden in data sources, then navigate and explore directly on data without the need for existing reports or metrics. This solution is available in four versions:

– *SAP BusinessObjects BI, Edge edition Standard Package*, which can provide enterprise and ad hoc reporting as well as world-class visualization.

– *SAP BusinessObjects BI, Edge edition with Data Integration*, which can deliver the ability to combine data from multiple sources; populate a data warehouse expediently; and leverage ad hoc, advanced, and drilldown analysis.

– *SAP BusinessObjects BI, Edge edition with Data Management*, which can enable data parsing, cleansing, and address synching.

– *SAP BusinessObjects BI, Edge analytics edition*, which enables analyzing massive volumes of data. The delivered analytics can be tailored to your industry and line of business need.

> **SAP BusinessObjects Edge Planning and Consolidation**
This application can help you simplify and streamline the budgeting, planning, and forecasting process, enabling all stakeholders to collaboratively participate in the process of allocating resources.

> **SAP BusinessObjects Edge Strategy Management**
This helps companies respond to and execute necessary strategy changes with agility. It allows everyone from executives to front-line workers to communicate plans clearly and translate them into priorities and tasks and then monitor and report on progress to any level of detail. The solution is built on the three pillars of strategy management: goals, initiatives, and key performance indicators (KPI).

This concludes the review of the SAP SME Business Intelligence offerings. Hopefully it served as a good overview of the great options available and you understand which solution could work for your company or your clients. Now let us take a look at what the small and midsize products, SAP Business One and SAP Business All-in-One fast-start program, might look like when implemented at a company.

Small Business and Midsize Company Case Studies

The following two case studies help you understand the strengths of each product and may help you determine which solution is the best fit for you.

The SAP Business One solution excelled in easy implementation and user acceptance for a small Chinese company, whereas the vertical solution and prepackaged Best Practices packages used to configure an SAP Business All-in-One solution delivered through the fast-start program made it a perfect fit for a midsize U.S. company.

SAP Business One, Case Study 1

Table 13.1 gives you a quick snapshot of a Chinese fishing equipment company's experience with SAP Business One.

Company	Chinese fishing equipment manufacturer and wholesaler
Existing Solutions	Non-SAP software
Challenge	To stay competitive in a strong market, to track sales and purchase orders, to monitor back orders dealing with a large number of SKUs, and to support multiple price tables; previous system incorrectly read bar codes and provided inaccurate month-end closings
SAP Solutions	SAP Business One
Benefits	Fast implementation, easy user acceptance, easy access to real-time information, better credit controls, visibility into inventory, reduction in order time and stock levels, improved customer service

Table 13.1 SAP Business One, Case Study 1

As a leading maker, distributor, and retailer of sports fishing equipment, this company sells more than 3,000 products. The company employs a total of 30 people but broadens its reach through 36 international distributors. The company was using an off-the-shelf software package for accounting, sales, and distribution, which used a batch method rather than working with real-time data. The old system could no longer support the company's growing business.

Tracking invoices and payments

In addition, the company was facing tough competition in key markets. The company looked at 15 possible vendors and chose to implement SAP Business One to improve the efficiency of its financial systems, reporting, and other key business processes. The company especially liked SAP Business One's scalability, ease of use, and features.

Reducing order-cycle time

The company worked with an SAP implementation partner and found the implementation of SAP Business One to be very smooth; it took only two months to implement it. SAP Business One enabled the company to provide updated information in real time. The ability to track invoices and payments was much improved, which resulted in tighter credit control. The company found they could close-out end-of-month books in half the time it used to take. Inventory management was also improved, because employees could view stock availability easily. The order-cycle time was reduced by 30%. The enablement of automatically generated bar codes and support for multiple price tables helped to support the 15,000 SKUs used by the business.

Employees found SAP Business One easy to learn and use. Furthermore, it provided all employees with customer and order information as needed. Management found real-time reports useful in helping them monitor current business and forecast future trends. In the future, the company hopes to integrate SAP Business One with its website for online ordering and integrate its systems with retail operations to provide access to real-time stock availability information.

SAP Business All-in-One Fast-Start Program, Case Study 2

Table 13.2 introduces you to another case study for a small business, a Hawaii-based sun-care-product manufacturer with 155 employees that manufactures and distributes its line of products internationally. This time, the focus is on the SAP Business All-In-One fast-start program.

Company	North American manufacturer and distributor of sun-care products
Existing Solutions	Non-SAP software
Challenge	To maintain a competitive position and integrate and optimize supply chain management with partners and to improve inventory management, coordinate production schedules, and improve customer satisfaction
SAP Solutions	Vertical SAP Business All-in-One fast-start program solution for the consumer packaged-goods industry with features for inventory management, production planning, and customer-relationship management
Benefits	More flexibility and efficiency in product distribution, resulting in a more competitive company with higher customer satisfaction, and efficient supply chain management, including production plans and inventory management

Table 13.2 SAP Business All-in-One Fast-Start Program, Case Study 2

The company had challenges in managing inventory, coordinating production schedules, and maintaining a high level of customer satisfaction. The company worked with an SAP vertical solutions reseller to implement an SAP Business All-in-One solution delivered through the fast-start program.

Added flexibility and efficiency in the distribution of its products, along with a better match to customer requirements, helped to improve customer satisfaction and competitive position. The company streamlined its supply chain management, improved inventory management, and generated better production plans and forecasts.

Conclusion

In this chapter, you learned about the various products that SAP offers small and midsize enterprises and SAP's approach to the needs of those markets. SAP, once perceived as providing solutions for only large companies, has now moved beyond that image with solutions for smaller businesses and midsize companies. These solutions, for which we provided an overview, include the following:

> SAP Business One for smaller enterprises

> SAP Business All-in-One program for midsize enterprises

> SAP Business ByDesign for midsize enterprises with a hosted solution

> SAP BusinessObjects BI, Edge edition

Next, we will provide an overview of the data tools and reporting applications that are available in SAP, starting in Chapter 14.

PART III
Essential SAP Tools

SAP Reporting and Analytics

Every time an event happens within the SAP Business Suite, transaction data is recorded and stored in a table. These events include every time an order is placed, every time an invoice is generated, and every time a payment is made. This information is very valuable: by analyzing the information in these tables, you can draw conclusions that can help you manage your enterprise better.

This chapter explores the comprehensive set of offerings that SAP has in the field of reporting and analysis. We will discuss the tools that help users extract, transform, explore, and distribute data, as well as tools that create compelling reports and ad-hoc queries that are delivered to users via their desktops and mobile devices.

Analytics in the Enterprise

The field of enterprise analytics is responsible for collecting information in the enterprise and storing, organizing, transforming, extracting, and reporting on it, which turns raw data into meaningful insights.

Over time, SAP has built a comprehensive set of enterprise analytics tools, covering all vital aspects. These tools include:

Analytics tools from SAP

279

> **SAP Business Warehouse (SAP BW)**
> This is SAP's original data warehouse solution, with end-to-end capabilities that allow enterprises to extract, transform, load, report, and analyze data.

> **SAP BusinessObjects reporting tools**
> These tools produce compelling reporting solutions using data from SAP BW, from the SAP Business Suite, from SAP HANA, from flat files, or even from external, non-SAP systems.
>
> These reporting tools can be used on the desktop or on mobile devices, delivering data in highly customized, predefined reports, or with ad-hoc queries, for which you can build the report on the fly to meet your specific needs.

> **SAP HANA**
> SAP's in-memory database and application server and, most importantly, a game-changing virtual data warehouse that virtually "transforms" data into reportable, meaningful data stored in-memory.

> **Budgeting, forecasting, planning, and consolidation tools**
> This includes tools such as SAP Business Planning and Consolidation (SAP BPC) and SAP BW Integrated Planning, which allow users to combine plans and forecasts with past history for consolidating, planning, and forecasting the finance of the organization.

> **ETL (extract transform load) tools**
> These include SLT (SAP Landscape Transformation Replication Server) and SAP Data Services, providing solutions to load data into SAP BW and SAP HANA from SAP and non-SAP sources.

Enterprise analytics is an ever-growing area. New tools are added to SAP's portfolio every day. We will discuss many of these tools further in this chapter, and Chapter 15, which is entirely devoted to SAP HANA.

SAP Business Warehouse

SAP Business Warehouse became part of SAP's portfolio in the late nineties—when the "New Dimension" products were launched to complement SAP ERP's original offering.

SAP BW operates out of its own separate SAP NetWeaver application server and has its own database server. It can use any relational database management system (RDBMS) applicable to SAP NetWeaver. This includes Oracle, IBM DB/2, and SAP products such as MaxDB and SAP HANA.

SAP BW is, by itself, a complete analytics solution. It incorporates the following:

SAP BW functions

> **Extract transform load (ETL)**
> Allows for extraction of data from a source system (SAP and non-SAP systems) and the transformation of data into the format of OLAP structures that can be reported inside the data warehouse.

> **Data warehouse**
> Once data is extracted into SAP BW, it is stored in different data storage objects: DSOs (data store objects), InfoObjects, and multi-dimensional structures called InfoCubes that implement a star schema.

> These objects are loaded in layers in accordance with an LSA (layered scalable architecture). This architecture future-proofs the data warehouse solution, makes it robust and better capable of supporting multiple business areas, and manages the interdependency between these areas.

> **Reporting**
> Queries are created on SAP BW to expose data in a reporting tool. When reports are run by users, the corresponding query is executed in the OLAP Engine (which is now called SAP BW Analytic Manager, as shown in Figure 14.1), and a report is published in one of the following reporting tools:

> - In Microsoft Excel, via SAP Business Explorer (BEx) Analyzer— a native SAP BW technology that offers sophisticated slicing and dicing capabilities with limited formatting and printing capabilities.

> - In SAP Portals, as a web application, created with WAD (web application designer) with sophisticated slicing and dicing capabilities and more complex formatting than the SAP BEx Analyzer.

> - Consumed by one of the many SAP BusinessObjects reporting tools—such as Web Intelligence, Design Studio, Explorer, or Crystal Reports—which offer a plethora of possibilities in formatting and various degrees of ability to slice and dice data.

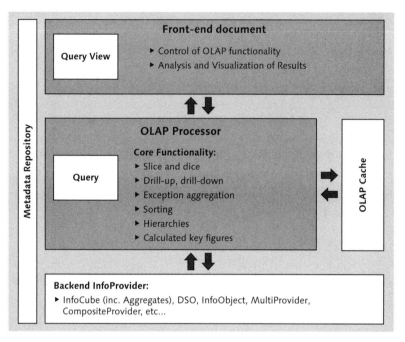

Figure 14.1 Reporting Using the OLAP Engine

> **Planning and consolidation**
> Data stored in BW can also be manipulated with one of the planning and consolidation tools of SAP: SAP BW Integrated Planning or SAP Business Planning and Consolidation (BPC).

In the following sections, you will become more familiar with the design, characteristics, and capabilities of each individual component of SAP BW.

SAP BW Business Content

One of the most powerful features of SAP BW, and perhaps the reason behind the enormous success of the system in the marketplace, is its business content. SAP BW Business Content comprises a set of pre-defined extraction, loading, and reporting objects. These cover the end-to-end reporting solutions for many business areas and in many cases are all the developers need to use in order to produce professional-looking, meaningful reporting solutions.

SAP BW Business Content is a powerful accelerator for the implementation of SAP BW solutions. The developer only needs to "activate" and "enhance" the business content by adding or modifying objects, or adding user exits in order to produce the required solution. Indeed, the great majority of SAP BW solutions running today use a considerable amount of enhanced SAP BW Business Content. Very few solutions use only customized objects.

Implementation accelerator

SAP BW Internal ETL—Extract Transform Load

Data that is reported out of SAP BW must first be extracted from the source system and then stored in an SAP BW data mart. We will go over these steps in the following subsections.

Extract Data

The very first step is to extract data from the source system. The extractor is made up of two portions: the DataSource (which resides in the source system), and the DataSource replica (which resides in the BW system).

Transformation

The conversion of data between the source object to the target object is performed by a transformation. A *transformation* is a generated program created inside the Administration Workbench.

Convert data between source and target object

A transformation allows you to map, cleanse, modify, and integrate data. Data from different sources can be semantically synchronized, aggregated, and prepared for reporting—for example, units of measure can be changed, or data from several business units can be amalgamated.

Load

The extracted data is placed in a data target object. Extracted data can be of one of the two basic types: transactional data or master data. Master data can contain text, attributes, or hierarchies. Transactional data is made up of any transaction that occurs in the source system, such as sales or accounts payable events, that normally occurs in a specific point in time.

An example of transactional data is the sales history for all products. The quantity sold, the unit price per time unit (let us say, per day)

Extracted data types

identified with a specific date, product code, product family, sales organization code, and warehouse code constitutes transaction data.

The descriptive texts of product, product family, sales organization, and other attributes of these fields are all examples of master data.

Other ETL Tools

Although SAP BW has powerful ETL tools, other, more powerful and flexible tools were added to the mix as SAP's analytical tools evolved, including:

> SAP Landscape Transformation Replication Server (SLT)
> SAP Sybase Replication Server
> SAP Data Services
> SAP Sybase Even Stream Processor
> SAP Sybase SQL Anywhere
> SAP HANA Smart Data Access

Two notable solutions, which will be further detailed next, are:

> **SLT**
> Offers powerful real-time and non-real-time replication capabilities to load data into SAP HANA and SAP BW.

> **SAP Data Services**
> Was incorporated into the SAP portfolio via the acquisition of Business Objects.

We will discuss some of these tools in the following sections.

SLT

Data replication to SAP HANA or SAP BW

SAP SLT is a tool designed for data replication into either an SAP HANA or an SAP BW system.

SLT is trigger based, which means that it initiates data replication whenever a pre-defined event (such as a database-level INSERT or UPDATE) occurs in the source system. It can perform data replication in real time or in scheduled mode. As a result, the data warehouse can be updated continuously and contain real-time data.

SAP SLT also has the ability to convert data into SAP HANA or SAP BW format while replicating data in real time, and it can be used with almost any type of ABAP-based SAP application (as of version SAP R/3 4.6C). It can also import data from non-SAP sources, provided the non-SAP system uses an SAP-supported database. SAP SLT can perform transformation functions, such as data filtering, enriching table structure, anonymizing data, and so on.

Data conversion

SAP SLT is the technology of choice for those companies that use SAP HANA for analytics. It is also becoming an important choice in SAP BW target scenarios, in particular as SAP BW on SAP HANA and real-time data warehouses become more prevalent.

SAP SLT operates out of its own server and is comprised of three components:

SLT components

> Read Engine
> Mapping and Transformation Engine
> Write Engine

Figure 14.2 illustrates the components of the technology.

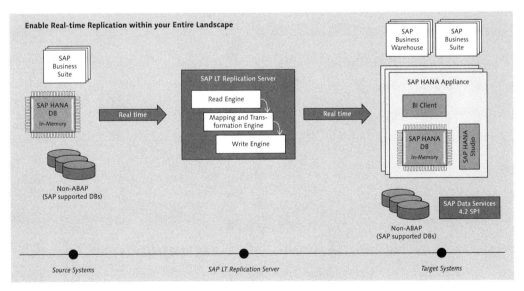

Figure 14.2 SLT Components (source: SAP Landscape Transformation Replication Server Overview Presentation, by AGS-SLO Product Management, SAP SE)

Let us discuss the different engines, as shown in the figure:

> The Read Engine is responsible for pulling data into the engine. It enables efficient replication via a database trigger. A *trigger* is a procedure that is created at database level and runs whenever a predefined event happens (such as a database-level INSERT or UPDATE) — hence the name "trigger."

> The Mapping and Transformation Engine is responsible for transforming data from its original format into the format that will be written to the target system. The developer configures the conversions required, such as filtering, enriching, or anonymizing.

> The Write Engine is responsible for posting data directly into a database table into the target system. The Write Engine also has two different types of connections to the target system, depending on whether the target is an SAP HANA system (non-ABAP) or an SAP BW system (ABAP).

 Note

Although SAP SLT is the ETL tool of choice for SAP HANA–based analytics solutions, there are other options for provisioning data into SAP BW through prebuilt Business Content extractors, which can be more effective.

SAP Data Services

Data Services is another ETL tool provided by SAP. It is a single solution for data integration, data-quality management, and text-data processing that allows users to integrate, transform, improve, and forward data to a data repository. This repository can be any SAP-supported database.

Components

Its components are:

> A development user interface (UI)

> A metadata repository

> A data-connectivity layer

> A runtime environment

> A management console

The Data Services server is usually installed on the same physical box as the SAP BusinessObjects platform; this simplifies version management and administration.

The other component, the Data Services Designer, is a fat-client application that enables data workflows that are classified in tasks to be monitored. Data Services Designer helps you define connections with the various data sources that are stored as separate data sources (as DataSources); all changes in a given connection are updated once, and any other occurrences of data sources will be updated automatically.

Monitor data work-flows with Data Services Designer

The Data Services application offers a number of predefined transformations and functional objects that allow modeling of the ETL flows, such as:

Model ETL flows

> Data merging (MERGE)
> Column mapping (QUERY)
> Performance of SQL queries (SQL)
> Validation of records (VALIDATION)
> Comparison of table contents (TABLE COMPARISION)
> Parent–child relationship management
> Surrogate and natural keys generation
> Conditional expressions that model the data flow

Figure 14.3 shows a typical Data Service data flow.

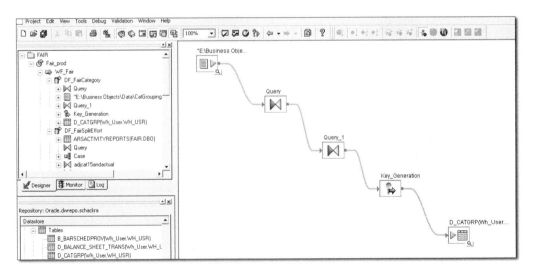

Figure 14.3 A Data Services Data Flow

One common use of Data Services is with rapid marts—preconfigured SAP BusinessObjects reporting and Data Services extraction jobs, which can use SAP HANA, Oracle, or SQL Server as the target repository.

Enterprise Performance Management

In its majority, the data present in a data warehouse has been generated outside its server (it has, for example, been generated by the OLTP system) and brought onto the data warehouse, reorganized, optimized for analysis and reporting, and reported upon.

This is true for most past transaction-related data, such as past sales volumes, past sales dollars, invoices received, accounts paid (or even payable), but not for information such as forecasts, plans, and budgets. These are, by nature, either created by humans who make assumptions and educated guesses, or by mathematical models using existing history to predict the future.

Forecasts, plans, and budgets

This information must be somehow entered into the system, and this is what "Enterprise Performance Management" systems have been created for. Forecasts, plans, and budgets are either entered manually, or inferred based on past history (or both) and merged into reportable data marts.

SAP's offers in this area include two major products (that, interestingly are being merged as this book is being written):

> SAP BW Integrated Planning (IP)

> SAP Business Planning and Consolidation (BPC)

We will discuss these products in additional detail in the following sections.

SAP BW Integrated Planning

SAP BW Integrated Planning is a central planning tool (i.e., a planning tool that manages one plan, stored in a central database, that can be entered and manipulated by several users within the organization). A user uses input-enabled BEx queries to manually enter and manipulate information. This input-enabled query can be presented to the user via BEx Analyzer (Microsoft Excel based), Web Application (built with the Web Application Designer), or via SAP BusinessObjects Analysis for Microsoft Office, Microsoft Excel version.

The core of an SAP BW Integrated Planning solution is as follows:

Core of an IP solution

> **A real-time InfoCube**
  This InfoCube—built as per the star schema—is marked as "real time" when it is being built. On this cube, *aggregation levels* are defined; these aggregation levels determine which characteristics and key figures will be used for planning.

> **An input-enabled BEx query**
  In this query, the value of certain key figures can be entered or altered by the user manually. They must contain the characteristics defined on the aggregation level.

> **Planning functions**
  These are organized or not as part of planning sequences—which run on demand (either by the user kicking them off manually or scheduled via Process Chains) to alter the data in the real-time InfoCubes. These functions are built in many different ways:

  – As standard functions, such as copy, delete, aggregate, disaggregate, repost functions—which have been predefined in SAP BW Integrated Planning and only need a few parameters to know what needs to be done.

  – As "Fox Formulas," which give the developer a lot more flexibility to manipulate data. Fox Formulas are sophisticated manipulation routines that the developer can use to manipulate data in any aggregation level. They tend to be very useful in moderately complex calculations.

  – As user-exit functions—which give the developer complete freedom as to how the data is to be manipulated and how to integrate with the database. These are useful in complex calculations, such as overhead allocations.

Figure 14.4 illustrates a typical planning application, based on an input-ready query, delivered via SAP BusinessObjects Analysis for Office.

Typical planning application

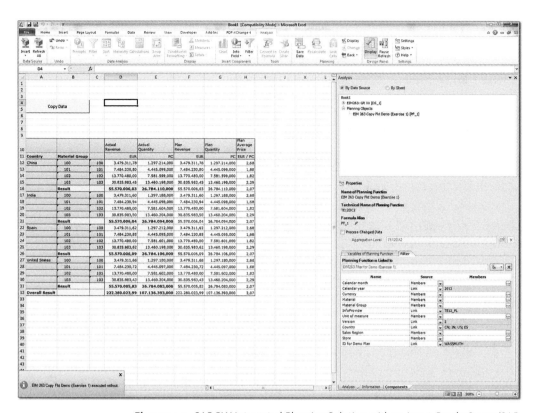

Figure 14.4 SAP BW Integrated Planning Solution with an Input-Ready Query (SAP TechEd 2012 EIM263—SAP SE)

SAP Business Planning and Consolidation

SAP Business Planning and Consolidation (SAP BPC) is a decentralized, flexible-planning, Microsoft Excel–based tool that allows users to create, simulate, and manipulate budgets, plans, and forecasts. Data either can reside in the users' PCs or can be a shared plan from a central SAP BW data warehouse.

SAP BPC versions   SAP offers two major versions of its BPC product: one that uses local data on the user's Microsoft-based PC, with local data for standalone operations, and one that integrates with the SAP NetWeaver environment, using and updating data stored on an SAP BW–based data warehouse.

Both solutions are very powerful and give the end user ultimate flexibility when producing their business plans and consolidations. They both:

> Let the user develop their own reports, enabling them to decide how to view their data.

> Can perform currency translation, intercompany elimination, allocations, account transformations, and validations and can carry forward opening balances.

> Work in multiple languages.

> Use Script Logic.

The differences between the Microsoft and the SAP NetWeaver versions of SAP PBC are as follows:

Microsoft vs. SAP NetWeaver differences

> The Microsoft version stores data on a spreadsheet, whereas the SAP NetWeaver version stores data on a central SAP BW database, enforcing the users' security profiles.

> The SAP NetWeaver version manages versions, whereas on the Microsoft version the user has to create separate files.

> The SAP BPC version allows for true collaboration, as it manages a central version used by several users; in the Microsoft Excel version, users send files to one another and have to manage change themselves.

> The Microsoft-based version uses K2 as the scripting language, whereas the SAP NetWeaver version uses ABAP—so the in-house skills can be used to reduce development time and lower total cost of ownership (TCO).

SAP BW IP and SAP BPC are two approaches to address the same problem: one centralized, reliant on the enterprise data warehouse, predefined, and pre-formed and the other flexible and decentralized (albeit using central data) and in which the user has more flexibility to create and manipulate the plans.

 Unified Solution

At the time of writing, SAP is working on an offering that will combine features of both solutions into one, a SAP BPC NetWeaver "unified" solution, as illustrated in Figure 14.5.

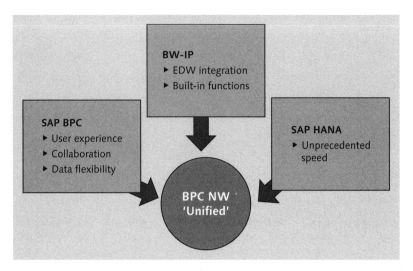

Figure 14.5 SAP BPC NetWeaver Unified

SAP BusinessObjects Reporting Solutions

SAP BusinessObjects has a portfolio of reporting, analysis, and data-visualization tools, and it brings a variety of reporting options to users. It is extremely versatile as a reporting platform and can be integrated with SAP and non-SAP systems.

SAP Business-Objects portfolio
The latest SAP BusinessObjects version is the Business Intelligence platform version 4.1. The following reporting tools are part of the SAP BusinessObjects portfolio:

> SAP Crystal Reports

> SAP BusinessObjects Dashboards (formerly Xcelsius)

> SAP BusinessObjects Web Intelligence

> SAP BusinessObjects Analysis for Microsoft Office

> SAP BusinessObjects Analysis for OLAP

> SAP BusinessObjects Design Studio

> SAP BusinessObjects Explorer

> SAP BusinessObjects Mobile BI

Note

Each has its own strengths and weaknesses. It is not uncommon for people to feel that they all seem to serve the same purpose, and that there is a lot of overlap among them. They do in fact perform similar tasks, and in many cases, the differences are a mere question of how they connect with the data source.

In many cases, it is also a question of personal preference. In fact, the best use of each tool is subject to lengthy debates, lectures, and presentations. As this book is being written, SAP has embarked on an effort of "portfolio simplification."

The following sections will further explore each of the reporting tools and how they communicate with the data warehouse. They will also shed some light on how they can be best used.

SAP Crystal Reports

SAP Crystal Reports produces highly formatted reports, typically presented with the appearance of preformatted forms or official documents. It is ideal for those reports that would be broadcasted or exported to PDF and sent from one person to another, providing static information. It can use data sourced from a special type of file called a universe, an SAP BEx query, SAP HANA, or by directly accessing tables from a database through an ODBC connector.

Crystal Reports can be accessed online and offline and can also be sent to users via email (broadcasting). You can see an example of a report in Figure 14.6.

When should you use Crystal Reports as a reporting tool? When you have:

> Highly formatted reports that need to be used as official documents.
> Reports that need to be printed.
> Reports containing highly textual information.
> Reports with date-specific aggregation.

Comparative Income Statement

	March 2004		Percent Difference
	Actuals	Budget	
Revenue			
Sales Revenue			
Bike Sales - Competition	94,572.06	29,655.58	-218.90
Bike Sales - Hybrid	15,799.35	22,763.99	30.59
Bike Sales - Kids	5,020.80	854.08	-487.86
Bike Sales - Mountain	62,599.69	39,232.42	-59.56
Sales Gloves	442.21	351.39	-25.85
Sales Helmets	1,634.82	2,192.99	25.45
Sales Locks	366.83	26.42	-1,288.63
Sales Returns	5,351.02	875.71	-511.05
Sales Saddles	532.13	568.43	6.39
Net Sales	175,616.87	94,769.58	-85.31
Expense	142,766.94	137,776.50	-3.62
Cost of Goods Sold	82,032.91	120,101.39	31.70
Bikes (Competition) Cost	42,927.30	75,147.08	42.88
Bikes (Hybrid) Cost	7,278.26	7,324.10	0.63
Bikes (Kids) Cost	2,259.36	1,346.24	-67.83
Bikes (Mountain) Cost	28,213.04	34,668.75	18.62
Gloves Cost	201.83	67.01	-201.20
Helmets Cost	739.98	1,092.47	32.27
Locks Cost	168.57	197.10	14.47
Saddles Cost	244.58	258.65	5.44
General & Administrative Expense	9,349.42	7,740.03	-20.79
Accounting & Legal	0.00	1,000.00	100.00
Advertising & Promotions	0.00	10.99	100.00
Amortization Expense (Building)	2,045.94	2,045.94	0.00
Amortization Expense (Machinery)	2,134.68	2,134.68	0.00
Bank Charges	29.16	2.35	-1,138.64
Courier & Postage	125.33	97.91	-28.00
Insurance	1,467.56	206.46	-610.82
Interest Expense	2,051.03	2,051.03	0.00
Internet	120.34	13.55	-787.94
Miscellaneous	62.43	1.25	-4,896.00
Office Supplies	0.00	100.17	100.00
Repair & Maintenance	552.71	0.00	0.00
Telephone	374.62	21.20	-1,666.79
Utilities	385.62	54.49	-607.74
Payroll Expenses	51,384.61	9,935.08	-417.20
Wages & Salaries	51,384.61	9,935.08	-417.20
Total Operating Expenses	142,766.94	137,776.50	-3.62
Net Income	32,849.93	-43,006.92	176.38

SAP

Figure 14.6 A Sample Crystal Report

SAP BusinessObjects Dashboards

Organizational metrics and KPIs

SAP BusinessObjects Dashboards is a tool designed to give users access to the organization's metrics and key performance indicators (KPIs). It drives business intelligence (BI) adoption across the organization by creating interactive, mobile-ready dashboards that can be deployed in Flash format to web portals, SAP environments, the SAP

BusinessObjects BI platform, and desktop applications such as Microsoft PowerPoint, Microsoft Word, or PDF format. This tool contains a large library of commonly used charts, maps, gauges, and scorecards.

An example of the use of SAP BusinessObjects Dashboards is a supply-and-demand dashboard that enables executives to easily access high-level inventory data (see Figure 14.7). In addition to viewing actuals, managers can drill down into product-level details. They can also see inventory reserves, aggregating data forward or backward through user-friendly charts and tables.

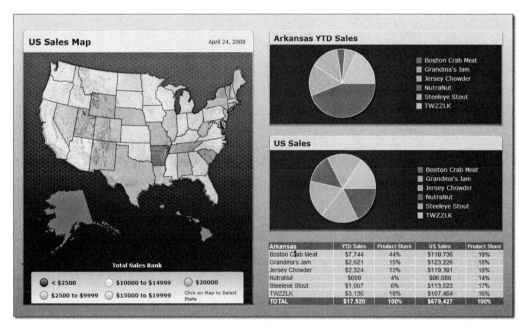

Figure 14.7 A Sample SAP BusinessObjects Dashboard (Source: SAP Solution Brief SAP BusinessObjects Business Intelligence Solutions—SAP SE)

SAP BusinessObjects Web Intelligence

SAP BusinessObjects Web Intelligence is a reporting tool that provides users with flexible, self-service access to ad-hoc reporting tools and intuitive analytics. It can be consumed on the web, on desktop or mobile devices, and either online or offline (see an example in Figure 14.8). It can also be sent to users via email (broadcasting).

Ad-hoc reporting

SAP BusinessObjects Web Intelligence supports heterogeneous data sources: universes, files such as Microsoft Excel or .CSV files, SAP BEx queries, and SAP HANA data. It is available either as a client tool of the SAP BusinessObjects portfolio or as a standalone product.

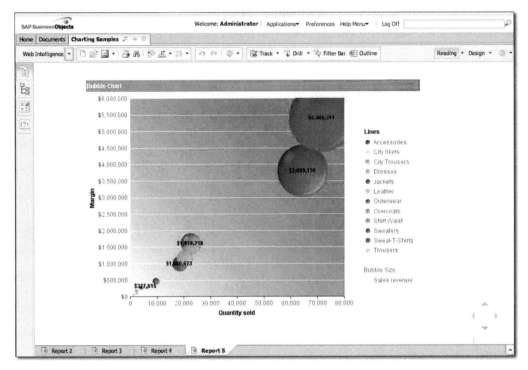

Figure 14.8 SAP BusinessObjects Web Intelligence Report

SAP BusinessObjects Analysis for Microsoft Office

Multidimensional analysis in Microsoft applications

SAP BusinessObjects Analysis for Microsoft Office is a Microsoft Office add-in that allows for interactive, multidimensional analysis of OLAP sources in Microsoft Excel and Microsoft Excel workbook application design (see Figure 14.9) and intuitive creation of BI presentations within Microsoft PowerPoint.

SAP BusinessObjects Analysis for Microsoft Office also supports planning data: you can enter planning data manually, or you can enter planning data automatically using Planning Functions and Planning Sequences in SAP BW Integrated Planning.

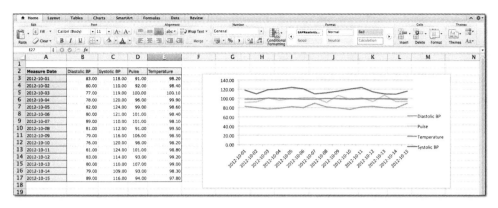

Figure 14.9 An SAP BusinessObjects Analysis for Office Workbook

SAP BusinessObjects Analysis for OLAP

SAP BusinessObjects Analysis for OLAP is an advanced, web-based analysis for OLAP tool. See an example in Figure 14.10.

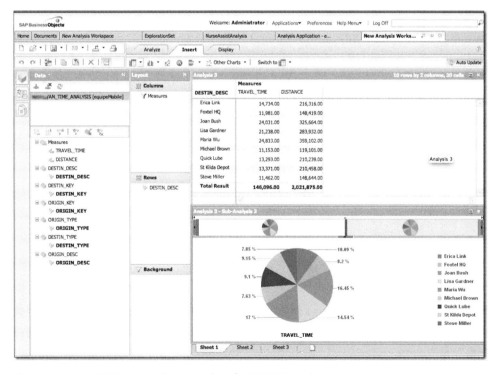

Figure 14.10 An SAP BusinessObjects Analysis for OLAP Example

| Data sources | SAP BusinessObjects Analysis for OLAP can source data from the following: |

> SAP ECC via Transient Providers (as of ECC 6 — EHP 5).

> SAP BW via SAP BusinessObjects BI Consumer Services

> SAP HANA (directly)

> SAP Enterprise Performance Management (EPM) providers: SAP BusinessObjects Planning and Consolidation, SAP BusinessObjects Profitability and Cost Management, and SAP BusinessObjects Financial Consolidation

> Non-SAP systems, such as Teradata, Oracle Essbase, Oracle OLAP, and Microsoft Analysis Services.

| Analysis applications that work with other reporting tools | SAP BusinessObjects Analysis for OLAP interoperates with other SAP BusinessObjects reporting tools. You can create analysis applications that can be improved with Design Studio, or you can report against analysis views with Web Intelligence and Crystal Reports. |

SAP BusinessObjects Design Studio

| Dashboarding and reporting | SAP BusinessObjects Design Studio is a dashboarding and reporting tool. Feature-wise, it is like a combination of SAP BusinessObjects Dashboards and SAP BusinessObjects Web Intelligence. The difference is that it was built from the ground up to work directly with SAP BW BEx Queries and SAP HANA analytical models. This makes it a very powerful tool. Furthermore, it was developed after the acquisition of Business Objects, so it contains the combined knowledge of people from both the SAP and Business Objects sides. |

| HTML5 and mobile apps | Its version 1.2 is an Eclipse-based application design environment that offers HTML5 rendering, making it the best tool in the SAP BusinessObjects portfolio for the creation of mobile applications (see Figure 14.11). It has predelivered iPhone templates for rapid implementation. |

The target audience for this reporting tool is IT personnel, key users, and designers. It is a premium alternative to SAP BusinessObjects Dashboards and SAP BEx Web Application Designer.

It has direct access to SAP BW, SAP HANA and universe (file extension UNX) data through SAP BusinessObjects BI Consumer Services.

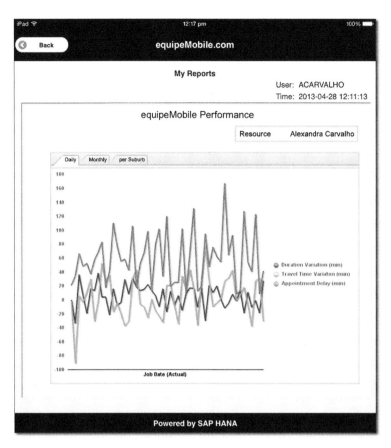

Figure 14.11 An SAP BusinessObjects Design Studio Mobile Application

SAP BusinessObjects Explorer

SAP BusinessObjects Explorer (BEx) is a data-discovery application that combines the speed of Internet search with the analytical capabilities of business intelligence for faster, more informed decision making. You can quickly understand your business through self-service data exploration with flexible visualizations.

Data discovery

When you perform a search, data is retrieved from "information spaces." Data in information spaces is organized in data sets called facets. A media facet, for example, could include values such as music, DVD, or book (see Figure 14.12).

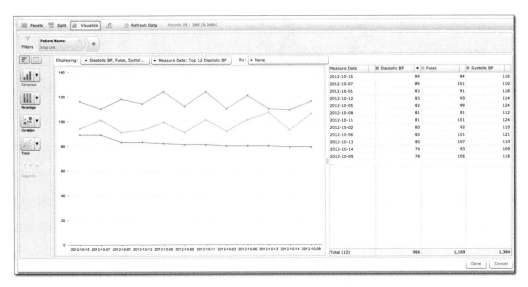

Figure 14.12   SAP BusinessObjects Explorer in Action

SAP BusinessObjects Explorer reports are extremely fast, because they leverage indexed data based on a pre-run query. They can:

> Connect to SAP BW through a universe, and a disk-based index for the data is created.

> Connect to SAP Business Suite through a universe and source data from InfoSets, ABAP Queries, or ABAP Functions.

> Access data directly from SAP HANA and leverage the prebuilt indexes from the SAP HANA system (in this case, it does not have to create another disk-based index for the data). It is also possible to connect SAP BusinessObjects Explorer to SAP HANA via a universe. In this case, the SAP HANA prebuilt indexes are not leveraged, but they create disk-based indexes for the data.

> Create disk-based indexes in Microsoft Excel spreadsheets. The spreadsheets can be uploaded on-demand or they can be stored as part of the SAP BusinessObjects Enterprise system (in this case, an information space can be created).

Free app in iTunes store   SAP provides a free SAP BusinessObjects Explorer mobile app in the iTunes store, enabling you to run your SAP BusinessObjects Explorer reports on your iPhone or iPad. This app is an intuitive data-discovery application that helps you identify trends in your data and quickly retrieve answers to your business questions.

SAP BusinessObjects Mobile

SAP BusinessObjects Mobile provides you access to the SAP Business-Objects BI content on your mobile device, allowing you to make informed decisions based on targeted, personalized information any-where and anytime. You can analyze key metrics and discover data trends with striking interactive visualizations. It works seamlessly both online and offline.

Business intelligence on your mobile device

You can run the following SAP BusinessObjects reports through SAP BusinessObjects Mobile:

> Crystal Reports (only for iOS—iPhone or iPad)

> SAP BusinessObjects Web Intelligence

> SAP BusinessObjects Dashboards

> SAP BusinessObjects Design Studio (only for iOS—iPhone or iPad)

> SAP Lumira and Lumira Cloud (only for iOS—iPhone or iPad)

> SAP BusinessObjects Explorer artifacts (only for iOS—iPhone or iPad)

SAP provides a free SAP BusinessObjects Explorer mobile application in the iTunes and Google Play store, enabling you to run your SAP BusinessObjects Mobile reports on your iPhone, iPad, or on any Android tablet or smartphone. See Chapter 16 for more information on mobilizing your enterprise.

The BI Launch Pad

Once SAP BusinessObjects reports are created, they are published in a page from which users can run them. This page is called the BI Launch Pad. In this page, the reports are organized in folders by sub-ject area—for example, finance, procurement, travel and expenses, and human resources.

Running the analysis reports

Users do not need to connect to the BI Launch Pad separately. The BI Launch Pad is integrated with the main SAP portal (for example, the SAP NetWeaver Business Client), and once users are logged into the

SAP portal, they can access all functions related to their profile, including the SAP BusinessObjects reports in the BI Launch Pad. This mechanism of authentication is called single sign-on.

SAP Lumira

SAP Lumira (formerly Visual Intelligence) is a self-service business intelligence tool that allows end users to create highly engaging visualizations, combining data from multiple sources into a single view. Figure 14.13 shows a typical SAP Lumira visualization.

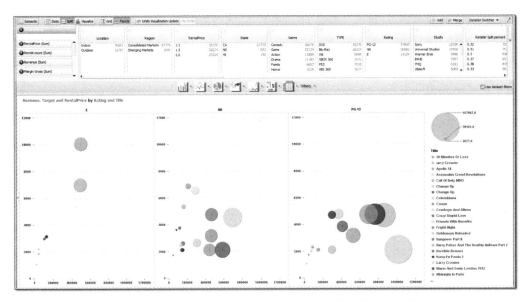

Figure 14.13 SAP Lumira (Source: SAP Visual Intelligence Solution Overview—SAP SE)

SAP Lumira can be installed locally on your desktop. It is also available in the cloud. SAP is currently offering the personal edition of SAP Lumira for free.

SAP Lumira can source data from a variety of sources:

> SAP BusinessObjects Universes (both 3.x UNX and 4.x UNV files)

> SAP HANA (by consuming SAP HANA views, which gives you instant access to massive data volumes)

> SAP BW on SAP HANA (by consuming SAP HANA analytical models based on SAP BW InfoProviders)

> Relational databases, such as Teradata, Sybase IQ, Microsoft SQL Server, Oracle, and IBM DB2

> Microsoft Excel and .CSV files

SAP Predictive Analysis

SAP Predictive Analysis is a complete data-discovery, visualization, and predictive analytics solution that enables you to identify trends and insights in your data, as well as discover hidden patterns in the data from which you can make predictions about future events.

Figure 14.14 shows a typical SAP Predictive Analytics visualization.

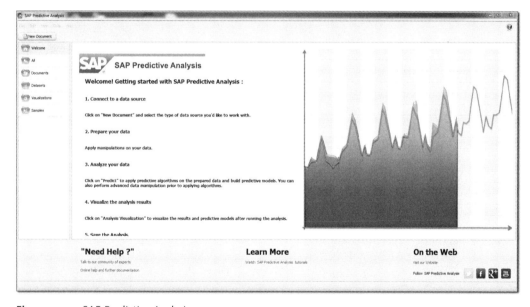

Figure 14.14   SAP Predictive Analysis

SAP Predictive Analysis shares its main interface with SAP Lumira, but features an additional workspace in which you can work with predictive algorithms. Like SAP Lumira, you can source data into SAP Predictive Analysis from the following (see Figure 14.15):

Interface with SAP Lumira

> SAP HANA (by consuming SAP HANA analytical views, which gives you instant access to massive data volumes)

> SAP BusinessObjects Universes

> Relational databases, such as Teradata, Sybase IQ, Microsoft SQL Server, Oracle, and IBM DB2

> Microsoft Excel and .CSV files

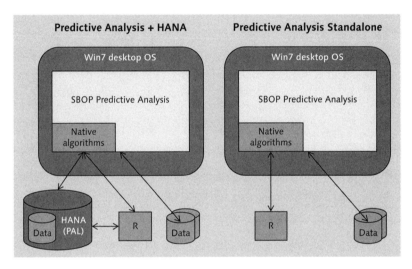

Figure 14.15   SAP Predictive Analysis

SAP Predictive Analysis offers a range of embedded predictive analysis algorithms, such as outlier detection, time-series forecasting, trend analysis, segmentation analysis, classification analysis, and affinity analysis.

Analyzing large data volumes

When using SAP Predictive Analysis with SAP HANA, you can use SAP HANA's built-in data-mining capabilities for handling large volume data analysis efficiently. These data-mining functions comprise the Predictive Analysis Library (PAL). PAL is embedded in SAP HANA via the Application Function Library.

Predictive Analysis Library

PAL includes classic and universal predictive-analysis algorithms in eight data-mining categories:

> Clustering

> Classification

> Association

> Time Series

> Preprocessing

> Statistics

> Social Network Analysis

> Miscellaneous

SAP Acquires KXEN

SAP acquired KXEN, a leading provider of predictive analytics technology, in September 2013 to complement SAP's existing advanced analytics portfolio. SAP plans to incorporate KXEN technology into its cloud and on premise applications built on SAP HANA.

InfiniteInsight is KXEN's predictive-analytics platform, and it provides an automated end-to-end modeling process, helping to deliver highly accurate and robust predictive models.

InfiniteInsight

KXEN's platform is aimed squarely at business analysts, not data scientists or data miners, but it offers no visualization functionality, so it is likely that SAP will meld the visualization power of SAP Lumira with KXEN predictive-analytics algorithms. Also, KXEN takes great advantage of automation and machine learning, which could be a great complement to SAP Predictive Analysis.

SAP and SAS partnership

In October 2013, SAP and SAS unveiled a partnership in which SAP and SAS will create a joint technology to run SAS advanced analytics algorithms on SAP HANA's in-memory platform, giving businesses the ability to handle large data sources while also supporting real-time analytics.

SAP HANA Analytics

SAP HANA is an important part of SAP's analytics offerings, and many see it as the future of analytics. It implements virtual star-schema objects in a way that replicate InfoCubes and InfoObjects, with the advantage that data does not need to be persisted to be reported on.

Furthermore, SAP HANA analytical models can be used with many SAP BusinessObjects tools.

Chapter 15 of this book is entirely dedicated to SAP HANA: its components, its analytics capabilities, and how it integrates with other SAP tools. Please refer to that chapter for more information on how SAP HANA complements the analytics offerings.

Conclusion

In this chapter, you learned about the different tools that SAP provides to help users analyze the large amount of data that exists in organizations and to present it in a visually engaging, attractive manner. Some of the tools discussed in this chapter include the following:

> SAP Business Warehouse, the oldest, most complete analytic platform that SAP provides

> SAP BusinessObjects tools, a suite of products that provides many options for reporting displays and many uses depending on business functions and requirements

> SAP Integrated Planning and Business Planning and Consolidation, which help with planning and forecasting

> SAP Lumira and Predictive Analysis

In the next chapter, we will discuss SAP's revolutionary platform: SAP HANA.

SAP HANA

It is almost impossible to be even somewhat involved with SAP and be unaware of its most recent addition that truly disrupted the database market: SAP HANA. SAP HANA is a highly innovative approach to the age-old problem of storing and retrieving data for applications and doing it quickly. This platform is designed to work fully in memory, taking full advantage of the multicore parallel processing of modern servers.

SAP HANA has made such a large splash because no software vendor has ever packed so much punch into a single product. Never have so many features been packaged into one product as now, and never have so many of SAP's products been positively impacted by one offering.

This chapter examines SAP HANA. We will provide a more in-depth explanation of this database-management system, explore the technology and benefits, and see some use cases. We will also explore the different uses for SAP HANA and its different versions.

SAP HANA: The Game Changer

SAP HANA was launched in 2009. It has many facets and purposes in enterprise applications, and it is much more than a mere relational database, although it is a very powerful one.

SAP HANA is used to do the following:

> **Acquire**
> Data is brought in via SLT, SAP BusinessObjects Data Services, or virtually through SAP HANA Smart Data Access (SDA).

> **Accelerate**
> By processing in-memory data preprocessed and acquired from Hadoop and other sources along with real-time feeds.

> **Analyze**
> Acting as a link between the database and ad-hoc SAP BusinessObjects tools, such as Predictive Analysis, Lumira, and Explorer, and visualization tools, such as Crystal Reports or Design Studio.

What SAP HANA does

But what is SAP HANA, really?

SAP HANA is a relational database management system (RDBMS). It can be used whenever a relational database is required. Where we had before MaxDB, DB2, Microsoft SQL, or Oracle, now can also have SAP HANA. Indeed, it is being used as the database for many SAP NetWeaver–based solutions, such as SAP BW, SAP ERP, SAP SCM, SAP CRM, and so on.

SAP HANA supports ANSI SQL and has a powerful scripting language (SQLScript)—so programmers used to developing Structured Query Language (SQL) procedures, or embedding SQL in ABAP or other languages, will feel right at home with SAP HANA.

It is a revolutionary solution. It functions fully in memory (we discuss what this means later in the chapter) with powerful parallel processing. It contains a column store and a row store. This combination results in an extremely fast database.

SAP HANA XS

It also contains its own application server, SAP HANA XS. In SAP HANA XS, using Server-side JavaScript (XSJS) as its primary language, developers can create and serve web-based applications directly on the SAP HANA server. This eliminates the need for a separate application server and leverages a direct database connection to the SAP HANA appliance.

SAP HANA is also an analytics platform. SAP HANA's objects—attribute view, analytic view, and calculation view—are used to build quasi-star-schemas that can be consumed directly by SAP BusinessObjects reporting tools as OLAP objects.

Analytics

Figure 15.1 illustrates the various components of SAP HANA, and how they fit together; SAP HANA is much more than just a fast database system.

SAP HANA components

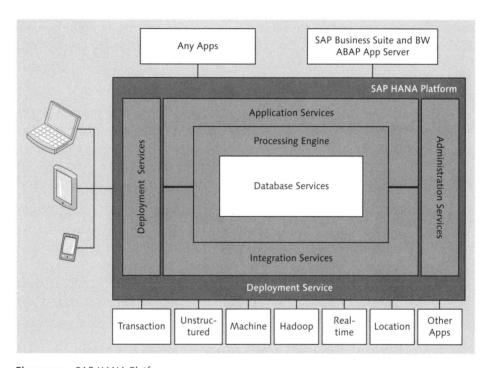

Figure 15.1 SAP HANA Platform

The History Behind the Product

SAP engineers have long held the belief that higher performance can be achieved by shifting database operations from disk to memory. For example, look at SAP ECC's original ABAP programs. In most cases,

Database consistency

the disk I/O bottleneck operations are reduced to a minimum. Data is read in bulk and placed in internal tables; all search, insert, and update operations are performed on those internal tables; and then data is written back to disk, in bulk, in one operation. The reasons for using in-memory operations at that time had more to do with SAP's engineers endeavoring to achieve consistency across the many different types of database (as SAP was built to be compatible with many different RDBMSs) than with striving for better performance by itself, but it did prove that by reducing the I/O bottlenecks the system performed better.

Prior Uses of In-Memory Computing

SAP has experienced at least two occasions during which in-memory computing came to the rescue of systems that required superior performance to be workable.

SAP APO Demand Planning

In the original SAP Advanced Planning and Optimization (APO) Demand Planning solution, data was stored in writeable InfoCubes, similar to the ones now used in Integrated Planning. The solution was reliable and sound, but not fast enough to handle the enormous volumes that a typical demand-planning solution requires.

When version 3.0 was launched, SAP listened to clients' feedback and moved the Demand Planning submodule to LiveCache—creating "planning areas" in which the transactional data was kept entirely in memory. The result was a system that performed 600 times faster, and this made it possible for companies such as Nestlé and Colgate to implement the solution across their many international operations, making SAP APO the true success that it is today.

Business Warehouse Accelerator

TREX   As BW implementations grew in size and complexity, queries became increasingly larger and slower. BW applications teams were running out of options for how to make the solution faster. What came to the rescue was a technology developed by a team in SAP's headquarters in Waldorf, Germany: Text Revival and Information Extraction, or TREX. The team was experimenting with crawling algorithms (similar to the ones used by Google), which resulted in indexes that were stored entirely in memory. They then worked on a way to use this technology to index InfoCubes. At the same time, Intel was called upon to provide dual-core processors that could process SAP commands natively in parallel.

The results were impressive; queries could run literally hundreds of times faster. The entire solution was packaged as a standalone appliance that would operate side-by-side with an SAP BW server, acting as a turbocharger. This solution was launched in 2005, and named Business Intelligence Accelerator (BIA), later renamed to Business Warehouse Accelerator (BWA).

Moving to Today's Solution

Having had these successes, an obvious question had to be asked: What if we put the entire database in memory? A top-secret project named "Tracker" was created in 2005 to address this question. By 2006, the Tracker project team had produced a workable database, which passed the SAP Standard Application Benchmark for 1,000 User SD—essentially matching the performance of the two leading certified databases at the time.

In 2010, Hasso Plattner himself announced SAP's vision for an entirely in-memory database and announced the birth of SAP HANA. The rest, as they say, is history.

The Technology Behind the Product

SAP HANA combines a series of innovations into one product; it is designed to function fully in memory, it combines a column store and a row store, and it takes full advantage of multicore, parallel-processing servers.

These three factors combined make SAP HANA a solution without parallel; it is designed for performance and to work with SAP's products.

In-Memory Computing

No other factor makes SAP HANA more unique than the fact that it runs entirely in memory. Whereas the average database will store and retrieve data from disk (caching it in memory), SAP HANA will operate entirely from the appliance's main memory.

No caching

Storing data in memory is not a new concept. Even on a PC, RAM-Disks have been available since the 1990s. What is new in SAP HANA is the fact that it was built from the ground up to deal with in-memory data. Most database systems use several layers of caching to reduce the number of round-trips to the disk (which causes bottlenecks). Moving data between the disk and these caches, between these caches and the main memory, and to the CPU and back is what takes time. A database that was ported to work in-memory would still have these caches moving data from one place to another. SAP HANA does not have that issue. It was built to move data from the main memory to the CPU for processing and back—and that is it.

Disks are still used in an SAP HANA appliance as a backup but are not the main memory. Writing to disk is performed asynchronously, so it does not impact performance of the main threads, which deal with in-memory I/O.

Column-Based Computing

According to Hasso Plattner's now famous paper "A Common Database Approach for OLTP and OLAP Using an In-Memory Column Database" (Hasso Plattner Institute on the SIGMOD, 2009, *dl.acm.org/citation.cfm?id=1559846?*), early tests performed by SAP's Tracker project team and by researchers at the Hasso Plattner Institute during 2005 and 2006 found that relational in-memory databases based on row storage did not perform significantly faster than leading RDBMSs with equivalent memory for caching. This puzzled engineers and forced them to look for alternative solutions. This gave rise to the idea of using column-based storage as an alternative. When column storage was added to the equation, they found what they were looking for; not only did the in-memory RDBMs perform much faster, but the memory usage requirements were reduced.

Column storage concept

The concept of column storage is not new, and it is relatively simple. Figure 15.2 illustrates the difference between row and column storage. Most databases would store the table 1 data in a row store, as displayed in table 2; that is, one internal RowID would be allocated to each row and the entire row with all attributes. The column store, instead, would store data as several individual tables for each individual attribute, with pointers to the RowID. Figure 15.2 also shows how an individual record for Joe Jones is stored in either case.

Data compression

Notice that whenever an attribute appears more than once (as in `LastName = Jones` or `FirstName = Bob`) the database does not store the attribute several times. Instead, it stores only the pointers to the `RowIDs`. This illustrates the first advantage of column storage; data can be compressed, because repeated values are not stored repeated times. Indeed, in the case of SAP HANA, the typical compression is by a factor of at least five.

Data retrieval

The second advantage comes to light when data is to be retrieved. To illustrate this, imagine that the following SQL query is to be executed to retrieve the names of all people in the database whose salary is higher than $45,000:

```
SELECT LastName, FirstName
WHERE  SALARY >  45000
```

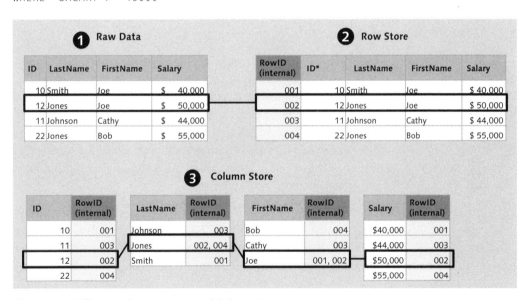

Figure 15.2 Differences between Row and Column Storage

First, let us examine the row store. In this case, assuming that no secondary index has been created on `Salary`, the database would have to scan the entire database (via sequential read), retrieving data record by record (entire records), select the attribute `Salary`, and compare it with the value `45,000`. Having determined that records `002` and `004` meet the criteria, the database will then select the required attributes `LastName` and `FirstName` and return:

LastName	FirstName
Joe	Jones
Bob	Jones

Column store Now let us look at the column store. In this case, the database would go straight to the `Salary` attribute table and select the values above 45,000. This task would be more efficient than scanning the entire row-based table, because the `Salary` attribute table is sorted. With the `RowIDs` for the rows `002` and `004` in hand, the database would perform direct reads on the attribute tables for `LastName` and `FirstName` and return the same result.

In the case of column storage, there would be a lot less data moving from one place to another, fewer calls to the database, and the entire process would be performed via direct reads.

One could argue that row storage could reduce the number of sequential reads by using secondary indexes—in our example, in `Salary`. However, this would come at a cost; whenever data is to be loaded, those secondary indexes must be updated. Furthermore, it is not practical to create secondary indexes in all columns of a database, because the size would increase exponentially. Column storage, on the other hand, behaves as if all columns were indexed, eliminating the need for secondary indexes in most cases.

The Hasso Plattner Institute's researchers and the Tracker project engineers found that by using column storage in memory, the performance of read and write operations was hundreds of times faster than in traditional, disk-based, row-storage databases.

Multicore Processing

Modern blade servers contain several CPUs with multicore processors. Multicore processors are essentially multiple processors located on one chip or in one package that use fast communication among themselves. These can perform hundreds of operations in parallel.

SAP HANA was built to take full advantage of these multicore blade servers. The database operations are divided among the available processors and sent to be processed in parallel. Hundreds of threads are performed in parallel. The results are then aggregated back and presented to the calling process.

The SAP HANA Appliance

SAP HANA is delivered as an *appliance*, a certified server with a fully installed operating system (SUSE Linux) and the SAP HANA server software. The hardware is provided by major manufacturers, such as Cisco, Dell, IBM, HP, Hitachi, NEC, or Fujitsu and using the latest Intel Xeon E7 processors.

A certified server means that it has all the technical specifications to allow SAP HANA to function in an optimum manner. It also means that SAP HANA has been built specifically to take full advantage of the capabilities of that server.

in "t-shirt" sizes, based on how much RAM is used in the

es are extra small (128 GB), small, medium, and

xtra large (2 TB).

can also be clustered—that is, several nodes

r to make up a larger appliance. We have come

ng a 32 TB cluster (a 16-extra-large-appliance

Us and 1,280 total cores.

Certified server

Benefits of SAP HANA: Beyond Faster Processing

By powering an SAP BW system with an SAP HANA database, the organization gets a data warehouse that is faster, more flexible, smaller, simpler, and easier to implement and maintain. It is not difficult to understand how these changes can have a profound impact on the bottom line of the businesses implementing this solution. For example, SAP HANA can help achieve the following:

SAP BW on
SAP HANA

> Reduce total cost of ownership (TCO)

> Reduce projects cost

> Enable solutions that would otherwise be impractical

> Enable self-service analytics

This section will explore these areas in more detail.

Reducing TCO

BW systems running on traditional databases will have, no doubt, several performance bottlenecks. These bottlenecks need to be addressed somehow for the existing systems to run fast enough and deliver analysis with adequate performance. Managing these bottlenecks has its costs: creating aggregates, maintaining precalculating queries, and caching.

Reduce workload When SAP HANA is implemented, the workload is reduced; aggregates no longer need to be created or maintained, and the need for precalculation and caching reduces significantly. Even steps such as deletion and recreation of InfoCube indexes and calculation of InfoCube statistics are no longer necessary. This has a significant, positive impact on the amount of workload of the BW support team. The process chains become simpler, faster, and easier to maintain.

Reducing Projects Cost

In general, analytics projects include a major performance-tuning component. Once the queries are defined and the required results are well understood, the project will spend some considerable time making sure these queries run within a time frame that is acceptable for end users. This is a project cost that comes directly from the fact that, in most cases, the existing technology is not advanced enough to cope with the current requirements of speed and data volume.

Project teams also spend valuable time analyzing data loads and extractors, creating secondary indexes, analyzing query performance, creating aggregates, and including them in process chains, all in the name of better performance.

Reduce performance tuning With the introduction of SAP HANA, the performance-tuning component of analytics projects reduces significantly. There is no need to analyze query performance with the view of building aggregates, and the process chains become smaller, easier, and faster to build and test.

The data model becomes simpler too; it is possible to report straight out of DSOs—so InfoCubes become redundant or smaller and simpler. This too has an impact in reducing and simplifying process chains.

Furthermore, project teams no longer have to spend time pinpointing the typical navigation states of queries and optimizing the configuration specifically for those navigation states. The user is free to navigate, interrogate, and truly slice and dice data in ways that were not practical before. This creates new possibilities; users are able to gain more and better insights from the information they already have.

The BW teams become a lot more efficient, deliver faster solutions, and meet a wider range of user requirements; this has a positive and lasting impact in reducing the total cost of the organization's BW team.

Enabling Solutions That Would Otherwise Be Impractical

The ability to crunch massive amounts of data at acceptable speeds or the same amount of data faster than ever imagined creates new possibilities. Some solutions, with high potential for monetary benefits, may have been thought of but never implemented, because they were just not practical. Some may have been abandoned, because they did not perform well. SAP HANA's superior performance brings these discarded solutions from mere fiction to the realm of possibility.

Every organization has analytics solutions that are no longer used (or rarely used) because their performance became too poor. They may have been originally designed with a specific amount of data, but as data grew or business units started to be incorporated, they became impractical. Queries started to be too slow, or users could no longer wait for the planning functions to run online.

Recycle abandoned solutions

Faster databases will breathe new life into these solutions and deliver the business benefits that were intended when they were first created.

Faster data-load processing means data load can run more frequently, virtual providers become feasible, and real-time data can be incorporated into analytics solutions (obviously, the performance of the extraction still depends on the performance of the source system).

Real-time analytics

A new type of analytical solution is now possible: solutions that enable the user to combine historical and real-time data.

Enabling Self-Service Analytics

In many organizations, IT managers have been reluctant to let users create their own analytics solutions, as this could cause the servers to slow down or even crash. With SAP HANA's performance and ability to deal with large amounts of data, this fear no longer exists—and the user can explore data using SAP BusinessObjects tools such as Explorer, Lumira, Analysis, or even SAP BW BEx.

This reduces the overall cost of IT for the organization, as users require less project work and fewer IT resources to achieve the results they need.

Using SAP HANA in the Enterprise

You now know what SAP HANA does. However, you may still be wondering how SAP HANA can work in your organization. This section explains the different use cases for SAP HANA.

SAP HANA as a Database

From the perspective of most applications, SAP HANA behaves exactly like your everyday RDBMS. It is comprised of tables, relationships, procedures, triggers, and so on, just like your average database.

SQL

Like other RDBMSs, SAP HANA speaks SQL. Its SQL is based on SQL 92 standard, enhanced—so it has everything SQL 92 has, plus additions that make sense in SAP HANA only. This means that it is possible to introduce SAP HANA as the database of an application with minimum disruption; everything that worked in the previous database will work on the new one.

This is certainly true with SAP applications. Most of the effort that SAP puts into "SAP HANAfying" its applications has to do with changing its applications to take advantage of the new technology rather than changing the application to cope with a change in database. All the existing ABAP commands will work with SAP—but it makes little sense to work with SAP HANA by bringing all the data into a memory-internal table and processing it when the database is already in memory.

It is true also for other, non-SAP applications. You can port mobile web applications from SQL Server to SAP HANA with minimum disruption; in most cases it is a mere case of updating the ODBC or JDBC library from SQL Server to SAP HANA, and voilá. The difference, in most cases, is significant performance gains. We are also able to take advantage of SAP HANA's analytic capabilities. So, now we are embedding BusinessObjects Design Studio applications in our apps, reading HANA Calculation Views directly.

Easy adaption

Additionally, the learning curve is not steep. Anyone familiar with SQL can use SAP HANA. The adoption of SAP HANA in other areas outside the SAP sphere, in particular in web and mobile applications, is due to this very factor; people are familiar with SQL.

The scripting language, SQLScript, is also very easy to learn—and developers feel right at home.

SAP Business Suite Powered by SAP HANA

Again, SAP HANA is an SQL-compliant relational database. Therefore, any SAP solution ported from certified database "A" to SAP HANA will function without a glitch.

However, it took SAP some time to "SAP HANAfy" its Business Suite because, like everything from SAP, it was originally written to circumvent the database bottleneck. The SAP Business Suite had been designed to keep to a minimum the number of times data was read or written and to process data in internal tables functioning as buffers. One look across the typical SAP Business Suite program will show that this was largely how the entire solution was built.

Therefore, by porting SAP Business Suite to SAP HANA, the impact would have been minimal; the limited number of I/O operations would have been made faster, but overall the performance would have been largely unchanged.

What SAP's engineers had to do was to take full advantage of SAP HANA: push data-intense processes to the database level, taking advantage of SAP HANA's calculation engine while significantly reducing the size of result sets flowing from the database server to the application layer and vice versa. This resulted in a much faster system overall; data-intensive processes run much faster in the SAP HANA database server than in the application server, and sending less data between the servers makes the overall performance even better.

With those changes, all SAP Business Suite applications, including SAP CRM, SAP ERP, SAP PLM, SAP SCM, and SAP SRM, became faster.

Transactions that had traditionally suffered from the poor performance of a traditional database turned into much faster operations; running increasingly growing CO-PA plans became feasible and long-running transactions and overnight batch processing became things of the past.

You can now couple transactions with analysis in real time in a single blended environment to get live insight about a fast-breaking situation. You can dramatically accelerate core business processes and evolve toward supporting real-time scenarios.

It also is now possible to create analytical models directly on the main SAP Business Suite database, unifying transactional and analytical processing on a single real-time platform.

SAP BW on SAP HANA (BoH)

Over time, SAP BW installations have grown to become the typical central data warehouse for SAP's clients, harmonizing several source systems, including non-SAP systems. As BW-based systems kept growing in size and complexity, it became obvious that two areas would have to be addressed.

Presentation · The first one was the presentation side: clients demanded more sophisticated forms of visualization, presentation, and sharing of information. This was addressed by SAP with the acquisition of BusinessObjects.

Performance · The second was performance. There was a need to make the now gigantic BW systems run faster and deliver results within acceptable time windows. SAP's initial response was to build SAP BWA. Portions of the data stored in SAP BW were copied onto a RAM-based column store running on a separate blade-based appliance, which could respond up to 100 times faster to users' queries.

Although BWA produced great results in terms of query run-time, it was hardly the best solution for the problem. For one, the cost was prohibitive for most companies. Furthermore, although it addressed well the query runtime problem response time was still not acceptable for other activities (such as writing data or performing data activation).

In 2009, an SAP parallel development (until then very secret) came to the rescue: a new database, running fully in memory, using the same column-store concepts and highly parallel processing that made SAP BWA such a great tool, but this time the entire database ran in memory. All inserts, updates, deletes, all select operations, all SQL procedures, everything, runs entirely in-memory; that is SAP HANA.

It is no wonder that SAP BW was the first of SAP's solutions to be "SAP HANAfied." It is a match made in heaven: an ultra-fast database running a solution that requires and demands fast responses on querying and writing enormous amounts of data.

SAP HANA as OLAP

On top of being a groundbreaking relational database system, SAP HANA is also a capable analytics platform. SAP HANA's native objects—attribute, analytic, and calculation views—are used to expose data to OLAP tools such as SAP BusinessObjects Explorer, Lumira, and Predictive Analysis and/or to customized applications via MDX—a query language for OLAP databases, much like SQL is a query language for relational databases.

Analytics platform

Figure 15.3 shows the SAP HANA attribute views. Here you can see separate modeling of descriptive (dimension) data from modeling of measure (fact) data.

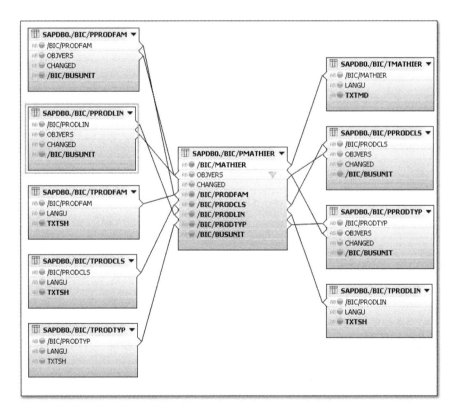

Figure 15.3 SAP HANA Attribute Views (Source: Modeling Basics for SAP HANA Modeler and SAP HANA Information Composer—SAP SE)

Figure 15.4 shows that more complex models can be created by combining two or more analytic and attribute views via graphical calculation views.

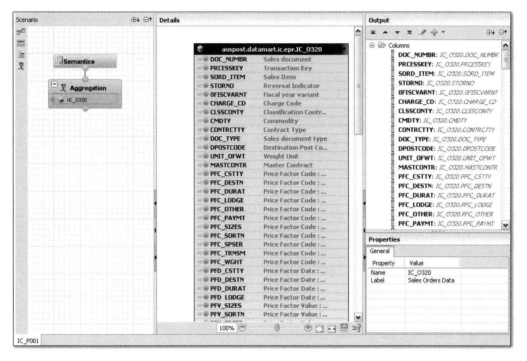

Figure 15.4 SAP HANA Calculation Views (Source: Modeling Basics for SAP HANA Modeler and SAP HANA Information Composer—SAP SE)

Compare objects It is almost impossible to resist the urge to compare SAP HANA's objects with SAP BW's modeling objects:

> An attribute view is like an InfoObject in BW; the difference is that data is not persisted—that is, the attribute view is really a view formed with underlying tables.

> An analytic view is like an InfoCube; it has measures (which function very much like key figures) and dimensions (which, in a sense, behave like SAP BW's characteristics). Again, data is not persisted. Analytical views are made up of database views.

> A calculation view could be a MultiProvider (if formed by unions) or a CompositeProvider (if formed by unions or joins). Once more,

data is not persisted but is formed by SAP HANA's powerful Calculation Engine.

The comparison helps a developer to build the models in their mind and understand how to use them—but it is too simplistic:

> SAP HANA's models can define calculated measures, currency conversion, and other features that can only be done via transformations in SAP BW.

> SAP BW's ability to persist data makes it more flexible in other ways; more customized and complex calculations can be performed as data is loaded.

Some organizations have opted for building their data warehouses entirely on SAP HANA without SAP BW. Other organizations, in particular those that already had SAP BW in place, are now adopting SAP HANA and will have their data warehouses built with data marts in both SAP BW and SAP HANA.

Data warehousing on SAP HANA

Those organizations that have implemented SAP BW and have taken full advantage of the SAP Business Content feel that the modeling capabilities of SAP HANA are not yet adequate for their requirements.

Those capabilities are getting better each day, though. Two areas have been helping SAP HANA stake its claim as the future technology of choice for the SAP analytics platform:

SAP analytics platforms

> **SAP HANA Rapid Marts**
Deliver data services–based extraction models and SAP Business-Objects reports for several areas of the business.

> **SAP HANA Live**
Prebuilt analytical models based on calculation views built on top of standard SAP tables within an SAP HANA database for SAP Business Suite.

We will discuss SAP HANA Live in the next section.

SAP HANA Live

SAP HANA Live delivers flexible, real-time operational reporting and analytics on SAP Business Suite on SAP HANA. It is installed as an add-on for SAP HANA.

Real-time operational reporting

There are two main options to leverage SAP HANA Live:

> Sidecar approach
> Integrated solution

Sidecar approach   In the sidecar option, the client uses SAP Business Suite in a traditional RDBMS database (non-SAP HANA) and replicates relevant reporting data into an SAP HANA platform through SLT to make use of SAP HANA Live (see Figure 15.5).

In this scenario, you are replicating data into an SAP HANA environment in order to accelerate the analytics component of your SAP Business Suite.

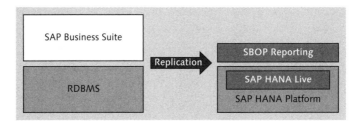

Figure 15.5   SAP HANA Live—Sidecar approach

Integrated solution   In the integrated option, the client is running SAP Business Suite directly on SAP HANA (see Figure 15.6).

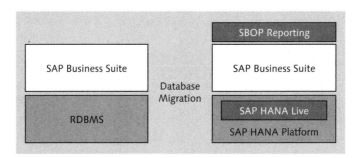

Figure 15.6   SAP HANA Live—Integrated Solution

The benefits of this option include the following:

> Reduce the TCO by consolidating your SAP landscape into an SAP HANA platform.

> Reduce data latency, because you do not need to copy data from your SAP Business Suite onto an SAP HANA platform.

> Accelerate your entire OLTP system by running SAP Business Suite on SAP HANA.

> Accelerate the operational analytics of your SAP Business Suite through SAP HANA Live.

The following SAP BusinessObjects Business Intelligence tools can be used to report on SAP HANA Live:

BI tools to report on HANA Live

> SAP Crystal Reports

> SAP BusinessObjects Analysis for Microsoft Office

> SAP BusinessObjects Dashboards

> SAP BusinessObjects Explorer

> SAP Lumira

> SAP BusinessObjects Design Studio

SAP HANA Live leverages a predefined set of tables and data models as delivered standard content for SAP HANA calculation views. Even though it is pre-delivered standard content, it can be customized to customer needs.

HANA Live virtual data models

The content is represented as virtual data models based on master data and transaction data tables of the SAP Business Suite applications.

SAP HANA Live's virtual data models are constantly evolving; you should check with your SAP representative before making any decisions.

SAP HANA Rapid Marts

Rapid marts are BusinessObjects reporting solutions, leveraging SAP HANA's analytics capabilities, without the use of SAP BW. They are typically delivered via a rapid-deployment, and cover areas such as the ones listed here:

Reporting solutions

> Financial Suite:
  - General Ledger Rapid Mart
  - Accounts Payable Rapid Mart

      – Accounts Receivable Rapid Mart

      – Cost Center Rapid Mart

      – Fixed Assets Rapid Mart

> Operational Suite:

      – Inventory Rapid Mart

      – Purchasing Rapid Mart

      – Sales Rapid Mart

SAP HANA Applications

SAP HANA was built for SAP and non-SAP communities. One of the most powerful features of SAP HANA is the ability that programmers have to create web and mobile applications that leverage the power of the data stored in memory in its servers. These applications can reside directly on the SAP HANA server or not. We will explore how this technology enables a new breed of applications.

SAP HANA Application Server (SAP HANA XS)

In line with SAP's truly revolutionary approach, SAP introduced a capability called SAP HANA Extended Application Services (also referred to as XS or XS Engine) as of SAP HANA SPS 5. In a nutshell, SAP HANA XS is a simple but powerful application server, web server, and web-development server all bundled in the SAP HANA server itself. It is not a separate server and it is not only another piece of software; it is an application and web server deeply integrated with the SAP HANA database.

HTML5   Its main purpose is to give developers the tools to build new HTML5-based applications that access SAP HANA data directly, removing the need for a separate application server and the latency that would result from integrating SAP HANA with the application via JDBC or ODBC drivers.

It is still possible for applications from other servers to connect to SAP HANA via ODBC and JDBC drivers—in particular, when porting other applications to SAP HANA—but SAP HANA XS becomes the preferred choice when new applications are being built.

Native and Non-Native SAP HANA Applications

Web or mobile web applications can be created directly on SAP HANA XS and served directly from the SAP HANA server. These are called native applications, because they run natively in the SAP HANA server. In these applications, the control-flow logic and the presentation logic both run from the same SAP HANA server as the database and calculation logic.

They deliver the best user experience; there is no latency in sending and receiving data between the application server and the database server, because they both reside in the same appliance. It is SAP's position that brand-new applications, written for SAP HANA, should be built using the native approach.

User experience

In this approach, the control-flow and presentation logic are typically written in server-side JavaScript, and OData REST services are used to expose data from the database into the application and to write data from the application onto the database.

On the other hand, the control-flow and application of desktop, web, or mobile web applications can be served out of a separate application server (which could be a dedicated server or the client itself). In this case, there are other options to develop the control logic of the program—ABAP, Java, JSP, .NET, and so on—and the communication between the application and the database server is done via open standards, such as JDBC or ODBC or even OData REST services.

Separate application server

In this case, the user experience is not as fantastic as in native SAP HANA applications, but there is an important gain in flexibility and portability. Existing applications originally designed for other database systems can be easily ported to SAP HANA, taking advantage of SAP HANA's performance and flexibility. It is important to highlight that even SAP HANA Studio was built with this approach.

Flexible and portable

Building Mobile Apps with SAP HANA

Mobile applications, be they web mobile, native mobile, or hybrid, can communicate with SAP HANA via OData REST services. Developers can build sophisticated mobile applications that read and write data onto an SAP HANA database, taking full advantage of SAP HANA's high performance and flexibility.

The communication between a native mobile app, such as the ones built in Java for Android or Objective C for iOS, is done via the OData API—that is, the application sends and receives data from an *http:// ...* address, which is created when the OData service is created on the SAP HANA server.

SAP HANA Versions: Beyond On Premise

Initially, SAP HANA was offered as an on premise solution. The organizations using it would have an appliance in their data centers and use it to power on premise applications. However, as the market matures and other uses of SAP HANA are found, in particular outside the original SAP shops, some other more innovative versions of SAP HANA are being made available.

We will explore some of these versions in this section.

SAP HANA One

Amazon Web Services

SAP HANA One offers SAP HANA via Amazon Web Services (AWS). The solution is licensed to be used for production systems via a small subscription fee plus AWS's infrastructure costs, for a 64 GB database. It is aimed at department-scale projects, system integrators, independent software vendors, and innovative startups.

This version has a very small startup cost and very low TCO. It can be used by organizations to prove a concept or to develop an initial idea at a fraction of the cost of an on premise appliance. It is also favored by startup organizations that use SAP HANA as the mechanism to deliver innovative web and mobile applications that scale out.

SAP HANA Developer Edition—AWS

Cloud

There are also several developer editions. SAP HANA is offered with zero license fee to be used by individual developers via the cloud. These systems are not aimed at productive use but to give developers access to SAP HANA to learn, evaluate, or build applications and demos. At the time of writing, the following cloud partners offered developer editions of SAP HANA:

> CloudShare

> AWS

> KT upcloud biz

> SmartCloudPT

SAP HANA Enterprise Cloud (SAP HEC)

SAP HANA Enterprise Cloud, also known as SAP HEC, offers SAP Business Suite on SAP HANA, SAP BW on SAP HANA, and SAP HANA innovative applications, all in SAP's cloud. They are production-grade solutions aimed at the enterprise. These systems can replace some or all existing in-house ERP solutions, using SAP HANA as a database.

Big Data Acceleration with SAP HANA

Big data is defined by the three Vs: variety, velocity, and volume. This term is new to the IT world and combines the need for customization in the customer-service experience with system logistics. Organizations have to deal with high volume of data, generated at high velocity, and available in a variety of sources to find and keep customers.

Variety, velocity, and volume

 Example

> To paraphrase Steve Lucas, president, Platform Solutions at SAP, as soon as a credit card is scanned, the name of the person doing the purchase and the credit card number are available to the smart organization there and then. Being able to match that individual with their previous purchases, tastes, likes, dislikes, and even comments that they have made in the social media gives the organization the opportunity to understand its consumers' behavior like never before. The intelligent organization can use that insight to drive even more business by providing highly personalized customer service, making customized offers, or improving its products and services.

Example: personalized customer service

How much data does a company need to crunch (i.e., high volume) and how many different sources does it need to go through to find meaningful insights (i.e., high variety) from so much data that is being generated in real-time (i.e., high velocity) to give, in that split-second that a card is being swiped and a transaction is being processed, an offer to a customer that makes sense, creates a true sense of value, makes the customer feel appreciated, and is not likely to be dismissed as a hard-sell tactic?

Big Data Technology

Big data databases generally deal with peta- or hexabytes, as opposed to the giga- or terabytes of the traditional databases; they are thousands to millions of times bigger.

Big data systems deal with structured data (traditional transactional data, such as sales orders, point of sale, bank transactions, etc.) and unstructured data (such as pictures, sounds, social media feeds, news articles, etc.) in the same database. They're fed by several sources at the same time. A social media source, for instance, is being fed from millions of people, all at the same time, from all parts of the world.

Revolutionize human interaction

Big data systems are revolutionizing all areas of human interaction: from improving customer experience in the retail industry to helping Homeland Security manage the country's borders to helping the banking industry prevent credit card fraud to helping in the diagnosis and treatment of cancer patients by performing genome sequencing in matter of minutes, rather than days, at a fraction of the cost.

Technology-wise, a common approach is to combine a database that can handle a vast amount of data, sourced from both structured and unstructured sources and storing it in low-cost servers, with a fast analytical engine capable of performing predictive and analytical what-if scenarios in real-time. This is how the marriage of Hadoop and SAP HANA came about.

 Note

Hadoop

Hadoop is an open-source project distributed by the Apache Foundation. The name is not an acronym, nor does it mean anything. Its name comes from the name given to the toy elephant owned by Doug Cutting's child. Doug Cutting is a former Yahoo programmer who created Hadoop by implementing the MapReduce framework (this framework was originally created by Google to crawl websites).

Apache Hadoop is not a single piece of software, but a collection of frameworks and APIs, as shown in Figure 15.7. Its core components are MapReduce—which handles distributed processing—and HDFS—which handles distributed storage. It is designed to scale up from a single server to thousands of machines with a very high degree of fault tolerance. Instead of relying on high-end servers, Hadoop is capable of detecting and handling failures at the application layer.

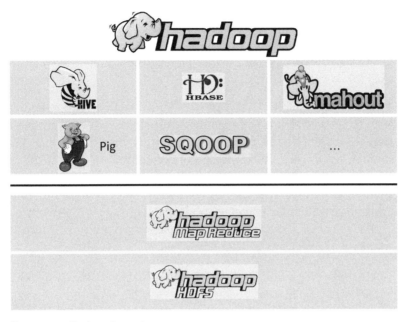

Figure 15.7 Hadoop Ecosystem

By using the MapReduce divide-and-conquer strategy, Hadoop handles processing of very large amounts of data using large clusters of commodity hardware. By using HDFS, it handles storage and retrieval of data in a large cluster of commodity hardware. Its power comes from parallel processing (sound familiar?) — distributing data and processing in a large cluster of commodity hardware.

Although Hadoop can handle large amounts of data and can deal with structured and unstructured data, it is very much a framework, so a lot of programming needs to be done for any solution to be built. Furthermore, although this is changing as the framework evolves and new libraries are created, Hadoop is very much built for batch processing, so it is not exactly the best choice for a real-time, time-critical analytical solution.

This is where SAP HANA comes in. Hadoop is used for its power to gather and store data sets of virtually any size, so it handles large

SAP HANA + Hadoop

amounts of data, preprocessing data for SAP HANA. SAP HANA is used for its ability to bring together data from diverse sources in real time and produce insights, what-if analysis, and predictions that can be changed at the speed of thought.

Furthermore, SAP HANA becomes the crucial link between data stored via Hadoop and SAP BusinessObjects frontend tools, which are used for data visualization.

As Steve Lucas puts it: "The SAP HANA platform and its integration with Hadoop have married together real-time insights with extreme storage, solving one of the biggest problems with current big data solutions, a fragmented landscape of solutions that are difficult to connect together. Our expanded big-data strategy provides customers a single, integrated approach to combine enterprise data and additional information to employees and consumers, as well as improve business processes such as customer engagement, preventative maintenance and responsive supply chain."

Figure 15.8 shows the typical architecture of SAP HANA and Hadoop integration.

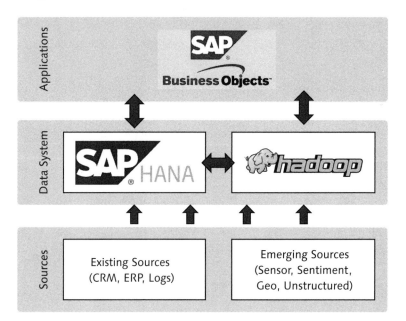

Figure 15.8 Typical SAP HANA–Hadoop Integration

SAP redistributes and supports the *Intel Distribution Apache Hadoop* and the *Hortonworks Data Platform*, both Hadoop implementations. Furthermore, SAP supports integration with IBM, Cloudera, and Amazon Elastic MapReduce.

Conclusion

SAP HANA is more than simply a fast, SQL-compliant, in-memory database. It is an application server, an Eclipse-based development platform, and a powerful analytics platform capable of supporting enterprise data warehouses and big data solutions. It is indeed a new chapter in SAP's story.

In this chapter, you learned that SAP HANA has achieved the following:

> Breathed new life into existing SAP solutions by making them faster, smaller, and more closely integrated with OLAP solutions

> Made SAP BW an infinitely more capable enterprise data warehouse solution: faster, smaller, capable of handling input from several sources in real time

> Created an entirely new ecosystem of startups that can deliver innovative solutions leveraging its power, speed, and simple approach to web applications development and deployment

> Enabled a new breed of big data solutions that can leverage the power of externally obtained structured and unstructured data combined with data available in the various systems of the organization

SAP HANA is indeed revolutionary, changing all SAP Solutions and impacting the entire IT industry.

In the next chapter, we will explore the mobile capabilities that SAP offers.

SAP Mobility

As more and more people carry their personal smartphones, tablets, and wearables, they have begun to expect to be able to interact with their corporate software via these devices. People no longer expect to be given a corporate "technology of choice," with limited abilities and no personal tools. They want to use their own personal devices, with their own personal applications, and perform their jobs on the go.

At the same time, "millennials" have the expectation that enterprise software interacts with them in the same way as the consumer apps they are so used to. The user interface must be beautiful, intuitive, and user-friendly to a degree that requires no training to use. They must be comprehensive in a way that does not bind people to their desks to perform their work.

Millennial expectations

Through acquisition, development, and research, SAP has developed an impressive portfolio of enterprise mobility solutions that gives organizations a comprehensive set of tools to manage all of these mobile aspects—from managing a vast range of different BYO ("bring your own") devices securely in a way that does not put the organization's precious data and hardware assets at risk, and allow employees to interact with their internal corporate software, performing common tasks on the go.

This chapter discusses the opportunities and challenges that organizations face in the journey to "mobilize" their applications, their workforce, and their customer experience. It also discusses many tools that SAP makes available, many of which are available through the SAP app store at *https://store.sap.com.*

Why Mobilize?

Everyone is talking about mobilizing their organizations, but what are the advantages, the business benefits, and the pitfalls of doing so?

Staying competitive

The need for mobility is a simple matter of competitiveness. In the same way that the early cell phones freed people from their desks and made them infinitely more effective, being connected on the go is making people more effective at their jobs. They gain the ability to have the correct information to make correct decisions wherever they are, they are able to interact with the organization to provide updates on the work they are doing, and they can approve expenses, transact, exchange information, update project information, update production statistics, enter sales orders, receive payments, and so on. All of this makes the organization as a whole more dynamic, more effective, and more responsive.

Purchased software, in-house development, or a mix of both?

The challenges of bringing this technology into the corporation are numerous. The first issue is a lack of solutions themselves. Corporate software vendors have traditionally focused on the desktop and, to some degree, on web-based technologies. Only recently have they awakened to the fact that people need to interact with their ERP systems through handheld devices. Furthermore, not all solutions are generic. Many are industry or even company specific and need to be tailor-made. So the first challenge is to identify which areas to address and what to use: purchased software, in-house development, or a mix of both.

The second challenge lies in the devices themselves. The mobile device market is highly dynamic, and products change all the time. There is no use in forcing everyone to use the same device, tested, approved, and certified by the organization. This had, until now, been the approach of most organizations regarding other types of hardware, but it does not work for this case. The organization must be able to support multiple types of devices and be dynamic enough to absorb new devices as they enter the market.

This in itself creates the next challenge—security. How can an organization keep unauthorized people from gaining access to its data and systems at the same time as it makes sure that the loss of a mobile device does not create a threat to the organization?

Security

The plan to mobilize must address these points: BYO devices, security, what types of applications to use, and what types of devices to support. All of these points are important and must have equal bearing on the choices made.

BYO devices

Types of Mobile Applications

Essentially, there are three types of mobile applications: web-based, native, and hybrid. They all deliver content to mobile devices, each through its own methods and with different benefits and pitfalls. We will cover the three different types in this section.

Web-Based Mobile Applications

Web-based mobile applications are essentially websites that are optimized to be accessed via mobile devices. In many cases, they look and feel like a mobile app, but they are in fact websites. For example, there are many mobile banking applications built as web-based mobile applications. Another case are applications that require a high degree of interaction with the backend system.

The advantage of this type of mobile application is that there is nc need to develop the same application several times to support several types of devices. One size fits all—that is, once the mobile website is built, it will function on any mobile device that supports HTML, CSS, JavaScript, and so on, and these days most popular devices support this technology.

One size fits all

The disadvantage of this technology is that it is very much dependent on the user being online for the app to function. In fact, users would find it very hard to run the application without access to the website. Another point is that web-based mobile apps' user interfaces are not as good as the ones built natively. It is difficult to build a user interface that functions well in all devices, that looks good in all devices,

Online connectivity and UI disadvantages

and, because the app has to send and receive data from the website all the time, that is as fast as a native application.

The takeaway is this: web-based mobile apps are fast to build and easy to deploy, but may not necessarily deliver the best possible user experience. Of course, as networks improve, mobile libraries become more comprehensive, and the devices themselves become more powerful, mobile apps become more and more a promising proposition.

Native Mobile Applications

Native applications are the ones that most of us are accustomed to use. They have taken the world by storm. We chat with our friends, check the weather, make purchases, listen to the radio, and so on, all with native applications we download from app stores.

Best user experience   These apps deliver the best user experience; they are fast, handle offline activities, access the device's utilities to read barcodes, play sounds, read and write credit cards via NFC ("near field communication"), interact with iBeacons, and find their geographical position via GPS. They are still able to talk to the web. They can still display HTML documents and read websites. They can still send and receive data via HTTP to RESTful services—the same as web-based mobile apps.

Harder to deploy   The disadvantage of this type of mobile application is that it is necessary to build one app for each type of device that is to be supported. One Android app, one iOS app (or maybe two—one for iPhone and one for iPad), one for Blackberry, one for Windows, and so on.

The takeaway is this: native apps deliver compelling user interfaces and access the devices' native capabilities but are harder to deploy and more expensive to build and maintain.

Hybrid Applications

One technology for all devices   Hybrid applications are built to take advantage of both options; they are built once using one technology—so they are faster and cheaper to build than native applications—and then are packaged and delivered to each type of mobile device. They deliver faster and better user interfaces and have direct access to the device's local capabilities.

Available technologies   There are several options and technologies to build hybrid applications. One of particular interest to SAP mobile developers is Apache

Cordova. The developer builds a web-based mobile app initially—for instance, using SAP AppBuilder and SAPUI5—and maybe this app leverages data access to an SAP NetWeaver system via SAP Gateway.

The hybrid app is then imported into an Apache Cordova folder in the developer's PC or Mac, where several builds of the same website are created: one for iOS, one for Android, one for Blackberry, one for Windows, and so on. Apache Cordova then generates native versions of the website and places them inside the native application, which is then compiled and enhanced with Apache Cordova libraries. These libraries use the device's local capabilities, such as the accelerometer, sound player, sound recorder, GPS locator, and so on. The result is: several native applications to be distributed via the devices' app stores.

The advantage of this type of mobile application is that the need to develop the same application several times is greatly reduced, whereas user experience and performance are better than with web-based applications.

The disadvantage, on the other hand, is that they are neither as cheap as developing one website only, nor as responsive as the equivalent native app. However, as more and more organizations demand this type of technology and more tools enter the market, the tendency is that hybrid applications will become better in both ways: easier and faster to use and build, while delivering better and better user interfaces.

What Type Is Best for Your Organization?

Deciding which type of development to use is a question of understanding your organization's needs and priorities. One size does not fit all.

If the solution requires an outstanding user interface or this solution will be the reason that consumers will choose your organization instead of a competitor, then maybe the best choice is to go for the higher investment of building and maintaining native applications.   UI

If cost is an important factor or if having the ability to use the solution in several devices is a more important factor, then the best solution may be to go for web-based development.   Cost

There can also be a question of maturity involved. If this is the first time your organization is toying with the idea of building a mobile application, then a first solution may be delivered as a web-based solution or as a native solution for a limited set of devices—say those devices that the target workforce is more likely to own.

Mobile Apps in the SAP Business Suite

Ready-to-use apps

SAP offers ready-to-use mobile applications via the SAP mobile marketplace. They cover a vast range of business functions and configurations. They can work on their own to perform discrete tasks or interact with the SAP Business Suite to allow employees and business partners to perform their work from anywhere in the world, at any time, from their own mobile devices. Figure 16.1 illustrates the mobile applications offered by SAP as part of the SAP Business Suite.

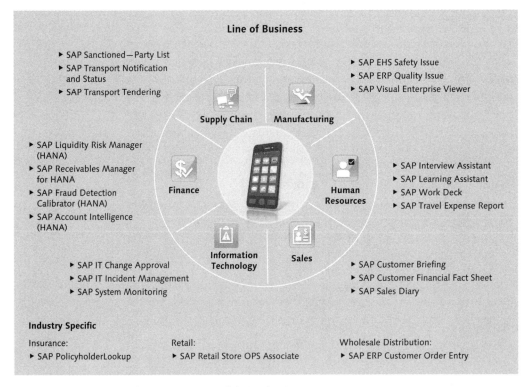

Figure 16.1 SAP Mobile Applications

These applications free employees from the need to use a computer to interact with their enterprise software to perform certain tasks. People can do part of their work on the go from a mobile device such as a smartphone or a tablet.

These applications are essentially mobile versions of functions that can normally be performed via a desktop or laptop computer, interacting with SAP Business Suite tools such as SAP ERP, SAP CRM, or SAP SRM.

Mobile versions of SAP functions

Applications are being added every day. More information on these applications can be found at *https://help.sap.com/bs-mobileapps? current=bs-mobileapps*.

We will go over some additional areas of specialties for mobile apps in the next sections.

Mobile Apps for Industries

SAP has developed more complex applications that are focused on resolving specific business problems within specific industries. Some examples of such apps include the following:

> **SAP Complex Manufacturing Accelerator**
> This is a tool for the shop floor. Users can collect operation-level data and display information on each production operation, including texts, documents, and images. They can collect traceability data, such as serial numbers and lot numbers, and monitor the production process as a whole.

> **SAP Direct Store Delivery**
> This app helps the store order and replenish goods on the fly. It enables mobile users, such as the field sales force and delivery drivers, to respond quickly to the customer's needs for new and revised orders while reducing inventory costs.

Mobile Apps for SAP Cloud Solutions

SAP offers mobile apps that interact with SAP Cloud solutions, including the following:

> Mobile apps for *SAP Business ByDesign*
> The SAP *Business in Focus* App
> Mobile apps for *SAP Cloud for Travel and Expense*

Mobile Apps for SAP HANA

Some of SAP's mobile apps are built to leverage the power of SAP HANA's in-memory database, delivering superior customer experience for performing complex or data-intensive tasks in highly responsive applications.

Some examples of these apps include the following:

> SAP Liquidity Risk Manager (HANA)
> SAP Receivables Manager for HANA
> SAP Fraud Detection Calibrator (HANA)
> SAP Account Intelligence (HANA)
> SAP Business Transparency (HANA)

SAP Fiori

Web-based apps for
ERP functions

SAP Fiori is a set of web-based applications that allow users to perform the most common ERP business functions via HTML-based mobile and desktop devices.

SAP Fiori's use of HTML technology and adaptive design makes it capable of seamlessly adjusting to most mobile and desktop devices. Indeed, it works on any HTML-based device, be it a tablet or a smartphone, such as iPhone, iPad, Blackberry, Android, Windows devices, and so on.

SAP Fiori's architecture leverages the existing SAP ERP infrastructure—on premise or in the cloud—and uses SAP Gateway to expose the SAP ERP data via the OData protocol. The frontend is built in SAPUI5—a technology that uses HTML5 and JavaScript to deliver a simple and easy user experience on a beautiful interface that makes any millennial proud to be using SAP.

Figure 16.2 shows the areas covered by SAP Fiori.

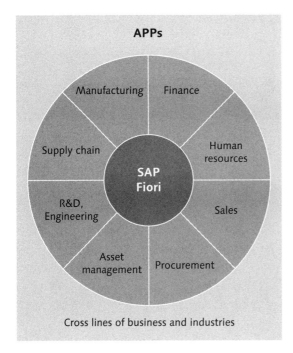

Figure 16.2 SAP Fiori Applications

SAP Fiori is supplied free as part of any SAP-licensed software.

Other SAP and Partner Mobile Apps

In SAP-delivered content, there are also several other apps written by SAP and partners. They can be paid for or free and can interact with SAP products directly, function or their own, or be part of applications hosted by partners.

Indeed, SAP has been very active in providing incentives for partners to develop innovative mobile solutions for known business problems. They can all be found on the SAP app store at *https://store.sap.com.*

Some example of other SAP-developed apps include the following:

SAP-developed apps: examples

> SAP 3D Visual Enterprise Viewer for iPad

> SAP 3D Visual Enterprise Viewer for Android

> SAP EMR Unwired for iOS

343

> › SAP EMR Unwired for Android

> › SAP Patient Management: Enhancements for SAP EMR Unwired

Mobile Security

What if a person loses a tablet or a telephone that contains information—possibly confidential information—pertaining to the company? How can an organization guarantee that only authorized persons with authorized devices have access to the appropriate information? Those concerns have kept many organizations from reaping the benefits of more widespread use of mobile technology.

Remotely manage mobile devices

SAP approached the problem from a different angle. It invested in technology that helps organizations embarking on a mobile journey to have complete peace of mind. These tools help IT departments remotely manage devices that have access to the company's systems, help with registration of devices, with management of who has access to the company data assets, how those devices behave, and which applications and features remain valid when the devices are connected to the company's network. Most importantly, these tools help to prevent unauthorized access should the device fall into the wrong hands; all of this can be done remotely from a central application.

We will discuss some of these SAP-provided security tools in the following sections.

SAP Afaria

SAP Afaria became part of SAP's portfolio in 2012. Afaria was originally developed as a tool to help IT departments manage resources remotely, such as disks, files, and sessions. The solution was acquired by Sybase in 2004 and became SAP Afaria in 2012, when SAP acquired Sybase and entered the mobile-application market on a grand scale. In 2011, Gartner identified Afaria as one of the top mobile-device-management platforms in the first Gartner Magic Quadrant report on the mobile-device-management market.

SAP Afaria is available both on premise and in the cloud. It is a mobile-device security application par excellence; it provides peace of mind for companies that let employees have access to their data assets on their personal devices. It manages devices of all types remotely, controls what resources these devices have access to, and erases applications and revokes access should the device end up in the wrong hands.

SAP Mobile Documents

SAP Mobile Documents is a productivity tool that takes advantage of mobile technology and allows people to do part of their work on the go while keeping one version of the work document. It lets users share files, view mobile documents, and collaborate on documents remotely from any type of mobile device. SAP Mobile Documents can be deployed on premises and as a "hybrid" solution, with documents available at the same time from on premise and secure cloud servers.

One version

SAP Mobile App Protection by Mocana

Mocana secures enterprise mobile apps—that is, those mobile apps built by the organization, for the organization, or by a third-party using the organization's data. It uses the concept of "wrapping around" the mobile app; the developers do not need to build into their applications the concepts of encryption, security, and application safeguard.

It can be used to secure applications on both managed and non-managed devices.

Mobile Analytics

As much as for transactional systems, SAP recognizes the need for people to have the information they need to make decisions available anytime and anywhere. SAP has been focusing on enabling the use of BI tools on mobile devices. With such technologies, the following scenarios become viable:

> Sales personnel can enter a meeting with a client with full knowledge of the client's order history, credit worthiness, applicable discounts, and so on, and be prepared to offer the best deal to the client based on real data. Sales personnel can also assess the impact

Mobile scenarios

on their business of each new deal they offer their client right on the spot.

> Sales people can access available-to-promise data while deciding whether to commit to a larger sales order or not with the knowledge that they will be able to meet that larger or changed order. What if the client's plans change? Sales personnel can check the impact on the spot.

> Procurement personnel can access spend information on a particular vendor, and this can help them negotiate a better deal for their company. They can then assess the impact of the new deal in future spend.

> Maintenance personnel can access the history of a particular piece of equipment while on the field.

What is the typical time between failures of this particular part or system? Which warehouse can I get a new one from, given my location? The answers to these questions are the very purpose of SAP's Business Analytics tools, such as BusinessObjects, SAP BW, and SAP HANA. However, they are tools that natively deliver analytics solutions to desktop and web.

SAP BusinessObjects Mobile was created to enable the delivery of SAP Business Analytics content to mobile devices.

SAP BusinessObjects Mobile

SAP BusinessObjects Mobile enables the delivery of SAP BusinessObjects Business Intelligence content on mobile devices, such as iPhone, iPad, Android, and Blackberry.

Secure access to corporate data

SAP BusinessObjects Mobile is a container that manages access to corporate data securely and delivers many SAP BusinessObjects solutions via a mobile device. The same SAP Crystal Reports, SAP BusinessObjects Web Intelligence, and SAP BusinessObjects Dashboards that can be normally visualized on the corporate network via a desktop or laptop computer is delivered to mobile devices, on the go, with the simple use of SAP BusinessObjects Mobile.

Figure 16.3 shows a typical dashboard delivered on an Apple iPad with SAP BusinessObjects Mobile.

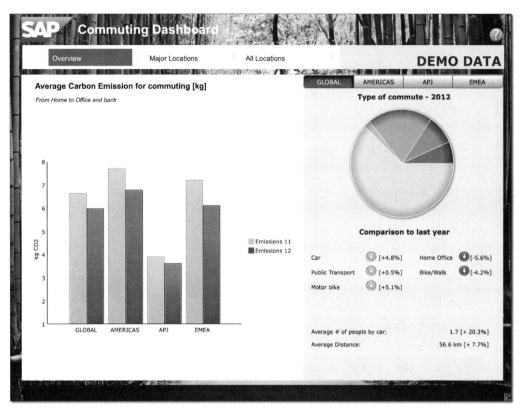

Figure 16.3 A Sample Dashboard Delivered via SAP BusinessObjects Mobile

SAP Mobile Platform

SAP Mobile Platform (SMP) is a set of technologies that help mobile developers to build, deploy, and manage secure and scalable enterprise-grade applications that connect the workforce with their organizations. The platform is a result of the evolution of a number of technologies acquired and developed by SAP, such as Sybase Unwired Platform, Syclo Agentry, and Sybase Mobilizer.

Technology for mobile developers

SMP enables end-to-end development of complete mobile solutions that leverage the corporate systems and databases securely, using open technologies, such as HTTP OData, HTML5, REST API, and Apache Cordova.

Components SMP's components include the following:

> SAP Mobile Platform Server (on premise)

> SAP Mobile Platform Cloud

> SAP Mobile Platform SDK

Figure 16.4 illustrates the architecture of SAP Mobile Platform.

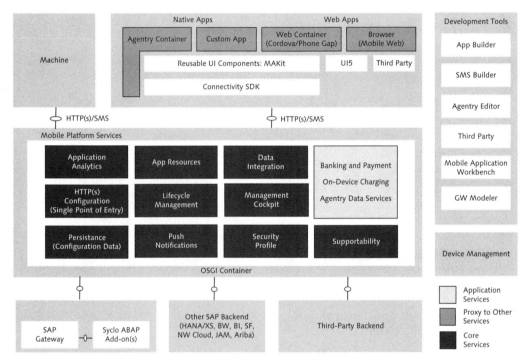

Figure 16.4 SAP Mobile Platform Architecture

We will go over the different components of the architecture in the following subsections.

SAP Mobile Platform Server (On Premise)

The SMP server is an application server that manages mobile applications, back-end synchronization, communication, security, transactions, and scheduling.

It helps the development team deploy applications and manage application security, and also acts as a gateway between the corporate systems and the mobile applications.

For the administrator, it provides a convenient way to manage tasks such as: who uses which application where, who has which version. It also gives the administrator an easy way to deploy applications in and out of the enterprise.

Some of its features include the following:

> Native push notification

> Authentication and secure onboarding (device registration)

> Administration, monitoring, application registration, and lifecycle management

> Reporting on mobile application usage characteristics

> Secure, reliable, and easy-to-consume access to business systems (both on premise and in the cloud)

> Centralized administration dashboard to configure and manage mobile applications

> Support for native and HTML5 application development using REST API services, Sencha, and Appcelerator

The secure onboarding is exposed as a RESTful service for client consumption. The platform enables proxy communication of any HTTP data source, such as SAP Gateway, SAP BusinessObjects, and SAP and non-SAP backend systems. SAP Cloud Connector serves as the link between on-demand applications in SAP Mobile Platform and existing on premise systems.

The SAP Mobile Platform Server runs on both Windows and Unix.

SAP Mobile Platform Cloud

SAP Mobile Platform Cloud delivers the same functionality as the SMP server, ready to be consumed in the cloud, offered by SAP as a platform as a service (PAAS). The availability of the platform in the cloud significantly reduces entry barriers, as it eliminates the need to install on premise mobile platform servers. This makes it cost-effective, easier and faster for companies of all sizes to deploy the solution with minimum disruption.

The platform enables interoperability with both on premise and cloud-based servers, both with SAP or non-SAP systems.

SAP Mobile Platform SDK

SAP Mobile Platform SDK is a set of client-side tools that aids the mobile developer in building solutions that integrate with SAP enterprise software and other non-SAP systems.

The SAP Mobile Platform SDK leverages open-source technologies and standards that most developers are familiar with. These tools lets the developer build web-based, hybrid, and native solutions, based on most common platforms, such as Android, iOS, Blackberry, and Windows.

Tools for the developer

Its components are several tools that increase the developer's productivity, including the following:

> **Native OData**
> The *OData SDK* provides an open and flexible framework for native applications to interact with OData services in both online and (as of SDK 3.0) offline applications. It is compatible with iOS, Android, Blackberry, and Windows.

> **MAF (Mobile Application Framework)**
> Provides reusable components to be used with native applications, including common features and functions, such as user authentication.

> **REST API**
> Enables standard HTTP client applications running in any platform (be they native, web based, or hybrid) to access SAP Mobile Platform REST services.

> **Kapsel**
> A set of SAP plugins built for Apache Cordova to develop hybrid applications. The Kapsel plugins enable the access to SAP Mobile Platform features, such as application lifecycle management, logon and single sign-on functionality, and push notifications.

> **Mobile Application Workbench**
> Eclipse-based editor to enable building resources that can be used to customize mobile applications without recompiling code.

> **Agentry Designer**
> Eclipse-based editor and SDKs to help the developer build meta-data-driven applications.

> **SMS Builder**
> Tools that help the developer visually compose and test SMS mobile applications.

> **Portal Templates**
> Reference web applications that help the developer understand available features and that can even be customized to meet clients' mobile-banking needs.

Although most SAP Mobile SDK tools are built for a Microsoft Windows client, there are some tools that are specific for Mac OS—in particular, those that support native development for iOS devices.

Mobile Application Development Tools

The field of mobile development for the enterprise is relatively new. Although consumer applications pop up all the time, applications for the corporate user are still being developed. SAP recognizes that many of the new corporate applications will be developed by the organizations that now use SAP ERP and by independent developers, so SAP has made several tools available that can be used to develop the applications that organizations need.

In this section, we will go over some of these tools.

SAP Gateway

SAP Gateway is an add-on to a company's ABAP-based SAP Net-Weaver system that allows developers to expose that system's data to other applications by creating open RESTful services based on OData standards. These RESTful services can then be accessed by web, mobile web, hybrid, and native applications via the HTTP protocol. These services can be exposed using JSON, XML, or ATOM standards.

All programming languages can communicate

In simple terms, any programming language that can send requests via HTTP protocol and interpret the response will be able to communicate with an SAP NetWeaver system. All they have to do is to to send and receive data to an SAP NetWeaver system, which has been exposed with the use of SAP Gateway.

This means that native mobile applications built with Java, Objective C, C#, and so on can easily communicate with SAP NetWeaver systems. The same is true for web- and network-enabled applications built with Python, Ruby, JavaScript, JSP, and most other modern languages.

OData, SAP NetWeaver, and SAPUI5

The person building the user-interfaced application does not necessarily have to be familiar with the SAP NetWeaver system's data dictionary to build "killer" apps that interact with SAP's systems; all they need is the knowledge of the OData services that have been exposed by the system connected to the SAP Gateway.

SAPUI5 libraries (which are based on JavaScript) make full use of OData services. Together, SAPUI5 and SAP Gateway form an important foundation for web and mobile development for organizations using SAP NetWeaver systems; they are tightly integrated and can dramatically increase the developer's productivity.

REST

REST (representational state transfer) is an architecture for the web. The REST service receives requests from the consumer process with one of four methods—GET, PUT, POST, or DELETE—and with parameters that define what is being requested and that identify the consumer process. For each method invoked, the RESTful service performs a defined task. The REST service then returns data to the calling process, typically in JSON or XML format.

OData

RESTful service

OData (Open Data Protocol) is an open web protocol that creates a RESTful service that allows the caller process to perform a database query (equivalent to SQL's Select, Update, Delete, etc.). The service returns data back to the consumer processes in JSON or XML formats and informs the result of executing the returns.

SAP AppBuilder

SAP AppBuilder is a browser-based rapid-development tool that allows the developer to build web-based mobile applications by simply dragging and dropping controls and using JavaScript to define their behavior.

Browser-based rapid-development tool

Its WYSIWYG (what you see is what you get) interface creates fully-functioning applications. It leverages standard technologies (HTML5/JavaScript) using SAPUI5 and can communicate with SAP and non-SAP backend systems with the use of OData and REST services.

AppBuilder is available for Windows and for Apple OS. Figure 16.5 shows some of the features of the user interface.

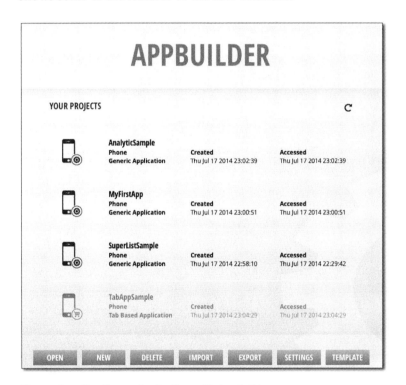

Figure 16.5 Creating an Application with AppBuilder

SAPUI5

SAPUI5 is a powerful productivity tool for the web and mobile SAP developer. It is comprised of a set of client-side libraries based on

HTML5 and JavaScript

HTML5 and JavaScript that can be used to build rich, web-based applications for both mobile devices and desktop computers. It uses open-source frameworks and well-known standards, such as HTML, CSS, JavaScript, and JSON.

It has a set of modern themes that can be used to build great-looking applications and rich, web-based and hybrid mobile applications. Some themes and libraries are specifically targeted to mobile devices—such as Android, iOS, Blackberry—and create applications that look and feel native.

SAPUI5 forms the basic building blocks of all of SAP's web and mobile web–focused development tools, such as SAP AppBuilder, SAP Fiori, and SAP HANA XS applications. It is also used by SAP internally to develop their web, mobile web, and SAP HANA XS applications.

OpenU15 is the open-source version of SAPUI5, supplied under the Apache 2.0 license and available from *http://sap.github.io/openui5/*.

Conclusion

The demand for enterprise and work-related applications is only going to grow. SAP has been aware of this trend and has been positioning itself to help the business and developer communities deliver the solutions that they need. In this chapter, you learned:

> How to deliver content on mobile devices: web-based, native, and hybrid applications.

> About options that will keep enterprise data secure on many devices.

> About developer tools for mobile development, such as SAP Gateway, OData, and SAPUI5.

SAP professionals can only feel excited about the opportunities that this trend brings and the ways in which all technologies will converge and how much more exciting working with SAP technologies will be.

In the next chapter, we will continue to discuss tools, but this time for employees who work with enterprise information.

17

User Productivity Tools for Information Workers

The interface and tools that an SAP solution presents to your employees and managers are very important parts of its usefulness. In this chapter, we will explore SAP's easy-to-use interface, combined with access to data and analytics offered by portals and roles. In addition, we will look at another powerful feature, the ability for employees and managers to use self-service workspaces to get work done based on their roles. Because SAP NetWeaver enables these technologies, they are available to many of SAP's applications to help boost your productivity. Finally, we will show you how access to data from mobile devices opens up opportunities for employees, regardless of where they are.

Portals and Roles

A portal is like a technology dashboard that IT can customize to contain certain pieces and that employees can personalize to access the centrally stored data they need—whether that data is analytics, order-status information, or customer records (for example). Depending on

Read Chapter 18 for more about SAP NetWeaver

the role a person plays in your organization, he will be given access to a certain set of data.

Understanding Portals

Portals are essentially based on the technology used in web browsers, and they offer an interface you can use to access and view information from different data sources. Instead of logging on to a variety of systems or opening several pieces of software, an employee can use a portal to get to all of the information he needs. Workers can also drill down through deeper and deeper levels of information, depending on the level of detail they need.

Beyond receiving data

When you put a portal together with the functionality of SAP applications such as SAP ERP, you can go beyond having employees simply receive data. They can use features of those applications to publish documents to team sites for collaboration, track project progress, and even perform searches that tap into several systems at one time to get results (see Figure 17.1).

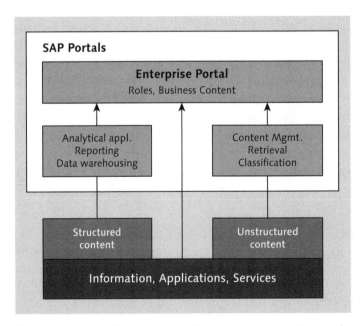

Figure 17.1 Portals Give Workers All of the Tools and Data They Need in One Location

Tip

The SAP Enterprise Portal (part of SAP NetWeaver) brings together the world of information, applications, data, and services for specific roles and topics:

> Internal and external information and services

> SAP applications and non-SAP applications

> Structured information (quantitative) and unstructured (qualitative)

> Data warehousing and analytical applications

> Content Management

The content in the SAP Enterprise Portal can be accessed through a variety of browsers and mobile devices.

Portals can even connect employees with systems outside of your walls, such as your business partners' or vendors' systems. This allows your partners to have access to up-to-the-minute information they can use to service your company's requirements (e.g., replenishing inventory of a component) and provides you and your partners with an environment for collaboration on various projects or initiatives.

Portals to third parties

Portals also can provide a window into the functionality of software your employees are already comfortable with, such as Microsoft Outlook for email and scheduling, right from within a single interface.

Portal to familiar functionalities/ applications

Portals, which are spaces where data is collected in one place, are one part of the story. The other part is how you can customize and personalize which information goes to whom. For that, you need to understand how roles work and the way that portals are connected to underlying information and functionality in your system.

Understanding iViews

With SAP Enterprise Portal, your IT employees can build and customize portals using templates along with HTML code and elements called *iViews*. These iViews are small applications that help connect the portal to the underlying data and applications in your system.

SAP offers hundreds of iViews that relate to industry segments such as aerospace or banking. iViews are the pieces that users can move around to personalize their own portals. You can think of these iViews as small boxes of predesigned content, which you can slot into

Hundreds of iViews

a portal interface. In some cases, one iView will call on another iView to provide related or more detailed content using a process called *eventing*. When you click on content in one iView, you initiate an event that might, for example, call on another iView to provide the backup data for the chart that you were just viewing.

Assigning Roles

Whether you work in a small or large company, each employee probably has a role. One person might work in the human resources department and need access to employee salary and benefits information; another person who supervises the shop floor has no business accessing employee salary information but absolutely must have information about materials inventory and sales orders at his fingertips.

Security and user access

By assigning a role to an employee, such as HR or production, you can also assign a set of accesses to data that an individual needs to get his job done. An HR professional might have access to personnel records, for example, whereas a manufacturing person might have access to customer orders or inventory levels. In an SAP system, those roles can be set up and modified to accommodate changes in position or responsibilities.

The ability of IT to customize and of employees to personalize portals helps you make each worker and manager more productive. Role-based capabilities are currently available in SAP ERP Human Capital Management (HCM), SAP ERP Operations, and SAP ERP Financials.

 Tip

SAP offers portal templates to get you started. These templates are based on typical business processes, such as sales. They give you a head start to personalizing templates for the various people in your company.

 Example

An IT person assigns a role to a worker and provides certain access privileges. Based on that role, an employee can, to a certain extent, personalize his own portals by selecting from a set of options. An assistant in the accounting department can choose the data and tools he needs, as can the CFO, based on his job in the enterprise. Just as you might personalize your ISP's home page by adding the weather report, your horoscope, and sports scores, you can personalize a portal to display different types of information and functionality from a single page.

A *guided procedure* is a user-interface component that represents a step-by-step process that a user follows to complete a process. Each step in the guided procedure might impact a different application. IT organizations can use guided procedures that help employees work through the steps of a typical business process, much as a wizard in a typical software program prompts you to move through the steps of setting up a new piece of hardware or changing browser settings.

Guided procedures

Now let us see how portals are built and why they are so flexible.

How SAP NetWeaver Supports Portals

SAP NetWeaver is the platform that runs SAP and non-SAP applications, data, and user interfaces, including portals. In the area of portals, it provides several essential elements.

First, SAP NetWeaver contains the repository of enterprise services. Enterprise services allow an SAP application to call on just the functions it needs rather than an entire application, because they break business processes down into bite-sized chunks.

Enterprise services

Next, the SAP NetWeaver Developer Studio (NWDS) tool and Portal Development Kit (PDK) can be used to design and deploy portal applications. During the design phase, you can use predefined, packaged portal content to expedite your portal implementation. This business content consists of iViews bundled into hundreds of role-specific business packages based on solutions from SAP.

The SAP Enterprise Portal component provides functionality that allows you to manage the portal infrastructure. The portal also supports knowledge-management functions, enabling users to find, organize, and access unstructured content stored in SAP and non-SAP data stores.

The SAP Enterprise Portal component is tightly integrated with other functionality in SAP NetWeaver, including SAP Business Warehouse (SAP BW) and SAP NetWeaver Master Data Management (SAP NetWeaver MDM). These components consolidate and harmonize data to deliver information and analytics through portals that users can work with in their daily tasks.

SAP Enterprise Portal integration

Tip

The SAP Process Orchestration component (SAP PO) is the tool that helps you exchange data between SAP and non-SAP applications.

Within portals, you can build self-service functionality that enables employees to handle common business processes themselves to save time. The next section looks at collaborative tools and self-service.

Collaborative Tools

To help you improve productivity in your enterprise, SAP makes several useful collaboration tools available. Let us review these in the upcoming subsections.

Workspaces

Workspaces are essentially portals where people working on the same project inside and outside of your company can share data and communicate. Workspaces come in two types: personal and team. Each type can include calendars and schedules, lists of tasks, areas for discussions and chats, and even the sharing of applications.

SAP E-Recruiting

Additional collaborative features—either built into SAP NetWeaver or available through SAP applications—include the ability to check others' calendars and schedule them for meetings, instant-messaging features, shared folders, and broadcasting report views to others via SAP BW. One great example of collaborative features is SAP E-Recruiting, with which a hiring manager and an HR professional can collaborate on the hiring process for a position or positions.

Discussion Forums and Wikis

SAP Enterprise Portal also enables organizations to set up discussion forums and wikis. These collaborative tools help users publish information and collaborate quickly in decision and documentation processes. Discussion forums allow people to share ideas about various topics and participate in group decision making. Wiki pages allow many users to reach consensus on definitions in projects, plans, and other key information. Simple, web-based user interfaces reduce learning time and make it easy to work with people securely both inside and outside of your organization.

Collaborative features such as workspaces and wikis are wonderful, but what about the employees who practically live on the road? For these employees, mobile productivity helps them get their work done and stay in touch.

Self-Service

There was a time in the business world when managers would dictate information to secretaries who would then type that information into a document. It took two people and sometimes a few drafts to get a simple memo written, approved, signed, and sent out. Not that long ago, this model changed and managers began to type their own memos and letters into computers, cutting out the middleperson and saving money and time.

A self-service workspace is a similar concept; it provides users with role-based access to applications and information required to perform certain tasks. Why should you have to play phone tag or email tag with somebody in a travel department to book your trip when you could just fill out an online form, pick your flights and hotel, and be done with it? SAP provides self-service capabilities that enable both employees and managers to streamline several areas of functionality.

Self-service workspaces

 Tip

There are two types of self-service applications: employee self-services (ESS) and manager self-services (MSS). Applications in ESS can be accessed by all employees who were granted access to the ESS iViews. Applications in MSS can only be accessed by managers who were granted access to the MSS iViews. Typically, MSS- and ESS-related iViews are present in the same portal and are accessed by clicking on the respective ESS or MSS tabs.

Employee Self-Service Workspaces

Via portals, employees can take advantage of several self-service activities (see Figure 17.2). Doing so saves duplication of effort and the errors that sometimes result from duplication of data entry. Once entered, those who deal with the data (e.g., travel-expense analysts or company travel agents) can access it in centralized databases.

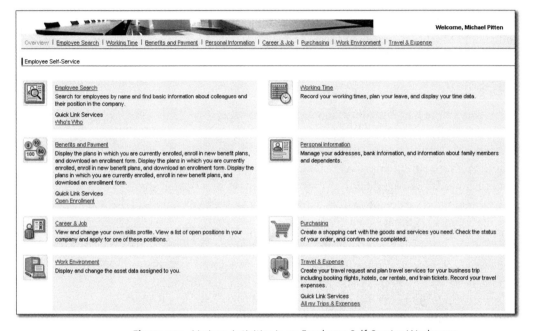

Figure 17.2 Various Activities in an Employee Self-Service Workspace

ESS components

Areas of ESS include the following:

> **Personal Information**
> Employees can access their personal information in HR databases and make changes to data such as home address or emergency contact.

> **Travel and Expense**
> Employees can set up business travel and record travel expenses.

> **Time Management**
> Employees working on projects or on an hourly basis can report the hours they worked, request leave, and review their working schedules.

> **Corporate Learning**
> Employees can access training schedules, get manager approval, and sign up for classes.

> **Corporate Information Management**
> Employees have access to general corporate information such as security policies and the employee handbook.

> **Benefits Management**
> Employees can enroll in benefits programs and view current benefits participation.

> **Life and Work Event Management**
> Employees can update data on life event changes, such as marital status or the birth of a child, and view their employment history.

> **Payment Administration**
> Employees can deal with various salary and compensation issues.

> **Internal Opportunities**
> Employees can review job openings, submit applications, and check on hiring status.

> **Procurement**
> Employees can buy products or services or request maintenance or repair for equipment using self-service.

ESS can be used by just about everybody in your company. MSS, on the other hand, is uniquely suited to those who wear manager hats.

Who can use ESS and MSS?

 Tip

A specialized self-service workspace is called a work center. Work centers allow employees to create portals that are focused on certain types of work—for example, particular business units or a group such as manufacturing or HR. Rather than adding this work-specific content to the employee's main portal interface (which typically includes the employees' schedule, commonly used applications, and analytics related to the overall job), you can create work centers.

For example, a manufacturing manager might include his schedule, contacts, and analytics about manufacturing productivity on the portal he opens every morning, but he might call up a management work center in which he accesses all job-performance information, staffing projections, employee vacation schedules, salary information, and so on when working on employee-related issues.

Manager Self-Service Workspaces

Managers will be on the receiving end of some ESS requests, specifically those that require approvals such as leave requests, training approvals, or purchasing requests. In addition, there are some manager-specific self-services that help to streamline any manager's job, including the following:

Access analytics

> **Budget**
>
> Budget planning and monitoring features help managers get their numbers in line. Managers can access analytics that help them keep track of variances and make corrections to posted budget numbers (see Figure 17.3).

Tools for workforce planning

> **Staffing**
>
> Recruitment and staff-review procedures are two HR-related self-service features. Managers can use tools for compensation planning, viewing attendance records, and handling future staffing planning.

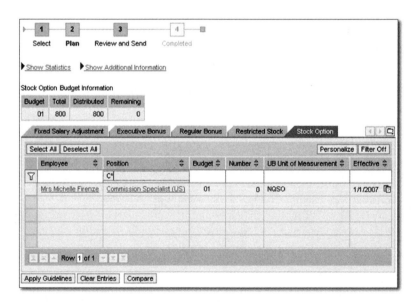

Figure 17.3 Compensation Planning

Tip

> With SAP ERP, you can create a personnel record for each employee with all of the relevant details, such as compensation, attendance history, vacation time available, and so on. You can make one set of data available to managers and another set available to the employee, depending on their need to know.

In addition to self-service workspaces, SAP provides tools that enable collaboration to make people more productive, which we will examine in the next section.

Mobile Productivity

Mobile computing is essential in a business world, where we rush from appointment to appointment and from one office to another—often in different countries. Staying in touch and being able to tap into your corporate home base has become imperative.

The SAP NetWeaver Mobile component provides an infrastructure that allows people on the move to use links from their mobile devices to SAP core systems. You install SAP NetWeaver Mobile on each mobile device and then, when used with SAP mobile applications, you can access many of SAP Business Suite's features from mobile devices. IT can work with users to customize a mobile setup that works for their needs. For more details about mobility options from SAP, refer to Chapter 16.

Link mobile device to SAP system

Mobile devices can use local business logic to process actions, such as entering an order, without having to access the home system. In locations where wireless or dial-up access is not available, this means that workers can still do their jobs on the road.

Back at the office, mobile users can synchronize their devices with the core system to ensure that data is kept current, orders are processed, and other transactions, such as generating invoices or customer confirmations, are initiated.

Mobile device synchronization

Voice recognition Finally, by using the voice-recognition capabilities built into SAP NetWeaver, workers can use cell phones to submit or request data or initiate transactions they used to have to handle back at their desks.

 Tip

Synchronization of SAP NetWeaver Mobile provides a secure encrypted transmission by using the HTTPS protocol that ensures that wireless connections are safe for your sensitive data. In addition, role-based authentication, authentication using passwords, and integrity protection keep your office systems safe fom outside attacks via mobile devices.

You can use a standard browser for mobile access, or you can customize a user interface via which your mobile workers can access your systems.

 Tip

If your company has to maintain and repair mobile assets, such as a vehicle fleet or utility stations, you may want to look into SAP Service and Asset Management. Workers in the field can use its features, along with SAP NetWeaver Mobile and SAP Mobile Asset Management (SAP MAM), to deal with asset installation, maintenance, or repair out on the road and track their activities back to your main system. You can even track maintenance activities based on counter readings (such as an electric meter reading at various locations) and schedule future maintenance.

Conclusion

In this chapter, we provided you with an overview of some very useful tools to make your workers more productive:

> Portals with role-based access for delivering information to and sharing information with users

> Collaborative tools, such as forums and wikis

> Self-service workspaces that allow people to access many common business processes, such as scheduling training for themselves

> Tools for mobile productivity to keep workers in touch with information while on the road

Now that you understand the useful tools that an SAP system can offer your workers, we are going to delve a bit deeper into the architecture and technology behind the tools.

In Chapter 18, we will discuss user-friendly SAP: Duet, Alloy, SAP Fiori, and Adobe Interactive Forms, the technology platforms that provide a way for Microsoft Office and Lotus Notes to interface with SAP Business Suite functionality from the familiar Office and Notes environments. In addition, we will see how SAP Fiori provides a consumer-grade usability experience and how paper-based forms can be replaced by Adobe Interactive Forms.

User-Friendly SAP: Duet, Alloy, Adobe Interactive Forms, and SAP Fiori

Enterprise computing software is constantly being upgraded with new features, easier-to-use interfaces, and more sophisticated capabilities. Although these features provide a wonderful starting point, there are several SAP tools that you may want to make more accessible to your employees.

For instance, you can encourage employees to use SAP tools and save time and money on training by allowing them to leverage the software programs and functionality to which they are accustomed. That's what Duet and Alloy are all about: providing a way for Microsoft Office and Lotus Notes users to interface with SAP Business Suite functionality from their familiar environments.

In addition, you can replace paper-based forms with HTML-based SAP Interactive Forms software by Adobe, which can be viewed by anybody. SAP Interactive Forms by Adobe make entering data easier and allow you to capture form data electronically. Implementing such forms inside or outside of your organization can make your employees' and customers' lives much easier and save you time and money.

Microsoft Office, Lotus Notes, and Adobe Interactive Forms interfacing with SAP Business Suite

SAP Fiori is another user-friendly tool. SAP Fiori is a collection of apps that provides a consumer-grade usability experience to the end user (we already touched on the mobility apps in Chapter 16). Fiori uses interactive, attractive UI elements and provides consistent usability experience across all device types without additional implementation requirements.

Let us begin the review of these practical tools with an overview of Duet and how it brings familiar interfaces into SAP functionality.

Duet: Providing Information Workers with What They Need

Microsoft and SAP

Duet is a joint offering of SAP and Microsoft that can work with many of the SAP applications, including SAP Customer Relationship Management (SAP CRM), SAP ERP 6.0, SAP Supply Chain Management (SAP SCM), and SAP Supplier Relationship Management (SAP SRM). Essentially, Duet allows office workers to take full advantage of SAP business processes and business intelligence through the Microsoft Office environment (see Figure 18.1). Workers can use features such as analytics delivered through Microsoft Excel, or scheduling tools via Microsoft Outlook. These functions are synchronized between Microsoft Exchange and SAP.

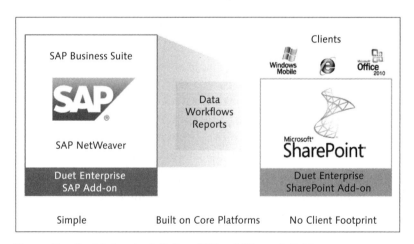

Figure 18.1 Duet Enterprise Is Built on SAP and Microsoft Platforms

By allowing workers to use the software they are familiar with, you cut down on training time and help people feel comfortable participating in new enterprise processes that you introduce. As a result, you can increase corporate policy compliance, improve decision making, and save time and money.

Key Functions and Features

The initial release of Duet software includes four scenarios for self-service functionality that you can access through Microsoft Office applications:

> **Time Management**
> Allows you to schedule, record time spent, and review project work and billable hours via Outlook's calendar feature. This data is then automatically updated in the SAP ERP system.

> **Budget Monitoring**
> Provides access to financial information that you use to create and monitor budgets and to alerts for budget variances and postings, transfers of budgets, and posting adjustments. This data can all be integrated with SAP ERP Financials.

> **Team Management**
> Allows users to update human resource records to which they have access and perform activities such as searching for open positions in the organization or entering management approvals through Outlook.

> **Leave Management**
> Enables users to submit leave requests in the Outlook calendar that can then be integrated with approval guidelines and HR processes in the SAP system.

Functionalities that were implemented and available in Duet Enterprise 2.0 include:

> **Travel Management**
> Allows employees to make travel arrangements for air, hotel, and car rentals using Outlook, ensuring compliance with company travel policies via SAP.

Duet scenarios

Duet Enterprise 2.0

> **Sales Management**
> Helps you manage sales activities, including making sales appointments, updating sales contacts, and obtaining pricing approvals through Outlook. You can access sales analytics from SAP CRM as well and even use Microsoft Word to generate purchase agreements.

> **Purchasing Management**
> Enables you to handle purchase order processes and supply chain planning in the familiar spreadsheet interface. You can also analyze supplier performance data via SAP SRM.

> **Reporting and Analytics**
> Allows you to request one-time-only reports and scheduled reports, and look at SAP analytics through Outlook or Excel. SAP BusinessObjects Live Office is a plug-in for the Office environment that allows the user to use the BI client tools inside Excel, Word, PowerPoint, and Outlook for reporting and analytics.

> **Demand Planning**
> Involves the use of Excel to create planning sheets and analyze demand data you obtain from SAP SCM.

> **Recruitment Management**
> Lets managers and HR staff view open positions, schedule interviews, and provide candidate feedback.

> **Workflow Approval**
> Enables managers to approve such things as invoices, new hires, marketing promotions, and merit increases through Outlook.

Reporting and analytics

These business process-focused tasks, which often involve a great deal of data entry and retrieval of data, are a good match for the capabilities of Microsoft Office applications. Performing these activities in a familiar interface requires little, if any, training. Moreover, the data is automatically integrated with SAP Enterprise products, thereby avoiding the need for rekeying and any resulting errors.

How Duet Works

Duet components

How exactly does Duet work? Essentially, it uses the web services architecture of SAP NetWeaver to allow direct calls from a client to a web service. Microsoft Exchange Server is used to route messages in the Duet system. For technically-minded readers, here are the details of Duet:

> A client add-on module for the Office environment includes a runtime engine, secure cache storage for data, and an output queue.

> An SAP add-on for the backend SAP ERP software provides an engine to bundle service requests to SAP Business Suite applications, configuration tools, and a metadata (data about data) repository.

> The Duet software server enables deployment of Duet and allows communication between the Microsoft and SAP components. This server includes a runtime metadata repository, an element that formats and routes information in the Microsoft Exchange Server, and a module that sends updates to client systems.

This architecture offers several layers of security that come from both Windows and SAP. This security is easy for employees to live with because it is available in a single sign-on (SSO), role-based system. When a user signs on, he is authenticated at the desktop, but Duet then maps the user token to the user profile in SAP. Then, depending on the user's role in the organization, he is granted certain access privileges.

 Tip

Duet allows offline web service calls, because the client add-on offers secured caching functionality, which stores sets of data to be used both offline and online. This means that a worker on the road can access information such as a contact form offline. If a user enters data while offline, it is automatically updated in SAP the next time the user logs on to the system. In addition, for the sake of security and privacy, you can designate sensitive information to only be available through online access.

Configuring Duet is relatively simple. There are several preconfigured templates, such as those for typical employee leave requests. When you install Duet, your administrator can simply choose the types of built-in requests to use for your organization.

Preconfigured templates

Examples of Duet in Action

Imagine Outlook as a window on a wide variety of activities, not just an email tool and a contact database. For example, if you work in a sales organization, your typical day using Duet in the Outlook interface might be something like the following.

A typical day with Duet
You make a morning sales call in a nearby town. In trying to close a big deal with the client, you decide to request approval from your boss to offer special pricing. Within minutes of entering the request as an Outlook task, you get approval.

On the short flight home, you track your time offline. When you get back to the office and log on to the system, your hours are automatically delivered to the SAP system in which billable hours are tracked.

Before you go into your sales appointment, you check your contact database through Outlook to be sure you have all of the necessary background information about your customer (i.e., spouse's name, interests, and past-order-related issues that help you connect during the sales call).

Back at the office, contract in hand, you request a report on your customer's payment history, which you receive via an email in your inbox. If you want to see more detail, you can drill down through levels of data stored in SAP from within Outlook. You can even export the report to Excel and modify and update it there.

Drilling through levels of data in SAP from Outlook
You spend some time scheduling meetings and appointments for the following week, and they are synchronized. Next, you have to make travel arrangements for next week's sales calls, so you submit travel requests via Outlook. The system automatically suggests itineraries that are in compliance with company travel policies for you to approve. In addition to the tools just outlined, you can use Outlook with Duet to approve employee requests, request and approve leave time, access budget data, authorize bonuses or vacation, and more.

Microsoft is not the only company that has found synergies with SAP. IBM has also found a way to integrate SAP into its products through a new application called Alloy, which we'll discuss next.

Alloy: Joining SAP and Lotus Notes

For more than 40 years, SAP and IBM have worked together to enhance the user experience of their joint clientele. For companies using Lotus Notes, SAP has teamed with IBM to create a new application called Alloy. Alloy, like Duet, allows your employees to continue using the tools they are already familiar with—in this case, Lotus Notes—while providing access to data within the SAP Business Suite (see Figure 18.2). Workers also have greater flexibility to view reports (online and offline), obtain procurement data, and use analytics through the integration of SAP Business Suite information into Lotus Notes. Your workers are more productive, because all of the information they need to make an accurate and timely decision is immediately available to them.

IBM and SAP

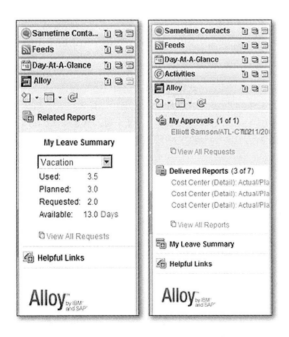

Figure 18.2 Using Lotus Notes to Access SAP Data

Alloy's Key Features

The first release of Alloy provides access to the following SAP functions through Lotus Notes:

Alloy 1.0 features

> **Reports Management**
  Allows you to personalize, schedule, and access reports from SAP Business Suite applications via Lotus Notes while maintaining data security. Reports can then be shared with and viewed (both online and offline) by coworkers without violating security.

> **Leave Management and Travel Management**
  Permit you to submit and approve leave and travel requests through Lotus Notes.

> **Lotus Notes sidebar**
  Workers can view appropriate contextual information so that processing leave and travel requests is done within the framework of the approval guidelines established by your company in SAP ERP.

> **Workflow Decision Management**
  Helps minimize the risks when you are making decisions by bringing your corporate decision steps from other SAP business processes (such as budgeting, recruitment, and purchasing) into the Lotus Notes client.

With Alloy, after you perform transactions or make decisions in Lotus Notes using the features described previously, the data transferred to the SAP enterprise products is automatically updated. This reduces the likelihood of errors introduced by manually reentering information.

Alloy components

Take a look at the nuts and bolts of Alloy. In essence, Alloy creates a gateway service used to pass messages between the SAP software (e.g., SAP Business Suite or SAP NetWeaver) and the IBM Lotus Domino server. These messages are passed through the gateway using web services and XML. To initiate this service, SAP and Lotus Domino need the following:

> Client plug-ins that improve performance and flexibility by handling metadata and the central Alloy sidebar.

> An Alloy add-on that is deployed on the SAP NetWeaver server to collect and bundle data received from SAP BW and SAP Business Suite. After this information is collected, it is passed to the Lotus Notes client.

> An IBM Lotus Domino Alloy add-on module that likewise collects and bundles data received from Lotus Notes, passes it back to the

SAP server, and then hands it off to the SAP Business Suite applications.

The Advantages of Alloy

Because of the type of architecture that is used by Alloy, workers only use a single sign-on. When a worker requests information from SAP via Lotus Notes, the Lotus Domino Alloy add-on validates the worker's signature against his profile stored in SAP. If there is a positive validation, the request is passed to the SAP system. This maintains security for your system and data and makes things easier for your employees.

Alloy advantages

Alloy also supports SAP workflows, which means that relevant information from SAP Business Suite applications displays in the Lotus Notes sidebar to help your employees make accurate decisions on the spot.

Although Alloy comes with a set of standard workflows and reports, it is easy to customize it to reflect the unique processes of your organization. When a manager needs to approve a travel request, for example, the Lotus Notes sidebar can display the current amount of money remaining in the travel budget so he can make the correct decision about the request.

With Alloy and Lotus Notes, if your employees are traveling and working offline, they can view existing SAP reports and make changes. The next time an employee connects to the network, those modifications will automatically be uploaded against the report stored in SAP so that everything stays in sync.

An Everyday Example of Alloy

Late Friday afternoon, one of your employees submits a request to take a trip via the SAP Leave Management application. The next step in the business process requires a manager to evaluate the request and determine whether or not it can be approved.

It is now Sunday evening, and you decide to get a jump on the workweek. When you open your Lotus Notes email, you see the message from your employee requesting vacation time. Because of the Alloy add-ons in SAP and Lotus Domino, the request that was submitted in SAP now appears as a form in your email.

Request via email

Before you approve this request, you review the relevant information provided in the Lotus Notes sidebar, which includes the department calendar that shows the other employees who have requested time off for this same period. In addition, you also see the deadlines for your projects that are coming due during this time. As a final check, you review the summary display of the leave time this employee has already taken and see how much time he has remaining.

Based on the information provided, you approve the leave request. The approval is then routed back through the Lotus Domino Alloy add-on and the SAP Alloy add-on, the changes are applied to the SAP Business Suite application, and the request is then submitted to HR as the next step of your business process.

Because you are about to enter a critical phase in one of your projects, you decide to generate a report to show how much time off remains for the people in your department as well as the dates of the upcoming project milestones. Your report displays in Lotus Notes and allows you to drill down through SAP to view all relevant data. This is a great application if you are using Lotus Notes with SAP.

Now let us move on to look at how Adobe's form technology provides another great match with SAP systems by allowing users to enter and share data easily.

The Paperless Office: Adobe Forms

SAP Interactive Forms software by Adobe

The office of yesterday was jam-packed with paper forms. Perhaps your office today is still groaning under the weight of antiquated forms processing. With SAP Interactive Forms software by Adobe, you are about to get a lot more efficient, at least in the realm of forms.

The Need to Go Paperless

Digital-asset management

A 2004 study by GISTICS, an analyst firm specializing in digital-asset management, estimated that a single paper-based form costs the average enterprise $75,000 a year in labor and materials. Count up the number of forms used in your organization, and the numbers can become staggering.

When a paper form is used for approvals, there is the ever-present danger that the form will go astray or get lost under piles of paperwork. If the approving manager is on the road, everybody waits until he returns to the office to sign off and get things rolling again.

In addition, paper-based forms require data to be reentered into systems, opening you up to the possibility of introducing errors and creating extra work for all involved. Paper forms require additional work to centralize, track, access, and audit data. It is almost impossible to extend your business processes to outside partners, customers, and suppliers without further manual processing.

If you have remote or mobile workers, they will not be able to retrieve up-to-date paper forms or make changes to them if necessary.

 Tip

> Think HTML forms are the answer? Think again. HTML forms may allow you to capture data from them, but they can't be used offline, and they're difficult to print.

Streamlining Business Processes

When you implement SAP Interactive Forms, you may not go entirely paperless, but you can become much more efficient in your handling of forms. These are interactive digital forms that you can actually integrate into the business processes that SAP supports.

The SAP Interactive Forms system creates a bridge between the very structured data that is stored within your enterprise database and the document-based processes you use every day. Data entered into a form by a customer, supplier, or employee can be sent directly to the core databases without further data entry.

 Tip

> Forms change on a regular basis, so it is useful that form design and modification is relatively easy thanks to Adobe technology connected to the SAP NetWeaver development environments for Java and the ABAP programming language.

In the past, if an internal customer placed a larger order, your purchasing clerk may have had to locate a requisition form, complete it, and send it on to another manager for approval. With SAP Interactive Forms, all forms can be requested online, and these forms can already be populated with the requestor's contact and cost center information. SAP's embedded workflow pushes such requests to the approver, ensuring a timely response.

 Tip

When your workers are on the road, they should have access to forms that connect to your backend system seamlessly. Remote users should be able to upload forms and expect that the home-based systems will update rapidly.

With SAP Interactive Forms, an employee on the road could connect to a system such as SAP CRM, upload forms, and instantly update the backend system. A salesperson could even use a downloaded form on a sales call, complete the form, email it to the home office, and print out a copy for the client to retain as a receipt. If the generation of that form triggers a next activity in the organization, such as pulling ordered items for shipment, the submission of the form can be set up to act as such a trigger.

Interactive Forms in the Workplace

What will SAP Interactive Forms look like in your workplace? Here are just some of the form processes that can be streamlined:

> Purchase requisitions
> Personnel administration (Figure 18.3 shows special payments being processed for an employee)
> Cost center change requests
> Expense reports
> Internal requisitions for products or services
> Job applications

Working with SAP Interactive Forms

Interactive forms can be prepopulated with common information, including the company contact information or client address and client number, saving time in generating such forms. By linking fields in the forms to SAP applications, you can automatically capture and distribute data, ensuring that your entire system is up-to-date and accurate.

Special Payment

Reference Number

SAP

Employee Name

Personnel Number

Personnel Area

Position

Purpose of Form

The purpose of this process is to give an employee Special Payment. The process consists of the following steps :

1. Requesting Manager : Enters a reason and an amount for the special payment.
2. Superior Manager : Approves, rejects or sends back to requester.

(In case of warnings or errors once the Superior Manager approves the item can be forwarded to   professional user in step . If now warnings or errors occur the process is completed with step 2)

3.HR Administrator (optional): Analyzes and resolves issues and informs other involved roles.

Form Area for Requesting Manager

Select the date for the payment and press the button   ***Update Display.***
Select   the Payment   Reason and enter an Amount.

Date of Payment

| Update Display |

Annual Salary

Annual Salary retreived with respect to Date of Payment

Figure 18.3 Initiate Special Payments for Your Employees

Forms can be securely sent via email, which is a much more effective way to communicate data than with fax or paper-copy distribution. If you have business partners that supply you with data, you can capture that data via forms and even add customer and partner forms into your own business processes. Forms can also be signed with electronic signatures.

 Tip

SAP Interactive Forms support multiple languages, so if you have an international presence or supplier base you will find it easy to use these forms for international transactions.

Interactive Forms Extend Outside Your Organization

The concept of using interactive forms does not have to stop at your front door. Imagine if you could use these forms for business processes outside of your organization. Implementing such external business processes reduces costs by eliminating the necessity for rekeying data. Examples include the following:

Interacting outside of your business

> A large insurance company can send out an interactive form to a customer to fill out an insurance claim. The form is already prepopulated with customer information, and all the claimant has to do is to fill out the information and send the form back. All information is then electronically stored and forms the basis of the claim.

> Universities are using interactive forms to plan courses. Students can simply mark checkboxes for their chosen subjects. The form can already have some intelligence to ensure that the correct number of study hours is entered. The student then submits the form, and class sizes are updated and appropriate rooms are allocated for the courses.

These are just two examples of how information can be integrated into business cycles using interactive forms technology.

SAP Fiori for SAP Business Suite

SAP Fiori is a collection of applications that provides greater usability experience for frequently used SAP functions. As of mid-2014, there are over 220 role-based apps that can be used by customers who are currently using SAP Business Suite on any database or SAP Business Suite powered by SAP HANA. As seen in Figure 18.4, SAP Fiori works seamlessly on any device; the usability experience is the same whether the app is accessed via a desktop, tablet, or a smartphone. You can find more information about SAP Fiori in Chapter 16.

Types of apps The apps are classified as follows:

> **Transactional apps**
Using these apps, you can perform transactions such as creating a leave request for an employee, creating a travel request, and so on.

> **Fact sheets**
You can these apps to get a display of the contextual information and key facts about central objects used in your business operations. From a fact sheet, you can drill into its details, as well navigate from one fact sheet to a related fact sheet. For now, fact sheets run only on the SAP HANA database.

Figure 18.4 SAP Fiori Apps Can Be Accessed from Any Device and Provide the Same Usability Experience

> **Analytical apps**
> You can use these apps to get real-time information on large volume data in a simplified frontend. These apps help you to monitor key performance indicators (KPIs) in real time and react to changes when required. These apps run only on an SAP HANA database.

 SAP Fiori Options

In SAP Fiori, there are over 60 transactional apps available, over 80 fact sheets, and over 80 analytical apps.

The SAP Fiori apps are organized by user roles, and the SAP Fiori Launchpad is the central entry hub to access all the SAP Fiori apps. From within the Launchpad, the user can access services for navigation, personalization, single sign-on, and search. The Launchpad and the tiles can be customized by the users to meet their needs.

SAP Fiori Launchpad

The Launchpad will display different tiles (see Figure 18.5). What tiles are displayed on the Launchpad depends on the roles and authorizations assigned to that user.

The Launchpad provides the following capabilities:

Capabilities

> **Personalization**
> When the user logs in, the Launchpad will display a home page that contains predefined content based on the user's role. The user can personalize his or her home page by adding tiles from the catalog or by grouping/deleting the tiles.

> **Responsiveness**
> The launch pad can be accessed from any device. The app adapts automatically to the respective screen size.

> **Search**
> The search functionality enables you to search for business objects across your SAP Business Suite applications and to search for apps in the SAP Fiori Launchpad. From the search entry field, you can see a listing of your recent searches or recently launched apps.

> **Session Management**
> You will be able to log in and log out of a session.

> **Single sign-on**
> SSO can be enabled to launch and access the respective systems.

> **Theming and branding support**
> The theme can be customized to reflect the corporate branding.

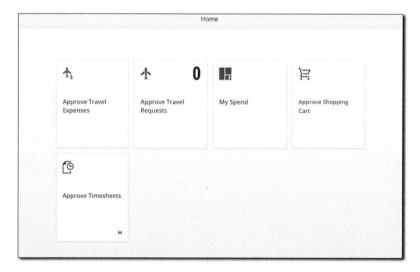

Figure 18.5 Accessing the Different SAP Fiori Apps from the Launchpad

Tip

You can leverage the previously defined roles and authorizations to define which apps and what data a user is allowed to access.

Accessing SAP Fiori Apps as a Manager

Managers can access Fiori apps to process workflow approvals, look up specific information, and perform any self-service tasks.

As an example, as seen in Figure 18.6, the manager accesses the APPROVE TIMESHEETS tile from within the SAP Fiori Launchpad (see Figure 18.5). Once the app is launched, the manager gets a view of all of his or her direct reports and the time recorded by them. The manager can approve or decline the time entries made by his or her direct reports.

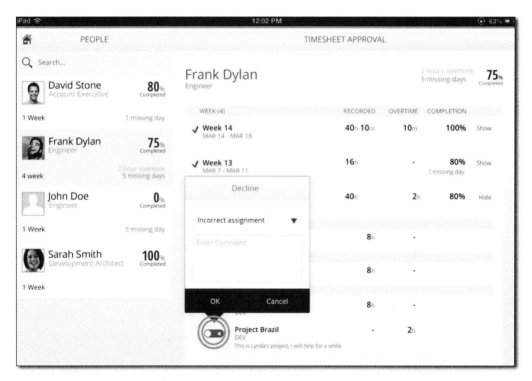

Figure 18.6 Timesheet Access by the Manager

Accessing SAP Fiori Apps as an Employee

Based on the roles and authorizations provided to an employee, the employee can access the apps from within the SAP Fiori Launchpad.

As shown in Figure 18.7, the employee has authorization and roles assigned to access the ORDER FROM REQUISITIONS tile from within the SAP Fiori Launchpad. Once the app is launched, the employee clicks on the ASSIGNED PRS option and reviews the purchase requisitions (PRs) and their status. The employee has the option to create a new purchase order (PO) from within the app as well.

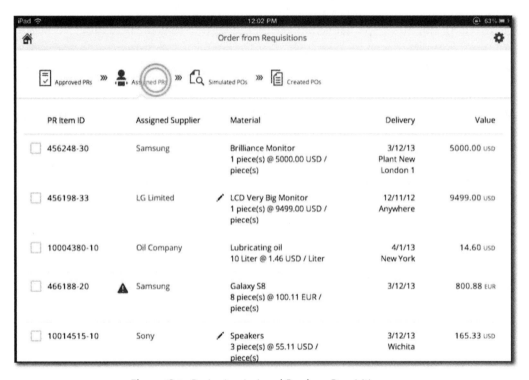

Figure 18.7 Reviewing Assigned Purchase Requisitions

 Note

You can get a full listing of the currently available SAP Fiori apps from SAP Help; visit *http://goo.gl/J1Goyo*.

Conclusion

In this chapter, we explored four technologies that SAP has incorporated to make end users' lives simpler:

> Duet represents a joint venture of Microsoft and SAP that seamlessly adds the familiar interfaces of Microsoft Office products into SAP business processes.

> Alloy, like Duet, allows your employees to continue using the tools they are already familiar with—in this case, Lotus Notes—while providing access to data within the SAP Business Suite.

> SAP Interactive Forms software by Adobe produces well-designed forms that can be built into your everyday processes to make data entry much more efficient.

> SAP Fiori is a collection of apps that provides a consumer-grade user experience. SAP Fiori apps can be accessed from any device and offer the same usability experience irrespective of which device they are accessed from.

Next, in Chapter 19, we will look at SAP NetWeaver, the technology platform for all SAP applications, and what is involved in its implementation.

19

SAP NetWeaver as a Technology Platform

SAP NetWeaver is the technology platform for all SAP applications. In the same way that Microsoft Windows is the operating system for the Microsoft applications you use on a daily basis (for example, Microsoft Office), SAP NetWeaver provides services that allow you to run both SAP and third-party products. A key capability of SAP NetWeaver lies in its integration options that allow various programs and applications in the IT systems to communicate with one another. This means that you can access data from various sources without having to open and close other software applications or log on to systems and log off again. It is also possible to run business applications across various departments and to run these faster, more efficiently, and more seamlessly than before.

This chapter describes how enterprises can use SAP NetWeaver, explains its various components, and provides an outlook for the future development of this technology.

The Role of SAP NetWeaver in Your Enterprise

SAP NetWeaver provides enterprises with a range of functions and tools for integrating and running SAP and third-party products. The platform also provides a technology basis for building and operating

Integrate/run SAP and third-party products

a service-oriented architecture. It comprises functions for creating new applications and services and for enhancing existing ones; these functions allow you to design your IT infrastructure in line with your business strategies. How exactly does this work?

This section provides an overview of the functions and application options provided by SAP NetWeaver. We will discuss the specific components of SAP NetWeaver, on which these functions are based, later in this chapter.

An Integration Platform

SAP NetWeaver integrates users, information, and processes on a single platform. It facilitates communication between users, the administration of and access to data in diverse IT systems, and the execution of business processes across these systems.

SAP NetWeaver integration

Using the existing IT infrastructure represents one way of using SAP NetWeaver's integration functions. It is irrelevant whether this IT infrastructure consists of third-party products, of SAP applications, or a combination of both. If the processes in your enterprise are executed in different types of systems and data is saved in various applications, SAP NetWeaver helps users to locate and consolidate the relevant data in these systems. SAP NetWeaver also takes account of the technical properties and requirements of the various systems and allows these to be managed centrally.

In this way, SAP NetWeaver supports access to all of the data in these systems and reduces technical complexity for users and system administrators. In addition, SAP NetWeaver enables the exchange of data between applications and allows the functions of all SAP applications and tools to be integrated. The section entitled "SAP NetWeaver Components," which appears later in this chapter, explains how this is achieved.

A Composition Platform

Sequencing of useful business applications

Another way to use SAP NetWeaver is to enhance the existing IT infrastructure and make it more flexible. SAP NetWeaver provides the tools that allow you to create new business applications based on existing applications using web services, the ABAP and Java programming languages, or other industry standards. SAP calls this process "composition."

You can, for example, develop new custom applications to meet specific requirements in your enterprise, create portals to enable central access to the functions and data that end users require to do their work, or use subfunctions from SAP applications to build composite applications that combine existing services in completely new business processes.

 Business Content

> In addition to tools for developing new applications, SAP NetWeaver includes business content, which is comprised of integrated templates and industry-specific applications that can be used "out of the box."

Enterprise Services Repository

SAP NetWeaver includes a repository of enterprise services, from which you can compile business processes of your own. An enterprise service is the smallest unit of an application that performs a business function; for example, the creation of an order or a check to determine the creditworthiness of a customer. Enterprise services have standardized interfaces, and their functions and components are described in a standardized form. This means that you can reuse the same enterprise service in various applications without needing to reprogram its function for each application.

Compile business processes for reuse

 Descriptions of Interfaces and Functions

> In terms of technology, enterprise services use recognized web service standards, such as XML (Extensible Markup Language), WSDL (Web Service Description Language), and UDDI (Universal Description, Discovery, and Integration), to describe interfaces and functions.

You can use modeling tools to create custom enterprise services without programming, which means that you need not concern yourself with the technical details of enterprise service implementation. When you use SAP NetWeaver, the underlying complexity is not visible to you because you do not need to use programming languages or web standards. Instead, you can model the individual functions in the language of the relevant business departments.

Create without programming

The latest version of the Enterprise Services Repository contains more than 2,000 enterprise services. In addition to service management, it also includes business process models and business object models, which provide templates to facilitate the creation of your own business processes.

Figure 19.1 depicts the role of SAP NetWeaver as a process and composition environment for SAP landscapes. Here, SAP NetWeaver is shown as a comprehensive environment for the integration of SAP Business Suite applications and external applications. The data that is to be accessed is "abstracted" so that it is no longer relevant which technology is used to access it. The composition platform and its tools enable the creation of individual, flexible, service-oriented applications, which—like the SAP Business Suite applications—access the services in the Enterprise Services Repository.

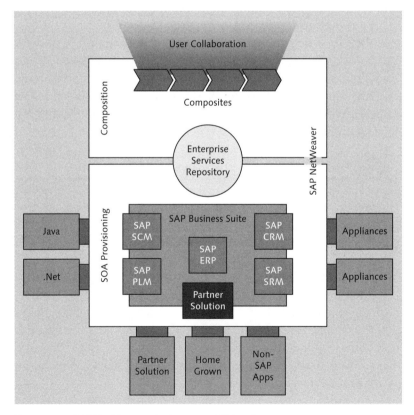

Figure 19.1 SAP NetWeaver: An Integrated IT Landscape

Management of Information and Reports

The third major field of application for SAP NetWeaver comprises the management of information and the creation of reports. The data warehousing and knowledge management functions of SAP NetWeaver help you to more efficiently structure the information that is distributed across all the various systems in your enterprise and improve access to that information. These functions can be used to search for data so that all employees in the enterprise can access consistent information.

In addition, SAP NetWeaver offers tools for analytical applications, which help managers make better business decisions based on up-to-date and meaningful reports.

Making better business decisions

Collaboration between employees is also enhanced through the shared use of data with SAP NetWeaver. Other functions enable, for example, mobile access to important data, which means that employees on business trips can still access the systems they need.

Now that you have been introduced to the functions of SAP Net-Weaver, we will turn our attention to the following section, which discusses the SAP NetWeaver solution map and explains the IT practices that are supported.

The SAP NetWeaver Solution Map

Figure 19.2 shows the SAP NetWeaver solution map. As you can see, SAP NetWeaver supports seven IT practices, which you can use directly or indirectly to tackle business-related challenges. Each of these seven IT practices in turn comprises several scenarios, which allow you to implement the practice step-by-step. If you take a look at the dynamic solution map on the SAP website (*www.sap.com*), you'll notice that each scenario also contains more detailed areas and components, which are required for the implementation of the individual IT practices.

IT practices and scenarios

The IT practices consist of the following functions:

Fields of application for SAP NetWeaver in an enterprise

> **User productivity**
User productivity enablement covers issues relating to the software user interface. It provides users with access to software applications

and information via an interface that is tailored to meet their requirements. User productivity enablement also includes functions for cross-enterprise *collaboration* and knowledge management—which means that you can even collaborate with external partners on a project, share documents, and have centralized access to unstructured data.

> **Information management**
> This functional area provides central master data management and a single repository for supplier, customer, and production data, including user-defined and third-party vendor data. Another tool in this area is the SAP Enterprise Search. Because knowledge drives today's business, users need a fast and secure means to access information and data regardless of the source or system on which it resides. The SAP Enterprise Search tool has a web-based interface that delivers results to your people when and where they need them.

> **Business rules management**
> These functions help you monitor your business processes so that you avoid duplication and reduce errors in complicated tasks. By embedding SAP Business Rules Management in your business processes, you ensure that your organization is able to align your processes with your overall business strategies. Business rules can be developed and then tested and modified by those departments impacted so that they can be refined to meet their needs. In addition, a repository controls the versioning and access to your business rules so that the business rules within your business processes are the most current.

> **Composition and application development**
> The composition tools allow you to create, deploy, and maintain applications that support your business processes. SAP NetWeaver supports application development with the Eclipse-based SAP NetWeaver Developer Studio, Adobe Interactive Forms, ABAP, and J2EE.

> **Lifecycle management**
> In this area of SAP NetWeaver, your organization can develop a more robust IT landscape through the elimination or consolidation of redundant IT systems and the archiving of old data. While you

streamline your IT systems, these SAP NetWeaver tools also ensure that records retention and data reporting are maintained for compliance purposes.

> **Security and identity management**
Although the amount of information and the demand for that information continue to increase, SAP NetWeaver's security and identity management tools help your IT department secure the identities of those who access this information (internally and externally) and protect your data and intellectual property from virus threats and hacking.

> **SOA Middleware**
These tools provide the smooth communication link between all of your organization's systems and data regardless of the platform or source.

The following sections discuss in detail the various components and tools in SAP NetWeaver that you need to implement and execute the various IT practices.

User Productivity	User Interface Technology	Portal and Collaboration	Search	Mobile
Information Management	Master Data Management	Content Management	Business Intelligence	Data Management and Integration
Business Process Management	Business Process Modeling	Human Interaction Management	Business Process Monitoring	Business Rules Management
Composition and Application Development	Composition	ABAP Development		Java Development
Lifecycle Management	Landscape Design and Architecture	Application Management	Software Logistics	Systems Operation
Security and Identity Management	Identity and Access Management	Compliance and Software Lifecycle Security		Secure Collaboration and Interoperability
SOA Middleware	Repository-Based Modeling and Design	Service Bus-Based Integration		SOA Management

Figure 19.2 The Solution Map for SAP NetWeaver Technology

SAP NetWeaver Components

SAP NetWeaver consists of seven technical components, which can be used individually or in tandem to meet various business requirements and implement various IT practices. These components, which cover everything from effective data management to enhanced integration, constitute the essential core of SAP NetWeaver.

SAP NetWeaver Application Server

Runtime environment

SAP NetWeaver Application Server (SAP NetWeaver AS) provides the runtime environment for all SAP applications. It therefore serves as a cornerstone for any SAP landscape without which no SAP system can operate. SAP NetWeaver AS consists of two tightly integrated parts, one serving as a programming and runtime environment for ABAP and the other for Java.

SAP NetWeaver AS provides similar services in both—for example, transaction administration, user administration, tools for creating custom applications, and an infrastructure that enables a distributed development of new applications by multiple developers at the same time.

Infrastructure for using web-service technology

The infrastructure of SAP NetWeaver Application Server also serves as a basis for using web-service technology, as well as tools for developing standards-based services and extremely flexible web applications. In this way, it supports the entire process of creating new applications, including completion of installation and setup. The key components of this infrastructure are briefly introduced next.

ABAP applications

> **ABAP Workbench**
> The ABAP Workbench is a highly integrated collection of tools for developing applications in the ABAP programming language. This language was developed by SAP over 25 years ago and has been in a state of continuous evolution ever since. ABAP is optimized to ensure efficient and secure processing of structured datasets and fulfills the requirements of modern software design thanks to the object-oriented programming capabilities of its ABAP Objects component. The ABAP Workbench provides all tools required to develop ABAP applications, including an editor, a debugger, a dictionary of data types, and a framework for interface design with Web Dynpro technology (for more details, refer to the section entitled "SAP Tools for Developers").

Java applications

> **SAP NetWeaver Developer Studio**
> The SAP NetWeaver Developer Studio (NWDS) is a development environment based on the Eclipse open-source framework. The tools in the Developer Studio allow you to develop Java/J2EE business applications and web-service applications. The Web Dynpro

Java component of the SAP NWDS provides you with the option of creating user interfaces for your business applications. For more information about the SAP NWDS, refer to the section entitled "SAP Tools for Developers."

> **Other Tools**
The SAP NetWeaver toolbox also includes a repository for version management and a data storage medium, which uses the local file system to save relational databases on a central server. Meanwhile, you can manage changes that occur due to business or organizational restructuring with the Change Management function and with transport services, which distribute new functions to the relevant systems.

> **SAP NetWeaver Application Server Security Standards**
The security standards implemented in SAP NetWeaver Application Server include HTTPS, SSL, and LDAP. Functions for secure communication between client and server, authentication and *single sign-on (SSO)*, modern user administration in the form of *centralized user administration (CUA)*, digital certificates, digital signatures, and audits (a method for system monitoring and reporting of all changes) are also provided.

 Open Standards

Thanks to the use of open standards (vendor-independent standards), you can install SAP NetWeaver Application Server on any open technology platform.

SAP Business Warehouse

It is of crucial importance to today's enterprises to have immediate, real-time access to the data required for management decisions. Unfortunately, the information stored by an enterprise is often distributed among various systems and data stores and, in some cases, is available in two or three different versions.

Making information available when needed

SAP Business Warehouse (BW) provides an infrastructure for all business-intelligence and data-warehousing functions. A data warehouse serves as a central store for historical enterprise data from various sources. Data from all business areas can be integrated in SAP BW and

Data warehousing concepts

can then be made available as needed in the form required for strategic decision making.

> **Data warehousing**
> The data warehousing function of SAP BW enables the retrieval of key data, business modeling of that data, the creation of data warehouses, modification of the data architecture to suit business structures, and the management of data from various sources.

Searching large
volumes of data

> **Analysis and data mining**
> The functions provided in the Business Intelligence area include *online analytical processing* (OLAP), *data mining* (a function that allows you to search for patterns in large volumes of data), and *alerts*. These functions allow you to access and represent data, identify patterns, and detect exceptions to standard procedures.

Microsoft Excel and
web-based planning
and budgeting

> **Framework for business planning**
> A framework for business planning allows you to establish a reliable planning workflow based on your business processes. You can execute planning from different perspectives (bottom up or top down) based on consolidated business data. Business-planning functions also support the use of Microsoft Excel, as well as web-based planning and budgeting.

> **Business insight**
> Business insight functions allow you to create queries, reports, and analyses. With the functions provided for designing web applications, you can create analysis reports and publish business intelligence applications on the Internet or on your enterprise's intranet.

Consistent data

> **Measurement and management**
> The SAP BW functions for measurement and management allow you to manage business content, metadata, and collaboration business intelligence. You can also create report templates to ensure data consistency.

> **Open-hub services**
> *Open-hub services* enable the distribution of high-quality, audited enterprise information to applications using web services. These services also include the exchange of mass data and modeling functions.

> **Information broadcasting**
> You can use *information broadcasting functions* to distribute information to a large number of users in a personalized and secure form. The information can be distributed according to a schedule or based on key events. This information may take the form of a document or a current report and may be attached to personal emails or published on the Internet.

> **SAP BW Accelerator**
> *SAP BW Accelerator* is used to enable fast access to business intelligence. The functions of SAP BW Accelerator make queries more efficient and accelerate background processes using compression, parallel memory processing, and search technologies.

SAP Enterprise Portal

The SAP Enterprise Portal is a component that allows users to unify all applications they use in their day-to-day work (for example, various SAP systems, third-party components, or Internet pages) in a single, browser-based interface. Users can define how these applications are displayed and organized so that each employee has his or her own unique, personalized user interface. Because the design of the user interface is usually determined by an employee's role and function within the enterprise rather than by his personal preferences, we refer to this approach as a role-based approach.

Role-based interface

With the SAP Enterprise Portal, information and applications are no longer confined to their original user interfaces, and can instead be accessed from any screen by any user in the enterprise in a standardized or personalized form. The SAP Enterprise Portal also supports the exchange of data based on very simple drag-and-drop functions. The benefits of this are clear; users can retrieve all of the information they need directly from their work stations and only need to log on to a single system (the SAP Enterprise Portal) to access a range of other systems.

Integration

The term "integration" is used to describe the way in which a single interface is used to unite various systems. Open standards and web services are used to integrate the various applications in the SAP Enterprise

Portal. Predefined business content enables a fast and cost-effective implementation of the portal and integration of existing systems.

Collaboration functions

The user interface of the SAP Enterprise Portal also allows users to collaborate on joint projects with colleagues, both within and outside of the enterprise, and, for example, to work on certain files at the same time. These collaboration functions allow users to exchange information in real time in virtual workspaces called *collaboration rooms*.

Finally, the Knowledge Management functions of the SAP Enterprise Portal help users to search, organize, and access content saved in the enterprise. Classification tools (for example, an index server and search engine) can be used to structure data, publish information in web-based applications, and manage business content more efficiently.

SAP Process Orchestration

SAP Process Orchestration (SAP PO) provides additional integration technologies. However, rather than integrating applications in a user interface, these enable process-oriented collaboration between applications—in other words, an automated exchange of data without user intervention.

SAP PO supports collaboration between SAP and non-SAP applications within and across enterprises. Process integration is based on standards-based XML messaging, and all process-dependent data is modeled using web-service standards.

Maintaining, storing, and changing integrated information

SAP PO is also delivered with predefined business content. This incorporates information about interfaces and assignments between applications, business scenarios, and business processes (referred to as *mapping*) in the central Integration Repository and Integration Directory. You can maintain, store, and change this integrated information using the modeling and development tools that are also provided.

You can use the adapters provided in SAP PO to set up a connection to systems from other providers; for example, with IDoc or BAPI interfaces or with file, messaging, database, or web-service interfaces. Finally, functions are also provided for *business-to-business* (B2B) integration. These functions support communication with business partners, even if they cannot access SAP NetWeaver.

 SAP Process Orchestration

> SAP Process Orchestration (SAP PO) bundles the SAP NetWeaver PI component with SAP Business Process Management and a range of Java-based tools in a complete package that is optimized for running service-oriented applications among individual systems.

SAP NetWeaver Master Data Management

Master data is data relating to products, customers, or employees that never or only rarely changes as part of day-to-day business (unlike transaction data). This data includes names, addresses, material numbers, and so on. *SAP NetWeaver Master Data Management* (SAP NetWeaver MDM) helps you manage this data and therefore provides a foundation for service and business process management.

Master data as a business foundation

SAP NetWeaver MDM allows you to consolidate and cleanse master data records relating to the same object from various systems (referred to as duplicates) and to then save these in a central repository. In this way, SAP NetWeaver MDM enables consistency of data across systems.

In addition, SAP NetWeaver MDM allows you to maintain master data and to distribute it to the various systems connected while also guaranteeing the quality of this data. Global attributes ensure the availability of identical master data in all systems. You can track and verify the active status during distribution, which gives you more control over the process.

Maintaining and distributing master data

You can use the SAP NetWeaver MDM user interface to perform administrative tasks, such as handling data exceptions and assigning access rights to business processes and role-based information. In terms of data administration, you can also use the interface to configure the merging of data sources, define business rules, and set distribution parameters.

You can choose among several tools for working with internal content. These allow you to manage images, texts, and PDF documents,

Catalog management

browse and publish web catalogs, modify and send print catalogs, and create reports based on synchronized data.

SAP for Mobile

Mobile applications
   SAP for Mobile provides the technology basis for developing and operating mobile applications based on SAP NetWeaver. This component also enables the use of composite applications for mobile business.

Remote employees
   Users can use the functions on mobile devices even if they are not connected to the system. Data can also be saved on mobile devices without a connection and then synchronized with backend systems later. A special development environment in SAP for Mobile helps developers create and modify mobile solutions. In addition, an administration console enables centralized administration of mobile solutions and access to these.

Client technologies
   The following three client technologies, which have been optimized for specific user roles and various mobile end devices, are provided in SAP for Mobile:

> **Mobile Java Client**
> This software is used by PDAs (personal digital assistants) or handheld devices that access online applications such as Mobile Asset Management.

> **Mobile .NET Client**
> This technology was designed for devices with Microsoft Windows systems that are used, for example, to run CRM applications for field-service employees.

> **Mobile Browser Client**
> Mobile devices that are permanently connected to a web server use this technology in conjunction with WAP, WLAN, Bluetooth, and GPRS.

SAP Auto-ID Infrastructure

This component provides RFID capabilities. *Radio frequency identification (RFID)* technology is used to create, store, and transmit electronic data via radio waves. This electronically communicated data can be read by IT systems. RFID is used for noncontact identification of objects by means of a reader that can read an RFID chip or transponder (for example, on a cardboard box).

The SAP Auto-ID Infrastructure creates a gateway that allows IT systems to access RFID data. Using this SAP NetWeaver component, you can integrate all automated communication and sensing devices, including RFID readers and printers, Bluetooth devices, and bar code scanners. The technology receives and controls automated signals to make this possible.

Integration of all device types

If you set up a connection between the SAP Auto-ID Infrastructure and the business processes in the backend system, then you can access data in real time, which significantly accelerates processing. The Integrator, an application in the SAP Auto-ID Infrastructure, incorporates RFID technology into logistics processes.

 Areas of Application for RFID

The Auto-ID Infrastructure meets the requirements of large retailing chains, which retag goods with RFID chips. RFID can also be used to track drugs electronically in the pharmaceutical industry.

SAP Tools for Developers

In addition to the main components of SAP NetWeaver described previously, the SAP technology platform also provides tools for implementing, developing, and managing your IT systems. These tools are introduced in this section.

The developers in your enterprise can use various SAP NetWeaver tools to modify or enhance the SAP solution. These include the large development environments for ABAP and Java and also specialized tools for modeling composite applications and user-friendly interfaces and for creating SAP Enterprise Portal content and analyses.

ABAP

ABAP is a programming language developed over 25 years ago by SAP for the development of business applications. It is the programming language in which the core applications of SAP ERP and most backend areas of the other SAP Business Suite applications were written. In the last ten years, ABAP has also provided developers with the ability to develop applications in accordance with the object-oriented

SAP's programming language

programming paradigm. ABAP's distinguishing features include transaction security, stability, a sophisticated data-type concept, and, of course, its extensive range of development tools.

ABAP Workbench

The ABAP Workbench provides a central point of access to all ABAP development tools. Unlike other programming languages (e.g., Java) the ABAP Workbench is the only development platform for ABAP, and it is only available as part of an SAP NetWeaver Application Server.

Tools The ABAP Workbench contains all of the tools you need to plan, develop, test, and compile ABAP programs.

These include:

> The ABAP Editor for writing code

> The ABAP Debugger for testing programs and detecting errors

> The Class Builder for creating and managing classes for object-oriented programming

> The Web Service Framework for creating and managing ABAP web services

> A range of other tools to help you test and improve all aspects of your programs

Development infrastructure The sophisticated development infrastructure of the ABAP Workbench means that different developers can work on the same project simultaneously without any conflicts. The ABAP Workbench is also connected to the "transport system," which enables fast and reliable distribution of newly developed programs to the relevant target systems.

Web Dynpro ABAP

Web Dynpro ABAP is a tool in the ABAP Workbench that provides a development environment for modern user interfaces. You can use this tool to create ergonomic interfaces that are based on the latest programming principles (for example, a clear division between business and presentation logic, the need for modeling, and so on) and can be used on a wide range of end devices. Web browsers, PDAs, and mobile cellular phones are supported.

Java

The Java programming platform was developed by Sun Microsystems and released in 1995. Java is freely available and free of charge. Java enables exclusively object-oriented programming. The language is particularly suitable for the development of multifunctional, web-based user interfaces and for applications that connect various systems or users in various applications (*composite applications* and *collaboration* functions).

SAP uses Java, for example, as a language for the SAP Enterprise Portal, for analytical applications, and for the development of *composite applications*.

SAP NetWeaver Developer Studio

The SAP NetWeaver Developer Studio (SAP NWDS) is the SAP development environment for J2EE-based, multilayer applications. This component is based on the Eclipse open-source framework, for which SAP offers a comprehensive collection of modeling, development, and maintenance tools. The following are a few examples of the many types of tools available:

Eclipse

> Tools for developing J2EE applications

> Tools for developing Java web services

> Tools for developing Web Dynpro applications

> Debugging tools

> Tools for managing distributed development projects (Java Development Infrastructure)

Web Dynpro Java

Web Dynpro interface technology is provided for Java, just as it is for ABAP (see the section on ABAP). The underlying functions of Web Dynpro Java are the same as in Web Dynpro ABAP. You can simply choose between the two variants depending on the developer's preferred development language or the language of the backend application.

SAPUI5

SAP UI Development Toolkit for HTML5 (SAPUI5) is a user-interface technology that is used to build and adapt client applications based on

SAP NetWeaver Neo. The SAPUI5 runtime is a client-side HTML5 rendering library with a large set of RIA-like standard and extension controls based on JavaScript (JS), and a lightweight programming model. The rendering control library is Open AJAX–compliant and based on open-source jQuery and can be used together with other client-side libraries.

SAP Composite Application Framework

Composite applications (which were previously known as xApps) are applications that consist of services from diverse applications. You can use the *SAP Composite Application Framework* (CAF) to create and use SOA-compliant composite applications. SAP CAF includes, for example, development tools, an abstraction layer for objects, a user interface, and libraries of sample processes, which you can employ to create and use composite applications.

With SAP CAF, you can combine business processes from existing objects from various systems rather than having to program code for objects and processes when you require a new application. The object access layer of SAP CAF allows you to run composite applications in any system landscape, regardless of the system in which they originated. The object-access layer is a central interface that controls system communication using web services and SAP PO.

Several other CAF tools are also provided—for example, tools that allow you to develop user interfaces and *guided procedures*—functions similar to wizards, which guide users through business processes—and predefined collaboration functions, which help you to quickly implement mechanisms for virtual collaboration between team members.

SAP NetWeaver Visual Composer

Portal iViews

The *SAP NetWeaver Visual Composer* (SAP NetWeaver VC) tool allows you to create model-based business applications. With this tool, you build user interfaces either based on templates or by using simple drag-and-drop functions and then defining the data flow between the individual components. In this way, you can create an application without writing a single line of code. When you create a model, the relevant code is generated automatically.

The SAP NetWeaver VC tool is integrated into the SAP Enterprise Portal and SAP BW.

SAP NetWeaver Composition Environment

The SAP NetWeaver Composition Environment (SAP NetWeaver CE) bundles SAP's tools for developing Java-based composite applications into a single product, which is relatively lightweight when compared to the SAP NetWeaver platform as a whole. SAP NetWeaver CE can run independently of other SAP NetWeaver tools in a separate development system and enables a particularly tight integration of all tools mentioned in this section.

It also includes two completely new SAP NetWeaver components, which are available for the first time with version 7.1.1 of SAP NetWeaver CE: SAP Business Process Management and SAP Business Rules Management. These tools are used for low-level modeling of complete business processes across physical system boundaries. This allows application development to move a significant step closer to the business departments.

SAP Solution Manager

SAP Solution Manager is discussed in detail in Chapter 23, but we will provide a short introduction at this point. SAP Solution Manager is a tool for implementing, operating, and upgrading IT solutions based on SAP NetWeaver.

SAP Solution Manager Availability

SAP Solution Manager is included in your annual maintenance fee for the SAP solutions installed in your enterprise.

SAP Solution Manager comprises a core palette of tools, which offers technical support for the operation of system landscapes.

Technical support for system landscape operation

The functions in SAP Solution Manager are primarily intended to enable the implementation, operation, and optimization of SAP solutions. However, SAP Solution Manager can be used for non-SAP software also. An essential part of the design of its functions is the connection between business processes and the underlying IT infrastructure. In other words,

SAP Solution Manager is not intended to be used solely for the monitoring of technical systems by administrations. It also always takes into account the functional interaction between various applications in a business process.

Its functions, which are described in more detail in Chapter 23, include the following:

> Roadmaps for implementing SAP Business Suite solutions within an enterprise as a whole and in a coordinated manner across various areas of the enterprise

> Documentation functions for all processes of your SAP solutions and all changes made to your systems

> Functions to accelerate the preparation and execution of software tests

> A Service Desk to help your IT support personnel record and process problems with applications

> Functions for central monitoring and analysis of systems, business processes, and interfaces

> An online connection to SAP support organizations, which allows you to request regular maintenance services and help from SAP in the event of serious problems

SAP NetWeaver Case Study

Table 19.1 provides an overview of the case study discussed in this section.

Enterprise	A large university
Existing Solutions	Various software applications from third-party providers and SAP ERP software based on SAP R/3
Challenge	To consolidate data and cleanse inconsistent data in the individual systems and applications
SAP Solutions	SAP Enterprise Portal and SAP BW
Benefits	Consolidated and consistent data, self-service functions, a single point of access for applications and data

Table 19.1 SAP NetWeaver Case Study

This large university has more than 6,000 employees and 30,000 students enrolled in a wide range of courses spanning various disciplines. The university needed a solution that would enable enhanced collaboration between the various departments and administrative uses and allow shared use of data.

The Challenges

Various IT solutions were implemented in the university over the years. The ERP software for finance, HR, and logistics that was implemented in 1994 was still based on an old release (SAP R/3). The university management recognized the need to consolidate the large volume of administrative master data and to eliminate inconsistencies. For this reason, it decided to implement SAP NetWeaver to integrate various data sources used by several isolated systems and applications.

The SAP Solution

Two SAP NetWeaver components were particularly well suited to meeting the university's requirements. Both SAP BW and SAP Enterprise Portal offer a single point of access (SpoA) to data. They also allow users to use self-services functions in the SAP Enterprise Portal to access data and create reports.

SAP BW and SAP Enterprise Portal

Because SAP BW accesses data structures in SAP R/3, retrieving data from the system did not present a problem. It was also a relatively simple matter to program reporting based on the underlying data for SAP BW. The first phase was completed in less than six months. This phase was shorter than originally planned, thanks to the use of existing business content, predefined reports, and analysis tools integrated into SAP NetWeaver. In addition, SAP NetWeaver tools accelerated the mapping of queries and reports in web applications.

Efficient reports

At the end of this phase, the university was able to access data relating to asset accounting, SAP Project System, settlement, room reservations, enrollment, course fees, and employee and student numbers. As a result, it was possible to create reports on HR and financial data. It was also possible to incorporate the staff/student ratio into the analyses.

With the SAP Enterprise Portal, users no longer needed to log on to several systems. Instead, they could use SSO to log on to the SAP

Single sign-on

Enterprise Portal once only. They then had easy and secure access to all of the information and applications they required. In addition, a portal-based interface allowed users to familiarize themselves with the system within a short space of time without any training.

Finally, the university museum used the search engine (*Search and Classification*) of the SAP Enterprise Portal to create catalogs for new exhibits in XML format. All employees with SAP Enterprise Portal access can use the integrated SAP search engine to search for the data they require.

Future Outlook

Following the implementation of SAP BW and the SAP Enterprise Portal, the university management now plans to extend their use of BI functions. It is planned that training and performance-management information will be added to the data warehouse, where it will be accessible to the HR department. Furthermore, additional areas are to be optimized using planning functions. These include the administration of assets, budgets, and spending. The Registrar's Office also hopes to use the functions of SAP BW to create reports and analyses based on student data.

The collaboration functions of the SAP Enterprise Portal would allow messages and information to be published on a website for students. The university is also considering using the SAP NetWeaver search engine to access information from file servers and other sources.

Conclusion

This chapter provided an introduction to SAP NetWeaver technology, which is a prerequisite for service-oriented architectures and supports other SAP applications. You are now familiar with the following aspects of SAP NetWeaver:

> Integration options

> Modeling tools

> Data administration and analysis tools

> Components such as SAP BW, SAP Enterprise Portal, and SAP NetWeaver Application Server

> Tools for developers, including ABAP Workbench and SAP NetWeaver Developer Studio

This technology platform, with its far-reaching functional scope, provides the basis for any SAP application you may implement.

Not let us move to Chapter 20, where you can learn how to prepare for an SAP on premise implementation. There, we will discuss the various resources and software packages that are available from SAP to help you prepare for an SAP implementation.

Preparing for an SAP Implementation

20

Whatever piece of the SAP solution landscape you are contemplating putting in place, doing so can take time, money, and effort. Before you jump in, you might want to get an idea of what is involved and also what resources exist to help you out. You will be glad to hear that you have a lot of options to take you step-by-step through an SAP implementation. This chapter covers some of the most useful support tools, methodologies, and programs.

> ▶ **Note**
>
> For a more in-depth exploration of preparing for an implementation, read *The SAP Project: More than a Survival Guide* by Gerald Sullivan (SAP PRESS, 2014).

Important Considerations

Before we explore the support and help available to you, take a moment to try to understand what a typical SAP implementation will involve. You need to understand four key elements before you proceed:

> The state of your own business
> How your business fits with industry best practices
> The potential costs involved
> How to anticipate and deal with change

Let us examine these elements one by one, starting with assessing your business.

Assessing Your Own Business

Understand your unique characteristics

Every business is unique in that it has its own structure, processes, industry-related procedures, customer base, geographic locations, and so forth. To put an enterprise solution in place, you need to understand your unique characteristics to find the right fit. Assessing your business and its needs is a very important part of taking the plunge with SAP. In fact, if you do not understand the goals of your company and where you want to go, you cannot implement any enterprise solution effectively. For example, you must identify your most pressing problem to decide which solutions to implement first. You have to understand and document your current processes to automate them, and so on.

Analyze industry needs

You should bring together all of the relevant people in your organization so that IT people understand the business strategies, goals, and priorities for solving business challenges and business people understand the existing IT landscape. Because SAP products can be incrementally integrated with your current systems, determining what changes will bring about the greatest benefit will help you to implement them strategically and cost-effectively.

Understanding How Your Business Fits in Your Industry

Even though every business is unique, each business also has some things in common with other businesses in their industry. Using SAP Best Practices, built into SAP Business Suite products, helps provide out-of-the-box solutions that have worked for many companies in your industry.

SAP Best Practices provide a prototype you can use to accelerate your move to SAP. You get a methodology for using the prototype, documented scenarios that reflect both a business and technical point of view, and preconfigured SAP solutions. There are SAP Best Practices for the following industries, among many others:

> Apparel and footwear
> Automotive
> Chemicals
> Consumer products
> Discrete Manufacturing
> Engineering, construction, and operations
> High tech
> Industrial machinery and components
> Life sciences
> Professional services
> Public sector
> Retail
> Utilities

Cross-industry best practices are those that are useful for most businesses regardless of their industry. These include the following:

Cross-industry best practices

> SAP Best Practices for Business Intelligence (SAP Best Practices for BI)
> SAP Best Practices for Business Planning and Consolidation
> SAP Best Practices for Business Warehousing (SAP Best Practices for BW)
> SAP Best Practices for Data Migration
> SAP Best Practices for Governance, Risk, and Compliance (SAP Best Practices for GRC)
> SAP Best Practices for Human Capital Management (SAP Best Practices for HCM)
> SAP Best Practices for Supply Chain Management (SAP Best Practices for SCM)

> SAP Best Practices for Customer Relationship Management (SAP Best Practices for CRM)

> SAP Best Practices for Strategy Management

SAP Best Practices prototypes are reusable and help you get an SAP ERP Business Suite solution in place faster and more cost-effectively.

In addition to the SAP Best Practices Solutions and SAP Industry Solutions, SAP also offers SAP Rapid Deployment solutions for an accelerated implementation. We discuss these solutions in Chapter 22.

Understanding Implementation Costs

Estimating the cost of your SAP implementation

It is not easy to help you estimate the costs of an SAP implementation. That would be like trying to guess what your vacation is going to cost without knowing your destination, how long you will be gone, how far you have to travel, how many family members will be joining you, or what activities you will participate in when you get there (although for small and midsized companies, you can increasingly find a *fixed price offer* depending on the scope of the implementation). But what we can do is give you some factors to consider that contribute to the final cost of your SAP implementation.

There are several pieces of an SAP implementation that you have to consider:

> Are you implementing a small business solution, such as SAP Business One, or are you customizing a combination of SAP Business Suite functionalities with SAP NetWeaver, a couple of pieces of SAP ERP, and one other package, such as SAP CRM?

> Are you gradually implementing pieces of SAP functionality, or do you want to implement a total solution as soon as possible?

> Do you have legacy systems that could integrate with SAP NetWeaver to save you money?

> Will you need a great deal of consultation to help you design and implement your solution or to customize processes, or do you have internal resources who can help with some of this work?

> Will your employees have to be trained in the new system?

> How many user licenses will you need, and what costs will you encounter in migrating data to the new system?

> How extensively will you want to customize the user interface?

> In which countries or regions will you be implementing the solution? Will localization be required?

An SAP account executive can work through all of these questions with you to help you estimate your total cost of ownership (TCO).

Dealing with Change

Do not forget to put a change-management plan in place. Change management involves preparing your organization for change by strategically introducing new technologies or procedures in a way that engages your employees and provides them with the tools they need (such as training) to be successful. When an SAP implementation encounters problems, it is often because the organization and its employees were not ready for the change and not because of the technology. There are two important things to remember about dealing with change:

Change management plan

> A new system for managing your business processes is likely to highlight areas of your current processes that are weak or even nonexistent. People can be offended by the suggestion that they are not handling things in the most efficient way possible. Remind them that to solve problems you have to identify them first. Identifying problems is not a process of assigning blame but of focusing on a better way to get work done. Involve your people in the process and they will feel like a part of your future success.

Change is a people issue

> Change is difficult, even for the most flexible among us. Keep that in mind as you find employees suddenly married to an old system that they used to gripe about. Provide clear justification for the change and information about the anticipated rewards. Document and celebrate milestones as you implement the new system.

Although you may have many partners involved in your implementation, your employees are the people who will work with the new system day in and day out, so do not forget them as you work through the process. Next, we will introduce you to a variety of resources that can help you begin planning for an SAP implementation.

Planning for Success

Adopting any SAP solution means that you are entering the world of service-oriented architecture (SOA), an approach to enterprise computing that brings a lot of benefits. You will be glad to hear that you are definitely not alone when you begin to implement an SAP solution. SAP has created an entire program to help you adopt the SOA model for your business called the *SOA adoption program*. In addition, there are people and organizations that can help you determine how to leverage SOA and begin to map out your SAP solution.

The SOA Adoption Program

SOA is designed to deliver benefits by using existing systems and reducing the costs of changing or developing new processes. However, an SAP approach to SOA is also designed to provide support for business processes through an entire organization, which is no small task. An organization does not put an SOA into effect overnight. You need more than a technology implementation; you need education, direction, and time to get all of the pieces in place.

 Tip

> SAP has introduced a program called *Standardized E2E* (End-to-End) *Operations* to help with the operations portion of SOA adoption. This is the phase in which you refine what you put in place. The first piece of this program is an organizational model that assigns roles to all involved stakeholders, including tools for collaboration and SLA-based support processes. Standardized procedures are also established. Tools are implemented for executing the described procedures.
>
> SAP Solution Manager, which you will learn more about in Chapter 23, supports the various SAP standards for solution operations, and individual work centers provide access to all functions that different stakeholders need to perform their role-based jobs. Finally, the stakeholders have to be educated to use the E2E Solution Operations procedures. SAP's role-based education and certification program for E2E Solution Operations meets this need.

The SOA adoption program was designed to help you envision an SOA environment for your business and find the best path to it. There are four phases to this program: *discovery*, in which you find out what

SOA can do for you; *evaluation*, in which you build a roadmap for making the move to SOA and SAP NetWeaver; *implementation*, the phase in which you plan, build, and run the services you will use as the foundation of your business processes; and *operations*, when you go live and refine what you have put in place.

The SOA adoption program includes the following:

> Roadmaps that are like blueprints for your SOA adoption. These roadmaps show you how you can merge SAP's enterprise applications with SAP NetWeaver functionality to achieve a services-based environment.

> Discovery Server is a preconfigured system that allows you to try out SOA and SAP NetWeaver in your own business.

> Enterprise Services Workplace (ES Workplace) allows you to browse through packaged enterprise services and test them to see how they might work in your enterprise. You can access the ES Service Workplace browsing environment directly at *http://esworkplace.sap.com*.

> Industry Value Networks help you collaborate with others to develop business solutions.

> The Business Process Expert (BPX) community has the goal of bridging the gap between IT and business strategies by helping these two camps find a common language. The role of the business process expert (also called business analyst, business consultant, or process consultant) in an organization is largely a result of introducing a service-oriented approach to business solutions.

> SOA Innovation is another community that offers information in the form of brochures, demos, and webcasts from experts to help you find your way to an SOA environment in your company.

The roadmap for SOA

A SOA adoption program can help, but what about those times when you need a one-on-one helping hand? There are several options from which you can choose, discussed ahead.

SAP and the SAP Community

In addition to the various planning and adoption tools outlined so far in this chapter, there is a virtual army of resources out there that can help you get started.

SAP account repre-
sentatives—more
than just sales
people

SAP account representatives are not just salespeople. They are your team leaders for designing a solution, assembling a team of advisors, and working with you to develop an analysis of your needs. An account representative will also stick with you throughout your implementation to ensure that you are getting what you need from SAP.

 Tip

> To find an account representative, go to *www.sap.com/directory/main* for a list of SAP offices around the world. Contact your closest office to begin working with an account representative right away.

SAP consultants —
consultant
certification

SAP consultants have been certified by SAP to help companies with their SAP implementations. There are more than 140,000 certified specialists, including application, technology, and development consultants, as well as solution architects. Currently, there are three levels of consultant certification: *associate* (fundamental knowledge), *professional* (proven project experience), and *master* (expert grasp and broad project experience within complex projects).

SAP third-party
certification

SAP supports third-party vendors who want to integrate their software with SAP software. SAP Integration and Certification Centers (SAP ICC) can offer help in connecting you with third-party solutions and advising you on integration issues. Visit *www.scn.sap.com* to find information on these ICC programs.

In addition to these people and groups, SAP provides help in the form of SAP Services, a broad program designed to provide you with what you need to have a successful implementation.

Enhancement Packages

Enhancement
packages

Full system upgrades and installations can be extremely costly in terms of time, money, and resources, not to mention the disruption to your day-to-day business activities. If your company already has SAP ERP installed and running but wants to improve general business functionality or specific industry functionality to remain competitive, consider an SAP Enhancement Package.

Enhancement packages bring you the flexibility to install only those portions of software that directly impact the process or function you want to improve. After these specific components are in place, you can then reactivate the impacted processes, and your system will react only to those changes.

Who Can Help You Implement?

SAP Services is an extensive network of people and programs that offers tools, consulting, and service plans to help your company get up and running with an SAP solution throughout the entire planning, building, and running process.

SAP Services

In this section, we look at SAP Services through the planning, building, and running phases of an implementation and then take a closer look at what SAP Consulting has to offer.

SAP Services Portfolio

SAP describes its service offerings in a model that breaks them down into three key phases of an implementation: planning, building, and running. Each of these phases is further broken down into categories of services: complete execution, expert guidance, quality management, and enablement (see Figure 20.1).

SAP Services portfolio

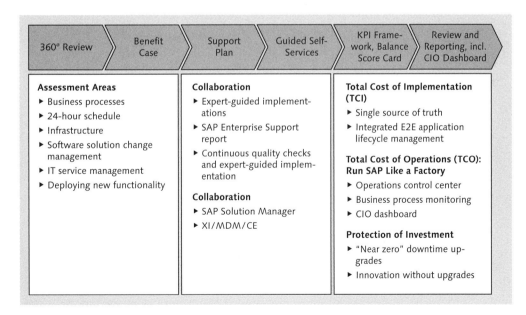

Figure 20.1 SAP Roadmap

In the next three sections, we explore the details of each of these phases.

SAP Services Portfolio: Planning Phase

The planning phase helps your business define what your processes are and where they need improvement. In this phase, you determine the direction for your IT strategy through a variety of services:

> **Program and Project Management**
> These services include program management, project management, and change management services. You work through initial planning, organizing, and staffing, as well as controlling the project.

> **Business Process Design**
> These services include process analysis, redesign, innovation, improvement, determining best practices, and quality assurance.

> **Custom Solution Development and Maintenance**
> These services include the development of applications and interfaces. The features include planning your help desk support, solution testing as part of installing support packages and upgrades, and software maintenance.

> **Business and IT Strategic Consulting**
> This is where you identify and quantify the business value that you can expect from improving the efficiency of your enterprise. In this category, you get solution planning, analysis of your business process and business requirements, and value assessment services.

> **Solution Architecture Design**
> These services involve helping to integrate your business solutions into your overall enterprise architecture. Activities in this category include developing an implementation approach; establishing scope, costs, and timelines; designing the process and application landscape; and setting benchmarks against which you can assess your operations.

> **Technology Architecture Design**
> This is where you break down high-level system architecture into the technical requirements of your implementation project. Activities include system landscape strategy, internal release rollout, determination of distributed and centralized systems, and software change management.

> **Support and Operations Strategy**
> This is the part of the planning phase in which you set up support structures, establish the appropriate level of support, calculate your TCO, and pinpoint the strategy for your system operation.

> **Solution Assessment**
> These services help you identify and minimize technical risk in your implementation, target integration issues, and check the technical feasibility of an implementation project. They also help you identify weak points in your existing solution.

> **Quality and Risk Management**
> These services help you identify and manage implementation risks, provide a review of the project's progress, and analyze the technical design.

> **Enablement and Assessment of Support and Operations**
> These services help you to assess and set up support structures and processes. Training workshops help your support organization understand how to analyze and solve system problems.

> **Education, Training, and Certification Services**
> These services help educate users, consultants, and project teams. Consulting, customized training, documentation, and computer-based tools are provided to users, including a range of courses and certifications on SAP solutions and infrastructure.

When you move beyond the planning phase, you are ready to begin building your solution, which is where the building-phase categories of services come into play.

SAP Services Portfolio: Building Phase

When planning is done, you are ready to begin to roll out new applications, customize interfaces, and integrate all of the pieces. The building phase includes several services, such as those that involve custom solutions, solution implementation, technical implementation, and solution assessment. Some of these categories overlap with those in the planning phase but with a focus on implementing the solution. Building phase services include the following:

> **Program and Project Management**
> These services include program management, project management, and change management services.

> **Solution Implementation**
These services support implementation and rollout of new applications. Activities include blueprinting business process requirements, tailoring applications to business requirements, resolving conceptual and technical issues, cycle testing, and load and stress testing.

> **Custom Solution Development and Maintenance**
These services involve customized development of applications and interfaces. In addition, you get enhancements to packaged applications and templates. Other services cover outsourcing of the maintenance for your development projects, helpdesk support, solution testing while installing support packages and upgrades, and software maintenance.

> **SAP Application Management Services**
These services include helpdesk and second-level support, process support and infrastructure design, and system management and monitoring. This category of services can also involve remote application administration for solutions that are run onsite or offsite.

> **Services for SAP Hosting**
These services include selecting hosting and application-management services that cover everything from evaluation to implementation to application hosting. Out-of-the-box solutions can be scaled to meet your specific needs.

> **Solution Expert Consulting**
These services involve dedicated SAP solution experts with direct access to SAP development. These resources are available onsite or operating remotely to address solution, process, and technical issues, and these experts work with your project team to instruct them in software features and functions. The ongoing evaluation of tools and processes helps you avoid problems as you begin building your solution.

> **Solution Integration**
These services deliver detailed design, implementation, and management services that link applications and integrate them with your IT infrastructure. SAP integration experts help to match up SAP and non-SAP solutions. These services help you optimize the architecture and interfaces of your solution and adopt strategies for converting your data.

> **Technical Implementation**
> These services support the technical implementation and rollout of new applications by providing tools, methodologies, and best practices. Consultants help you translate high-level system architecture into implementation project technical requirements. Activities include configuration of your IT environment, definition of an IT security policy, and movement of data, operating systems, and databases from legacy systems to the SAP solution.

> **Implementation and Optimization of Support and Operations**
> These services deal with system administration, which includes reviewing the main aspects of your operations, such as interface settings, database administration, backup, recovery, and security settings. In addition, data volume management services help to reduce the size and growth of your database and offer a customized archiving strategy.

> **Solution Assessment**
> These services help you identify integration issues and risks during the building phase and to check the technical details of your implementation infrastructure, sizing, and volume.

> **Quality and Risk Management**
> These services manage implementation risks, examine your project's progress, and ensure your solution design aligns with your overall business needs.

> **Enablement and Assessment of Support and Operations**
> These services help you build a solution support organization. You set up support structures and processes and train your support organization.

> **Education, Training, and Certification Services**
> These services bring consulting, customized training, documentation, and the latest computer-based tools to your users.

SAP Consulting

One of the major support efforts of SAP Services is SAP Consulting. SAP Consulting offers two programs to help you: Technical Implementation and Solution Implementation. Here, briefly, is what each program delivers to your enterprise.

SAP Technical Implementation

To get the technical aspects of your implementation up and running, SAP Consulting provides the following services:

> **SAP Technical Analysis and Design**
> This helps to relate your high-level system architecture to project-specific technical requirements. SAP Consulting looks at your system landscape strategy, software-change-management approach, and how you will deal with business continuity throughout the implementation.

> **SAP Technical Installation**
> This provides technology tools for your installation, makes sure your hardware is configured optimally, and checks your system settings and speeds.

> **SAP Globalization and Language Consulting**
> This helps international companies with global implementation, setting up the right system architecture, and dealing with localization issues. Multiple-language and time-zone support are included.

> **SAP Security Concepts and Implementation**
> This consulting service helps you get your information security policy defined and in place. Your security policy will be analyzed, and suggestions will be made. In addition, detailed documentation helps you configure and set up your systems for improved security.

> **SAP Technical Migration**
> This helps you determine a strategy for migrating to a new solution or technology. You get guidelines and documentation for every stage and help with migrating your system with tools such as the SAP Legacy System Migration Workbench (SAP LSMW).

> **SAP ABAP and Java Consulting**
> This helps your company develop and integrate your own specific applications to work with SAP solutions.

Now let us move on to the other half of SAP Consulting: solution implementation.

SAP Solution Implementation

Your solution needs more than technology, which is where the solution implementation portion of SAP Consulting comes in. This area of support includes the following:

> **SAP Solution Implementation Consulting**
> This helps you map out your implementation by identifying your business and system requirements, performing analysis and design tasks, running requirements workshops to determine your needs, and creating both a business blueprint and a process plan to help model your business-process goals.

> **SAP Solution Expert Consulting**
> This brings best practices and proven methodologies to your solution implementation. In this area of solution implementation, SAP Consulting offers help with understanding all of the features of SAP software and provides tools for minimizing risk.

> **SAP Configuration**
> This gives you guidance and support in customizing SAP solutions to your specific business needs. You get specific requirements for your project and development specifications, a baseline configuration to give you a starting point, and a final configuration strategy for system deployment.

> **SAP Test Management**
> This keeps the cost of testing activities low and helps you automate test procedures. SAP Consulting provides a roadmap for your testing activities and uses SAP NetWeaver tools and proven testing methodologies.

SAP Consulting offers a wide range of services, including one for midsize companies called *ASAP Focus methodology*, which you will learn about in the next section.

ASAP Focus methodology

ASAP Focus Methodology

For midsize companies, the ASAP Focus methodology from SAP Consulting (see Figure 20.2) can make it possible to put an SAP Business Suite solution in place in a little over three months. This program streamlines the processes used by larger companies for IT implementation to meet a midsize business model. The focus in this case is on keeping costs down and keeping the disruption of your business's operations to a minimum. If your organization cannot afford any disruption to its core processes and you are concerned about controlling costs, this is a good option.

Based on SAP Best Practices, such as the SAP Business All-in-One fast-start program and other packaged solutions, this program includes the following:

> A roadmap for putting a predefined solution in place quickly

> Predefined processes that enable you to perform business activities and data-conversion tools to help you work with your existing data within the new system

> Documentation for business processes

> Predefined reports, printed forms, roles for your employees, and test programs

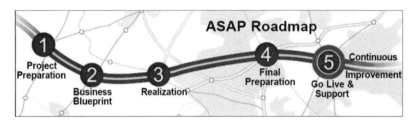

Figure 20.2 The ASAP Focus Methodology

In addition, the ASAP Focus methodology allows your people to put certain pieces of the process in place before you begin working with an SAP team, which can save you money right from the beginning. For midsize businesses, having a way to predict both the timeline and cost of an SAP implementation can be important, and the ASAP Focus methodology is designed to do just that.

In the next section, there is some information that can help prepare you for your first contact with SAP so that you will be prepared to ask the right questions and make an initial determination about which route might be best for you.

SAP Services Portfolio: Running Phase

The running phase offers several of the same types of services covered in the other phases, such as project management, solution optimization, integration, support organization implementation, and quality and risk management—but with the emphasis on a functioning implementation. At this point, you are monitoring your new solution, ensuring that any new development or outsourcing needs are met, and supporting your implementation with daily helpdesk support. Specific conceptual and technical areas are addressed to ensure that all of your SAP projects are completed successfully.

There is an ongoing evaluation to ensure that your solution is working and incorporating any new technologies or products. Conversion, Migration, and Landscape Optimization services help you make the move to your new system by integrating solution landscapes, which helps to ensure corporate governance. In this phase, there is a review of operations, including interface settings, database administration, backup, and security. There is also ongoing quality and risk management to ensure that your solution reflects the needs of your business.

Now that you understand the scope of services offered throughout the planning, building, and running phases of an SAP implementation, we will take a moment to review some specific tools and programs that deliver them.

SAP Operations Support Options

After you are up and running in the operations phase of an SOA adoption, there are several maintenance options and a support offering from SAP Services. These include SAP Enterprise Support services, the customized SAP MaxAttention program, and a portfolio of support offerings for project-based engagement.

> **SAP Enterprise Support**
>
> This provides the holistic management of your SAP solution through 24-hour global support. At this level of support, you get the best business practices and technology required to support your SAP implementation. This support program includes three components: Run SAP Methodology, Mission Critical Support, and Global Support Backbone.
>
> Enterprise Support also includes the resolution of issues through a service-level agreement (SLA). In addition, you get annual assessments that result in recommendations for actions you can take to lower your risk and improve your processes. A support advisor continuously provides guidance about your implementation and makes suggestions to keep things moving along smoothly.

SAP support offerings

24-hour global support

429

> **SAP MaxAttention**
> This is for those companies that need more customized support and maintenance options. Onsite specialists work to optimize your SAP software and provide you with ongoing quality management.

> **SAP Safeguarding**
> This is a technical quality management program. It provides a portfolio of assessments, tools, and services that can make your implementation, upgrade, migration, and finally the operation of your IT infrastructure more cost-effective and risk free. SAP Safeguarding services help you manage your core business processes and offer a risk management and service plan.

Find the program best suited for your organization

Your SAP account manager can work with you to determine the program that is best suited for your organization, depending on the size of your implementation and its related risks and costs. In the next section, you will learn more about the tools that are used in each of these programs.

SAP Services Tools and Programs

Many of the services described previously are delivered through specific tools and programs that you will encounter during your implementation, so we will provide a brief overview of these tools and programs here. Some of the tools and programs that provide many of the benefits of SAP Services include the following:

> **SAP Active Global Support (SAP AGS)**
> This includes services for planning, implementation, and operations, with an emphasis on helping to continually improve your business processes.

> **SAP Business Process Outsourcing (SAP BPO)**
> This helps you outsource peripheral business processes so you can focus on core business processes. SAP links you up with business process outsourcing (BPO) providers and offers what they call "enabling solutions and services."

> **SAP Custom Development**
> This uses SAP expertise to help you customize solutions. The program includes the services of development architects, project man-

agers, and developers to modify applications, create entirely new applications, or provide advice on application maintenance.

> **SAP Education**
> This helps companies implement solutions faster, reduce the risks of migrating to the new system, lower support costs, and speed up their adoption of new SAP releases. Curricula can be standard or customized, and cutting edge e-learning methods, simulation tools, and support tools help you save money.

> **SAP Ramp-Up**
> This is not for every SAP customer, but only for those who are involved with helping SAP test new products and providing input. This can put your company ahead of the curve technologically.

You may use different pieces of this support toolkit at various stages of your implementation. Again, your SAP account manager can help you orchestrate the best solution for your business.

In the next section of this chapter, we offer some sources for additional information about SAP and implementing an SAP solution.

Getting Information

There are several sources of information about SAP, its products, and its services that might help you get the most current information about, plan for, and work through an implementation. Some useful resources for information are briefly described here:

> *www.sap.com* is the SAP website; it offers an almost overwhelming wealth of information about SAP's products and their features and benefits, in addition to the articles and white papers, the latest news about SAP, and information about various SAP and SAP community services and support.

www.sap.com

> *SAP Community Network* (SCN) is an online community where those who develop, consult, integrate, or are just curious about learning more about the technical side of SAP can connect. You can access SCN by visiting *http://scn.sap.com/welcome*.

SAP Community Network

> *SAP Service Marketplace* is an extranet service platform run by SAP and used by SAP, its partners, and customers to collaborate. You

SAP Service Marketplace

have to be granted access to this area, but if you are a partner or customer, you will find this to be a helpful, portal-based environment. SAP Service Marketplace can be accessed by visiting *http://service.sap.com*.

SAP User Groups

> *SAP user groups* are nonprofit groups that are independent of SAP. They are made up of SAP partners, customers, and consultants, and they help to provide SAP with information about users' needs as well as providing education to their members.

Books and publications

> SAP PRESS offers an additional resource on SAP implementations: *The SAP Project: More than a Survival Guide (2014)*. Check out this book and other helpful titles at *www.sap-press.com*.

 Note

See Appendix B for a list of SAP resources and their websites.

Support in Action: A Case Study

To truly understand how an SAP implementation works in the real world, let us look at a case study. Review Table 20.1, and then proceed through the rest of the section.

Company	Large European bank
Existing Solutions	Multiple SAP applications
Challenge	To change its business processes to ensure compliance with Basel II capital accords and gain more flexibility from automated processes and centralized reporting
SAP Solutions	SAP Bank Analyzer applications, SAP BW, SAP Consulting support, SAP Custom Development, SAP Education, SAP Safeguarding, SAP Ramp-Up, SAP Active Global Support
Benefits	Enabled short-term and long-term compliance with Basel II, improved risk management and new functionality for trend analysis, and centralized monthly credit data and reporting procedures

Table 20.1 SAP Implementation Case Study

With more than 16,000 employees in 8 countries, this bank needed a way to quickly move into compliance with the complex Basel II accord. Technology was one piece of the puzzle, but the support to quickly implement that technology with a minimum amount of disruption required significant support from SAP and its partners.

It helped that SAP has a long history working with the banking industry. The company had just implemented SAP ERP, which helped to streamline its core business. SAP Consulting took the lead early on, bringing industry knowledge, technical expertise, and a familiarity with the client's data needs to the table. SAP Solution Manager facilitated technical support for various systems, helping to create an audit trail for deployment, operation, and maintenance. SAP Safeguarding services, through the SAP Active Global Support organization, orchestrated performance testing and fine-tuning of the hardware involved in the new system.

SAP and banking

The SAP Custom Development organization (part of SAP Services) created a proprietary application to deal with risk-related loan pricing. The new pricing system that SAP experts helped to implement provides improved templates for Basel II compliance. Lastly, a third party that SAP brought in provided a tool for data loading as part of the SAP Bank Analyzer implementation to help with high-volume data processing needs.

SAP Custom Development

Conclusion

In this chapter, we provided you with an overview of the various resources that exist for information and support as you begin to implement an SAP solution. We recommended that you perform an initial self-analysis of your business to understand its goals, industry-related considerations, and how you will deal with the costs and changes that an SAP implementation involves. We also introduced you to the following programs and resources:

> SOA adoption program
> SAP Services Portfolio
> ASAP Focus methodology
> SAP Consulting's various programs and support services

Now, let us proceed to Chapter 21, where you can learn how to prepare for implementing SAP Cloud Applications such as Ariba and Success-Factors. In that chapter we will discuss about the project methodologies that can be followed while implementing SAP Cloud Applications.

Preparing for an SAP Cloud Implementation

For a customer with years of experience in legacy on premise solutions, implementing a cloud solution means retraining the HR Information Systems team, new recruitment for positions for which internal resources are not available, budgeting, and dedicating members for the project team. Similar to any SAP implementation, implementing SAP Cloud solutions will require planning, budgeting, and identifying the right implementation partner.

 Note

> SAP offers a range of software as a service (SaaS) applications that are hosted in the cloud, and SAP offers cloud applications to help manage your entire enterprise business in the cloud. The SAP Cloud suite includes applications for human resources, financials, procurement, customer service, and sales. SAP Cloud applications can be integrated with your current on premise SAP applications to provide for a seamless integration and exchange of data.
>
> SuccessFactors, Ariba, and SAP Cloud for Travel and Expense are some examples of SAP Cloud Applications that are currently available for customers.

In this chapter, we will discuss how customers can prepare for an SAP Cloud implementation. Although we discuss this chapter from a customer perspective, project team members can also benefit from this chapter. Where helpful, we will specifically call out what is required from an implementation team.

Important Considerations

In this chapter, we will help you understand what a typical SAP Cloud implementation will involve. You need to understand these key elements before you proceed:

> The maturity of your own business processes

> How your business fits with industry trends and best practices

> The potential costs involved to implement and migrate to cloud applications

> How to anticipate and deal with the changes that are required when your applications are in the cloud

Usability Before you embark on your cloud journey, review the enterprise business processes for which you are implementing cloud applications. Many customers look at cloud solutions to leverage the usability experience that the cloud applications provide and the support for current trends.

For example, if you are implementing SuccessFactors Recruiting, take a deep look at your current recruiting process and identify the following topics.

Current Pain Points and Limitations in Your Process

While reviewing the business processes, identify bottlenecks that make the process less efficient and cumbersome. These pain points need to be removed and reengineered to gain efficiencies while implementing the cloud applications.

In a recruiting process, some of the pain points will include applicants not able to complete their job application, hiring managers not seeing a list of applications shortlisted by the recruiter, recruiters generating offer letters without sign off by the hiring manager, and so on.

Strengths of Your Business Process

Similar to identifying the pain points, it is very critical that the strengths of the current business processes are identified. These strengths need to continue to exist when the applications are migrated to the cloud. You can also explore whether any of the strengths can be reengineered to leverage the latest business trends or even to remove a pain point.

Missing any of the identified strengths in your new cloud application will not lead to project success, so work with your implementation and verify that the identified strengths continue to exist in the cloud application. An easy way to perform this verification will be to develop test scripts that capture the identified strengths. When the business users test the application with the developed test scripts, they can verify that the cloud application performs the way it is designed to.

Test scripts

Cloud Application Wish List

While reviewing the business processes, the users and business owners might come up with a wish list of items they would like to be included in the implementation. Review the wish list and identify if any of the items in it correspond to a current business trend. If they do, work with the implementation team to see if they can be included in the implementation. Also identify items that will improve end-user effectiveness and items that might bring efficiencies to your business processes. Among the items from the wish list that are included in the implementation, identify if any of the items can be implemented in the early phase of the project. Early wins greatly generate support for the project from the business community and end users.

Business trends and best practices

Cost of the Implementation

For many customers, cost savings is a primary motivation to move to the cloud. As a best practice, it is recommended that you perform a five-year cost horizon comparing the costs to maintain an on premise application versus a cloud application.

Note

Cloud applications eliminate many fixed costs related to hardware and software. Another advantage of cloud applications is that you pay as you go, meaning you can add and remove user seats as needed.

On premise vs. cloud

Table 21.1 summarizes the difference between on premise and cloud applications against parameters such as software licensing, location of the systems, and maintenance/subscription costs. Gain a good understanding of cloud applications and the costs/benefits associated with them before you embark on your cloud journey.

	On Premise	Cloud
Software license	You own it	You rent it
System location	You own or rent it (i.e., data center)	You rent it
Hardware	Provided by you	Included
Maintenance/ subscription fees	Purchased annually	Included, renewed every three to five years
IT Resources	In-house or consultancy	In-house or consultancy
Support	In-house, vendor, or consultancy	In-house, vendor, or consultancy

Table 21.1 Comparison of On Premise and Cloud Applications

Integration with your current on premise application and other cloud applications

Integrating your cloud application with other on premise and/or cloud applications will take a significant amount of time and budget. Do plan for these integrations (if they are required to sustain your business processes) while planning for the project.

SAP is continuously delivering integrations for their cloud applications. Check with SAP whether delivered integrations are available that meet your needs.

 Who Can Help You Implement?

SAP Consulting can support your implementation of the cloud applications. You can also reach out to the ecosystem and approach any SAP-approved implementation partner for implementing the cloud applications. Work with your SAP account executive to help identify a suitable implementation partner.

Project Planning and Methodology

Similar to SAP on premise implementation, you need to plan and follow project management methodologies for cloud applications implementation.

 Note

Only Ariba and SuccessFactors have their own methodology. Other SAP Cloud applications do not (because they are all developed by SAP themselves). Customers can use these methodologies as guidance while implementing other SAP Cloud applications.

BizXpert for SuccessFactors

If you are implementing a SuccessFactors solution, BizXpert (see Figure 21.1) is the project management methodology that you will need to use to manage and deliver SuccessFactors-related projects.

Figure 21.1 BizXpert Methodology for Managing SuccessFactors Projects

 Note

The Sales phase in the BizXpert Methodology Map (Figure 21.1) is not an official customer-facing BizXpert phase. It is included in the BizXpert methodoloy map to reiterate the importance of sales in the success of the project to the implementation team.

Table 21.2 describes the critical tasks in each phase of the Success-Factors project that uses the BizXpert project management methodology.

Critical tasks

Phase	Deliverables
Sales	› Lead determination › Set project scope & pricing › SOW process—determine functional and technical scope › Transition from sales to project-implementation team › Provide customer-access provisioning
Prepare	› Complete project-team orientation (PTO) › Project kick off and kick-off meeting › The customer works with the implementation team to conduct project planning and resource booking › The implementation team conducts requirements-gathering workshops
Realize	› Configuration and requirements refinement › Legacy data migrations, if any › Extensions/technical developments, if any › Data imports/exports (integrations) › Unit testing/configuration verification
Verify	› Integration testing › User-acceptance testing (UAT) › Go-live training for the user community
Launch	› The team plans for the go-live › Cutover plan is developed › After the go-live, the application is transitioned to the customer success team at SuccessFactors › Go-live support provided by the implementation team › Project closeout and lessons learned

Table 21.2 Deliverables in Each Phase of the BizXpert Project Management Methodology

Checkpoints

During each phase of the BizXpert project management, there are checkpoints. Checkpoints are milestones at which the project stakeholders agree that the identified deliverables for that phase meet the project requirements and, consequently, the project can continue.

Table 21.3 describes identified checkpoints at each phase of the BizXpert methodology.

Phase	Checkpoint	Description
Sales	Transition from sales to implementation team	Once the sales are completed, the implementation partner is identified. The implementation team will work with SuccessFactors sales team to understand what modules are purchased. The implementation team will also be given access to the customer-provisioning account.
Prepare	Scope and project readiness	Ensure the customer is ready to engage in project activities.
Realize	Configuration acceptance	Ensure configuration matches and is aligned to the captured business requirements.
Verify	Integration testing acceptance	Ensure configuration, data, and integrations (if any) support the business processes.
Launch	Production readiness acceptance	Ensure the customer is ready for the go-live.

Table 21.3 Checkpoints in Each Phase of the BizXpert Project Management Methodology

Ariba

Similar to SuccessFactors, Ariba (first discussed in Chapter 10) has its own project management methodology. Figure 21.2 shows the different phases in Ariba's project-management methodology. These phases are as follows:

> **Phase 0: Sales support**
> **Phase 1: Project management and prep for deployment kick off**
> Standard project management methodology and tools are used to define project scope, resourcing, and timeline.
> **Phase 2: Deployment kick off**
> Project scope, approach, and timeline are shared with the team. Roles and responsibilities are discussed with the team. An overivew of the as-is state is discussed. Configuration workshops are started.

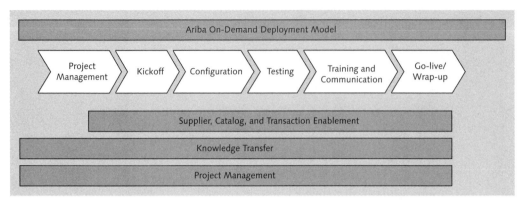

Figure 21.2 Ariba Deployment Framework

> **Phase 3: Functional and data configuration**
> Ariba is configured as per customer requierments. Master data is loaded into the Ariba application. System configuration and data loads are validated. Preparation is started for testing phase.

> **Phase 4: Testing**
> Integration test and user acceptance testing are conducted during this phase. Customer will sign-off on configuration and data loads.

> **Phase 5: Training and communication**
> Training is developed and delivered to the identified teams. Communications regarding the go-live are published.

> **Phase 6: Go-live**
> Ariba solution is moved to production.

> **Phase 7: Wrap up and transition to Ariba customer support**
> The application (project) is transitioned to operations and customer support. The customer provides the final sign-off.

Change Management

Change management is an important process that is required to make the transition to the cloud a success story.

Best practice: have a change management team

As a best practice, it is suggested to engage a change management team from the start of the project. The change management team can be included in business workshops as well. These will provide an opportunity for the change management team to understand the scope of the project and the complexities involved in the change process. The change management team can also provide inputs on what features and usability experiences can be easily rolled-out. The change management team might also be able to provide input on what features can be included in the first wave and what can be considered for later waves.

The change management frameworks that can be followed are discussed in the next sections.

Communications

Develop a communications strategy on how to communicate the transition to the cloud to the end users and stakeholders. Typically, this would mean developing a terminology sheet, a sheet that provides an overview of the changes in business processes (if any), informing your vendors who use the system or whose applications interface with your cloud application. You should also communicate about the advantages and benefits the new application provides to the user community and to the organization.

Stakeholder Management

Provide periodic updates on the progress of the project, status of the open items, resourcing issues (if any), and the project budget to the stakeholders. These can be on a formal level, such as steering committee meetings, as well as on an informal basis.

As part of the change management process, identify key employees who can function as champions of the project and who can highlight the benefits the project will bring to the organization. These champions can be from the executive level or can even be key business users.

Workforce Transition

Identify any changes in employee policies or processes that are due to the implementation of the cloud application. Identify any changes to security roles or policies that need to be addressed.

Prepare the organization and the workforce for the successful deployment of the cloud application.

When you transition from on premise applications to cloud-based applications, some of the employees might possibly need to be reskilled. Make plans for this as well when you are preparing for a cloud implementation.

Training

Train the trainers and documentation

Provide required training to the end users and to the administrators of the cloud applications. One typical training method is to "train the trainers." During train the trainers, the identified employees are trained on the application and given a walkthrough of the business process to make them fully equipped to provide support during the rollout of the application. These trainers will act as points of contact for other employees if they need any help or have any questions about the application. You can also consider developing end-user documentation and making it available to the end users. Customers can also consider developing a training video and making it available for the end users. Do note that well-planned training is essential to support an implementation. Often, the longevity of an application is shortened due to a badly planned training rollout.

Knowledge Transfer

Ensure that there is proper knowledge transfer from the implementation team to the end users and to the administrators of the cloud applications. The knowledge transfer should ensure that the users are comfortable in maintaining the application without any downside to the business processes. Typical documentation that needs to be completed and walked through during the knowledge transfer (KT) includes the configuration workbook, security workbook highlighting the security settings that were made, process flow maps, functional specifications that detail the customizations and extensions that were developed, and documentation related to integrations. Integrations and customizations are usually complex in many cloud implementations. Lack of complete documentation or KT might result in spending time researching what was done or in difficulty in maintaining the applications.

Note

The knowledge transfer and training can be facilitated as a combination of on-the-job and one-on-one trainings. As a suggested best practice, encourage your team to shadow the implementation team consultants. Shadowing the implementation team would mean more hands-on experience of the cloud application and a greater opportunity to learn. Shadowing is always a better training option than a classroom-oriented KT or training. However, this does not mean that you should do away with KT or training. Both KT and training can add to the shadowing experience.

To see how to prepare for SAP Cloud implementation, read through the following case study.

SAP Cloud Implementation Case Study

Table 21.4 gives you a quick overview of the case study exemplifying how to prepare for a SAP Cloud implementation. Go through it before you read the rest of this section.

Company	A global life sciences company
Existing Solutions	The company is an existing SAP customer that recently moved its on premise HCM applications to the cloud. The company has applications such as Financials and Logistics still on premise.
Challenge	Existing travel and expense solution is on premise; the legacy travel and expense application is proving expensive to maintain, and the company is not willing to invest any further in an on premise solution.
SAP Cloud Solution	SAP Cloud for Travel and Expense
Benefits	SAP Cloud for Travel and Expense enables employees to use their smartphone cameras, location services, and date defaults to capture travel and expense receipts on the dates they are incurred. This feature greatly reduces the chance of lost receipts and delays in submitting expense reports.

Table 21.4 SAP Cloud Implementation Case Study

A life sciences company has offices distributed globally. Its employees travel frequently. The company is currently using a third-party on premise travel and expense application. Although the current T&E application fully meets their business processes, the users are not happy with the application. The legacy T&E does not fully support mobility, there are frequent issues related to workflows, and the HRIS team spends large amounts of time to maintain the application.

With the successful implementation of SuccessFactors behind them, the HRIS team felt a need to migrate T&E to the cloud. They did an initial study of SAP Cloud for Travel and Expense and saw a demo of the application as well.

HRIS made a decision to implement SAP Cloud for Travel and Expense and sunset their legacy T&E application.

The Challenges

The company has an employee base of 4,000 employees working from various global offices and another 3,000 employees working in different factories. Many employees, including managers and senior executives, travel frequently. Travel request forms have to be approved by the appropriate line manager, and receipts for expenses incurred need to be submitted within 15 days of completion of travel.

The company decided to replace the existing legacy T&E application with an application that supports mobility, easy workflow approvals, and ability to upload receipts, as well as easy integration with the SAP FI-CO solution.

The SAP Cloud for Travel and Expense Solution

The customer has retained SAP Consulting as the project implementation partner. SAP has implemented SAP Cloud for Travel and Expense for other customers in the recent past and has access to the best practices that the customer is looking to implement as part of the solution implementation.

The customer identified that employee travel records and other data that currently exists in the legacy T&E application should be migrated to the new SAP Cloud for T&E application.

The customer identified that a training budget needed to be allocated to develop ready-to-refer videos that would walk the user through how to use the new application, conduct training classes for the HR team involved in processing travel expenses, and conduct training for the managers explaining the benefits of the new application and ways to approve travel requests through mobile devices.

Training and change management

A change management lead was assigned to the project team to develop change-management processes to support go-live of the new application.

The change management lead noticed that SAP Cloud for Travel & Expense is fully supported by mobile devices and that employees using this application can capture receipt information in real time and manage expenses while travelling. She noted these functionalities as being critical for the success of the application and that these functionalities should be communicated to the employee population.

During the blueprinting phase of the project, the implementation team identified the business requirements and shared the industry trends and best practices with the customer.

The implementation team collaborated with the customer to determine and implement the different integration points between SAP Cloud for T&E, SAP HCM (required to integrate employee information), and SAP FI-CO (required to integrate budgeting and cost center information). The implementation team discussed testing strategies with the customer, and test scripts were developed jointly with the customer.

SAP's ASAP project methodology was used to implement the project. All project documents were stored and tracked in SAP Solution Manager. The customer had a successful go-live, and the initial feedback from the user community was very positive.

The immediate benefits from the successful go-live are that the employees are able to submit their travel expenses on time and the HR team are able to process the submissions within five to seven working days after submittal. Managers can now approve all travel requests from their mobile devices and are no longer constrained by the need to access the workflows from their laptops.

Immediate benefits

Looking toward the Future

The customer is very impressed with the successful go-lives of their SuccessFactors and SAP Cloud for Travel & Expense applications. The user community is very pleased with the usability and mobility experiences that cloud applications provide. The HRIS team is able to concentrate on more immediate needs rather than being involved in support and maintenance of the on premise applications.

Conclusion

In this chapter, we provided an overview of how you can prepare for SAP Cloud implementation. The chapter discussed the following:

> The various resources that are available for you to prepare for the SAP Cloud implementation.

> The need for you to review your current business processes and see if they can be reengineered to gain better efficiencies provided by cloud applications.

> The project methodologies that are followed while implementing SAP Cloud solutions, and the need to integrate your cloud applications with your current on premise applications.

> What to consider for change management.

Now let us proceed to Chapter 22, where we will discuss a recent development in SAP implementation options, call SAP Rapid Deployment solutions.

An Introduction to SAP Rapid Deployment Solutions

As with any software implementation, it's unfortunately not atypical to see an SAP implementation with project time and budget overruns. Among other things, these overruns can be due to poor requirements gathering, staff training, and migration issues. Blueprinting alone can take up to a year before the actual software is even touched.

After seeing that customers can struggle to configure a full deployment to their unique needs, SAP has developed a new offer: SAP Rapid Deployment solutions. These solutions enable customers to quickly deploy specific SAP solutions at a lower service-to-software ratio. These are preconfigured, topic-specific software offerings that are developed and tested by SAP, containing industry best practices. Individual rapid-deployment solutions can be implemented at customer locations in as little as six to eight weeks.

In this chapter, we will explore the concept behind SAP Rapid Deployment solutions, look at what is delivered with a rapid-deployment solution package, and look at a quick case study.

The Concept

Software from scratch vs. standardized best practices

Traditionally, an organization wants a software solution that meets its specific needs. This means that every aspect of the software solution needs to be designed from scratch, which can take a very long time, as we have already mentioned. And just think: by the time a year has gone by on blueprinting, your organization may have made some drastic changes, which requires even more time spent on modifying the blueprint!

This is where SAP Best Practices come in. We have already mentioned that SAP has developed a standard set of industry best practices, which are recommended to customers during implementation. Now, SAP has taken their best practices and developed standardized, pre-configured software packages.

Engineered solutions and customization

After learning about a software package that is preconfigured and standardized, you may be skeptical. A fast implementation sounds great, but what about tailoring the solution for specific business needs? SAP has thought of that, too. Like SAP Business All-in-One, a rapid-deployment solution bundles SAP software with SAP Best Practices. However, a rapid-deployment solution also provides engineered services that can be provided by an SAP consultant or qualified partner. In contrast to a traditional, "build-to-order" delivery approach, engineered services enhance and expand the existing SAP Rapid Deployment solutions philosophy in order to provide faster time to value for customers.

SAP provides different versions of rapid-deployment solutions, as well. These solutions are available for full cloud, full on premise, and hybrid solutions deployment.

Solutions across SAP's portfolios

Figure 22.1 shows that a rapid-deployment solution is available across many of SAP's product portfolios. SAP and SAP Partners are adding new rapid-deployment solutions every week. You can check online for their ever-changing list of solutions, and also refer to the book *Rapid Deployment of SAP Solutions* by Bernd Welz et al. (SAP PRESS, 2013).

Mobile and User Experience

- Simplify user experience
- Deploy mobile platforms easily
- Mobilize enterprise applications
- Secure mobile access
- Provision mobile devices fast
- Extend access anywhere, anytime

Cloud

- New cloud SaaS solution deployment
- Rapid migration to cloud
- Integration for hybrid cloud and on premise landscapes

Business Applications

- Asset management
- Corporate strategy
- Finance
- Human resources
- Manufacturing
- Procurement
- Sales, service, marketing
- Supply chain management
- Industry-specific processes

Analytics

- Accelerate business intelligence adoption
- Powerful planning and consolidation
- Increase transparency and governance

In-Memory Capabilities

- Rapid migration to SAP HANA
- New in-memory-based solutions with content designed for SAP HANA
- Advanced predictive analytics
- Content for accelerated insight and business intelligence

Figure 22.1 SAP Rapid Deployment Solutions across SAP's Portfolio

Note

You can get more details about SAP Rapid Deployment solutions by logging into SAP Service Marketplace and accessing *www.service.sap.com/ rds*. You need to have an S User ID to be able to log in to SAP Service Marketplace. Your BASIS administrator will be able to create an S User ID for you.

Assets That Are Available with a Solution Package

When you implement a rapid-deployment solution package from SAP, it comes available with preconfigured implementation content that is based on industry best practices that are tested by SAP and ready for customer deployment. A rapid-deployment solution package contains the following (see Figure 22.2):

> Documentation such as business process procedures (BPP), detailed step-by-step deployment guides, and scope/project documentation

Contents of the solution package: documentation

> Configuration and technical documentation that explains what configuration settings need to be completed

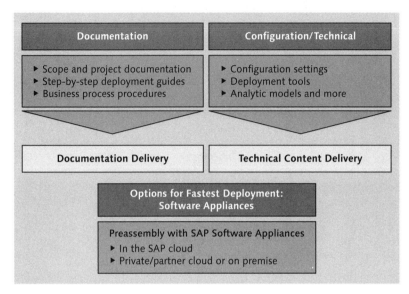

Figure 22.2 Contents of a Rapid-Deployment Solution Software Package

 Note

SAP Rapid Deployment Solutions software package can be implemented by the customer or can be implemented by SAP Consulting or by any of the SAP implementation partners.

Typically, when a customer is implementing a rapid-deployment solution, the following assets (see Table 22.1) are provided and made available to the customer or implementation team.

Asset	Description
Building block configuration guides	Describes in detail how to manually configure the system
Building block descriptions	Describes in detail the content and functions covered by the building block
Content library	A listing of the building block ID numbers and the building block titles
Manual activation and configuration page	A generated page that groups together information about manual activation and configuration

Table 22.1 List of Assets Available in a Rapid-Deployment Solution Package

Asset	Description
Prerequisites matrix	A listing of the required building blocks and their implementation sequence
Master data procedures	This document describes how to create master data that supports the preconfigured content
Activation content (if possible)	All content that is used to activate a solution in the customer's landscape (the exact technology used depends on the chosen rapid-deployment solution)
Automated activation page (if possible)	Provides information about activation with SAP Best Practices Solution Builder
Solution (scope) file (if possible)	A definition of the solution scope provided as an XML file that is used to activate preconfiguration in the target system with SAP Best Practices Solution Builder
Quick guide for package implementation	Provides documentation to implement the complete package scope after the technical landscape has been defined according to the software requirements
SAP Note	A compilation of released SAP Notes that provides additional information or corrections for the installation and documentation of the solution
Software requirements	A table that lists all software required to implement and run the chosen rapid-deployment solution
Business process documentation page	This page groups information about the business processes in the solution
Function list	A listing of transactions in scope
Process diagrams	Describes the sequence of steps in each scope item in the solution
Scope item descriptions	Describes the business context and process flow of each business process or key feature

Table 22.1 List of Assets Available in a Rapid-Deployment Solution Package (Cont.)

Asset	Description
SAP Solution Manager template	A container for the implementation content for one or more solutions in an area
SAP Solution Manager template description	A list of solutions contained in the template describing dependencies within each solution
Business process documentation	Describes each business process as it is realized in the chosen rapid-deployment solution

Table 22.1 List of Assets Available in a Rapid-Deployment Solution Package (Cont.)

Rapid-Deployment Solution Implementation Case Study

Table 22.2 gives you a quick overview of the first case study showing how to prepare for a rapid-deployment solution implementation. Review it before you read the rest of this section.

Company	A public sector customer in Europe
Existing Solution	A third-party recruiting ATS solution. This ATS is integrated to the customer's SAP HCM solution. The SAP HCM solution is on ECC 6.0 EHP5.
Challenge	The recruiting ATS was not providing the efficiency the customer was expecting; there were candidate drop-offs, recruiters were not able to report on applications, and the solution was not candidate friendly.
SAP RDS Solution	SAP E-Recruitment rapid-deployment solution was the solution decided upon by the customer to replace the legacy ATS application.
Benefits	SAP E-Recruiting rapid-deployment solution software offered the best solution for the customer, because it is a preconfigured software solution, and met the customer's business requirements.

Table 22.2 SAP Rapid Deployment Solutions Implementation Case Study

A public-sector customer based in Europe is currently using a third-party applicant tracking system (ATS) as their recruiting solution.

E-recruiting

The recruiting solution is integrated to their SAP ERP HCM application. The employee data (internal candidates) is integrated to the ATS, and the hired candidate data is sent back to the HCM application for the hiring and onboarding processes.

The Challenges

The recruiters feel the current ATS does not fully support their business needs. Candidates are not able to register for job alerts (it does not exist in the ATS application), and the job-application process is long and cumbersome.

The ATS does not have a ranking of candidates based on their qualifications, so the recruiter has to manually review the candidate applications and rank them prior to the prescreening process.

The ATS does not have a good reporting and analytics capability, and the customer had to develop SAP BW–based cubes for their reporting needs.

The customer chose SAP E-Recruiting rapid-deployment solution software as their go-to recruiting solution.

The Rapid-Deployment Implementation Solution

The customer had just invested in their ATS application, and was not comfortable going through another long implementation cycle. When they reviewed the SAP E-Recruiting rapid-deployment solution software, they felt comfortable with the solution.

The rapid-deployment solution software offered a preconfigured software package and a complete set of configuration documentation with details on how to download the package, what business functions should be activated, and what switches need to be configured.

The customer retained SAP Consulting, which had prior experience with implementing rapid-deployment solution software applications and implementation methodology (see Figure 22.3), which the customer felt would greatly help in implementing the rapid-deployment

Methodology

solution software package. This methodology provides a roadmap for implementation, as well as a team to guide the execution of the selected rapid-deployment solution from Start (initial preparation) to Run (go-live).

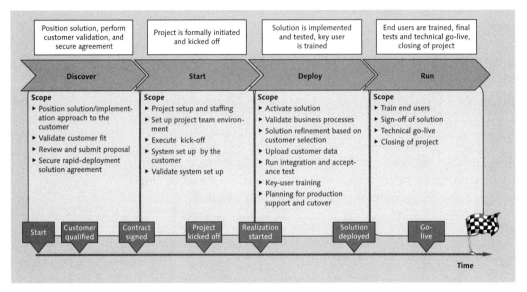

Figure 22.3 SAP Rapid Deployment Solutions Implementation Methodology

The customer took the responsibility of modifying the business process maps (which were available with the rapid-deployment solution package) where required to meet their requirements. The SAP team ran a blueprinting workshop to capture the requirements, downloaded the rapid-deployment solution package, set the configuration (as described in the configuration document asset), and made the changes as requested by the customer. Testing of the application was completed, and the go-live was 10 weeks from the start of the project.

Looking toward the Future

The customer was very impressed with the rapid-deployment solution implementation methodology and the assets that were available with the package. The assets were descriptive, and the documentation explained (refer back to Figure 22.2) what modules were mandatory versus optional. SAP Consulting was able to reach go-live within the agreed-upon time frame. The customer is now planning to implement rapid-deployment solution packages for FI-CO requirements.

Conclusion

In this chapter, we provided a short introduction to SAP Rapid Deployment solutions and the assets that are available when you use a rapid-deployment solution software package.

Through the case study, we introduced the concept of rapid-deployment solution implementation methodology and how a rapid-deployment solution software package can be implemented.

Now, we will proceed to Chapter 23, where you can learn about SAP Solution Manager and how it can help support your SAP implementation.

SAP Solution Manager

SAP Solution Manager is SAP's central platform for application management and collaboration, provided to SAP's customers at no additional cost. You have to use SAP Solution Manager to implement SAP solutions, and with good reason. This very useful platform helps you manage your implementation, and also helps you manage ongoing requirements throughout your solution's lifecycle.

In this chapter, we look at what SAP Solution Manager is, the benefits it offers your business, and the specific functions it delivers. Finally, we explore a case study in which you can see SAP Solution Manager in action.

What Is SAP Solution Manager?

SAP Solution Manager contains tools to support your SAP implementation, monitor your system after it is in place, request support from SAP's support organization, and upgrade your system when you need to grow and change. Quite simply, SAP Solution Manager takes you from the beginning to the end of your SAP experience (see Figure 23.1).

Implementation, monitoring, support, upgrade

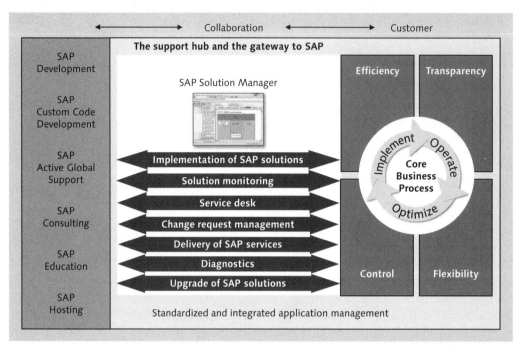

Figure 23.1 Solution Manager Has Many Roles (Source: SAP Solution Manager [2006] Schäfer & Melich. SAP PRESS)

SAP Solution Manager Overview

Included and required

SAP Solution Manager is included in the cost of your yearly maintenance contract, and you have to use it to implement SAP NetWeaver (and all of the SAP products that rest on SAP NetWeaver) in your organization. SAP Solution Manager provides three categories of offerings, as shown in Table 23.1.

Tools	Application/Technology Management and Maintenance, including:
	› Document
	› Implement
	› Train
	› Test a Deployment
	› Support and Maintain
	› Monitor and Optimize

Table 23.1 SAP Solution Manager's Offerings

Tools (Cont.)	› Control Change
	› Manage Incidents
Content	› Methodologies
	› Roadmaps
	› Services
	› Best Practices
Gateway to SAP	› SAP Active Global Support
	› SAP Development
	› Service Delivery Platform

Table 23.1 SAP Solution Manager's Offerings (Cont.)

As you begin to plan your implementation, SAP Solution Manager provides roadmaps (see Figure 23.2) that you can follow to work through the various phases of the installation or upgrade process. It also provides frameworks, tools, and services that are useful not only during your implementation, but also long after.

Roadmaps and other tools

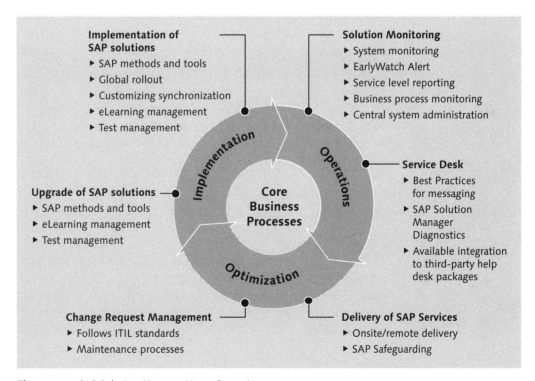

Figure 23.2 SAP Solution Manager Usage Scenarios

SAP Solution
Manager documen-
tation repository
Another role of SAP Solution Manager is to document your implementation in detail in a process-oriented documentation repository. The documentation can then be used by support groups or your own IT people to get a view of your IT enterprise computing landscape. If the people involved in your implementation or upgrade leave, you will still have a wealth of historical data for others to draw on as they maintain, upgrade, or troubleshoot your solution. Many SAP implementation teams also use SAP Solution Manager to document business requirements and generate the blueprinting document.

 Tip

> SAP Solution Manager contains a functionality called Business Process Repository (BPR). BPR is the central storage of an integrated, cross-component business scenario. From within the BPR, select your business scenarios or business processes. Modify to fit your requirements, and use them for requirements capture, configuration, and testing.
>
> Once you complete capturing the business requirements, you can generate the blueprinting document containing the captured business requirements from within SAP Solution Manager.

SAP Solution Manager provides certain functionality that helps to document and expedite your implementation, but those features are based on an underlying approach to how you put pieces of your solution into place, which we will explore in the next section. Finally, SAP Solution Manager ties you into SAP's support organization, generating information they can use to help you over any bumps that you may encounter on the implementation road.

The SAP Solution Manager Approach

There are six key ideas that provide the foundation for SAP Solution Manager and its various features:

Business process
focus
> ▶ SAP Solution Manager is designed to help IT employees link technology tools to fit the needs of various business units in a company. It helps IT employees communicate with business users and hide the technological details from them, focusing instead on their business needs.

> When you implement software in your organization, it has a lifecycle that might last years. Applications that spread across your entire enterprise will not only need to be implemented but will also require updating and maintaining. SAP Solution Manager helps you monitor the entire lifecycle of your solution.

Openness, coordination of IT processes, tools, and documents

> SAP Solution Manager helps you integrate the various pieces of business processes and account for the various components and interdependencies that are involved. In addition, SAP Solution Manager helps you integrate software from other vendors by providing dedicated integration packages.

Integration

> SAP supports an open environment spanning any number of systems and platforms. SAP Solution Manager also supports the implementation of SAP products in a way that allows for a variety of products and helps you resolve issues among those products.

Lifecycle support

> SAP Solution Manager coordinates the IT processes, tools, and documents that you need to implement and operate an SAP solution.

Single point of access

> SAP Solution Manager gathers a variety of information about your SAP implementation together and makes it available in one location. This is useful not only for you to locate information about your systems but also to comply with information-transparency requirements (see Figure 23.1).

Transparency

SAP Solution Manager is the platform that, based on these six underlying ideas, enables you to implement standards for end-to-end (E2E) solution operations. This means that after an implementation, you have the experience from thousands of successful projects at your fingertips.

End-to-end (E2E)

Now that we have given you a rough idea of what SAP Solution Manager is, we will look more closely at the features and tools you get with SAP Solution Manager.

SAP Solution Manager Contents

SAP Solution Manager gives you technical support for deploying solutions, operating your systems, and upgrading your solutions long term. SAP Solution Manager supports both SAP and non-SAP software and will dovetail nicely with upcoming SAP solutions.

 Tip

> Typically, you wnill enjoy a lower cost of ownership by having SAP Solution Manager in place.

Connect IT to business

SAP Solution Manager is strongly focused on your core business; it provides tools and features for your IT people to connect technology to your business processes and strategies (see Figure 23.3). From installing a new piece of enterprise software to managing your existing systems, SAP Solution Manager was designed to make everything work together and help you solve problems rather than create new ones.

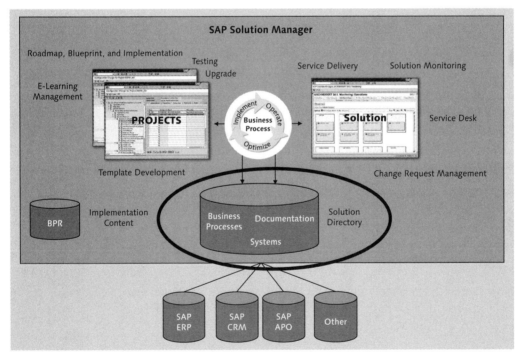

Figure 23.3 How SAP Solution Manager Fits in an Implementation Environment

Functionality

SAP Solution Manager offers a lot of functionality to support your implementation:

> Configuration information and a processcentric implementation strategy help you create an implementation blueprint, configure your system, and deal with the final preparation phases of your implementation. SAP Solution Manager has tools that help you administer your project and deal with cross-component implementations. For example, Figure 23.4 displays what needs to be done to manage business blueprinting in SAP Solution Manager.

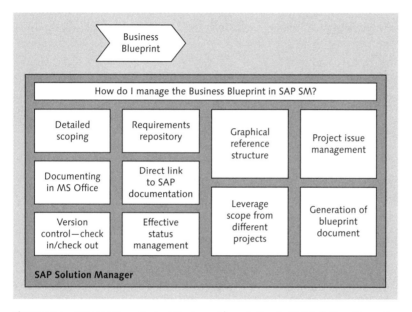

Figure 23.4 *Manage Your Project Business Blueprinting in SAP Solution Manager*

> Rollout tools to support standardization of your processes throughout your enterprise with methodologies and predesigned functionality. You can build Business Configuration Sets and put standardized settings in place at your various sites without having to reenter configuration settings locally.

> Support desk functionality that helps you deal with support incidents quickly and saves you money in the area of support costs.

> Monitoring for your systems, business processes, and interfaces, including any dependencies among your various systems.

Monitoring features constantly check for problems and help you avoid disasters. SAP Solution Manager also sends automatic notifications of problems and helps you know whether SAP ERP is functioning as it should.

SAP Safeguarding SAP Solution Manager provides tools for preparing system tests and making their execution faster. You get one point of access to your entire system and centralized storage of testing material. Service recommendations and connections to SAP support services, such as SAP Safeguarding for dealing with technical risk, are also included.

 Note

For more information on the specific help functions in SAP Solution Manager, refer to the book *IT Service Management in SAP Solution Manager* by Nathan Williams (SAP PRESS, 2013).

How do these features work in practice? Take a look at a case study to see exactly how SAP Solution Manager fits into a typical SAP implementation.

SAP Solution Manager Case Study

Table 23.2 provides you with a snapshot of a case study. Review the table and the remainder of this section to learn more about how SAP Solution Manager worked for one company.

Company	European natural gas supplier
Existing Solutions	Standardized on SAP ERP, SAP BW, SAP Enterprise Buyer (SAP EB), and industry-specific SAP solutions
Challenge	To implement a CRM solution quickly while keeping the solution cost-effective
SAP Solutions	SAP Solution Manager and SAP CRM
Benefits	Fast implementation with documentation repository to help support maintenance and future upgrades of system; predefined content provided a foundation for customizing

Table 23.2 SAP Solution Manager Case Study

A Norwegian company that supplies natural gas to European customers is also a major supplier of crude oil. With 24,000 employees and offices around the world, the company was growing and enjoying great success but needed to plan now for future growth. To support its success, the company felt that SAP CRM was a logical fit for its future.

The Challenges

The company needed a CRM solution, including mobile sales features to support about 200 field salespeople in Norway, Denmark, and Sweden. Extensive downtime was not an option for this $37 billion company, so the company wanted to roll out SAP CRM quickly and efficiently. The company hoped to save money through various methods, including having its own employees assist with the implementation.

The SAP Solution

SAP Consulting worked with the company to structure an SAP CRM solution and suggested using SAP Solution Manager to streamline the implementation. SAP Consulting conducted a two-day workshop with the company's IT employees. Implementation accelerators and an entire set of preconfigured business processes in SAP Solution Manager helped the company get a head start. SAP Solution Manager also gave the IT staff an understanding of both the functionality of SAP Solution Manager and how its tools could support relevant business processes.

CRM solution

The centralized repository for implementation documentation that SAP Solution Manager provided has proven to be a valuable resource for future changes and maintenance. In addition, predefined configuration settings served as a great starting point for customization.

The Benefits

The SAP solution set up the blueprint for SAP CRM and configured the entire system. The costs were half of what the company spent on its entire legacy CRM system. SAP Solution Manager enabled an implementation that took less than a year to complete.

SAP CRM blueprint

In fact, the company's employees could handle more of the process without consultant input because of SAP Solution Manager and the tools it provided. The company's next step is to implement an Internet sales model in partnership with SAP to leverage the features and tools of SAP Solution Manager further.

 Tip

> SAP Solution Manager provides a variety of centralized services for implementing your SAP projects and operating your SAP solutions.
>
> Some of the advantages include the following:
>
> › One central point of access
> › End-to-end process control
> › Guaranteed consistency within your system landscape

Conclusion

In this chapter, we provided an introduction to SAP Solution Manager, which is integral to any SAP implementation, with the following:

> ❯ An overview of the features that SAP Solution Manager offers you to make your implementation more efficient and effective

> ❯ The six key ideas underlying SAP's approach to using SAP Solution Manager

> ❯ A discussion of the SAP Solution Manager scenarios that deliver key features of SAP Solution Manager

> ❯ A case study of SAP Solution Manager in action

As mentioned at the start of the chapter, you are required to use SAP Solution Manager, because it is part of SAP NetWeaver. You will find that it automates your implementation documentation in very helpful ways.

The Next Step

We hope the information in this chapter, as well as the information provided in the preceding chapters, has provided you with a solid foundation for understanding what SAP, the company, is; what products and technologies it offers; and what tools and services it delivers to support you through an SAP implementation.

We hope that this book makes your experience with SAP and its products a smoother and more productive one, letting you make informed choices. Throughout this book, we have tried to give you the latest and most accurate information possible about the specific products, services, and driving concepts behind SAP so that you have a solid grounding in enterprise computing and SAP's offerings. Of course, SAP is known for being responsive to its customers' needs, which means that they constantly update products and services or offer new innovations, so be sure to check some of the resources listed previously, and contact an SAP representative to discuss your needs when you are ready to implement an SAP solution.

Appendices

A   Glossary

ABAP   (Advanced Business Application Programming) The programming language developed by SAP to develop applications for SAP systems.

Abstraction The act of representing essential features without including the background details or explanations. In the computer science and software engineering domain, the "abstraction" principle is used to reduce complexity and allow efficient design and implementation of complex software systems.

Access management The process used in organizations to grant or deny employees and others authorization to secure systems and network elements.

Adobe Interactive Forms (SAP Interactive Forms software by Adobe) A digital forms technology used in SAP software for collaborative electronic forms documentation.

Alloy An application developed through the joint effort of SAP and IBM to allow Lotus Notes users to access data within the SAP Business Suite.

Analytics The combination of skills, technologies, applications, and processes used by organizations to gain insight into their business. It typically involves collecting, cleansing, transforming, and reporting on data collected by their transactional systems during their day-to-day activities.

ASUG (Americas' SAP Users' Group) A nonprofit organization of SAP customer companies dedicated to providing educational and networking opportunities in support of SAP applications and implementation. ASUG also works with SAP in its Partners in Education Program offered at the annual SAP TechEd conference.

Authentication The process of verifying the identity of a computer user to provide access to a system, data, or network area.

Best practice A management concept that involves devising a method or process that most effectively produces a desired outcome. SAP applications use business best practices to automate common business processes. See also SAP Best Practices.

Business Application Programming Interface (BAPI) An application programming interface (source code that systems use to request services from computer applications) with certain business rules attached.

Business content Predefined sets of business analytics artifacts, such as extractors, data marts, InfoObjects, queries, and web templates, predefined by SAP and delivered as part of SAP BW and covering a wide range of business areas.

Business object Items in an object-oriented computer application that match an abstract business concept, such as an order, invoice, or product. Business objects are used as part of a domain model to encapsulate their associated behavior in programming.

Business process outsourcing Contracting with an external vendor to perform a discrete set of business processes, such as payroll processing, procurement, accounts payable, and so on.

Business process A set of related steps performed to create a defined result in a business setting. SAP applications support typical business processes, such as invoicing.

Business to business Services or products delivered by one business to another business, that is, not directly to individuals.

BusinessObjects A business intelligence company purchased by SAP in 2008 (see Chapter 14 for details). Also refers to the products that were incorporated into SAP's Business Intelligence portfolio, as a result of the acquisition.

Change management A structured approach to the process of strategizing and managing change for individuals, teams, and departments in an organization.

Collaboration room Online portals where members of a team can collaborate by sharing documents, applications, schedules, and tasks, along with communicating via chats or discussions.

Compliance The process businesses use to comply with regulations such as Sarbanes-Oxley or health and safety regulations.

Composite application An application that rests on other applications or components to use their service-enabled functions and data to build business scenarios.

Corporate Services One of the four main applications areas of SAP ERP; Corporate Services offers tools such as

real estate management, enterprise asset management, and travel management.

Dashboard A Business Intelligence interface that provides metrics, statistics, insights, and visualization into current data. It allows users to view instant results of the live performance state of business or data analytics. It also refers to SAP BusinessObjects Dashboards — an SAP BusinessObjects data visualization component.

Data warehouse A collection of corporate data derived from operational systems and external data sources, designed to support business decisions by allowing data consolidation, analysis, and reporting at different aggregate levels. A data warehouse is populated through the processes of extraction, transformation, and loading.

Database An electronic collection of information organized for easy access by computer programs.

Digital signature A form of authentication in SAP in which a user enters an SAP password to validate information entered or decisions made.

Document Management System A component of SAP that integrates with logistics, operations, supply chain, and product lifecycle management to manage all of documentation.

Duet A joint venture of Microsoft and SAP that allows the use of SAP functionality and business intelligence through the Microsoft Office environment.

Embedded analytics Incorporating business intelligence within operational applications and business processes.

Employee Self-Service (ESS) One of two self-service features provided by SAP NetWeaver that enables employees to access data and complete processes related to their roles in a company, such as submitting vacation leave requests or signing up for employee training. See also Manager Self-Service (MSS).

Encryption The process of using an algorithm to encode information, making it unreadable for unauthorized users. The encoded data may only be decrypted or made readable with a key and the reverse algorithm.

Enterprise computing Computer systems and processes used within an enterprise.

Enterprise resource planning (ERP) A type of application that is used to integrate all of the data and processes of a business or organization with the goal of maximizing the efficiency of operations. See also SAP ERP.

Enterprise service A web service used to execute one step of a business process. Enterprise services can be used and combined to build business processes. See also web service.

Enterprise Services Repository (ES Repository) The centralized storage place in SAP NetWeaver for services, business objects, and business processes along with metadata (data that provides information about the characteristics of other data).

Enterprise Any business or organization.

Governance Strategic directives for an enterprise to follow; corporate policies and procedures.

Granularity An approach to defining services that breaks them down in relation to the steps of a business process. See also business process.

Guided procedure A wizard-like workflow tool in SAP NetWeaver that guides users through collaborative business processes using templates.

HTML (Hypertext Markup Language) A markup language used to create web pages; HTML describes the characteristics of text in a document involving a request from a client to a server and a response.

HTTP (Hypertext Transfer Protocol) An application-layer protocol used primarily on the World Wide Web. HTTP uses a client–server model in which the web browser is the client and communicates with the web server that hosts the website.

HTTPS A variant of the standard web transfer protocol (HTTP) that adds a layer of security on the data in transit through a secure socket layer (SSL) or transport-layer security (TLS) protocol connection. See also HTTP, encryption.

Independent Software Vendors (ISV) Software vendors who have had an SAP-related software solution certified, thereby earning the right to participate in SAP's Industry Value Network process in support of larger SAP customers.

Industry solution map Industry-specific maps from SAP that guide users and help them focus on core processes and functions relevant to their types of business.

Industry Value Network Any of eight industry-focused organizations that involve customers, partners, and

SAP employees who work together to innovate solutions within particular industries.

Integration The data and business processes that flow from one SAP component to another to bring greater organizational efficiency.

Interactive forms See Adobe Interactive PDF Forms.

Interface The ability for data generated by one software application or device to be used by another device or software application.

Intermediatory Document (IDoc) A medium of communication that automatically transfers data from one system to another.

Invoice Monitoring System (IMS) A feature of SAP ERP that preprocesses invoices to deal with a variety of invoice exceptions.

iView Small applications that typically run in a portal and connect to the underlying data and applications in your system.

JavaScript Scripting language developed initially by Netscape that enables web developers to build interactive websites. JavaScript is used as the basis for development of SAPUI5 sites.

jQuery A free and open-source JavaScript library used by web developers to navigate HTML documents, handle events, and so on. jQuery is licensed under the MIT License and the GNU General Public License.

Key performance indicator (KPI) Both financial and nonfinancial measurements that help to quantify and analyze strategic performance objectives of an organization.

Knowledge management Various efforts by an enterprise to create, classify, and represent information and distribute it throughout the organization.

Lifecycle Data Management A part of SAP Product Lifecycle Management related to using SOA to manage product-related data.

Lifecycle Process Support A part of SAP Product Lifecycle Management for integrating SAP PLM with other SAP Business Suite applications.

Manager Self-Service (MSS) One of two self-service features provided by SAP NetWeaver that enables managers to access data and complete processes related to their management roles in a company, such as hiring or creating budgets. See also Employee Self-Service (ESS).

Master data management See SAP NetWeaver Master Data Management.

Modeling A system of programming that describes what a software application's function is by defining relationships between components.

Online analytical processing (OLAP) An approach to answering multidimensional analytical (MDA) queries. OLAP is part of the broader category of business intelligence, encompassing relational databases, report writing, and data mining. The term OLAP was created as a modification of the term Online Transaction Processing ("OLTP").

Online transactional processing (OLTP) A computer system built to efficiently manage and facilitate transaction-oriented applications. Most transactional business applications, such as ERP systems, are considered OLTP systems.

Outsourcing See business process outsourcing.

Portal Typically, a main site on the web or on an intranet that provides capabilities users can personalize for their needs.

Procurement Acquiring goods or services at the optimum price and quality.

Protocol In object-oriented software applications, protocols are used to help objects communicate with each other.

RFID (radio-frequency identification) Tags that enable a device to remotely read data; used for activities such as inventorying stock in stores or warehouses.

Risk management Identifying and planning for potential risk in business, including performing risk analysis, monitoring, and developing responses for possible risk scenarios. SAP GRC Risk Management is a portion of an SAP solution for governance, risk, and compliance.

Role based The concept of providing information and services to end users based on their role in an enterprise.

SAP Advanced Planning & Optimization (APO) An advanced solution to the SAP ERP Production Planning component to cater to complexities of production and detailed planning, demand management, and supply-network planning.

SAP Best Practices A set of preconfigured business templates based on industry best practices to accelerate

implementations and upgrades. Used substantially in the SAP Business All-in-One fast-start program.

SAP Business All-in-One fast-start program An integrated software system built on business SAP Best Practices for the small to midsize company.

SAP Business ByDesign The SAP hosted offering for mid-market customers. A complete, integrated solution with easy configuration, targeted specifically for the mid-market.

SAP Business One SAP's offering for the smaller end of the mid-market.

SAP Business Suite A comprehensive business solution from SAP that includes SAP ERP, SAP CRM, SAP PLM, SAP SCM, and SAP SRM.

SAP Business Warehouse (SAP BW) A component of the SAP NetWeaver platform that offers data warehousing functionality via repositories of data and tools for information integration.

SAP BusinessObjects A set of business intelligence components that cover data visualization, reporting, discovery, and acquisition; a major component of SAP's Business Analytics offering that was initially incorporated into SAP's portfolio via the acquisition of Business Objects in 2008.

SAP Community Network (SCN) SAP's official user community in which SAP users, developers, consultants, mentors, and students get help, share ideas, learn, innovate, and connect with others. SCN has over 430 spaces (subgroups) dedicated to SAP products, topics, technologies, industries, and programming languages. It can be found at *http://scn.sap.com*.

SAP Composite Application Framework (SAP CAF) A part of SAP NetWeaver; development environment for services used to create composite applications.

SAP Customer Resource Management (SAP CRM) Part of the SAP Business Suite that deals with managing the business interactions and relationships with customers.

SAP enhancement package A periodic release from SAP that contains new features and functionalities. Customers can review the release notes that accompany each SAP enhancement package and decide if they want to implement it or not.

SAP ERP A suite of software applications from SAP that focuses on the core business requirements of mid-size to large companies, including areas of Human Capital Management, Financials, Operations, Supply Chain Management, and Corporate Services.

SAP ERP Corporate Services The area of SAP ERP that provides centralized management of cost-intensive corporate processes, including real estate; enterprise assets; project portfolios; corporate travel; environment, health, and safety compliance; quality; and global trade services.

SAP ERP Financials The area of SAP ERP that helps you predict performance, manage compliance, and automate financial accounting and supply-chain management.

SAP ERP Human Capital Management (SAP ERP HCM) The area of SAP ERP that helps you manage human resources processes, including talent management, workforce deployment, and core HR processes, such as hiring and training.

SAP ERP Operations The area of SAP ERP that involves managing procurement and the flow of materials, the manufacturing lifecycle, and sales and service and also integrates with associated payments to vendors or from customers.

SAP HANA SAP's innovative software that features an SQL-based in-memory RDBMS (relational database-management system), an analytics engine, and a web server; SAP HANA uses massive multiprocessing and column storage to perform highly efficient database operations.

SAP Manufacturing An SAP software package that enables you to integrate manufacturing with other areas of your business operations and detect exceptions in your operation. It covers all forms of manufacturing, such as discrete, process, repetitive, and Kanban.

SAP Mobile A part of SAP NetWeaver that provides an open standards platform used to give access to data and processes via a variety of channels. SAP NetWeaver Mobile is the technology that works with SAP Mobile Business to provide access to mobile devices. See also SAP Mobile Business.

SAP Mobile Business SAP software that enables you to access SAP Business Suite solutions via mobile devices.

SAP NetWeaver SAP's technology platform for most of its solutions. It allows for the integration of various application components and for composing services using a model-based approach. SAP NetWeaver is also the location of a centralized services repository whereby technologies enable activities such as mobile computing.

SAP NetWeaver Master Data Management (SAP NetWeaver MDM) A system for managing data that receives and sends out data to the various databases in your enterprise. With SAP MDM, you can create a universal database and even store information about relationships between databases.

SAP NetWeaver Visual Composer A modeling tool included in SAP NetWeaver and used to create customized user interfaces.

SAP Process Orchestration (SAP PO) A feature in SAP NetWeaver that allows you to integrate processes, thereby allowing applications to communicate with each other.

SAP Product Lifecycle Management (SAP PLM) An SAP software solution that helps a company manage product development, management of projects, product structures, and quality.

SAP R/3 The SAP client/server architecture-based software introduced in 1992; SAP R/3 was a predecessor of SAP ERP.

SAP Rapid Deployment solutions Preconfigured SAP systems based on SAP Best Practices that are quick and efficient to deploy.

SAP Service and Asset Management An SAP software solution for managing service delivery and management and optimization of assets.

SAP Solution Manager A solution support set that includes tools, content, and access to SAP to help companies deploy SAP technical and functional products.

SAP Supplier Relationship Management (SAP SRM) An application that is part of the SAP Business Suite, which helps organizations manage the procurement process.

SAP Supply Chain Management (SAP SCM) An application that is part of the SAP Business Suite used to coordinate supply and demand; monitor the supply chain to manage distribution, transportation, and other logistics; and provide collaborative and analytical tools.

SAP TCO Model A framework for modeling total cost of ownership for SAP ERP software, which provides an analysis of specific customer data to support SAP implementations.

SAP TechEd && d-code An annual SAP conference spotlighting technical knowledge and skills related to SAP technologies, including hands-on workshops and technical lectures.

SAPPHIRE SAP-run annual conferences that take place in a variety of cities and countries to expose business decision makers to SAP's latest offerings.

Sarbanes-Oxley Act (SOX) A U.S. regulation initiated in 2002 to regulate financial reporting and accountability in response to corporate scandals such as Enron and WorldCom.

Scalability The ability of a system to be grown or built on easily.

Scenario A set of business processes that can be performed in sequence to reach a desired outcome. An example of a scenario in SAP is Procure2Pay, managing an entire procurement process.

Service See web service and enterprise service.

Service-oriented architecture (SOA) A software architecture that allows for the use of services with an exchange relationship to build business processes. In SAP, SOA refers to SAP's blueprint for implementing a service-oriented architecture to use services as building blocks for business processes based on open standards. See also Enterprise service.

Shared services center A method of sharing pieces of business-process scenarios via a centralized location; often used in outsourcing business processes to third parties.

SOA adoption A support program offered by SAP to help enterprises move toward a service-oriented architecture environment.

Solution Composer An SAP tool used to manipulate SAP Solution Maps and Business Solution Maps to visualize, plan, and implement various IT solutions in an enterprise.

Solution map A table of SAP software applications organized within a single solution category that define a set or requirements either within or across industries.

SQL (Structured Query Language) A standardized query language for storing and retrieving data information from a relational database — supported by products such as SAP HANA, MaxDB, Oracle, or DB2.

SQLScript Procedural language that can be used to build server-side database procedures within SAP HANA.

Standardization Setting up a single technical standard that various entities can agree to.

SuccessFactors A cloud-based HCM solution from SAP.

Talent Management An area of the SAP ERP HCM application that provides features for managing HR-related processes, including recruitment, hiring, training, performance, and compensation management.

User interface (UI) The visual definition of a communication between a software program and a user.

Value-based services for SAP solutions A method of evaluating the potential value of the implementation of SAP products or product enhancements.

Vertical solution An industry-specific solution. See also industry solution map.

Web Service Description Language (WSDL) A way of describing web services using XML to hide complexity and focus on functionality.

Web service Web application programming interfaces (APIs) that can be accessed via a network. Web services encapsulate a function of an application in such a way that it can be accessed by another application.

Work center A type of user portal that focuses on a certain set of tools or data that supports one kind of work or functionality.

Work trigger A role-based initiation of data or other functionality being pushed to a user based on a need to know.

Workflow A form of automation in which the system routes the assigned tasks to relevant business process owners.

XML Extensible Markup Language, used to share data across a variety of information systems.

B   SAP Resources

Many resources for helping you with your SAP implementation are discussed in detail in Chapter 20 and Chapter 21. Here we present a useful list of resources broken down into categories, with associated website addresses included.

SAP Communities and Alliances

Several organizations exist both within SAP and independently to provide free information or for-a-fee consulting, including business alliance partners and user groups:

> Americas SAP Users Group (ASUG): *www.asug.com*

> Business Process Expert Community: *http://wiki.scn.sap.com/wiki/display/BPX/Business+Process+Expert+Home*

> IBM/SAP Alliance: *http://www.ibm.com/solutions/sap/us/en/*

> Intel/SAP Alliance: *www.intelalliance.com/sap/*

> SAP Australian User Group (SAUG): *www.saug.com.au/*

> SAP Enterprise Services Community: *www.sap.com/platform/ecosystem/escommunity/index.epx*

> SAP Industry Value Network: *www.sap.com/platform/ecosystem/ivn*

> SAP Community Network (SCN): *www.scn.sap.com*

> SAP News Center: *http://www.news-sap.com/*

> SAP User Groups: *http://www.sap.com/communities/user-groups.html*

Certification

If you are interested in SAP certification, you can get information from SAP or from the company that administers the tests. You will find the following websites helpful:

> Pearson Vue: *www.vue.com/sap/*

> SAP Education: *www.sap.com/services/education/certification*

Websites and Blogs

There are many useful websites with information about topics such as enterprise resource planning (ERP), customer resource planning, ERP analytics, and topics specific to SAP products, including the following:

> SAP ITToolbox: *www.sap.ittoolbox.com*

> SAP ITToolbox Blogs: *www.sap.ittoolbox.com/blogs*

> The SAP Fan Club: *www.sapfans.com*

> The ERP Fan Club and User Forum: *www.erpfans.com*

> SAP Online Events: *www.sap.com/community/pub/events.epx*

> CIO Magazine Enterprise Resource Planning page: *www.cio.com/research/erp*

> ERP Guide: *www.managementsupport.com/erp.htm*

> SearchSAP: *www.searchsap.com*

> SearchManufacturing: *www.searchmanufacturing.com*

> SearchCRM: *www.searchcrm.com*

> 2020Software: *www.2020software.com*

Publications

Several print and online magazines provide regular articles on topics such as ERP, and SAP PRESS, the publisher of this book, offers a broad range of books on SAP-related topics. Some sources for publications include the following:

> Business 2.0: *www.business2.com*

> SAP Info: email *press@sap.com* to ask about subscribing

> *SAP Insider*: *www.sapinsideronline.com*

> *SAP Professional Journal*: *http://sapexperts.wispubs.com/SAP-Professional-Journal*

> *SAP NetWeaver Magazine*: *www.sapnetweavermagazine.com*

> SAP SCM (Supply Chain Management): *www.sapexperts.com/scm*

> SAP BI (Business Intelligence): *www.sapexperts.com/BI*

> SAP CRM (Customer Relationship Management): *http://sapexperts.wispubs.com/CRM*

> SAP Financials: *http://sapexperts.wispubs.com/Financials*

> SAP HR (Human Resources): *http://sapexperts.wispubs.com/HR*

> SAP PRESS, offering a range of books on SAP and its products, solutions, and technologies: *www.sap-press.com*

Conferences

If you are interested in attending an SAP or ERP-focused event, there are several of these events that occur throughout the year, including the following:

> SAP SAPPHIRE: *www.sapsapphire.com*

> SAP World Tour: *www.sap.com/company/events/worldtour2007*

> SAP Technology Tour: *www.sap.com/company/events*

> AGS Road show: *http://www.sap.com/about/events/agsroadshows/index.epx*

> SAP conferences and seminars from WIS: *http://sapinsider.wispubs.com/Conferences-and-Seminars*

> SuccessConnect, an annual customer conference organized by SuccessFactors: *http://www.successfactors.com/en_us/events.html*

> AribaLive, an the annual conference organized by Ariba for their customers, users, and partners: *http://www.aribalive.com/*

SAP Services

Many SAP organizations and programs exist to help you succeed. Here are some that you should check out:

> SAP Active Global Support: *http://www.sap.com/services-support/support.html*

> SAP Business Process Outsourcing: *www.sap.com/services/bpo*

> SAP Consulting: *www.sap.com/services/consulting*

> SAP Custom Development: *www.sap.com/services/customdev*

> SAP Education: *https://training.sap.com/us/en/*

> SAP Service Marketplace: *https://service.sap.com* (partner or customer ID required)

> SAP Solution Manager: *http://www.sap.com/pc/tech/business-process-management/software/solution-manager/index.html*

SAP Offices

If you are ready to contact SAP and discuss your needs further, use the following listing of offices worldwide to find the appropriate resource.

Office Directory: United States

Regional SAP Headquarters

SAP America Inc.
Strategic Planning & Support Office
3999 West Chester Pike
Newtown Square, PA 19073
Phone: +1-610-661-1000

US Products and Services
Phone: +1-800-872-1727

SAP Business One Response Center
Phone: +1-888-227-1727

Worldwide Country Sites

There are two useful sites that will help you locate SAP offices worldwide; you can send them an email and let them put you in touch with the right person:

> International SAP offices:
www.sap.com/usa/contactsap/countries/index.epx

> Contact SAP via email: *www.sap.com/contactsap/index.epx*

C   SAP Solution Maps

Throughout this book, we have provided information on SAP products and the highest level solution maps for these products. Each of these solution maps has additional information within its major categories that can be a handy reference for you as you consider various SAP solutions.

In this appendix, we provide you with detailed listings of product features for SAP ERP, SAP Customer Relationship Management, SAP Supplier Relationship Management, SAP Product Lifecycle Management, SAP Supply Chain Management, SAP Business One, SAP Analytics, SAP In-Memory Computing (SAP HANA), and SAP Mobile. We have also noted the relevant chapters to which you can refer for detailed information about each of these products.

 Important Note

> Some of the features mentioned here are available through SAP partners or are planned but not yet available at the time of this writing. Check with your SAP representative to find out how to obtain all the features you need for your particular enterprise situation.

SAP ERP

See Chapter 4, Chapter 5, and Chapter 6 for more information about SAP ERP, whose features are detailed in Table C.1 through Table C.8.

Category	Application
Talent Management	› Competency Management › Recruiting › Employee Performance Management › Talent Review & Calibration › Employee Development › Enterprise Learning › Succession Management › SAP Talent Visualization by Nakisa (STVN) › Compensation Management › Talent Management Analytics

Table C.1 SAP ERP Human Capital Management

Category	Application
Workforce Process Management	› Employee Administration › Organizational Management › Global Employee Management › Benefits Management › Healthcare Cost Management › Time and Attendance › Payroll and Legal Reporting › HCM Processes and Forms › Employee Self Service/Manager Self Service › Employee Interaction Center › Workforce Planning › Workforce Cost Planning & Simulation › Workforce Benchmarking › Workforce Process Analytics & Measurement › Strategic Alignment › SAP Org Visualization by Nakisa (SOVN)
Workforce Deployment Management	› Project Resource Planning › Resource and Program Management › Retail Scheduling
End User Service Delivery	› Manager Self-Services › Employee Self-Services › Shared Services Framework for HR (SSF-HR)

Table C.1 SAP ERP Human Capital Management (Cont.)

Financial Supply Chain Management	
› Electronic Bill Presentment and Payment › Collections Management	› Credit Management › Dispute Management

Treasury	
› Treasury and Risk Management › Cash and Liquidity Management	› In-House Cash › Bank Communication Management

Table C.2 SAP ERP Financials

Financial Accounting

› General Ledger	› Inventory Accounting
› Accounts Receivable	› Tax Accounting
› Accounts Payable	› Accrual Accounting
› Contract Accounting	› Local Close
› Fixed Assets Accounting	› Financial Statements
› Bank Accounting	› Travel Management
› Cash Journal Accounting	

Management Accounting

› Profit Center Accounting	› Product Cost Accounting
› Cost Center and Internal Order Accounting	› Profitability Accounting
	› Transfer Pricing
› Project Accounting	
› Investment Management	

Corporate Governance

› Audit Information System	› Whistle Blower Complaints
› Management of Internal Controls	› Segregation of Duties
› Risk Management	

Table C.2 SAP ERP Financials (Cont.)

Product Deployment

› Product Development	› Development Collaboration

Product Data Management

› Product Structure Management	› Specification Management
› Recipe Management	› Change and Configuration Management

Product Intelligence

› Product-Centric View	

Product Compliance

› Product Compliance	› REACH Compliance

Table C.3 SAP ERP Product Development and Collaboration

Document Management	
› Document Management	
Tool and Workgroup Integration	
› CAD Integration	

Table C.3 SAP ERP Product Development and Collaboration (Cont.)

Purchase Requisition Management	
› Purchase Requisition Processing	
Operational Sourcing	
› Sourcing	› Compliance Management
› Purchasing Optimization	
Purchase Order Management	
› Purchase Order Processing	› Commodity Management
› Delivery Schedule Processing	
Contract Management	
› Operational Contract Processing	› Trading Contracts
› Scheduling Agreement	
Invoice Management	
› Invoice Processing	› Flexible Invoice Reconciliation
› SAP Invoice Management by Open Text	

Table C.4 SAP ERP Procurement

Sales Order Management	
› Account Processing	› Contract Processing
› Internet Sales	› Billing
› Managing Auctions	› Incentive and Commission Management
› Inquiry Processing	
› Quotation Processing	› Returnable Packaging Management
› Trading Contract Management	
› Sales Order Processing	› Consignment
	› Commodity Management

Table C.5 SAP ERP Operations: Sales and Customer Service

Aftermarket Sales and Services	
› Service Sales	› Warranty and Claims Management
› Service Contract Management	
› Customer Service and Support	› Field Service
› Installed Base Management	› Depot Repair

Table C.5   SAP ERP Operations: Sales and Customer Service (Cont.)

Production Planning	
› Production Planning	› Lean Planning
› Capacity Planning	
Manufacturing Execution	
› Manufacturing Execution	› Supervision and Control
› Shop Floor Integration	› Manufacturing Analytics
Manufacturing Collaboration	
› External Processing	› Quality Collaboration

Table C.6   SAP ERP Operations: Manufacturing

Investment Planning and Design	
› Business Planning	› Maintenance Engineering
› Investment Management	› Interfacing CAD Systems
› Asset Portfolio Management	› Project Management
› Collaboration Specification and Design	
Procurement and Construction	
› Supplier Qualification and Candidate Selection	› Project Management
	› Collaborative Construction
› Bidding and Contract Management	› Project and Investment Controlling
› Procurement Process	› MRO and Services Procurement
› Document Management	

Table C.7   SAP ERP Enterprise Asset Management

Maintenance and Operations

> - Technical Assets Management
> - Workforce Management
> - Preventive and Predictive Maintenance
> - Maintenance Planning and Scheduling
> - Work Order Management
> - Approval Processing
> - Contractor Management
> - Refurbishment

> - Mobile Asset Management including RFID Enablement
> - Service Parts and Inventory Management
> - Interfacing CAD, GIS, and SCADA Systems
> - Work Clearance Management
> - Shutdown Planning
> - Asset Tracking with RFID
> - Takeover/Handover for Technical Objects

Decomission and Disposal

> - Asset Transfer and Disposal
> - Document Management
> - Collaborative Disposal Management
> - Project Management

> - Waste Management
> - Asset Compliance
> - Asset Remarketing

Asset Analytics and Performance Optimization

> - Integrated Asset Accounting
> - Asset and Maintenance Reporting
> - Asset Performance Management
> - Reliability Centered Maintenance
> - Asset Lifecycle Costing
> - Damage Analytics

> - Object Statistics
> - Spend and Supplier Performance Analytics
> - Predictive Condition Monitoring
> - Operator Dashboards
> - Budget Tracking
> - Maintenance Cost Planning

Real Estate Management

> - Portfolio Management
> - Commercial Real Estate Management

> - Corporate Real Estate Management
> - Facilities Management

Fleet Management

> - Fleet Administration
> - Fleet Maintenance
> - Transportation Logistics

> - Capacity Planning
> - Fleet Analysis

Table C.7 SAP ERP Enterprise Asset Management (Cont.)

Quality Management

› Quality Engineering
› Quality Assurance/Control

› Quality Improvement
› Audit Management

Environment, Health, and Safety Compliance Management

› EHS Management

› Recycling Administration

Inbound and Outbound Logistics

› Inbound Processing
› Outbound Processing
› Transportation Execution
› Freight Costing
› Product Classification

› Duty Calculation
› Customs Communication Service
› Trade Document Service
› Trade Preference Processing

Inventory and Warehouse Management

› Cross Docking
› Warehousing and Storage

› Physical Inventory

Global Trade Services

› Export Management
› Import Management

› Trade Preference Management
› Restitution Management

Project and Portfolio Management

› Portfolio Management
› Project Management

› Resource Management

Table C.8   SAP ERP Operations: Cross Functions

Marketing Resource Management

› Market Research
› Budget Planning
› Scenario Planning
› Marketing Planning and
  Budgeting
› Budget Control
› Product and Brand Planning

› Cost and Volume Planning
› Marketing Plan Analysis
› Marketing Calendar
› Marketing Organization
› Workflow and Approval

Table C.9   SAP CRM Marketing

493

Segmentation and List Management

› Multiple Data Source Access	› Data Mining
› High Speed Data Search	› Decision Trees
› Preview Lists	› ABC Analysis
› Prefiltered/Personalized Attribute Lists	› List Management—List Format Mapping
› Sampling and Splitting	› Duplicate Checks
› Embedded Predictive Modeling	› Postal Validation
› Personalized Filters	› Data Cleansing
› Quick Counts	› Data Enrichment
› Segment Deduplication	› List Quality
› Suppression Filters	› Lead and Activity Imports
› Target Group Optimization	› List Analysis
› Clustering	

Campaign Management

› Campaign Planning	› Real-Time Response Tracking
› Graphical Campaign Modeling	› Cost/Financial Reporting
› Campaign Optimization	› Personalized (E)Mails
› Campaign Simulation	› Bounce Handling
› Marketing Calendar	› Call Lists Campaign ROI
› Campaign-Specific Pricing	› Interactive Scripting
› Multichannel Campaign Execution	› Target Group Analysis
› Multiwave Campaign Execution	› Campaign Analysis
› Event-Triggered Campaign Execution	

Real-Time Offer Management

› Offer Portfolio Management	› Data Mapping Tool
› Real-Time Event Detection and Recommendation	› Configuration and Migration Tool
› Interaction Assistance	› Offer Performance Analytics
› Self Learning and Optimization Mechanism	› Agent Performance Analytics
› Offer Simulator	› Channel Performance Analytics

Table C.9   SAP CRM Marketing (Cont.)

Lead Management

› Multiple Interaction Channels	› Mass Generation
› Automated Qualification	› Response Recording
› Rule-Based Distribution	› Lead Surveys
› Lead Dispatching	› Automatic Generation of
› Web-Based Lead Generation	Follow-Up Activities
› Lead Partner Management	› Lead Analysis

Loyalty Management

› Loyalty Program Management	› Membership Management in
› Loyalty Campaign Management	Interaction Center
› Reward Rule Management	› Membership Management in CRM
› Membership Management in Web	WebClient UI
Channel	› Member Activities and Points
	Management

Table C.9 SAP CRM Marketing (Cont.)

Sales Planning and Forecasting

› Strategic Planning	› Planning-Cycle Monitoring
› Flexible Modeling	› Performance Reviews
› Rolling Forecast	› Sales Planning and Forecasting
› Collaborative Planning	Guides
› Supply Chain Integration	› Account Planning
	› Opportunity Planning

Sales Performance Management

› Pipeline Performance Management	

Territory Management

› Market Segmentation	› Rule-Based Synchronization for
› Territory Assignment and	Mobile Devices
Scheduling	› Sales Analysis by Territory
› Territory/Organizational Mapping	› Interface to Third-Party Territory
	Planning Tools

Table C.10 SAP CRM Sales

Accounts & Contacts

› Visit Planning	› Marketing Attributes
› Fact Sheet	› Customer-Specific Pricing
› Interaction History	› Account Planning
› Activity Management	› Customer Analysis
› Email and Fax Integration	› Account Classification
› Relationship Management	› Data Quality Management

Opportunity Management

› Opportunity Planning	› Product Configurations
› Team Selling	› Anticipated Revenue
› Competitive Information	› Buying Center
› Account-Specific Sales Processes	› Sales Project Management
› Automatic Business Partner Assignment	› Opportunity Hierarchies
› Pricing	› Sales Process and Selling Methodologies
› Activities	› Opportunity Analysis
› Follow-Up Transactions	

Quotation & Order Management

› Quotations	› Product Authorization and Restriction
› Package Quotation	
› Order Capture	› Product Configuration
› Automatic Business Partner Assignment	› Bill of Material
	› Availability Check
› Order Status Tracking	› Rebates
› Pricing	› Billing
› Price Change Approval	› Fulfillment Synchronization
› Order Validation Check	› Quotation and Order Analysis
› Credit Management and Credit Check	› Cross-/Upselling
	› Reordering/Listings
› Payment Card Processing	› Web Catalog
› Automated Follow-Up Processes	

Table C.10 SAP CRM Sales (Cont.)

Pricing and Contracts

- Value and Quantity Contracts
- Sales Agreements
- Authorized Customers
- Contract Completion Rules
- Collaborative Contract Negotiation
- Release Order Processing
- Cancellation Handling
- Fulfillment Synchronization
- Automatic Business Partner Assignment
- Product Configuration
- Contract Status Tracking
- Credit Management and Credit Check
- Pricing
- Customer-Specific Pricing
- Promotional Pricing
- Contract Analysis

Incentives & Commission Management

- Direct and Indirect Sales Compensation
- Incentive Plan Modeling
- Configuration Templates
- Roll Up Hierarchies/Indirect Participants
- Contracts and Agreements Handling
- Individual Plan Exceptions
- Target Agreement
- Adjustments
- Posting and Settlement
- Commission Simulation
- Commission Status Management

Time and Travel

- Time Reporting
- Expense Reports
- Receipt Itemization
- Track Receipts, Mileage, Deductions, and Border Crossings
- Integration with Activity Management
- Cost Assignment

Table C.10 SAP CRM Sales (Cont.)

Service Sales and Marketing

- Service Catalogs
- Service Marketing and Campaigns
- Service Opportunity Management
- Service Solution Selling

Service Contracts and Agreements

- Service Agreement Management
- Service Contract Management
- Usage Based Contract Management
- Service Level Management

Table C.11 SAP CRM Service

Installations and Maintenance	
› Installed Base and Objects Management	› Counter and Readings Management
› Installation and Configuration	› Service Plan Management

Customer Service and Support	
› Service Requests Processing	› Case Management
› Knowledge Management	› Complaints Processing

Field Service Management	
› Service Order Management	› Service Confirmation Management
› Resource Planning	

Returns and Depot Repair	
› Returns Processing	› In-House Repair Processing
› Loaner Management	› Quality Management Integration

Warranty and Claims Management	
› Warranty Management	› Recall Management
› Warranty Claims Processing	

Service Logistics and Finance	
› Logistics Integration	› Financial Integration
› Service Parts Management	› Billing

Service Collaboration, Analytics, and Optimization	
› Multichannel Integration	› Business Workflow, Alerts, and Rules
› SOA Ready Service Processes	› Service Forecasting, Planning, and Analysis

Table C.11   SAP CRM Service (Cont.)

Global Spend Analysis	
› Consolidated Spend Reporting	

Category Management	
› Category Strategy Planning	› Program Management
› Category Definition	› Project Management
› Methodology Setup	› Buyer Performance Management

Table C.12   SAP SRM Purchasing Governance

Compliance Management	
› Purchasing Policy and Compliance Analysis › Buyer Compliance Reporting › Business Unit Compliance Reporting	› Supplier Compliance Analysis › Embargo Screening › Contract Compliance Management

Table C.12 SAP SRM Purchasing Governance (Cont.)

Central Sourcing Hub	
› Automatic Source of Supply Allocation › Procurement Consolidation Workbench	› Demand Aggregation

RFx/Auctioning	
› Project Preparation › RFx Preparation › RFx Processing › RFx Multi-Round Processing	› Integrated Design Collaboration and Validation › RFx to Auction Conversion › Reverse Auction

Bid Evaluation and Awarding	
› Analyze Responses › Award of Bid	› Event Reporting › Bid Simulation and Optimization

Table C.13 SAP SRM Sourcing

Legal Contract Repository	
› Create Master Agreement Template › Create Master Agreement	› Upload Contract Document › Search Contract Repository

Contract Authoring	
› Clause and Template Library › Legal Contract Authoring with DUET	› Legal Contract Authoring without DUET › Internal Legal Contract Collaboration

Table C.14 SAP SRM Contract Management

499

Contract Negotiation	
› External Collaboration for the Legal Contract	› Renegotiation of an Operational Contract

Contract Execution	
› Integration of Legal and Operational Contract in ERP › Central Operational Contract Repository › Using Contracts for Source of Supply Assignment › Flexible Pricing and Discounts › Integration Between Contract and SRM Catalog	› Quota Arrangements › Records Management Integration › Contract Distribution for Global Outline Agreements › Enhanced Control and Risk Mitigation of Currency Fluctuations

Contract Monitoring	
› Contract Compliance Management › Monitoring Expiration of Contracts	› Maverick Buying Analysis

Table C.14 SAP SRM Contract Management (Cont.)

Self-Service Procurement	
› Manual Requirements Definition › Approval of Requisition › Goods Receipt	› Invoice Processing › Analyzing Self-Service Procurement

Services Procurement	
› Service Request Management › Integrated Requisition Creation – Materials Management › Service Delivery Entry	› Invoice Processing › Analyzing Services Procurement

Direct/Plan-Driven Procurement	
› Planned Requirements Processing › Goods Receipt	› Invoice Processing › Analyzing Plan-Driven Procurement

Table C.15 SAP SRM Collaborative Procurement

Catalog Content Management	
› Managing Catalog Content	› Supplier Managed Content
› Catalog Data Search	

Table C.15 SAP SRM Collaborative Procurement (Cont.)

Web-Based Supplier Interaction	
› Order Collaboration	› Invoice Processing
› Design Collaboration	› Financial Settlement
› Confirmation	› Supplier Managed Content
Direct Document Exchange	
› Order Communication	› Invoice Communication
› ASN/Service Entry	
Supplier Network	
› Supplier Onboarding Services	› Document Exchange Services

Table C.16 SAP SRM Supplier Collaboration

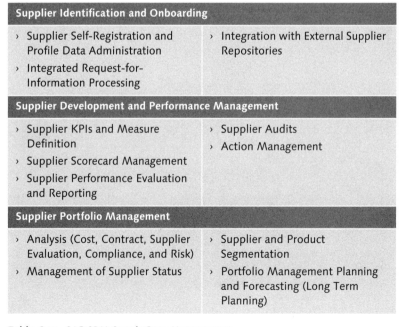

Supplier Identification and Onboarding	
› Supplier Self-Registration and Profile Data Administration	› Integration with External Supplier Repositories
› Integrated Request-for-Information Processing	
Supplier Development and Performance Management	
› Supplier KPIs and Measure Definition	› Supplier Audits
› Supplier Scorecard Management	› Action Management
› Supplier Performance Evaluation and Reporting	
Supplier Portfolio Management	
› Analysis (Cost, Contract, Supplier Evaluation, Compliance, and Risk)	› Supplier and Product Segmentation
› Management of Supplier Status	› Portfolio Management Planning and Forecasting (Long Term Planning)

Table C.17 SAP SRM Supply Base Management

Product Strategy and Planning	
› Product Strategy and Planning	› Product Risk Management
› Product Roadmap	› Product IP Management
Product Portfolio Management	
› Product Portfolio Management	
Innovation Management	
› Idea and Concept Management	
Requirements Management	
› Requirements Management	
Market Launch Management	
› New Product Introduction	› Postlaunch Review

Table C.18 SAP PLM Product Management

Engineering and R&D Collaboration	
› Product Development	› Engineering (ETO)
› Development Collaboration	› Engineering (MTO)
› Engineering Change Collaboration	
Supplier Collaboration	
› Sourcing and Supply Planning	› Supplier Scorecard Mangement
› Supplier Audits	› Supplier Performance Evaluation and Reporting
› Supplier KPIs and Measure Definition	
Manufacturing Collaboration	
› Prototyping and Ramp-Up	› Interfacing CAD, GIS, and SCADA systems
› Integrated Product and Process Engineering (iPPE)	
Service and Maintenance Collaboration	
› MRO and Services Management	› Asset Management
› Warranty and Claims Management	
Product Quality Management	
› Quality Engineering	› Failure Mode and Effects Analysis (FMEA)
› Quality Improvement	

Table C.19 SAP PLM Product Development and Collaboration

Product Change Management	
› Change and Configuration Management	

Table C.19 SAP PLM Product Development and Collaboration (Cont.)

Product Master and Structure Management	
› Product Structure Management	› Conceptual Product Structure
› Integrated Product and Process Engineering (iPPE)	› Variant Configuration
› Routing Management and Process Development	› Sales Configuration Management
Specification and Recipe Management	
› Recipe Management	› Specification Management
Service and Maintenance Structure Management	
› Phase-In Equipment	› Phase-Out Equipment
› Corrective Maintenance	
Visualization and Publications	
› Dynamic Publications	
Configuration Management	
› Catalog Management	› Classification and Search
› Part Management	

Table C.20 SAP PLM Product Data Management

Product Compliance	
› Product Compliance	› Hazardous Substance Management
› Global Label Management	
› Audit Management	› Dangerous Goods Management
› Product Safety	› Waste Management
Product Intelligence	
› Reporting, Query, and Analysis	› Providing Business Object Search
› Enabling Enterprise Search	

Table C.21 SAP PLM Foundation

Product Costing	
› Product and Service Cost Management	› Cost and Quotation Management
Tool and Workgroup Integration	
› MDA Integration	› Digital Manufacturing
› EDA Integration	› Packaging and Labeling
› CASE Integration	› Media and Artwork
Project and Resource Management	
› Project Planning and Scoping	› Strategic Portfolio Management
› Resource and Time Management	› Strategic Resource Management
› Project Execution	› Phase-Gate Management
Document Management	
› Document Management	

Table C.21 SAP PLM Foundation (Cont.)

Demand Planning and Forecasting	
› Statistical Forecasting	› Collaborative Demand Planning
› Causal Forecasting	› Macro Calculation
› Composite Forecasting	› Planning with Bills of Materials
› Lifecycle Planning	› Characteristics-Based Forecasting
› Promotion Planning	› Transfer of Consensus Demand Plan
› Data Handling	› Customer Forecast Management
Safety Stock Planning	
› Basic Safety Stock Planning	› Advanced Safety Stock Planning
Supply Network Planning	
› Heuristic	› Subcontracting
› Capacity Leveling	› Scheduling Agreement
› Optimization	› Aggregated Supply Network Planning
› Multilevel Supply and Demand Matching	

Table C.22 SAP SCM Demand and Supply Planning

Distribution Planning	
› Distribution Planning	› Vendor Managed Inventory (VMI)
› Responsive Replenishment	

Service Parts Planning	
› Strategic Supply Chain Design	› Parts Supply Planning
› Parts Demand Planning	› Parts Distribution Planning
› Parts Inventory Planning	› Parts Monitoring

Table C.22 SAP SCM Demand and Supply Planning (Cont.)

Strategic Sourcing	
› Long-Term Planning	› Catalog Management
› Bid Management	› Source Determination
› Contract Management	

Purchase Order Processing	
› Conversion of Demands to Purchase Orders	› Procurement Visibility
› Confirmation and Monitoring Purchasing Activities	

Invoicing	
› Receiving an Incoming Invoice	› Release of Blocked Invoices
› Verifying and Incoming Invoice	

Table C.23 SAP SCM Procurement

Production Planning and Detailed Scheduling	
› Production Planning	› Multilevel Supply and Demand Matching
› Detailed Scheduling	› Material Requirements Planning

Table C.24 SAP SCM Manufacturing

Manufacturing Visibility, Execution, and Collaboration

› Make-to-Order	› Process Manufacturing
› Repetitive Manufacturing	› Batch Management
› Flow Manufacturing	› Manufacturing Intelligence
› Shop Floor Manufacturing	Dashboard
› Lean Manufacturing	› Manufacturing Visibility

MRP Based Detailed Scheduling

› Production Planning	› Detailed Scheduling

Table C.24   SAP SCM Manufacturing (Cont.)

Inbound Processing and Receipt Confirmation

› Determination of External Demands	› Goods Receipt
› Acknowledgment of Receipt within Logistics	› Material Valuation
	› Kit to Stock
› Advanced Shipping Notification	› Goods Receipt Optimization
› Value-Added Services	› Internal Routing
› Yard Management	› Deconsolidation
› Delivery Monitoring	

Outbound Processing

› Delivery Processing and Distribution	› Proof of Delivery
› Delivery Monitoring	› Fulfillment Visibility
› Value-Added Services	› Warehouse Order Processing
› Yard Management	› Kit to Order
› Goods Issue	› Production Supply

Cross Docking

› Planned Cross Docking	› Retail Merchandise Cross Docking
› Opportunistic (Unplanned) Cross Docking	› Opportunistic Cross Docking
› Transportation Cross Docking	› Production Cross Docking and Production Supply Cross Docking

Table C.25   SAP SCM Warehousing

Warehousing and Storage

- › Strategies
- › Slotting/Warehouse Optimization
- › Native Radio Frequency Processing
- › Task Interleaving and Resource Management
- › Multiple Handling Units
- › Inventory Management
- › Storage and Stock Management
- › Quality Management Integration
- › Production Supply
- › Visibility of Warehouse Activities
- › Decentralized Warehouse
- › Labor Management
- › Warehouse Cockpit
- › Material Flow System
- › Graphical Warehouse Layout
- › Decentralized/Centralized Deployment Options

Physical Inventory

- › Planning Phase of Physical Inventory
- › Counting Phase of Physical Inventory
- › Monitoring of the Physical Inventory Activities

Table C.25 SAP SCM Warehousing (Cont.)

Sales Order Processing

- › Rules-Based Available-to-Promise (ATP)
- › Multilevel ATP Check
- › Capable-to-Promise (CTP)
- › Product Allocation
- › Backorder Processing

Billing

- › Creation and Cancellations of Invoices
- › Transfer Billing Data to Financial Accounting

Service Parts Order Fulfillment

- › Parts Marketing and Campaign Management
- › Parts Order Processing
- › Complaints Processing

Table C.26 SAP SCM Order Fulfillment

Freight Management	
› Capture Transportation Requests	› Send Confirmation
› Dynamic Route Determination	› Distance Determination Service
› Credit Limit Check	› Workflow Management
Planning and Dispatching	
› Load Consolidation	› Transportation Visibility
› Mode and Route Optimization	› Shipping
› TSP Selection	
Rating, Billing, and Settlement	
› Supplier Transportation Charges	› Transportation Charge Rates
› Customer Transportation Charges	› Integrate Invoice Request to FI/CO System
Driver and Asset Management	
› Asset Maintenance	› Driver Maintenance
Network Collaboration	
› Collaboration Shipment Tendering	› Trigger Customs Procedure
› Seamless Integration	

Table C.27 SAP SCM Transportation

Auto-ID (RFID) and Item Serialization	
› Partner Applications and xApps	› Serialization Data Management
› Preconfigured Business Processes	› Hardware and Device Management
Event Management	
› Procurement Visibility	› Supply Network Visibility
› Fulfillment Visibility	› Outbound/Inbound RFID
› Transportation Visibility	› Railcar Management
› Manufacturing Visibility	› Container Track/Trace

Table C.28 SAP SCM Real World Awareness

Strategic Supply Chain Design

› Supply Chain Definition	› Alert Monitoring
› Supply Chain Monitoring	

Supply Chain Analytics

› Service Fill Monitor	› Key Performance Indicators
› Service Loss Analysis	› Supply Chain Performance
› Supplier Delivery Performance Rating	Management
› Inbound Delivery Monitor	› Operational Performance Management
› Collaboration Performance Indicator	› Supply Chain Analytical Applications
	› Supply Chain Analytics

Supply Chain Risk Management

› Identify Risks	› Manage Risks
› Measure Risks	› Monitor Risks

Sales and Operations Planning

› Demand Analysis and Update	› Executive S&OP Analysis
› Supply Analysis	

Table C.29 SAP SCM Supply Chain Visibility

Supplier Collaboration

› Release Process	› Kanban Process
› SMI Process	› Delivery Control Monitor Process
› Purchase Order Process	› Invoice Process
› Dynamic Replenishment Process	› Self-Billing Invoice Process

Customer Collaboration

› Responsive Demand Planning	› Min-Max Replenishment
› Responsive Replenishment Planning	› Demand Forecast Collaboration

Outsourced Manufacturing

› Contract Manufacturing Purchasing	› Work Order Process
› Supply Network Inventory	

Table C.30 SAP SCM Supply Network Collaboration

Demand Planning in MS Excel	
› Planning Online	› Planning Offline

Table C.31   SAP SCM Supply Chain Management with Duet

General Ledger	
› Journal Entries	› Project Management
› Journal Vouchers	› Fixed Assets
› Reverse Transactions	› Datey FI Interface (Germany)
› Recurring Postings	› Folio Numbers (Mexico and Chile)
› Posting Templates	› Revaluation (Mexico, Chile, Costa Rica, and Guatemala)
› Posting Periods	› Financial Reports
› Exchange Rate Differences	› Transaction Journal
› Conversion Differences	› Document Journal
› Chart of Accounts	› General Ledger
› Account Segmentation	› G/L Accounts and Business Partners
› Account Code Generator	
› Purchase Accounting	› Aging Reports
› Budget Management	› Customer Statement Report
	› Transaction Report by Projects

Tax	
› VAT (Value Added Tax)	› Acquisition Tax (Europe)
› VAT Calculation (Europe)	› Tax Declaration Boxes
› VAT Correction (Portugal and Belgium)	› Tax Exemptions
	› ELSTER Integration (Germany)
› Withholding Tax	› Tax Only Documents
› Deferred Tax (Spain, France, Italy, Mexico, and South Africa)	› Multiple Excise/Service Tax (India)
	› Excise for Inventory Transfer (India)
› Stamp Tax (Portugal)	
› Equalization Tax (Spain)	

Table C.32   SAP Business One Financials

Banking	
› Incoming Payments	› Payment Engine
› Check Register	› Bank Statement Processing
› Credit Card Management	› Internal Reconciliation
› Deposits	› Bank Reconciliation Process (USA, Canada, and UK)
› Outgoing Payments	
› Checks for Payment	› Bill of Exchange (Belgium, Chile, France, Italy, Portugal, and Spain)
› Prenumbered Checks	
› Voiding Checks	› Dunning System
› Automatic Payment System	› Cash Discount
› Future Payments Monitoring	› Handling Small Differences in Payments

Cost Accounting	
› Profit Centers	› Profit Center Report
› Distribution Rules	

Table C.32 SAP Business One Financials (Cont.)

Sales	
› Sales Quotation	› Retailer Chain Stores (Israel)
› Sales Order	› Gross Profit Calculation
› Delivery	› Structured Marketing Document
› Returns	› Item Availability Check
› A/R Invoice	› Intrastat (Europe)
› A/R Credit Memos	› Down Payments
› A/R Correction Invoice (Czech Repulic, Hungary, Poland, and Slovakia)	› Drop Shipment
	› Open Items List
› A/R Reserve Invoice	› Sales Analysis Report
› Document Generation Wizard	› CCD Numbers (Russia)
› Creation of Sales Target Documents	› Tax Only Documents
› Backorder Processing	

Table C.33 SAP Business One Logistics

Procurement

› Purchase Order	› Multiple Shipping Addresses
› Split Purchase Order	› Customs Bill
› Goods Receipt PO	› Purchase Accounting
› Goods Return	› Down Payments
› A/P Invoice	› Freight Charges
› A/P Credit Memo	› Purchase Proposals
› A/P Correction Invoice (Czech Republic, Hungary, Poland, and Slovakia)	› Open Items List
	› Purchase Analysis Report
	› Creation of Purchasing Target Documents
› A/P Reserve Invoice	
› Landed Costs	› Tax Only Documents
› Vendor Invoice for Assets	
› Warehouse Segregation	

Inventory Management

› Batch Management	› Pick and Pack
› Serial Numbers Management	› Alternative Items
› Stock Transfer	› Inventory Revaluation
› Goods Receipts/Goods Issues	› Price Lists
› Customer/Vendor Catalog Numbers	› Special Prices
	› Inventory Reports
› Perpetual Inventory Management	

Production

› Bill of Material	› Production Orders

Material Requirement Planning

› Material Requirement Planning Forecasts	› Order Recommendation Report
› Material Requirement Planning Wizard	

Table C.33 SAP Business One Logistics (Cont.)

Activities Management

› Activity	› Activities Overview

Table C.34 SAP Business One Customer Relationship Management

Opportunity Management	
› Opportunities › Opportunity Analysis Reports	› Opportunities Pipeline

Service Management	
› Service Call › Customer Equipment Card › Service Contract	› Contract Template Management › Solutions Knowledge Base › Service Reports

Calendar	
› Calendar	› Microsoft Outlook Integration

Table C.34 SAP Business One Customer Relationship Management (Cont.)

Payroll	
› Payroll Accounting	

Employee Data Management	
› Employee › Human Resources Reports	› HR Connector

Table C.35 SAP Business One Human Resources

Getting Started	
› Creation of New Company › Document Numbering	› Document Numbering (Belgium) › Determining of Default Values

Financial Initialization	
› Currency Types › Foreign Currency Management › Rounding Methods › Opening Balances	› Foreign Currency Exchange Rates and Indexes Table › G/L Account Determination › Financial Report Templates

Table C.36 SAP Business One Implementation

General Settings	
› Company Details	› Future Posting Date in Documents
› Accounting Data	› User Shortcuts
› Display Settings	› User and Authorization
› Block Documents with Earlier	Management
Date	› Data Ownership

Alert and Workflow Management	
› Approval Procedures	› Alert Management

Application Integration	
› SAP Business One Integration for SAP NetWeaver	› SAP Business One Integration Partner Enablement Package (PEP)
› Email	

Table C.36 SAP Business One Implementation (Cont.)

Extension and Personalization	
› User-Defined Fields	› Advanced Layout Designer
› User-Defined Menus	› Multi-Language Support
› User Tables	› Export to File
› User Trigger	› Launch Application
› Layout Designer	› Screen Painter

User Defined Object	
› User-Defined Object	

Formatted Search	
› Formatted Search	

Analysis Tools	
› Query Wizard	› Drag and Relate
› Query Generator	

Table C.37 SAP Business One Customization

Support Tools	
› SAP Business One EarlyWatch Alert	› Context Sensitive Help
› Support Desk for SAP Business One	› Field Level Help
› User Documentation	
Migration	
› Data Transfer Workbench	› Copy Express
› Data Migration Wizard	

Table C.37 SAP Business One Customization (Cont.)

User Interface API	
› User Interface API	› FormData Event
Data Interface API	
› Data Interface API	
Data Interface Server	
› Data Interface Server	

Table C.38 SAP Business One Software Development Kit

SAP Analytics

See Chapter 14 for more information about SAP Analytics, whose features are detailed in Table C.39.

Business Intelligence	
› Reporting	› Mobile BI
› Dashboards and Apps	› Applications and Data Sources
› Enterprise Self-Service	› BI Platform
Data Warehousing	
› SAP BW	› Business Content

Table C.39 SAP Analytics

Enterprise Performance Management	
› Accelerate Financial Close › Financial Planning and Analysis Solutions	› Manage Operational Performance

Table C.39 SAP Analytics (Cont.)

SAP In-Memory Computing (SAP HANA)

See Chapter 15 for more information about SAP HANA, whose features are detailed in Table C.40.

SAP HANA	
› Analytics › Applications	› Platform › Cloud Deployments

Table C.40 SAP HANA

SAP Mobile

See Chapter 16 for more information about SAP Mobile, whose features are detailed in Table C.41.

Mobile Apps	
› Analytic Mobile Apps › Consumer Mobile Apps › Custom Mobile Apps	› SAP Store › Lines of Business Mobile Apps › Industry Mobile Apps
Mobile Commerce	
› Retail › Banking › Consumer Products	› Utilities › Transportation
Mobile Platform	
› Mobile App Development Platform › Develop Mobile Apps	› Cloud › Partner Programs

Table C.41 SAP Mobile

Mobile Secure	
› Secure Devices	› BYOD
› Secure Apps	› Managed Mobility
› Secure Content	› Afaria KNOX

Mobile Services	
› Enterprise Services	› Consumer Insights
› Operator Services	

Table C.41 SAP Mobile (Cont.)

D   The Authors

Venki Krishnamoorthy is an SAP ERP HCM and SuccessFactors functional consultant. Venki has over 13 years of experience as a functional lead, project manager, and program manager in HCM transformations projects. Venki has performed over 15 full lifecycle implementations of SAP and SuccessFactors Employee Central, Recruiting, Performance & Goals, Learning, and Succession Management solutions for customers in the U.S. and beyond. Venki is an author of three SAP PRESS books, a regular speaker at SAPInsider and ASUG conferences, and has published a number of white papers related to current HR trends and talent strategies. You can follow Venki on twitter at *@venki_sap*, and he can be reached on email at *venki.krish@ymail.com*.

Alexandra Carvalho is the head of analytics at BI Group Australia and an SAP Mentor who is focused on applying cutting-edge technologies in the business intelligence and data visualization space. She has great passion for delivering innovative solutions that create business value.

Alexandra has led the development and implementation of several SAP BI projects, and continues to innovate and apply new ideas that complement the SAP BI platform. She has been involved with the latest technologies around analytics such as BW on HANA and LSA++, SAP HANA (in-memory database) and real-time analytics, big data acceleration, predictive analytics, mobility, and cloud computing.

Contributors

Jawad Akhtar earned his chemical engineering degree from Missouri University of Science & Technology, USA. He has 18 years of professional experience, of which 10 years are in SAP ERP. He has completed 8 end-to-end SAP project implementation lifecycles in the areas of PP, QM, MM, PM, and DMS in the steel, automobile, chemical, fertilizer, FMCG, and building products industries. He has also worked as an SAP Delivery Head, SAP Integration Manager, and an SAP Project Manager, and has been proactively involved in a business development and solution architect role for 7 years. Jawad is the author of the SAP PRESS book *Production Planning and Control with SAP ERP*. He's also a technical adviser and a prolific freelance writer for *SAPexperts* (SCM Hub) and SearchSAP. His profile on LinkedIn is *http://pk.linkedin.com/in/jawadakhtar*. You may follow Jawad on Twitter *@jawadahl* or write to him at *jawad.akhtar@live.com.*

Justin Ashlock has spent half of his 20-year career in technology at SAP America, serving as the lead consultant for hundreds of SAP customer projects and engagements supporting over $100 billion in procurement and logistics activities. Justin currently leads a procurement practice for North America, focused on SRM, Sourcing, CLM, MM, and Ariba solutions. He holds a bachelor's degree from the University of California, Berkeley, and a master's degree in Business Administration from the University of Notre Dame.

Paul Ovigele is the CEO of Ovigele Consulting, LLC. He has worked as an SAP Financials consultant since 1997 in both North America and Europe, specializing in implementing the Financial Accounting and Controlling components, along with their integrated areas in various industries, including chemical, logistics, pharmaceuticals, apparel, manufacturing, consumer goods, beverage, and steel. Paul regularly speaks at SAP conferences around the world, is a technical adviser for *Financials Expert* journal, blogs regularly on his website providing unique SAP financials tips at *http://ovigele.com/*, and has written articles and spoken on topics including Material Ledger, SAP Taxation (domestic and International), SAP New General Ledger and Profit Center Accounting, and Cost of Sales Accounting. Paul is a certified chartered accountant and holds an MBA.

Index